Hopping

FREIGHT TRAINS

—— *In* ——

AMERICA

Hopping

FREIGHT TRAINS

—— *In* ——

AMERICA

by

Duffy Littlejohn

1993
Sand River Press
Los Osos, California

Published by Sand River Press, 1319 14th Street, Los Osos, California, 93402.

Copies of this book may be obtained by sending $13.95 + $1.95 postage and handling to: Sand River Press, 1319 14th St., Los Osos, California. 93402. California residents please include ($1.01) sales tax.

Designed by Bruce W. Miller

ISBN 0-944627-34-X

Printed in the United States of America

DISCLAIMER

This book presents subject matter which is illegal to engage in. Therefore both the publisher and the author must disavow and disclaim any responsibility for acts or omissions, purposeful, negligent or otherwise, which result in damages and are or may be claimed to be a result of information provided herein. In short you are on your own. Be careful.

ACKNOWLEDGMENTS

As you'll see this book was a labor of love. I am deeply indebted to and wish to acknowledge the following people, without whose generous assistance this book would not have become reality. I know lengthy acknowlegements are boring. I was exceedingly insecure however about the book's content and eleven friends agreed to read and critique the manuscript. Each contributed generously in his or her turn.

Amanda Elioff is a friend who now works as a geotechnical engineer out of Dallas Texas (and points beyond). We took a number of rides in the old days and AE gave me invaluable insight into a woman's perspective on riding the rails. She also set me straight on a number of transportation matters where I had strayed. To AE I say "many thanks."

George "Doc" Ablin is a psychiatrist at the California Atascadero State Hospital. We see things eye-to-eye and that's why I don't live there. Doc and I met at age eighteen when he was studying at Berkeley and I was studying the road. We took many freights together in the old days and Doc went on to work as a brakeman for the Southern Pacific. His inside knowledge of things railroad proved invaluable, as did his gratifyingly thorough critique of the manuscript.

Tom "Whirling Dervish" Weverka works as a translator and language instructor in Tokyo. Tom is a true expatriate who keeps promising to come home to his family of writers. He provided well-needed assistance on style and approach. Tom knows America better than most folks I reckon and I hope to return the favor some day but not in Japanese. Come home Tom.

Roxane "Banja" Polidora is approaching partnership in the San Francisco law firm of Pillsbury, Madison and Sutro. Banja helped keep my spirits up when I despaired of this most. She always liked my letters and encouraged me to try a book. Her constant exhortation that I continue with the pen won't soon be forgotten. Good luck Banja and keep litigating.

My brother Tony Littlejohn teaches Earth Sciences at Eagle View Middle School in Colorado Springs. Tony knows me better than anyone and gave me great advice about what was interesting and what wasn't. I've never taken him on a freight train ride so he's still a bit out of his element. Nevertheless he pointed out things which stuck in his craw. One of these days we'll catch out together and take a ride across Monarch Pass to the Western Slope. He's writing also and we enjoy great pollenization.

Marie-Paule Vadunthun is a *correctrice* (journalistic editor) for a series of fashion and perfume magazines in Paris. We lived together during the finalization and proffering of this piece. Her unflagging support both literary and financial (not to mention emotional) is in large part responsible for the book's existence. Her comments on style were adhered to better than she knows.

I've worked many hours with my publisher Bruce Miller of Los Osos California to buff and hone this text. Bruce was the only publisher of over 550 contacted who had the guts and insight to handle a book about this subject. I suppose it's because he rode the rails himself in the old days that he spotted an exciting idea. To the other 550-odd publishers who got cold feet I say read 'em and weep.

Photography in the text was graciously provided by Pat Holden of *Big Foot Hobbies* in Atascadero California. Pat is a dyed-in-the-wool train nut. He knows railroads inside and out and has been photographing engines and cars since 1982. Pat waded through 30,000-odd slides to come up with the best representative depictions. He took me on a photo journey over to Bakersfield, Tehachapi and Mojave for the track and signal photos. He was also a great source of information about freightcars and motive power.

Guitar Whitey out of San Luis Obispo is probably the nicest man you'd ever hope to meet. Whitey's been hoboing since the Depression. He spent long hours combing through the manuscript and calling BS on things he didn't agree with. He also reemphasized I hallmark the woman's rail-riding experience, which of course is every bit as fundamental to the tradition and adventure of riding rails in North America as any man's. He's 71 now, sharp as a tack and has been an incredible inspiration. I've spent many hours basking in his wisdom. If you ever want to meet "the genuine item" you'd do well to look him up.

I'd also like to acknowledge Captain Cook of "Hobo Times" and the National Hobo Association. The Captain has given me a number of ideas as to what this book is all about. He's courageous enough to print a newsletter about hobos and spits at the powers-that-be on the railroad.

Last but not least is my father Fred Littlejohn. Without question this book would not meet your eyes without his dogged assistance. I spent months in Paris 1991 and 1992 seeking out publishers through his aid. I tailored enquiry letters of solicitation which he paid photocopying expenses and postage on while advising him which chapters to enclose. He became great friends with the photocopy services in Boulder. Due to his patient and diligent efforts I yet receive letters of interest from dilatory publishers. He also sent me scads of second-hand railroad books which augmented my own research. You and I are each a benefactor of his caring labor.

To each I say thank you and God speed. Your efforts will not late be forgotten.

DEDICATION

This book is dedicated to my mother,
Dorothy Louise Kihm Littlejohn (1917-1989).
She saw to it that I learn my A B Cs, and hopefully you'll
be the beneficiary of her tutelage. She never liked that I rode freight trains
but always welcomed me home—dirty though I was. I miss her and wish her
a very deep, peaceful sleep.

TABLE OF CONTENTS

THE 100 COMMANDMENTS OF RIDING THE RAILS

1.   RIDING THE RAILS IS DANGEROUS. DO NOT APPROACH THE SUBJECT LIGHTLY. **SAFETY** IS THE MOST IMPORTANT CONSIDERATION.

2.   WEAR DARK, COMFORTABLE CLOTHES WITH LOTS OF POCKETS, AND ALWAYS BRING DARK GEAR.

3.   ALWAYS BRING ALONG A STURDY PAIR OF GLOVES AND BOOTS.

4.   ALWAYS BRING ALONG WATER OR OTHER LIQUIDS.

5.   DON'T FORGET YOUR RAILROAD ATLAS AND/OR HIGH-WAY MAP.

6.   BRING A WARM, WATERPROOF JACKET.

7.   BRING A BACKPACK YOU CAN THROW AROUND AND SIT ON.

8.   AVOID BRINGING SHARP OR BRITTLE GEAR.

9.   BRING LIGHT, PRACTICAL, COMFORTABLE, WARM AND DARK-COLORED BEDDING.

10.   USE DISCARDED CARDBOARD (1000-MILE PAPER) TO CUSHION YOUR RIDE AND KEEP YOU CLEAN AND INSULATED.

11.   BRING FOOD WHICH IS LIGHT, WILL KEEP AND DOESN'T NEED COOKING.

12.   KEEP ALL GEAR UNDER 25 POUNDS MAXIMUM.

13.   IN DECIDING WHEN TO COMMENCE YOUR JOURNEY, CONSIDER THE POSSIBILITY OF DELAYS CAUSED BY PASSENGER AND COMMUTER TRAINS, WHICH DAY OF THE WEEK IT IS, AND WHETHER RAILROAD LABOR PEACE IS AT HAND.

14.   REMEMBER - EVEN IF NO TRAINS ARE LEAVING OUT OF YOUR YARD SOMETHING IS ALWAYS COMING TOWARD YOU OVER THE ROAD.

15.   THE WEST AND SOUTH ARE SOMEWHAT EASIER THAN THE EAST AND NORTH FOR HOPPING FREIGHTS.

16.   CATCH YOUR FIRST FREIGHT TRAINS IN RURAL TO SEMI-RURAL AREAS UNTIL YOU GET THE HANG OF IT.

17.   FIND FREIGHTYARDS BY USE OF COMMON SENSE, STUDYING MAPS, KNOWLEDGE OF THE TOWN YOU'RE CATCHING OUT OF, WATCHING WHERE THE TRACKS GO AND USE OF LANDMARKS.

18.   EVERY RAILROAD FENCE HAS AT LEAST ONE HOLE IN IT.

19.   RAILROAD WORKERS ARE OUR FRIENDS, NOT OUR ENEMIES. THEY LIKE WHEN WE RIDE THEIR TRAINS *IF WE DO IT RIGHT*.

20.   FIND OUT WHAT YOU NEED TO KNOW BY ASKING RAILROAD WORKERS.

21.   ALWAYS ACCEPT FAVORS EXTENDED TO YOU BY RAILROAD WORKERS.

22.   ASK RAILROAD WORKERS ABOUT THE BULL (RAILROAD POLICE).

23.   RAILROAD BULLS ARE MORE BARK THAN BITE.

24.   NEVER RIDE BLIND BAGGAGE, THE BUMPERS, THE ROD OR THE DECK.

25.   CAPITALIZE UPON THE BULL'S INHERENT VISUAL DIFFICULTIES WHEN MOVING AROUND IN THE YARDS.

26.   ALWAYS PLAY NICE AND DUMB WITH THE BULL. REMEMBER THE ATTITUDE TEST.

27.   ONE MOMENT OF CARELESSNESS CAN CAUSE A LIFETIME OF SORROW. RIDE SAFELY.

28.   ALWAYS STOP, LOOK AND LISTEN BEFORE PLACING YOURSELF IN A POSITION WHERE YOU MIGHT COME INTO CONTACT WITH A MOVING CAR OR TRAIN. KEEP AS MUCH DISTANCE AS POSSIBLE BETWEEN YOURSELF AND THE TRACKS.

29.   NEVER CROSS A TRACK WITHOUT STOPPING, LOOKING AND LISTENING FIRST.

30.   WATCH OUT FOR SNAGS HANGING OFF THE SIDES OF FREIGHTCARS.

31.   WHEREVER PRACTICAL, WALK AROUND STRINGS OF FREIGHTCARS TO CROSS A TRACK BEFORE GOING OVER THEM.

32.   FREIGHTCARS CAN MOVE SUDDENLY AND AT TIMES VIOLENTLY. IF NOT CAREFUL YOU CAN BE THROWN DOWN ON OR OFF A FREIGHTCAR.

33.   ALWAYS CROSS OVER A TRAIN EXPECTING IT TO MOVE AT ANY MOMENT.

34.   ALWAYS GET OFF A TRAIN WHICH IS BEING HUMPED AND STAY AWAY FROM THE HUMP.

35.   NEVER TOUCH A FREIGHTCAR UNTIL YOU KNOW WHAT ITS AIR BRAKES ARE DOING - OR NOT DOING.

36.   FREIGHT TRAINS ARE EVERY BIT AS HARD TO STOP AS TO START.

37.   NEVER CLIMB UNDER A CAR OR COUPLER TO GET ACROSS A TRACK.

38.   ALWAYS FIND AN OPEN CAR TO JUMP UP ON AND WALK ACROSS BEFORE CROSSING OVER COUPLERS.

39.   WHEN CROSSING OVER COUPLERS, ALWAYS FIND A CAR WITH SAFE FOOTHOLDS AND HANDHOLDS. USE BOTH HANDS AT ALL TIMES.

40.   ALWAYS STICK SOMETHING SOLID IN THE OPEN DOOR OF A BOXCAR TO PREVENT IT FROM SLIDING SHUT ON YOU.

41.   IF ALL BOXCAR DOORS ON ONE SIDE OF YOUR TRAIN ARE SHUT, CHECK THE OTHER SIDE.

42.   LEARN HOW TO USE A BOXCAR'S DOORLATCH TO SWING UP INSIDE.

43.   ALWAYS RIDE THE BACK PLATFORM OF A HOPPER CAR.

44.   WHEN STANDING ON A HOPPER PLATFORM ALWAYS USE THE HANDHOLDS.

45.   RIDE BEHIND THE TIRES ON THE LEEWARD SIDE OF A TRUCK TRAILER ON A PIGGYBACK.

46.   ALWAYS TRY TO FIND A PIGGYBACK WITH AN APRON ALONG THE EDGES OF THE FLOOR.

47.   ONLY RIDE A GONDOLA IF YOU DON'T CARE ABOUT THE SCENERY. YOU WON'T SEE MUCH.

48.   AVOID RIDING FLATCARS UNLESS THEY HAVE BULK-HEADS OR LOADS WHICH CAN'T SHIFT.

49.   NEVER RIDE A TANKCAR. BOTH THEIR CONFIGURATION AND CONTENTS CAN BE HAZARDOUS.

50.   BE EXTREMELY CAUTIOUS ABOUT RIDING IN A NEW AUTO ON A TRAIN.

51.   NEVER MESS AROUND WITH RAILROAD COMPANY PROP-ERTY.

52.   ONLY RIDE IN BACK ENGINES AT NIGHT.

53.   IF YOU'RE RIDING AN ENGINE AT THE HEADEND, MAKE SURE IT'S THE BACKMOST ENGINE.

54.   DON'T CLIMB INTO AN ENGINE UNTIL THE LAST POS-SIBLE MOMENT BEFORE DEPARTURE.

55.   GET DOWN IN THE BATHROOM OF THE ENGINE UNTIL SAFELY OUT OF THE YARDS.

56.   IF YOU GET KICKED OUT OF AN ENGINE BY THE CREW, RUN BACK AND FIND A CAR QUICKLY.

57.   NEVER TURN ON THE LIGHTS IN AN ENGINE CAB AT NIGHT.

58.   NEVER BLOW THE WHISTLE OR TOUCH ANY EQUIPMENT INSIDE AN ENGINE.

59.   BELIEVE IT WHEN A RAILROAD POSTS A DANGER SIGN. THEY MEAN IT.

60.   ALWAYS KEEP ALL DOORS SHUT WHEN RIDING IN AN ENGINE.

61.   ALWAYS ACT DECENTLY AND FORTHRIGHTLY ON THE RAILROAD.

62.   LEARN HOW TO PLAY HIDE-AND-SEEK WITH THE CREW WHEN RIDING IN AN ENGINE.

63.   GET INTO THE ENGINE BATHROOM WHILE PASSING BY DEPOTS OR THROUGH YARDS.

64.   GET OFF AN ENGINE AT THE EARLIEST POSSIBLE OP-PORTUNITY AND LOWLINE.

65.   AVOID RIDING PEDDLAR OR DRAG FREIGHTS.

66.   REGULAR FREIGHTS COMPRISE MOST OF A RAILROAD'S BUSINESS AND PROVIDE A THOROUGHLY DECENT RIDE.

67.   HOTSHOTS ARE THE HALLMARK OF RAILROAD WAY-FARING.

68.   ALWAYS KEEP AN EYE OUT FOR UNIT TRAINS, DEDI-CATED PIGGYBACK TRAINS AND LAND BRIDGE TRAINS.

69.   PRIORITY OF TRAINS ON LARGE RAILROADS IS GOV-ERNED BY FREIGHT PROFITABILITY, DIRECTION OF TRAVEL, DAYTIME/NIGHTTIME, DAY OF THE WEEK AND/OR UPHILL/DOWNHILL.

70.   ALWAYS TRY TO RIDE TOWARD THE BACKEND OF A TRAIN.

71.   NEVER PLACE TRAINMEN IN A POSITION WHERE THEY HAVE TO EXPLAIN YOUR PRESENCE.

72.   POUR WATER ON AND BREATHE THROUGH THE ARM OF YOUR SHIRT OR JACKET IF YOU'RE STUCK IN A LONG SMOKY TUNNEL.

73.   WAIT FOR A TRAIN 2/3RDS TO 3/4THS OF THE WAY BACK FROM WHERE THE HEADEND WILL STOP.

74.   NEVER COMPROMISE YOUR SAFETY AND WELLBEING BY RIDING ON AN UNSAFE CAR. IT'S BETTER TO BE DE-LAYED THAN DEAD.

75.   FAMILIARIZE YOURSELF WITH THE LAYOUT OF THE YARD YOU'RE WAITING FOR A TRAIN IN.

76.   ALWAYS LIE DOWN OR SLEEP AGAINST A FORWARD WALL OR FLAT VERTICAL SURFACE.

77.   ALWAYS STAY AS FAR AWAY FROM THE OPEN SIDES OF A FREIGHTCAR AS POSSIBLE.

78.   NEVER HANG YOUR LEGS OFF THE SIDE OF A MOVING FREIGHTCAR.

79.   WHEN STANDING UP OR WALKING ON AN OPEN MOV-ING FREIGHTCAR, ALWAYS HOLD ONTO SOMETHING FOR SAFETY.

80.   PROTECT YOUR HEAD WITH YOUR HANDS WHENEVER IT'S NEAR A HARD SURFACE.

81.   NEVER STAND AT THE FRONT END OF A PIGGYBACK OR ANY OTHER OPEN CAR.

82.   IF YOU RIDE WITH A LOAD ALWAYS STAY BEHIND IT.

83.   STAY OFF LOADED FREIGHTCARS UNLESS YOU'RE POSI-TIVE THE LOAD WON'T SHIFT.

84.   PRE-POSITIONING IS CRUCIAL WHEN RIDING THE RAILS.

85.   NEVER RIDE BETWEEN A LOAD AND ITS FRONT WALL OR EDGE.

86.   WATCH OUT FOR BAD ORDER TRACK AND EQUIPMENT.

87.   NEVER RIDE IN A LOADED GONDOLA.

88.   IT'S EASIER THAN YOU THINK TO GET THROWN OFF A MOVING TRAIN. NEVER GET OVERCONFIDENT.

89.   WHEN YOUR TRAIN STOPS, IN CASE OF DOUBT WHEN IT WILL LEAVE STAY WITH THE TRAIN.

90.   THE SIGNAL IMMEDIATELY TO THE RIGHT OF THE TRACK YOU'RE ON IN YOUR DIRECTION OF TRAVEL CONTROLS YOUR TRAIN.

91.   ALWAYS CHECK ALL THE SIGNALS YOU CAN SEE AROUND YOU. THE WAY THEY CHANGE IN RELATION TO EACH OTHER GIVES YOU A COMPLETE PICTURE OF WHAT YOUR TRAIN WILL DO NEXT.

92.   ALWAYS THROW YOUR GEAR OFF FIRST BEFORE GETTING OFF A MOVING TRAIN - UNLESS YOU NEED IT TO BREAK A FALL.

93.   DON'T RISK YOUR PERSONAL WELLBEING ANY MORE THAN YOU THINK IS WARRANTED GETTING OFF A MOVING TRAIN.

94.   STEP OUT OF THE STIRRUP ON A MOVING TRAIN WITH YOUR BACK FOOT FIRST.

95.   WATCH OUT FOR ROCK-THROWING KIDS WHEN TRAVELING OVER THE ROAD.

96.   PATIENCE IS THE MOST IMPORTANT VIRTUE YOU CAN BRING TO THE RAILROAD.

97.   ADMIRE THE NATURAL BEAUTY OF AMERICA FROM A FREIGHT TRAIN.

98.   ANYBODY WITH A SENSE OF ADVENTURE CAN RIDE THE RAILS.

99.   ONLY BUILD A FIRE IN THE JUNGLE AND ONLY IF YOU REALLY NEED ONE.

100.   THERE ARE EXCEPTIONS TO EVERY RULE.

INTRODUCTION

Let's go on a step-by-step exploration of techniques we use to hop freight trains. Why ride freight trains? Because we have a ball and at the same time *beat the system in every way*. Riding the rails is the last pure red-blooded adventure in North America.

This is not a book simply for men. Women can and do hop freights all across the continent. For women contemplating this adventure please turn right now to page 263. You can play this sport every bit as easily as a man.

This book is unique - the first in-depth presentation of its kind. It shows you how to get on a freight train and ride. It's a how-to book with supporting reference material. Other folks have written books about their *personal* experiences riding the rails. This is not one of those books. Here we'll stick to the basics.

I had to learn how to ride freight trains the hard way - i.e., courtesy of the School of Hard Knocks. Luckily I never got myself killed (had a couple of close calls though). I was fortunate enough to receive timely advice from seasoned hobos on how to avoid the more dangerous aspects of the sport. I learned the rest from experience. You however will learn how to hop freights in the comfort of your armchair, or when the boss isn't looking.

Riding the rails *is* dangerous. Much of the book is devoted to the subject of safety. Safety on the railroad is paramount. We'll return repeatedly to safety topics - not because they necessarily interest me, but because they'd damned well better interest you. Hopping freights is not only dangerous, it's illegal - and thus not to be taken lightly.

The main reason I wrote this book is because I wish there had been something like it for me - a book I've reached for a dozen times which was never there. Hopefully you'll benefit from the experience of those who've passed this way before.

Just so you're confident you've latched onto the right book on this subject, compare it to anything else you can find (check the bibliography at the back of the book). In addition to the nuts-and-bolts of what to bring along, when, where and how to ride a freight train we'll cover additional information designed to enhance your railroading experience.

There's never been a book written about hopping freights which gives you the whole picture - from the inside. I'm writing this book out of basic frustration over the lack of substantive, reliable information about an adventure which reaches down to the very foundations of the North American experience. Riding the rails is one of the last pure adventures available in post-frontier America.

I'm from California. Being a Westerner I've ridden the rails through every state west of the Mississippi dozens of times. Back East I've traveled through each and every one of them at least three times. Conservatively estimated I've ridden about 350,000 miles on freight trains in America and Canada. I've probably hitchhiked around 400,000. I've never figured out the driving, etc., part of it, but the total is already over one million miles. As a young fellow I spent *five years* bumming around and I've returned to the road many many times. In short enjoy what you're reading because it's the real thing.

And "Happy Highball."

I

WHY RIDING FREIGHT TRAINS IS FUN

Why do so many people love to ride freight trains? First off, when a freight train gets going, it *gets going*. And it doesn't stop for much. In fact it doesn't stop for *anything* unless the crew wants it to stop. Take a second look at your next freight train and think about trying to "stop" it. Good luck.

Trains are the complete master of their own terrain. Nobody tells a freight train what to do. Freight trains run on their own track by their own rules. When you pass through a town or cross a road, *everything* stops for you. Whole towns get cut in half by a freight train. When it comes to "The Boss" transportation-wise, freight trains are in the executive suite.

Riding the rails is a real kick in the pants. You get on board this huge, hulking amalgamation of metal weighing tons and tons and tons, then take off across the great American Wilderness. You get a feel of power and purpose. It's like riding the back of a giant steel dragon lumbering across the land. You rock along in the metal cradle you're riding. Enormous physical forces are at work: heat, light, sound, gravity, inertia, momentum and centrifugal force. Metal grinds, bends and heats as engines and cars pound over the track - tens of thousands of tons of massive material in motion. You sense the shifting rhythm and flow of travel - the rocking rhythm of metal blessed with speed. You tap your foot in rhythm to wheels which incessantly beat on the ribbons of steel - lullingly hypnotic, yet punctuated by staccato bursts of brilliant jointed-metal high point. The rattle, boom, bang of the big wheel pounding the rail is like two lovers' impassioned kiss, repeated again and again with ardent fervor, and forgotten.

The smell of burnt diesel permeates your nostrils as you explode into a tunnel and light inks out. The wind rushes past with steady, ceaseless energy. The ground whizzes past and disappears in a blur. Faraway objects - signs, houses, fields and fences - march steadily toward you, loom up, then fly past as if compelled onward by a relentless earthbound conveyor belt. Vista upon vista approach, whirl past and disappear behind.

Nighttime has a special feel riding a freight train. It's startling to roll through the darkness then burst into a city of light - a sudden explosion of dancing, piercing brilliance. The solitude borne of darkening distance is interrupted by fleeting imposition of light and shadow, followed again by return to the enveloping night. Almost a life metaphor: Where were we before (who can tell)? Where are we now (passing through light). Where will we get to (who can tell)?

Freight trains are also *the* best way to see America. You may have your doubts. In fact, I hope you do. One reason I present this subject is because I figure you have your doubts. That's good. A healthy degree of skepticism never hurt anybody. Hang onto it as you continue reading.

Let's jump right into it now and begin by taking a look at what you want to bring along with you on this odyssey.

II

*O.K. - I WANT TO RIDE A FREIGHT TRAIN -
WHAT SHOULD I BRING?*

Planning your adventure is important. What you wear and bring along will make the difference between fun and folly. Here's a handy list of things to bring along:

CLOTHING

- Dark, comfortable clothes with lots of pockets
- Dark warm jacket
- Dark hat (optional)
- Sturdy gloves
- Sturdy boots
- Dark backpack
- Dark sleeping bag, 1000-mile paper or dark blanket(s)
- Plastic tarp or poncho
- Water (or other liquids)
- Toiletries
- Atlas and/or map
- Compass (optional)
- Penlight
- Food
- Utensils

Let's flesh out this list by talking about clothing. Then we'll move on to travel accessories.

The traditional hobo style of dress was a baggy dark suit which frequently had one or more holes in it, a battered floppy hat and walking boots which had no laces and were often held on the traveler's feet with rope or big rubber bands. Formal attire also required wearing a clean white shirt. Today the only part of this uniform we need to emulate is the dark clothing.

Dark clothes are a definite plus. Make your clothes dark, comfortable and utilitarian. Also bring dark clothes because freight trains are dirty.

Freight trains are caked with grit and grime built up from years of faithful outdoor service. Like the Miranda warning everything you touch can and will rub off against you - until you develop a technique for touching or sitting on things the right way.

This technique involves not grabbing onto things or sitting on them the way you do at home. Hold things tentatively, gingerly, gently - *unless you might fall off.* Don't slide your bottom over things like you do in the livingroom. Kneel carefully on things like at the altar rail. This way you'll minimize accumulation of grime.

I also suggest dark clothes which have lots of pockets. You'll need to have a number of small items close at hand.

When deciding what to wear, gauge what will happen in terms of weather. If unsure of what's ahead check the weather reports on TV or in the newspapers before taking off. I say this because just as on any other trip we want to travel as lightly as possible.

Always bring a jacket, preferably waterproof. Even if it's 100+ degrees outside today we never knows what's coming. There's nothing worse than being stuck on a freight train without adequate clothing.

As far as extra clothes go this is pretty much up to you. You know roughly how many days your expedition will take and how often you need to change socks, shirts and skivvies. I suggest bringing along a dark hat if you want to keep the sun or your hair out of your eyes and keep dirt out of your hair.

Some hobos suggest dressing like railroad workers. I don't think this is necessary nor do I know how railroad workers dress exactly. Perhaps wearing a pair of coveralls ("dashboards") would be a good idea but isn't really necessary. The main thing is to wear clothes which are practical and comfortable.

Bring along a pair of good, sturdy gloves made out of cowhide, or at least thick wool or cotton. Railroading is tough on hands. There are plenty of hot, cold, sharp, splintery and dirty things to grab onto. You'll never see a railroad man without them. Look for gloves which don't get slippery when they're wet. If it's foggy, raining or snowing you can lose your grip climbing around on freightcars. Keep your gloves close at hand.

Shoes are another important consideration. Ballast (the rock rails and ties are laid on) can mess up your feet in short order if you're wearing tennis shoes. Wear shoes or boots with sturdy soles which can withstand the rigors of walking on crushed rock. Vibram soles are good.

ACCESSORIES:

Traditionally most hobos traveled pretty light - a blanket, one or two changes of clothes, a pencil and some paper, a toothbrush, some socks and maybe something to cook with. The less one carried the more of a " streamliner" one became. Other hobos carried heavy baggage, perhaps the tools of their trade, work clothes and boots - perhaps everything they owned and carried in a "Montana bindle." Times have changed.

Today the most important concern is a knapsack or backpack. I'd recommend nylon or a similar synthetic material in case it rains. A backpack can get snagged easier than a jacket because it sticks out from you. An Army-Navy Surplus rifle bag is a good bet or anything which is sturdy and affords a big open pouch with shoulder straps. What's more important is to bring a backpack you can sit on and throw places without damaging it or its contents. In other words your gear shouldn't have any frame.

Railroads have been inconsiderate enough to neglect to equip their facilities with lounge chairs, sofas, futons or whoopee cushions. If you have a backpack to sit on you're automatically provided with a seat. And if your car really gets rocking when the train gets smoking (when they "ball the jack" or "rattle the hocks off her") you'll be glad you have the cushioning to sit on.

You need gear which can withstand impact - something you can throw on, off or over a train without messing things up. In fact you need a pack which if necessary can break your fall if you lose your footing getting on or off.

Not only should your backpack be collapsible, its contents shouldn't be breakable. Leave the chinaware at home. Avoid bringing sharp or brittle items. You can bring along most anything if it's repackaged in something soft. Plastic bags and containers are great. Tin cans and glass jars are out unless *extremely* well-cushioned by other soft things. Go with the Tupperware but be prepared for a few grins when you break it out.

Let's talk about bedding. Your bedroll should be five things: Light, practical, comfortable, warm enough and dark in color. You should be able to grab it and roll it up or stuff it into something quickly, because at times you have to move quickly. Don't bring the $400 superlight hi-tech Himalaya-type sleeping bag. If you break this kind of bag out around other hobos they might get the wrong idea. It's like breaking out the Moet Chandon when everyone else is drinking white port and lemon juice (WPLJs). Remember to fit in with the people around you. If you show up with thousands of dollars worth of food and equipment you won't fit in.

I suggest investing in a nice, $20-50 sleeping bag with enough warmth to withstand the worst weather you anticipate. Buy a cheapo, throw-away type bag for these expeditions, found in any Army-Navy Surplus store, discount store, sporting goods store, etc. Mummybags in particular are great. They keep wind and cold air from coming in the top of your bag.

Buy a dark sleeping bag. This follows our general color scheme and helps mask dirt. If you want to spend some bucks bring a bag which is washable - for your next trip. One neat trick to keeping a sleeping bag clean is to bring along a light plastic tarp which doubles as a poncho. A plastic tarp/poncho won't pick up much dirt, provides cushioning in your pack and represents almost no additional weight. If the weather turns you can loop it over your head and stay dry, or put it over your gear.

Here's another trick to staying clean - *and* increase insulation and cushioning. Find a discarded piece of cardboard or crating paper lying around the yards or in a car. Hobos call this stuff "1000-mile paper." Some hobos call it "500-mile paper." Perhaps they aren't quite as ambitious. Originally it was made of heavy brown craft paper or thin cardboard and was used to paper boxcar walls to keep grain from spilling out. Alternately it was made of two layers of paper with a thin layer of tar in between used to cover lumber or heavy equipment. Boxcars lined with 1000-mile paper were preferable to bare-walled cars. They were cleaner and perhaps a bit less windy.

Today this cardboard is found everywhere, discarded from modern-day crating and shipping schemes ripped apart by offloading warehouse-men. A nice piece of cardboard keeps you cleaner, warmer, increases cushioning and is thoroughly disposable at the end of the line.

If you want to get down and do it the traditional way, take a tip from homeless people all over the world. Wrap yourself up in a big piece of paper or cardboard - the same 1000-mile paper. One, two or three blankets also does the trick quite handily. There's nothing wrong with bringing dark blankets instead of a bag. Tie them up with a piece of leather or rope, leaving a loop to use as a shoulder strap. You can pick up blankets for about $4.00 a pop at most Goodwill/Salvation Army stores.

After the backpack and sleeping gear the next most important thing to bring is water - or some other type of life-sustaining liquid. Over the road you'll be cut off from a source of water. Without question the next worst thing to freezing your ass on a freight is to be dying of thirst. Bring water in a plastic container which is light and can withstand impact without puncturing. A metal canteen is alright but unnecessarily heavy. Go with a plastic canteen. Traditional hobos often used a well rinsed-out Clorox bottle. Or you can pick up a half-gallon or gallon jug of water at any convenience store. Make sure the cap can't pop off. Screwtops are preferable.

Another important accessory is toiletpaper. We won't elaborate on this too much. Let's just say it's handy and without it life's no fun.

Toiletries are optional. There are no drug stores on the railroad.

One very important thing to bring is a map. If possible pick up an inexpensive paperback railroad atlas of the country. You may have to special order one. Rand McNally publishes a good one for around $10-15. It shows all the routes, towns and junctions so you can follow along with what's happening during your trip. Try to find a recent edition because the North American railroad system is constantly contracting as railroads abandon main lines and tear up double track.

One note of caution about having a railroad atlas along: Be discreet about who's around while referring to it. Don't come off like a greenhorn. Maintain an aura of experience. Railroad atlases are great but keep them to yourself.

An atlas is truly great because it minimizes the panic which sets in after taking a wee siesta, then waking up to realize you don't have the foggiest idea where you are. If you know the territory or recognize a local landmark, fine. But if you're on new turf an atlas keeps you posted on where the train is, and educates you as to where you've been and where you're going.

A railroad atlas is more helpful than a highway map when you don't know where you are exactly - or at all. Every time you come into a town, somewhere you'll see its name posted - usually on a store, water tower, hotel, public park or building, or the railroad depot (if there is one). Hardware stores, cleaners, movie houses and hotels are often named after a town. You'll develop a talent for spotting the town's name on a billboard, neon sign, etc. Then simply whip out the atlas and - *Voila*! You know where you are. Another helpful location-finder is roadsigns. If you spot the number of the highway or see a mileage sign with distances to the next burgs you can find your coordinates in the atlas.

If you don't want to bother buying a railroad atlas at least get a decent highway map of the area you'll be visiting. Maps are acceptable even with professional hobos. They often have one. Maps are cheap and expendable.

Another reason I emphasize atlases, or at least maps (besides the fact I like them) is that oftentimes especially out West a railroad won't follow any particular road or highway. The more radical the terrain the more likely the railroad will part company from a road. There are several reasons for this.

Almost without exception railroads laid down tracks long before established highways were built. They got first choice on the easiest, most gradual route to get through the up-and-down parts of the country. Often this was along a creek or riverbed. Many times after laying track there wasn't enough room for a road.

Railroads often take off on another route to go the same direction. In the five deserts, the Rockies, the Sierras or the Cascades in the West, the Adirondacks, Alleghenies and Appalachians in the East, the Ozarks and swamplands of the Deep South and even out on the flat prairie the railroad will run along for miles far away from any road.

Common sense or a basic understanding of gravity leads to the conclusion a train can't climb or descend a grade as easily as a car or truck. Whereas tracks have to wrap around up-and-down regions, roads blast right through them. The curving nature of the North American railroad distinguishes it from its European counterpart. In Europe they blasted to make tracks straight. In America we built around things quickly. Not surprisingly either - it was cheaper and we were young nations. But today railroads pay for the increased distances and curve maintenance.

One vexing thing about highway maps (except those made by non-auto club and non-oil company concerns like Rand McNally and National Geographic) is that we never find railroad routes on them. I suppose automobile people like to think railroads don't exist. By the same token I've never seen a railroad atlas which had highways on it. Maybe it's a function of mutual disdain.

But this means when referring to a highway map, sometimes the best we can do is extrapolate where the railroad is in relation to the roads. The obvious solution is to bring both a railroad atlas and a highway map. They're paper and very light.

I mention this because there are times when you're literally out there in the middle of nowhere, without any town, road or other clue as to where the train is. If you've studied an atlas and/or map you can make an educated guess where you might be - or at least deduce the train's still going the right direction.

A pocket-sized compass isn't a bad idea if you're not confident in your sense of direction. Even if you have good directional sense there will be cloudy days and moonless or cloudy nights when you can't see anything to gauge direction from. Sometimes, particularly out in the wide open spaces of the West, you can wake up and have no idea if the train's still headed the right way. I've never carried a compass but there were times I wish I had. Beyond adding to a sense of adventure a compass could have saved my ass more than once. A compass is optional. Get away from metal before using it.

A handy compassless way to tell direction at night is the Big Dipper (Ursa Major) to find the North Star (Polaris). First find the Big Dipper. It's the constellation in the northern sky which looks most like its nickname. Next, isolate the two stars in the ladle farthest away from its handle. Using these two stars as an arrow, draw a line with your eyes upward and very slightly to the right. You'll run into a star of average brightness which is isolated from its neighbors. That's Polaris, which points nearly due north. With the North Star you can tell which way you're traveling. Ancient sea and desert mariners have been using this technique for centuries.

Remember this little trick. It might save your life someday - whether on the railroad or otherwise.

Another handy item to bring along is a lightweight, inexpensive flashlight. It gets dark out there under the starry skies of America, especially at night in the corner of a boxcar. Remember to bring a light to avoid the sinking feeling of realizing you can't see a bloody thing around. Matches are O.K. except for the wind factor. A light assists in checking maps or locating things which roll or bounce away on the car at night. Penlights are best because they're not heavy and fit in most pockets - and their light can be more easily concealed.

FOOD:

Here are some suggestions for good, healthy, all-weather preservable foods for riding the rails:
-Bread
-Dried meats and fruits
-Any kind of nuts
-Cheese (if it will keep without refrigeration for a couple of days)
-Peanut butter
-Anything canned (but put it in something else or pack it carefully)
-Fresh fruit (again, consider the weight-per-nutrition factor and impact-survivability)
-Crackers.
It's the same stuff we eat when camping where fires aren't allowed.

If you plan to cook you be the judge of what to bring. You can cook with a small frying pan ("banjo") on a sterno stove, portable gas stove or even with a "fusee" (flares found in engines and cabooses).

If you want to get authentic and make hobo stew (the basic mulligan stew) *you* lug the meat, potatoes, carrots and onions and *I'll* bring the spoon. (Mulligan by the way was a real person. He was a "gang cook" on the Union Pacific building the first transcontinental railroad across the Midwest. His concoction consisted of huge chunks of beef - buffalo when available - and large slices of potatoes, carrots, other vegetables and various herbs found along the route. Hobo stew was made from the same ingredients but with one major distinction. The "crumb boss" cut the meat into smaller pieces so everyone got more or less the same portion. The boss also put stones in the bottom of the pot to keep the stew from sticking to the metal and spoiling the meal.)

Today's canned soups and stews are good. They're heavy but provide a lot of nourishment per weight. Canned foods can be eaten without heating.

UTENSILS:

Bring a can opener unless all your cans have the latest ring-top technology. A knife is always handy. A basic Swiss Army knife with 4 to 6 functions is perfect - two sizes of knife, can opener, corkscrew, screwdriver and bottlecap opener. If you want to use a regular kitchen knife that's fine, but a folding knife is safer and pocketable. A spoon is also handy, as is a fork if cooking. Remember - anything you can eat with a fork you can eat with a spoon - even steak. A hard plastic cup comes in handy. Consider bringing a Boy Scout messkit. If you want to make tea, coffee or soup you can heat water in a softdrink can or even an empty wine bottle! The bottle will withstand one or two heatings. With either container when you're done you just throw it away.

You can easily bring all the gear mentioned and still keep your backpack down to 20-25 lbs. Anything else you want to bring along for the ride is up to you. Books are nice to while away the time. I've even heard some hardy souls bring along their *bicycle*. A bike could be handy for getting around.

I would like to reemphasize you're miles ahead when traveling light. Often you'll have to walk long distances. There's also a safety factor in carrying too much gear. You can jeopardize your well-being getting on, off and over trains. We'll discuss these ideas in depth further on.

III

WHAT'S THE BEST TIME TO CATCH A FREIGHT TRAIN?

Timing is a concept pertinent to any activity. Timing is one of the most alluring and enduring intangibles invented by man. Timing is so fundamental to the human understanding of Nature we've raised it to a level of unparalleled importance. Ponder for example the intriguing metaphysical universality: "What are the two things *everything* in the universe is doing?" Answer: "Taking up space and *growing older*."

The first timing concept I'd like to emphasize is patience. As with other sports we need patience to ride freight trains. It's the only sport where reports are not available for the freight *aficionado*. Unfortunately freight train movement information has never been made available to the public. I suppose this has to do with preventing sabotage, train-wrecking and the like. In fact during our many wars it's been absolutely *verboten* for a railroad employee to divulge information about the comings and goings of freights.

The habit of being secretive about freight train movement has become the order of the day for railroad folks. They don't *publicly* advertise where and when their trains go. (Note: They do however in industry journals. If you're serious about planning your trip accurately I suggest subscribing to two publications: (1) "The Official Railway Guide, North American Freight Service Edition," P.O. Box 1750, Riverton, NJ 08077 (1-800-888-0636); and (2) "CTC Board," P.O. Box 55, Denver, CO 80201. Another handy publication is "Trains" Magazine, found on most newsstands.) You can easily foil railroads' hide-the-cards approach by asking the friendly

14

employee or knowledgeable hobo when that next train to Kalamazoo is heading out. You'll soon be on the inside track.

Hitchhiking presents a timing perspective *somewhat* akin to riding freights. In either sport we wait for something to happen which *will* eventually happen. A train or a car will eventually come by and stop. The main distinction between hitching and hopping freights is there's an element of *begging* involved in hitching. Not begging in the traditional sense; rather, enticing or cajoling someone to stop. To get a ride it's helpful to try to look interesting, cute or clever. None of this is necessary to hop a freight train.

On the railroad if we're in the right place all the trains stop. If we're not none of them stops. Thus the only timing similarity between hitching and riding freights is to select times when the greatest number of rides - cars, trucks or trains - is available. The question becomes: When are most trains rolling?

It's hard to make hard and fast date- or time - specific suggestions about when to head out for a ride - unless you named a specific railroad for me. When it comes to getting trains rolling every railroad has its unique policies and priorities. Each road is constantly changing its arrangements to accommodate traffic requirements. We can however develop some broad generalities which help us figure out when *more* trains are made up and running over the road.

Three governing principles help us decide what times are most likely to get results. These are: 1) movement of passenger/commuter trains; 2) the agro-industrial workweek; and 3) union pay scales. Let's take these in order.

1. Movement of Passenger/Commuter Trains

Without exception passenger and commuter trains take priority over freights. Unlike at the airport where our flight to Bangkok sits on the runway waiting for takeoffs by DHL, Flying Tiger, UPS and Federal Express, railroads are a bit old-fashioned in the belief that people come before parcels. On single-track mainlines they regularly knock freights "into the hole" to let "Amtrak," "VIA Rail," "Caltrain" or "RTA" trains pass. ("Into the hole" means onto a siding to let another train pass.) In fact the Federal Railroad Administration ("FRA") has a rule which *requires* freight trains to get out of the way for passenger trains.

The first thing is to figure out is whether you're in an area which has a lot of passenger/commuter train activity competing for the same track. Actually there aren't many such regions left in America after the oil/auto/tire conspiracy of the 1930s-50s. Public transit is a sore subject in the corporate boardrooms at General Motors, Goodyear and Exxon, who with their cronies went about meeting America's transit needs *their* way - by buying up and retiring urban rail systems.

The rare metropolitan areas which had brains enough to hang onto their rail transit systems include cities along the Eastern Seaboard from Boston to Washington D.C., the Chicago area and the San Francisco Bay Area. These rail transit systems are distinguishable from newer urban rail systems which run on "dedicated track" (track used solely for passenger transit).

The older systems run on track used for long-distance commuter/ passenger service *and* freight trains. These include New York's Metropolitan Transportation Authority ("MTA"), Long Island's Long Island Rail Road ("LIRR"), New Jersey's New Jersey Transit ("NJT"), Chicago's Regional Transportation Authority ("CRTA" or "Metra"), Northern Indiana's Commuter Transportation District ("NICTD"), Boston's Massachusetts Bay Transit Authority ("MBTA," or "Charlie of the 'MTA'" - Peter, Paul and Mary), Maryland's Transit Authority ("MDOT") and the San Francisco-San Jose peninsular "CalTrain." Canada's Toronto (Government of Ontario, or "GO Transit") and Montreal (Montreal Urban Community Transport Commission, or "CTCUM") also have extensive commuter systems. Don't forget Amtrak's Northeast Corridor trains from Washington to New York running on Amtrak-owned or operated track, upgraded to provide 456 miles of 125 MPH service. Much as we support these systems as commuters, as adventurers they get in the way.

In the hobo department wait until typical commute hours are over in these areas. Mind you, it's fine to be *looking* for a train or car to ride during these hours. Just don't expect your train to pull out or get very far until all *paying* passengers have reached their destination. Passenger trains play hod with fast freight in these few areas of dense commuter traffic. Six to 9 a.m. and 4 to 7 p.m. are the times to be patient during the workweek, and Sunday evenings.

The underlying principle behind this advice is two trains can't pass each other on the same track - or what's know in the business as "single-track mainline." We know this from early childhood when we staged our first model train wrecks. Throughout much of the North American system railroads were cheap, or hadn't the foresight to build double-track to allow trains to slip past each other. Railroad buffs claim single track is "real railroading," because of the skill and hassle in getting trains around each another. *We* know it's a function of stupidity, near-sightedness and greed.

When two trains meet on single-track the question of which train is the *baddest* arises. The less-bad one has to go onto a siding to get out of the badder train's way. A "mainline meet" (when two trains bear down on each other on the same track) is one of any engineer or conductor's worst nightmares. Today railroads use signals, telephones and microwave to prevent these occurrences.

When one train goes onto a siding to let another pass this is called "going into the hole." The phrase reflects a natural inclination to assume one's train is Number One, and being required to acknowledge otherwise is a diminution in professional esteem. After all we try to avoid holes in life, don't we? Going into the hole has a negative connotation. To begin with most railroaders are a Happy Highball kind of crew. We'll talk about "Highballing" later but it means going fast.

There are ways to figure out how long we'll be in the hole - by listening to air brakes, reading signals and watching engines and crew. We'll discuss these tricks in later chapters once we have you up on a freightcar. Choosing times which don't conflict with commuter outpourings cuts down on the time spent waiting in the yards or in the hole for people who "ride the cushions" or the "varnish."

2. THE AGRO-INDUSTRIAL WORKWEEK

Monday begins the week. Just as in any business railroads have certain volumes of freight they can handle. Each railroad's ability to absorb its share of the nation's production output is limited by the number of engines, cars, tracks and employees it has standing ready at a given moment. This is particularly true with freightcars.

Heavy industries like mining and manufacturing have relatively constant material and delivery needs. Unlike the old days when small businesses shipped by rail, today most rail shipments involve predictable movements from *quantity* (large-scale) producers to their customers.

In contrast agriculture is seasonal and has wide swings in shipping requirements. Therefore at one time of the year a railroad might have too many of a certain kind of car per volume, while at others - like harvest time - too few. Agro-industry has been forced to consider railroads' capacities in determining when and how much of their product and material to ship.

As a general rule large railroad customers have a railhead, siding or series of sidings which come off the railroad's main line over to their factory, mine, lumberyard or grain elevator, etc. Customers can only afford to keep so many freightcars on their property due to space limitations and "demurrage" (rental) charges. Before they reach their spacial or demurrage limits they ask the railroad to come get the full cars and drop off empties.

The railroad shows up at the factory, etc. with a train and crew to haul the goods to market and bring the empties and raw materials to the plant. Railroads *try* to consolidate their techniques and procedures by carting things to and from a particular customer with the same engines and crew. But the left and right hands tend to overlook each other in large corporations. After the halcyon days of straight monopoly railroads have been dragged kicking and screaming into the era of competitiveness - due primarily to the trucking industry and interstate pipelines.

So one day a railroad might come by to pick up loaded cars. The next day they'll deliver empty cars or cars loaded with raw materials. The long and short of it is railroads still have aways to go before they can really compete on an efficient, cost-effective basis.

A typical railroad operates as follows: Yard crews "make up" local "work trains" over the weekend (especially late Sunday night and early Monday morning) to take out to local customers. On Monday crews take out slightly fewer empty cars than they bring back loaded ones. Industrial operations are usually closed over the weekend and don't begin filling their cars until late Monday or Tuesday. If a work train heads out to customers *early* on Monday the customer's loaded cars can't be brought back to the yards until Tuesday. In contrast during harvest season agricultural customers often request two "pick ups" per day to prevent delay. Agro customers also work weekends during harvest season and their cars are full by Monday morning. Monday work trains need to pick these cars up.

The key idea is everybody recommences the program on Monday, including the railroads. Except during harvest, on Monday customers start filling up freightcars and railroads begin hauling loaded cars back to the yards and empty or loaded ones out to the plants.

This means on Monday in the yards the railroads have a lot of *local* trains running but won't have many long-distance trains ready. They're parceling out and picking up business. They need time through the workweek to kick the cars around in the yards and make up long-haul trains. It's also a known fact in worker productivity studies Monday is not a banner day of industrial production (everybody knows not to buy a car manufactured on Monday morning or Friday afternoon). So Mondays are slow for us.

But agro-industrial activity continues and intensifies through Tuesday, Wednesday and Thursday. Once the railroads start picking up and delivering on Monday and increase this activity on Tuesday through Friday, we see much more action in the yards. Once they've got hold of enough cars, railroads "bunt" trains together to send out "over the road."

The rate of speed with which a railroad makes up trains and sends them out depends on factors beyond when they get hold of the cars. One important criterion is the *kind* of freight they're entrusted with. Is it perishable (like lettuce), or valuable (like new cars or appliances), or a rush shipment (like anything needed yesterday or mail); or is it something they can take their own sweet time with? Other factors affecting a railroad's promptitude include labor-management relations, the weather, availability of rolling stock, track conditions, whether the customer is paid up, harvest seasons, etc. We have no control over any of this. I mention these factors so you get the sense you're participating in an enormous conglomeration of inter-corporate transactions.

On Tuesday things start picking up. Wednesday, Thursday and Friday are action days. On Saturday things start fast but then slow down, and Sundays are often dead. Consider this description of the workweek in its very broadest perspective.

Another important thing to remember is you can catch a train out *over the road* any day of the week. Many trains have origins or destinations hundreds and even thousands of miles away. They don't get there overnight. Say a train is made up and sent out from the large port in Norfolk Virginia on a Thursday or Friday. It may not make it to your neck of the woods until Saturday or Sunday. If you're on a mainline in North America trains are coming through all the time.

3. RAILROAD UNION PAY SCALES

Another factor affecting timing is unionization. Railroads are almost 100% unionized. In fact the history of the railroad union movement is a microcosm of unionism in America. Railroad workers formed unions earlier than any other major industry. Railroads more than any other large-scale industry - even steel - have remained thoroughly unionized for over 70 years and in many railroad trades much longer.

Why is it unlike anyone else railroad employees manage to stay unionized? How have they kept management from undercutting their grip on the industry? Two basic reasons: 1) they have highly-skilled, dangerous jobs and are hard to replace, and; 2) when they go out on strike *everything* grinds to a halt. Query however what might be the distinction between them and air traffic controllers? I guess you could always take a train.

If for example railroad labor peace is at hand railroad workers make an effort to see the game goes smoothly, without a lot of official timeouts or appeals. They slap trains together and expedite them in "relatively" short order. If however labor *war* ensues they work "By the Book" (or "To Rule" in the U.K.) and everything slows to a snail's pace. ("By the Book" refers to the ICC/FRA/union/management book called the Book of Rules. The Book outlines the proper, safe way everything should be done on the railroad.) The Mother of All Rules in the "Book of Rules" and on all railroads is to work *safely*.

If each and every one of the book's procedures is followed however the makeup and dispatch of trains slows to a crawl. Here's a typical safety rule: "The most efficient speed for a switchman is 2-1/2 MPH, which is walking speed." Do you know many people less than retirement age who walk at 2-1/2 MPH? When the union works by the book it punishes management for its intransigence by insisting members work "safely" - which means everything slows down and traffic snarls occur.

In other words as far as we're concerned if everything is hunky-dory labor-management-wise the workers knock out trains and we don't have to wait around. But if they're disgruntled be prepared to get *patient* waiting for the anointed hour when the railroad finally "calls" a train and proceeds.

Railroad employees are a specialized group of workers - and they know it. The job takes skill and precision because it's flat-out dangerous.

Working in a North American freightyard was and *still is* the most danger-ous job we do even if all regulations are followed.

Watch railroad workers out doing their jobs. One false move and it's goodbye to that hand, leg or foot. Thousands of railroad women and men have been killed or maimed in the last 160 years, often due to someone's confusion, inattention or insobriety. Until invention of the automatic cou-pler and air brake it was commonplace to see railroad workers with one or two fingers missing from each hand - or only one hand left. They called it getting "pinched." In 1888 for example (the first year for which reliable statistics were compiled in America), 315 railroad passengers were killed and 2,138 injured, while 2,070 employees were killed and *20,148* injured! (As a basis of comparison, in 1988, 2 passengers were killed and 337 in-jured, while 43 employees were killed and *22,573* injured.) This is why railroad workers were one of the first groups (like pilots and truckdrivers) singled out by lawmakers for substance-abuse testing.

Between 1898 and 1908 (the first decade of non-employee injury compilations) 47,000 "railroad trespassers" were *reported* killed. Probably twice that number perished and were buried in "hobo graveyards" alongside the tracks. Railroading continues to be a dangerous job and that includes us.

Armed with the knowledge they have skilled and dangerous jobs, railroad employees have slowly but surely learned they can hog-tie the na-tion by going out on strike. They truly can. They truly have. And if they're ever allowed to strike again America's 200,000 railroad workers truly will.

For example in June 1992 a railroad machinists' union called a strike against the giant CSX Corporation under the terms of the Railway Labor Act. The strike was the culmination of nearly 5 years of negotiations over huge corporate bonuses vs. "featherbedding" of union jobs which have no real work. Thirty-nine of the 40 member railroads of the Association of American Railroads (AAR - the industry's trade group, statistician, lobbyist and coordinator) bargaining unit locked out their unions and shut down. Transportation Secretary Andrew Carn estimated the strike would cost the nation 1 *billion* dollars a day and declared a 30-day cooling off period. Secretary Carn ordered the unions to either negotiate, go to binding arbi-tration or submit their grievances to a three-member arbitration team and accept the last best offer extended within 20 days. If the unions rejected the arrangement the arbitrators would pick a package and give it to the Presi-dent for his signature. Ninety percent of the union members rejected the arbitrated settlement. Nevertheless CSX employees were handed 16% cuts in wages and health benefits. In effect the railroads shut themselves down to prompt government intervention.

All of which means railroad unions have great impact on our timing. Over the years the unions (mainly today's "UTU" - United Transportation Union, an umbrella group for the traditional railroad trade "Brotherhoods") have cut deals with management which determine how much workers get paid during the three workweek shifts, Saturdays and Sundays. Like other industries wages go up on swing shift and graveyard - nighttime "differentials" which compensate for working strange hours. Saturdays and Sundays are a veritable goldmine where workers can make up to 2-1/2 to 3 times the flat rate. This runs into a lot of dough shelled out by management. All told labor costs (wages, health, welfare, pensions and payroll taxes) represent over 40% of a bigtime Class I railroad's annual operating expenses.

Thus we see the constant struggle to eliminate jobs through technology - like doing away with firemen ("ash cats") in the 1970s and cabooses ("bouncers," "buggies" or "crummies") in the 1980s. If they ever invent robots for brakemen like in the auto industry things will change again.

This means if you're planning to catch out on a newly-marshaled train ("Marshall" is freight parlance for putting a train together. Railroads "make-up" and "break-up" trains like lovers. Older railroaders and management types call freightyards "marshaling" or "classification yards"), you'll see many more freights made up on Tues*day* through Fri*day* than most nights, Saturday afternoons or Sundays - except during high summer and fall. Many may be the woeful weekend when you traipse down to the yards only to be told there won't be anything coming out until a day or two later. The combination of agro-industrial production and union pay scales makes Thursday morning through Saturday morning the best bet. Friday night is always busy even though workers are paid more. Freight stacks up after the workweek. (This is the best time for low senority workers to be "marked up" on [being at the top of] the "Spare" or "Extra" Board. They'll likely be called.) By Saturday afternoon most trains have been sent out and pay scales are high. The yards get quiet.

But be not of despair. Don't hang your boots up simply because it's late Sunday night. Remember those over-the-road trains moving everywhere every day.

Bear in mind these timing tips are *general* in nature - shot through with myriad exceptions. Your favorite railroad (or at least your local one) may march to the tune of a different drummer. America and Canada have close to 500 freight railroads although only the big 14 have major through-routes. Within legal limits American railroads can operate any way they find profitable since the Staggers Act deregulation of 1980. Many seasonal and manufacturing variants arise throughout the far-flung regions of the continent. Late Spring, Summer and Fall will always be busier than Winter and early Spring. Commuter trains and unions make timing more challenging. When in doubt whether you've picked the right time to hit out, find out everything possible from people in the yards before being satisfied nothing exciting is happening.

IV

WHERE DO I GO TO CATCH A FREIGHT TRAIN?

Maybe you haven't got hold of that railroad atlas we were talking about earlier. If you're serious about this sport I strongly suggest you do. But if you don't have one, open up a national roadmap.

The railroads *generally* follow the same routes we see on the roadmap. In the East you'll notice the basic directional patterns run in both directions - north-south and east-west, whereas in the West it's mainly east-west.

This is more vividly demonstrated with a railroad atlas than a roadmap. West of the Mississippi there are few north-south railroads. Why? West of the Big River settlement and shipments moved from east to west. In America and even more so in Canada, our long train rides are east-west, not north-south.

One important question is which parts of the country are easier to ride freights through? Answer: The West and South rather than the East and North. Much of this has to do with weather, but also with the more relaxed approach to life people seem to have in the South and West. Railroads in the Sunbelt are and always were more tolerant of the adventurer than they've been back East.

Another reason riding trains is easier in the South and West is because more agricultural, mineral and forest products are produced there. Particularly in agricultural and lumber operations, industry needs unskilled workers on a *seasonal* basis, e.g., during harvest times or periods of low fire danger. The traditional North American hobo has been unskilled except during major economic contractions.

An unspoken peace has existed between many - but not all - railroads and industries in the South and West to enable the hobo to get to seasonal jobs. This is particularly true on the Burlington Northern and Southern Pacific, which stretch in a big circle from Chicago to Seattle to Los Angeles and back to New Orleans - and now crisscrossing the West back to Chicago. Miners, loggers and farmers throughout this hub need workers and railroads need business. With exceptions western and southern railroads give a wink and nod when hobos hop their trains.

This is not to say you can't ride trains in the East and North. You most certainly can to your heart's content. It's easy to catch bulls (Railroad Police) napping Back East because there are so many more miles of track and yards compared to the number of hobos. The only real problem with the northern *Plains* is weather. Any time from September to April in eastern Washington to Michigan you can be in for a very unpleasant surprise, like a Blue Norther'.

In the northeast (east of the Great Lakes and north of Maryland) it's a problem of passenger and freight congestion and railroad people having a bit of an attitude problem. South of the Mason-Dixon things get easier. Again there are many exceptions - railroad by railroad. You're more than welcome to catch a freight from downtown Pittsburgh if the spirit moves you.

Another cardinal truth is Western and Southern railroads (which primarily go through agricultural areas or relative wilderness - mountains and deserts) are more relaxed about people riding their trains (except the Santa Fe and Union Pacific). In these regions it's not such a big deal if we hop on. As a general rule we're more likely to encounter a hassle in a big urban area than out in the middle of God's country. But this is true of *life in general*, right?

Another concern is the danger encountered in big-city yards. Between the professional thieves and the volume of traffic rolling around you're in a more precarious position. All other things being equal I recommend making your first outings in rural or semi-rural areas. Go out where it's more peaceful and quiet to catch your first freights.

Please turn to the Appendix for a list of cities and towns in America and Western Canada where you're most likely to find a freight train to climb on and ride.

V

HOW DO I FIND A FREIGHT YARD AND GET INTO IT?

East of the Mississippi many towns were established before railroads reached them (an exception is Atlanta Georgia, which was consciously staked out as a railroad junction town). Boston, Hartford, New Haven, New York, Philadelphia, Baltimore, Washington D.C., Richmond, Norfolk, Savannah, Charleston and New Orleans were all well-established before the railroad arrived.

In general when a railroad arrived at an Eastern town, civic fathers were called upon to make a decision where to put the yards. Often this was accomplished through civic-mindedness and pride. Just as often it was accomplished with well-worn railroad money placed in the right civic-minded palms.

For Eastern municipalities railroads meant commercial boom and jobs. When the railroad arrived the town was connected with other commercial centers. This brought immediate economic expansion - always a welcome development.

On the other hand civic fathers had a downside to contend with. The railroad's arrival meant urban blight. Freightyards were noisy, smoky, sooty, dark and dangerous places in the days of steam. So the first question for Eastern cities and their new visitor was: "Where do we put this thing?"

And the answer was "Downtown." If a railroad actually *paid* for downtown property its owners bought the cheapest part they could lay hands on. More often through government's ultimate right of eminent domain civic fathers simply booted people off their turf, tossed them a few shekels for their trouble and turned the property over to the roads.

26

Failing this however a second alternative was to set aside some vacant property *adjacent* to the city limits, then assume the town would grow up on the other side of it - which usually happened. New neighborhoods which grew up across the tracks from the established part of town are what we call "The wrong side of the tracks." Americans have known where the wrong side of the tracks are ever since railroads first sidled up to Eastern towns before the Civil War. Tracks often delimited native-born from immigrant neighborhoods and red tape from red light districts. Boston, Hartford, Philadelphia, Chicago and Alexandria Virginia are examples of this kind of freightyard placement and "wrong side of the tracks" urban growth.

A third yard placement alternative evolved in cities where geographical limitations ruled out coming in downtown with anything larger than a passenger depot. New York, Boston and San Francisco are examples of this (San Francisco has always been an Eastern - even European - city at heart). Since Manhattan is an island and Boston and San Francisco are on the tips of rather confining peninsulas, railroads had to locate their big yards across a body of water - Hoboken and Jersey City in the case of New York, Somerville and Medford in the case of Boston, and Oakland and Santa Clara in the case of San Francisco. (Actually at one time San Francisco had some fairly extensive yards located south of town - the Bayshore yards. But they were abandoned long ago and were sold in 1989 for $108 million. S.F. is still a good example however because when the Bayshore Yards were established the town hadn't extended that far south. And in the tradition of the wrong side of the tracks the neighboring area became a ghetto.)

West of the Mississippi most towns owe their existence exclusively to the railroads. In extending their lines west railroad builders staked out where towns would be and brought in the people. In fact the builders' opinion of the value of particular regions of the West largely determined which regions were developed first. West of the Mississippi the major roads decided where towns would be located, except for Denver, Salt Lake, Provo, Santa Fe, Taos, Seattle, Albuquerque, Las Vegas (N.M.), El Paso, Astoria, San Francisco and Los Angeles - all of which existed before the railroads arrived. Otherwise once having staked out a region for development railroad owners literally said "O.K., we'll put towns here, here and here." In these towns the railroads put their divisions, shops and freightyards wherever they pleased - which usually was and still is downtown.

But not always. In some instances (especially in anticipation of the westward expansion of the Santa Fe) enterprising individuals made calculated guesses at which direction a railroad was headed and staked out towns and freightyards in advance. If the railroad agreed and came in, all well and good. If it didn't the town would die. In either event railroads - not land speculators - made the final decision which towns they would serve and set up shop in. These decisions were made with little input from government officials, either local, territorial, state (often because they were barely in existence) or the federal government.

Some western towns *did* owe their creation to influences other than the railroads (e.g., the federal government - usually for military purposes). Western military forts, garrisons and Indian Agencies were founded for reasons other than railroad interests. These include Forts Atkinson, Belknap Agency, Benson, Benton, Bidwell, Boise, Bragg (in California), Bridger, Calhoun, Clark, Cobb, Cody, Collins, Davis, Defiance, Dodge, Gallup, Garland, Gibson, Griffin, Hall, Hancock, Huachuca, Jones, Kearney, Klamath, Laramie, Larned, Lincoln, Lupton, Lyon, Mackenzie, McKavett, Morgan, Peck, Pierre, Rice, Riley, Ripley, Robinson, Rock, Ross, Scott, Seward, Sheridan, Sill, Steele, Stockton, Sumner, Supply, Thomas, Tompson, Towson, Union, Washakie, Worth and Yates.

Other towns came into being where two settlers' trails met along the Oregon, California, Mormon, Spanish, Santa Fe (and Cimarron Cutoff) Trails. These include towns like Topeka, Las Vegas (N.M.), El Paso and Independence Missouri. Some towns sprang up where a railroad hit a navigable river or lake for transfer of freight from train to boat and vice versa. This explains Midwestern cities like Duluth, Minneapolis-St.Paul, Milwaukee, Chicago, Detroit, Cleveland, St. Louis and Kansas City.

Still other towns owed their existence to the route taken by the Overland Mail Company land grant of 1862. Green River Wyoming is a good example. Green River was originally an Overland Mail town incorporated in Dakota Territory in 1868. When the Union Pacific arrived two months later with automatic land grant ownership it demanded from $70 to $100 for each city lot. The citizens agreed on proviso U.P. put its winter terminus for passenger and freight trains in town.

The U.P. refused to dig in at Green River and staked out the town of Bryan 12 miles west for its winter haven. All but 100 of Green River's 2,000 residents moved to Bryan to work. In 1872 Bryan's water dried up however and the U.P. moved back to Green River. Green River Wyoming is a typical example of the jockeying which went on between preexisting towns and railroads. Another is Nickerson Kansas. When the Santa Fe tore down its division there nearly all of the 300 employees were forced to move to Newton. Nickerson had been deemed a "backwater." Today Nickerson does not appear on the map of Kansas.

All this has great bearing on where to find freightyards, because there's an important distinction between an Eastern and a Western town. Back East it's problematic reasoning out where the yards are by knowing the history of the town. Out West where the railroads called the tune they took the select portion of riverbank or coastline, or a low-lying area for their yards, or a high-lying area for their mansions. In general they took whatever part of town best suited their needs.

Conclusion? Whether East or West, look at a map of the town you'll be catching out of. If nothing else you can consult a map in a local gas station. You can conjure up where the yards are simply by evaluating the town's terrain and how it's configured.

In a riverless flat town the only bridges in town will be for streets going over the tracks. A nighttime technique is to listen for trains booming around in the distance. Or as you come into town keep an eye on the tracks coming in to figure out where they head. Most tracks parallel the main road coming into a town, then branch off.

If it's a hilly town the yards will be in the lowest part. If it's a river or port town the railroad will be close to the water. In a factory or company town the railroad will be near the plant. In a farm or mineral town the yards will be near the grain elevators, mine or mill. In religious towns the railroad will be as far away from the main house of worship as possible. In a boom town (except San Francisco) the railroad will be downtown - even Denver.

Going back to a map if one part of town has streets laid out in uniform squares or rectangles - especially running north-south and east-west - the yards are often next to one side of them. Railroads loved to lay out streets in boxes running to the points of the compass. Chicago, Minneapolis, Denver, Sacramento and Phoenix are good examples of railroad-square towns. Towns with numbered and lettered streets give a strong clue, which may be a sad commentary on the empire builders' creativity. The yards are near the start or finish of the numbers or letters. If there's a blank space which looks like it shouldn't be there the yards are there. One dead giveaway is if there's a street named "Railroad Avenue" with a big blank space next to it. Always look in the Street Index for a "Railroad Avenue, Street," etc. or a street named after the local railroad (i.e., "Cotton Belt Street").

Initially the best way to find the freightyards is to ask a townsperson who looks like he or she's in the know. Getting directional information from the sun or Polaris and studying a map in advance will prevent you from making a forced foot-tour of the entire municipality.

Once you've got your bearings and are headed toward the yards, notice the street you're on usually deadends at the edge of the yards. Most streets do this unless they're major thoroughfares which cut through the yards or go over on a bridge. If your street deadends you'll likely be confronted with a fence at the edge of the yard. Fences are an annoying and vexatious part of our sport. Let's talk fences for a minute.

Like most property owners railroads go in heavily for walls, barricades and fences - but mainly fences because they're *cheap*. Railroads are cheap and are wild about fences - especially the *cheapest* kind - the chain link fence.

The funny thing about fences is unless a large landowner is *really* serious about keeping us out, there's always a hole in the fence right where we need one. Why? Because people take a very common sense approach to fences. They realize fences are stupid, antisocial, elitist - and above all ineffective. Armed with this wisdom people trash fences with unceasing regularity. Nowhere is this more true than around a freightyard. Everyone knows you can't hurt a freight train. The worst thing you can do as an individual is start a fire or pass out on the tracks. Yet railroads have this overwhelming desire to demarcate their terrain with fences.

Think about the chain link fence for a minute. Aside from barbwire it occurs chain link is not only the cheapest but the *dumbest* kind of fence you can erect. Here are its inherent problems:

Problem Number One, we can see right through it to what we want or where we want to go. Problem Number Two, it provides its very own means of being scaled (we stick our feet through the holes and away we go). Problem Number Three, any ten year old kid can cut through one with a decent pair of bolt cutters.

At times railroads get fancy with barbed wire strung along the top, taking their cue perhaps from concentration camps and range wars. But we all know how often barbed wire is cut, snapped, rusted away and dangling uselessly. Even with the new nasty curly-cue stuff barbed wire rarely presents a consistent, down-the-line obstacle. And barbed wire only solves Problem Number Two. Problem Number Three is usually the fate of barbed wire as well as chain link.

In short almost without exception we can find a conveniently pre-established *hole* in the fence at every major place where people seek access to the yards. Usually holes are found where streets in a town terminate at the edge of the yards. Sometimes they're in a nook or cranny where no one can see us slip through. Oftentimes they're where people in the neighborhood need to get through to visit friends on the wrong or right side of the tracks. Wherever the hole is you'll soon find it, because railroad fences are *shot through* with holes. Just stroll alongside the fence, keep your eyes open and soon you'll find your inroad.

Not to mention these fences are never continuous. At some point you'll find a gap where an access road or spur line enters. Railroads can't fence out their workers and customers, can they? Or the gap is where a bridgeless public thoroughfare crosses the right-of-way. Running into a fence is not the end of the world. Just walk along and sure enough, you'll find a way through, over or around it.

Once in the yards be on the lookout for someone who can tell you where your train is. Find a worker who looks like he knows what he's doing. With your ever-ready charm and congenial personality warmed up, ask this person where that next train to Seattle is. He'll either tell you or find out with a radio or squawk box.

If it's a hobo you run into you're also in luck. He'll know where you want to go to catch out. If it's a worker you're in luck. He'll have the information about which track to find and what time the power's "called for" (i.e., when the "over-the-road" crew comes on duty - your train usually won't leave for another hour or so). If you meet both such personages you're on a roll. You'll be able to figure out the best way to get from where you are to where you want to be, using all the time-tested techniques outlined ahead.

VI

WHO IS WORKING ON THE RAILROAD?

Aside from fellow wayfarers the other people we meet hopping freights are railroad employees. Let's examine who railroad workers are and how to relate to them because they play an indispensable part in our adventure. Let's begin with the bonafide workers we meet out in the yards. Then we'll talk about the bull.

RAILROAD WORKERS

Railroad workers are our friends, not our enemies. Believe it or not 98% of them *dig* it when we hop a freight. At first blush you may find this surprising. You might think railroad workers are a collection of rough-and-tumble hell-bent-for-leather workers who'd just as soon toss us out on our ear as look at us. Nothing could be further from the truth. In fact if you stop to think about the friendliness of Americans and Canadians in general it's only natural railroad employees are friendly.

In addition there's a *specific* reason why railroad workers are a nice group of people. The best way to illustrate this is to focus on the nature of the job itself.

Imagine for a moment the typical railroad worker. What does he or she do for a living? (S)he schedules, monitors, dispatches, reroutes, repairs, maintains, locates, arranges, rearranges, signals, switches, hooks up, breaks up and shunts huge, inanimate objects (i.e., freightcars) for huge inanimate railroad companies (i.e., the 14 big ones) who *try* to make huge profits off the back of her or his union-employer-government-regulated labor. In other

32

words workers are out there risking their necks to make profits for a company which probably doesn't even know they exist. And they do this at relatively modest personal income.

Let's be blunt - it's even worse than that. In the corporate world - and especially in a corporate enterprise as large as a modern-day North American railroad - somebody is always on your back. Shopforemen, supervisors, union reps, quality control people, arbitrators, safety management teams, contract/work dispute resolution teams, management directives, blah, blah, blah. The corporate worker is constantly being pushed and pulled by faceless interests over which he or she has little or no control. One result of all this pushing and pulling is that an employee in a gigantic corporation obtains little feeling of personal accomplishment from his work.

So while working on the railroad as a brakeman, carman, engineer, conductor, engineman, carknocker, switchman, tower operator, dispatcher, trackwalker, shopworker, rip-track worker, gandy dancer, dirt stiff, bridge hog, stake artist, mud chicken, snipe, jerry, rust eater, dino, bender, hump master, retarder operator, callboy, shop carpenter, section hand, janitor, car foreman, section foreman, yard foreman, hostler, wiper, trucker, trainmaster, shopmaster, roadmaster, boilermaster, signal maintainer, telegrapher, shopman, telephone lineman, track patrolman, flagman, yardman, ash cat, herder or waybill checker - the employee walks around silent, rolling monoliths of corporate commerce known as freightcars, thinking or muttering to himself about sex, strikes and whether it's gonna rain today.

The freightcars don't respond. They watch in silent witness to his trials and tribulations. The rails, ties and ballast stand by muted. The earth and fences solemnly watch as he traverses his course through the day. And this guy or gal knows his buddies are off somewhere doing pretty much the same thing.

Most railroad employees - especially the large majority who are yard workers - are all alone during much of their shift. Most things which need doing can be done by one person. The large distances involved in getting from one job to the next and single-operator stations or towers keep people isolated. The typical railroad employee is out there pondering the imponderable and perhaps feeling a bit lonely. While feeling blue he's surrounded by symbols and slogans of wealth, success and corporate prowess plastered on the sides of freightcars: "Old Reliable," "Shit IT on the Frisco," "Southern Serves the South," "Next Load, Any Road," "For Greater

Efficiency," or "The ACTION Road." In other words very often he's out there by himself, constantly being reminded he's a very small cog in a very large wheel.

All of a sudden out of the blue in the middle of the yards he meets you. There you are walking toward him, just a regular sporting kind of person who wants to ride his train. The worker thinks to himself: *"A real-live human being!! Out here with me!!"* It's a bit of a surprise - but probably a nice one *if* you approach him or her the right way.

For starters don't startle a worker. If he's preoccupied with work, make some type of noise a respectable distance away like kicking the ballast or coughing. Make sure he's aware of your presence before you get up close.

Once aware you're in the yards the worker thinks to himself, "Hey, this gal wants to ride my train!" Believe it or not there's more than just a bit of flattery attached to this modest revelation. Maybe it makes him a bit more proud of his work. Thus, railroad workers help us get where we need to go.

I'm not making this up. If you're friendly railroad employees are friendly and helpful back. Basic intuition might tell you they're upset we're on their turf. Not true. If anything they're *happy* to see us out there.

Look at it from another angle: Railroad workers know what they're doing. They know what you're doing is illegal and against company policy. And after reading this you'll know what you're doing. You also both know it would be nice to take the day off and ride a train out to the end of the line. You appreciate their work because you know they're doing important and dangerous stuff. They know you appreciate their work because you'll benefit from it. It's a spontaneous little *conspiracy* you enter into out there in the wide open spaces of the yards.

Traditionally riding as an unpaid passenger or "free-loader" was not allowed - supposedly. Hobos knew it and railroad men knew it. But it went on largely with the tacit approval and assistance of the men in the yards, irrespective of Jack London's tall tales to the contrary in *The Road*. The same is true today. Workers figure as long as you simply want to ride no harm's done and it's fine with them.

When you meet these folks capitalize on the encounter by finding out what you need to know. If you don't know which train to look for ask them. They'll know which track it's on and which track you're standing on (tracks are always numbered). You can count tracks over to where your train is. When you ask the woman where that next train to Tuscaloosa is she'll say: "Well this is track 26. Your train's on 47. It's that way (pointing)." Then you thank her, start walking and count over tracks.

Let's say you want to know when a certain train will leave. She'll tell you when the power is called for. As indicated this is when the tower or stationmaster radios for "units" (diesel-electric locomotives, or "power") to come out of the "roundhouse" or "enginehouse" (yard where "off-shift" engines sit, idling or shut off), couple onto the cars and are readied for departure. If she doesn't know she'll call in with a hip-holster walkie-talkie she uses to keep in touch with the office or a nearby squawk box. She'll ask an innocent question such as: "Oh, and uh, by-the-way. When did you say that train for Jacksonville is called?"

The people in the office know what's going on. They know this worker has nothing to do with the train she's asking about. They know she's helping direct a "trespasser" to a train. It doesn't matter. The office always answers back. I've *never* asked a question of a railroad employee which wasn't promptly and courteously answered, and I don't think I'm any exception. If they don't know the answer they'll find it out.

The latest craze is to bring along your own electronic scanner and listen to dispatchers talking to yard workers and over-the-road crews. I've never tried this technique but it sounds intriguing. Hi-tech hoboing is probably here to stay.

If you're reasonably presentable and exude a pleasant, non-threatening attitude you can even *walk right into the office* and ask about trains. The folks in the office will look around apprehensively for a moment, then come across with the information as business-like as if you were the boss. In general try to avoid people wearing ties or white hats (supervisory personnel). Look for the gals and guys in the dashboards. Also look for "call sheets" (train schedules) lying around or ask for one.

You may even find employees to be so helpful they'll tell you to follow them over to where you need to be, or tell you to get in the truck or locomotive and *take you* there. This is absolutely true. People in switchengines will invite you to climb on and ride with them over to where your train is. And that's real railroading. Or they'll tell you there's nothing called or "made up" (i.e., no string of cars coupled together with hoses hooked up ready to go), and you should come back later, or tomorrow or whatever. The point I want to emphasize is to view railroad workers as our friends. They are vicarious adventurers.

The Bull - Square Peg in a Round Hole

Because railroad employees are happy to see us ride their trains, like most things in life there has to be a countervailing factor - someone who's *not* happy to see us on railroad property. There is. There's only one guy we consistently have to watch out for. His name is "The Bull." We need to develop the parameters of this railroad personage so you're fully prepared to deal with him *if* you ever meet him.

The bull is a private railroad employee who's job is to ensure mischief is not made with company property - land, equipment or freight - and to put fear into the hearts of trespassers along the right-of-way. The bull is to railroad property as the scarecrow is to the cornfield. He's commonly referred to by employees and sportsmen alike as either the bull, or "dick." "Bull" is current hobo lexicon for the fellow. "Dick" is an archaic predecessor which once included the police and other private-eye types. Other nicknames were "fly cop," "spotter" and "stool pigeon."

Company officials and the bull himself refer to the job with highfalutin' appellations like "Railroad Police," "Special Agent," "Railroad Security Agent," "Railroad Detective" or some other similarly-interchangeable combination of awe-inspiring titles. This awe-inspiring kind of job description sounds more impressive than "Bull" of course, although much less descriptive of what he actually does. Bull describes it best.

Fortunately North America has grown more civilized since the Depression, which was the heyday of the bull. Bulls were once brutal, sadistic railroad police who patrolled the freight yards, preying on hapless wanderers. Many were former city and state police who had been dismissed for brutality. Some railroads sought them out for their training and disposition toward an underdog. They used to shoot people, beat them up, go into the jungle and make trouble and do other equally deranged things - all in the name of private property. Even today's most frothing railfans aren't much enamored of the bull.

The old days were bad with the bull. Perhaps you've seen movies like *Emperor of the North*, where Ernest Borgnine plays the Depression-era Union Pacific freight conductor trying to keep Lee Marvin the hobo off his trains. One technique was to tie a big metal nut on the end of a rope. The game was to let the nut bounce up and down under a moving train off the ties and undercarriage of the cars (underside of the floor) trying to nail hobos "riding the rod" underneath (see below).

This kind of thing is not mere Hollywood. Old hobos have stories like this. Bulls used to take people out into the fields and beat the tar out of them, and all other manner of unmentionable things. Happily all this has changed. But bulls still try to keep us off their trains.

Many rail-riding expressions come from techniques hobos devised to avoid being caught by the bull. Since these expressions are illustrative of the hide-and-seek nature of our relationship with the bull, four are described here.

Riding "blind baggage" or "riding the blinds" was a way of hopping a passenger train, literally by the seat of your pants. Hobos took a seat on the back footboard of the wood, coal or oil tender (the fuel car behind a steam locomotive), facing backwards and staring at the front car of the train, the baggage car. (A "footboard" is a small catwalk provided for brakemen to stand on to ride with an engine or car while switching.) "Riding blind" referred to the fact the baggage car had no door on its front end. Thus since you sat with your back against the rear wall of the tender while facing the sealed front wall of the baggage car, you couldn't see anything except out each side. Hence riding blind baggage or riding the blinds.

The footboard was narrow and this was a dangerous uncomfortable ride. You had to hang on tight. Even dead tired sleeping was out of the question. In case of a dispute as to who got to ride a passenger train this way "the blinds" were reserved for the most experienced hobo.

Another blind baggage variant I've heard about was riding between two passenger cars. The walkways between cars were covered with a flexible material designed to protect passengers passing from one car to the next. Hobos clung to the outside of the material or "the blind" and hung on for dear life. I'm not sure I believe this. According to Jack London passenger trains a century ago had several blinds to choose from. Check out his short story "Holding Her Down" in *The Road*.

Although dangerous and rigorous, any way you did it riding the blinds was a quick way to get on and off a passenger train. You could latch onto your train at the very last minute as it picked up speed and the bull was neutralized. But after sitting on a bucking, bouncing footboard or blind for 200 miles you'd had a day's work.

A more dangerous variation on riding the blinds was "riding the bumpers." "Bumpers" are the draft gears which hold out the "hands" or "knuckles" of the couplers at each end of a car. Draft gears (or in the old days "draw-heads") are called "bumpers" because they're spring-loaded or otherwise cushioned to absorb shock between cars. Hobos climbed on trains - again, optimally at the last possible moment - and straddled the draft gear to ride. With less space to sit on than a footboard and nothing to hang onto, this ride was like bronco busting. If the train suddenly stopped or started the rider could easily be crushed or hurled under the train.

But there was an even *more* dangerous way to ride called "riding the rod." The "rod" was a series of metal struts running underneath the undercarriage of older freightcars which reinforced the structural integrity of the car. Roughly eighteen inches of space existed between the topside of a rod and the undercarriage of the car. Another place to ride was on the narrow brake rods that stretched just above the car's trucks - the four-wheeled units at each end of the car. Perched here the rider was in constant danger of losing his balance and falling under the wheels.

Hobos crawled in underneath cars, climbed up on top of a rod and rode for miles and miles. When they got down they'd be deafened from the car's concussions and covered with grease, soot and dust. It was a rough, dangerous ride. The advantage of riding the rod was you couldn't be seen under there. To flush out hobos the bulls used the nut-on-a-rope trick.

Another favorite technique, "riding the deck," involved climbing up onto the roof of a passenger or freightcar. Out over the road hobos were free to sit up and enjoy the scenery. But when the train came into a yard they'd flatten themselves face-down on the roof. Earthbound bulls couldn't see them up there. The danger was always the same - falling asleep. One healthy rock and you'd fly.

Lastly yet another spot frequently used to ride passenger cars was inside an empty battery box slung at the bottom of the car. The wayfarer was in peril of being thrown out of the container and under the wheels if the car suddenly jerked or took a sharp turn.

Today these evasive measures are no longer necessary. I've never seen anybody riding blind baggage (since tenders are a thing of the past) or the rod (since freightcars with rods have long since been scrapped) or the bumpers (although I wouldn't be surprised if some of our more desperate visitors from south of the border use this technique). Battery boxes no longer exist since passenger trains are fully electrified. Every now and then someone rides the deck - usually a kid or a greenhorn. I wouldn't recommend it. It's a long way down.

Instead of being hired to rough people up, today the bull is entrusted with the sole and edifying responsibility of ensuring railroad property interests aren't interfered with. To do this he's equipped with a car/truck, a gun, coffee, a badge, an 11th grade education and a radio. If he finds trouble he's supposed to stop it. Not a very complicated job and certainly not a very interesting one.

What the bull is entrusted to do is really no different than your average bank security guard. Don't move, do nothing and make sure nothing happens. He doesn't produce, create, facilitate, fix, serve, solve, transfer or invent anything. He merely spends 8 hours' time ensuring nothing happens.

If anything *does* happen, 9 times out of 10 he's not there to stop it. That's why railroads suffer millions of dollars in theft annually. Unless someone *else* apprehends the thieves or figures out when a theft occurred the bull can claim it didn't happen in his yard or during his shift. So he rarely stops anything serious.

The reason he's not there to stop anything is his unparalleled sloth and laziness. Although the railroads will claim otherwise, no one supervises his work. He can do pretty much whatever he wants - which very often is sleep. Most bulls take the "You Call Me" approach. They hide out in the office until notified something's happening which warrants their attention - which almost never happens. Workers never call a chronically lazy bull out of the office to deal with us as long as we're behaving ourselves. *If* someone calls, the bull quickly guzzles down the coffee, grabs the gun off the desk, climbs into the car/truck and roars out to make sure everything's O.K. We don't have to worry about this typical kind of bull.

A few bulls actually drive around the yards through some of their shift looking for suspicious activity - which they rarely find. This type of bull (who does what he's paid to do) is the one we have to concern ourselves with. The bull who drives around is the kind of bull whose kids (if he has any) say "Dad loves his work." Let's call this kind of bull the "gung-ho" bull.

How do gung-ho bulls patrol? They drive around on access roads which run through freightyards. These roads are ordinarily used by workers to get where they need to be if they can't use the narrower "runways" between the lines of track. But gung-ho bulls use access roads to drive around and hunt for trouble. And in their book, *we* are trouble.

The gung-hos drive up and down the yards "all day" (maybe 4 hours max.) then head for lunch. It's one of those lonely, dirty jobs which - according to the railroads at least somebody has to do. Bulls simply check to see what's going on. They think they know where the "action" spots in the yards are including the jungle. They design their "patrol" to go from one action spot to another.

Among the rather obvious reasons somewhat strange people are attracted to this job (can you imagine wanting to protect things thousands of times your own weight?), one reason bulls hang in there is because they have to endure the unflagging disgust of all other railroad workers. The workers detest them.

Bulls represent the Boss. Ever since the 1870s (when they were called spotters) they've accused workers of union participation and theft (often rightly so). They're non-union. And they *try* to dress like white collar wonders (but wind up looking like door-to-door salesmen). This isolates them from the rest of the railroad world. And they can feel it. The beauty of all this is *we* can use this inherent hostility to good advantage.

In fact to prevent the possibility of meeting up with the bull ask workers if your yard has one. Many don't or are spottily covered. If yours does today find out what kind of car/truck he drives and what his routine is.

The workers will tell you all about the bull and will often help you in your efforts to avoid him. For example, "Oh, he drives a white Suburban and he pretty much stays on that road over there (indicating). He's probably at lunch now. He's no problem. Just stay down there (again indicating) and you won't run into him." Remember the conspiracy phenomenon which takes place out in the yards. The workers don't want you to get caught. They look sad on the rare occasion when you do - especially after they've helped you out.

So bulls may or may not drive around during some part of their shift, aimlessly wasting time and money. They attempt to maintain security by developing a "keen eye" for legs walking on the other side of freightcars. They're on a search-and-destroy mission and we're the target. This may seem hard to believe but it's true.

To illustrate the point, visualize what a person looks like walking on the other side of a string of freightcars from you. All you can see are legs moving except at the ends of cars directly in front of you. Here for a brief moment you can see the whole person before he's eclipsed by the next car. Mainly we only see legs walking. That's all the bull can see too.

Now visualize a person walking on the other side of *three* strings of cars. What can you see? Nothing unless you have X-ray vision or bend over and put your head down near rail level. When a bull does this he's assumed his primary position of authority. His vision is further impeded by having to watch his driving while being too far up off the ground to see our legs. In other words he has *inherent visual difficulties* we can easily exploit.

One major visual difficulty bulls have is nighttime. Nighttime is the *shits* for the bull. Almost all the theft and vandalism he's employed to curtail happen at night (and God help the bull if he ever runs up against a professional gang of thieves - day or night). Unless he has great night vision chances are he never sees what's going on. Even in "hot" yards (which employ gung-ho bulls) he's relatively powerless at night. The reason is simple.

As a rule freightyards are not well-lit at night. In fact they're usually pitch black. Only the most modern, up-to-date yards have neon or halogen lighting. The majority of yards are black, except for the distant light way off somewhere by the tower, yard office or roundhouse. Darkness is one of our major assets in giving the slip to an exceptionally gung-ho-bull. Look at this aspect of the sport as the closest thing to "hide-and-seek" adults can play.

Here's where dark clothing and gear give us an assist. At night we're incognito vis-a-vis our surroundings. The majority of freightcars are painted dark colors - rusts ("railroad red"), browns, blacks, grays or faded oranges. If we blend in with this color scheme the bull can't see us against these backdrops until he's right on top of us.

Another advantage we have over the bull is his lack of mobility. Unless he gets out of his car/truck his movement is limited to the access roads. Access roads are relatively few in number - say, one for every five tracks. We can always chart a course through the yards which avoids getting close to these roads.

Bulls never, repeat *never*, get out of their car/truck until they think they're hot onto somebody's trail. Have no concern about them moving through the yards on foot. Walking is not part of their job description. It's too much like work.

If we have the additional protection of one or more strings of cars between us and his access road we're way ahead of the game. We can use dark embankments, walls, buildings and trees to provide additional cover and limit our movement to times when no vehicles are approaching. If we see a car we quickly duck behind something. There are myriad ways to frustrate the bull's attempts to interfere with us.

We have yet another advantage over the bull. Railroads only have one on the job per shift. I've never seen more than one at a time no matter what size the yard is (although I've been advised in a few yards they work in pairs). When you go into the yards and see how enormous they are you'll realize a lone individual simply can't cover the territory.

Every now and again you might see a gung-ho bull parked next to a train entering a yard at night. He'll have his headlights and spotlight aimed at the train. This is the type of bull who *thinks* he's flushing people out. I've seen this technique used a number of times. Yet no matter what kind of car I've been on I've *never been caught*. Bulls tend to focus attention on trains consisting primarily of piggybacks or auto racks and "stack trains." "Junk trains" consisting of coalcars, tankcars or mixed low-priority freight draw little to no attention (see within).

Here's a suggestion: IF you think you've been seen by a bull AND the train stops soon thereafter, get off on the other side from him and make tracks ("lowline") out of the yards. He'll never get across the train in time to catch you.

In general then, talk to the workers about the bull, wear dark clothes, wait until night if necessary, walk two or three strings over from roads, use whatever camouflage, cover and other vision-impeding obstacles are available, watch your matches and smokes and avoid overhead lights.

What's the poop if you *do* get caught? Nine times out of 10 all the bull will do is jot down your name and other information then tell you to "Leave and don't come back." He'll tell you if he catches you again he'll take you to jail. He usually quotes a term of 30 days county jail. If it was up to him it would be 6 years on the rockpile. If he tells you to leave do it - for 8 hours, or go to the next division (see within). If the same bull finds you twice the same day odds are you go to jail. This is a high insult to his frail ego. But you won't be in the can very long.

Here's how getting caught works: Let's say through some incomprehensible foulup a bull stumbles upon you. He sets down the coffee in his "Cozy Cup" holder, radios in he's got a "Subject" (God only knows who he radios in to; nobody cares), gets out of the car/truck and strides over to you or tells you to "Approach The Vehicle." He'll ID you and write down your name and other information he thinks is important. While doing so he might ask some vapid questions about what you think you're doing down here. *Never make a damaging admission* like you know you've done wrong. Then he'll give you back your ID, tell you you're on railroad property and to leave. Try not to act too shocked when he tells you you're on railroad property. He'll screw up the sternest, meanest, ugliest eye he can muster and tell you if he catches you again it's gonna be 30 days.

Sometimes you have to read between the lines of what a bull says. For example, what would you make of: "I'm workin' out here 'til 6:30 an' I don't wanna see you in here again"? I'd say try seven.

The bull usually sums up by saying he's going to put your card on file. That way if he catches you again you go to jail. But I've been caught in the same yards more than once - even by the same bull - and they never recognized me or went back to the office to check. It's too much like work and his recitation is basically hot air. Politely stand there and watch him go through his song-and-dance and do what he says - for 8 hours. Then come back and try it again - at night.

Politeness and "Respect for Authority" are key here. What I'm suggesting is *if* you get caught, play *nice* and play *dumb*.

First of all be respectful. Acknowledge the bull has a thankless, courageous job protecting things five zillion times his size. Be grateful he stopped you before you did something horrible. Be friendly.

Look at it this way: Everybody in a cop or quasi-cop type profession has to deal with people who are less than excited to deal with him. As we've all seen many folks make the mistake of mouthing off at cops. Just ask your local parking enforcement official. So over the years cops have developed what's known in the business as the "Attitude Test." The attitude test is something we either pass or flunk, usually within the first 30 seconds.

For example while writing up your moving violation you can chat amicably about current law-and-order issues, maybe even admit the light *might* have been yellow (when you were in the middle of the intersection), and generally be friendly about the whole thing. You pass the attitude test every time. Maybe the cop will relent and let you off with a strong "Verbal Admonishment" not to do it again.

Or you can be surly and contentious, tell him you have a bigshot lawyer, he hasn't heard the end of this, you have friends in high places, jot down his badge number and generally make his day even more of a drag than it already was. You *flunk* the attitude test. Your test results determine what happens to you.

This is as true with a bull as any other kind of cop. It's up to you. If you want to be a jerk, so be it. But if you simply want him to take your name and tell you to leave this is up to you too. Sometimes if you're nice enough he'll drive you somewhere to get rid of you - like the Greyhound Station - or offer you some coffee. Seriously. Bulls aren't 100% bad folks. Just 100% lame. I've even met a couple of rather nice ones. The main idea is don't get cute and you'll get your hand slapped, not your butt kicked.

Here are a couple of suggested routines to keep filed upstairs if you meet up with the bull:

"Well gee, Officer. My friend told me it was O.K. to try to get on a train."

Or "Ever since I was a kid I loved trains. I just wanted to try to ride one one time."

Then there's "Well, actually, I'm a football coach at Local Tech, and I was just doing this for a little exercise" (this one is highly recommended).

A sure-fire tear-jerker is "Well see, my Mom died Friday, and I've been looking for a job for about two months. I gotta get to Wichita to be with the family. I'm afraid to hitchhike - too many weirdos on the road. I don't have any other way to get there."

And so forth.

Let's say worst comes to worst and the bull hauls your sporting self off to the klinker. The Penalty Box if you will. This of course is never a good development. But since I want to get you *excited* about freights, not paranoid, let's say a few things about hobo prosecutions.

Many bulls have no more legal authority than a bar bouncer. They have to make something like a citizen's arrest to have the force of law behind them. And they get very excited *if* they actually get a case into court. Going to court makes them feel like a real cop. But the chief reason they get excited is because it's a rare day when their efforts get prosecuted. The first hurdle is called the jail.

As we all know American jails are packed to overflowing. America is continually running out of cell space for the 1,000,000 or so inmates locked up on a day-to-day basis - 72% of whom *haven't been convicted* of anything (they just can't make bail). The entire situation is out of control and many jails are under Court Order to keep the population under a certain number. Exceeding the court-ordered number has been ruled Cruel and Unusual Punishment (by way of comparison, putting people to death isn't).

So with federal and state judges breathing down their necks jailers have to prioritize the types of dastardly criminals they actually *keep* locked up. They basically look at what you supposedly did, how big or little of a rap-sheet or "Criminal History" you have, or whether they know you and you're a jerk. Then they prioritize you for release on such-and-such a day.

Some of the more popular "Inmate Population Control" programs are weekend or work furloughs (remember Willy Horton?), good-time/work-time credits, halfway houses and early release. Depending on how packed the jail is the criminal element in America gets back on the street after serving somewhere between 30 and 70% of their sentences. It doesn't really matter how much more time legislators tack onto the popular crimes. People get out when the jail can't handle them any more. Parole and probation boards take care of the paperwork. These arrangements don't bother law enforcement people nearly as much as the man on the street. Law enforcement folks figure "He'll be back." And of course they're usually right.

But three other "get-rid-of-the-inmate" programs are of greater interest to us. One is where they let us out on our "Own Recognizance" ("OR") of our solemn obligation to return to court ("Yeah, I'll be there [*OR* I won't]"). For villains like us it's a serious commitment nobody really expects us to keep. Just stay away from the area for a while and your case will wither and drop off the vine (being a "line-jumper").

The other program is release after posting a nominal amount of bail - usually around 10% of $300 dollars or so. Jailers are not happy having to do all the paperwork for such a whimpy crime so odds are they'll put us in touch with the friendly bail bondsman. This civic luminary will be more than happy to take us to the nearest ATM machine and get us sprung for his "nominal" fee. Another typical disposition is release by noon the following day with time and fine suspended. You see, being in jail as Arlo Guthrie so eloquently put it in the movie *Alice's Restaurant* for doing something even less serious than littering, we're "In there with mother-rapers and father-stabbers, father-rapers and mother-stabbers, and all kinda mean, horrible, ugly people" - which means chances are good we'll be released quickly under some arrangement or another.

Now let's assume for some silly reason they won't release you and you're still in the Penalty Box after the first three hours or so. The next hurdle the bull faces is called the District Attorney's Office. D.A.s get just about as excited about a hobo case as we do about trash night. After all would *you* like to present such a case to a jury of your peers? Probably not. So the bull has to go to the D.A.'s Office to plead with somebody - anybody - to charge the case. Actually bulls love begging the D.A. to charge us because it's another real-cop activity. Moreover there's always plenty of free coffee and donuts to keep victims and witnesses from passing out after waiting three straight, thankless days to testify.

Now to be sure the Feds and every state have crimes against the railroad on the books. Some are quite serious like "Trainwrecking," "Sabotage," "Disclosing Information on Cargo Shipments to the Enemy," "Moving of Locomotive," "Tampering with Air-Brakes or Other Railroad Apparatus" and "Injury to Railroads and Railroad Structures." That sort of thing. These laws make sense.

But for simply *riding* a freight train the statutes follow the general trespassing genre of laws. The first such law was enacted in Pennsylvania in 1876 and was commonly known as the "Tramp Law." Today sometimes they call it "Endangering the Lives of Railroadmen and the Operation of Their Equipment," or "Obstructing Interstate Transport." California for example has a fairly typical one:

[Trespassing on railroad trains] Every person, who shall, without being thereunto authorized by the owner, lessee, person or corporation operating any railroad, enter into, climb upon, hold to, or in any manner attach himself to any locomotive, locomotive-engine tender, freight or passenger car upon such railroad, or any portion of any train thereon, shall be deemed guilty of a misdemeanor, and, upon conviction thereof shall be punished by a fine not exceeding fifty dollars ($50), or by imprisonment not exceeding 30 days, or by both such fine and imprisonment. (Penal Code § 587b - 1909 A.D.)

Other states run with the old vagrancy laws such as "Being In Danger of Leading an Idle, Dissolute, Lewd and Immoral Life," or "Loitering On or About Private Property with No Apparent Legitimate Business

Thereon." These turgid statutes are titles of laws from several states - high-sounding offenses which have absolutely nothing to do with sitting on a freightcar. Unbelievably you can be charged with theft *of services*. I'd argue with this one because they're providing *freight* service, not passenger. But these laws are on the books and every gung-ho bull knows them by heart. And loves them.

The next working day after our arrest the bull calls the jail to see if we're *actually still there*. If our luck is bad and we are he goes down to the D.A.'s office and tries to convince someone to charge the case.

Adept as they are at ducking work it's tough for a D.A. to escape the bull when he comes a'callin'. Instead the "Charging D.A." (who's usually a rather plodding soul who never goes to court) empathizes with the weightiness of the bull's responsibilities. Then he says he's got to get over to court right this minute. He'll get back to the bull after reading his 8-page single-spaced typewritten report about how we were caught standing next to a railroad train. Odds are he'll dismiss the case in court on arraignment day then duck the bull's follow-up telephone queries.

Even if you're in a very backward part of the country where D.A.s file on hobo cases you have one last ally - the judge. Be nice to the judge and maybe he'll be nice to you. Your judge will have 52 other father-raping type crimes on the calendar this morning and will seek a quick disposition of your high crime. Maybe he'll ask if you'd care to contribute $50.00 to the county coffers, or if you'd like a suspended sentence and don't do it again. Take these kinds of deals. People reviewing your rap-sheet in the future will undoubtedly conclude you're some sort of garden variety homeless person - certainly not a heavy-hitter.

If the principle of the matter is at stake and you won't take any deals the judge will hunker down on the D.A. to ascertain whether he's serious about going forward. If the D.A. is a real anal-retentive (and unfortunately many are) the judge can usually take the case out of his hands. He'll offer you something like credit for time served and glower at the D.A. if he doesn't agree. Everyone involved in the criminal justice system likes to stay warm and friendly. The D.A. will agree. In other words for probably the only time in our life a judge will help us out when all else fails. Of course none of this will have anything to do with us.

So yes it's illegal to ride freight trains. And yes people will try to catch us and make us pay. In general though the criminal aspect of our sport is so minimal as to be legally *de minimis* (which means "So what?"). But again we must accept the fact we can encounter unsportsmanlike conduct out there by people who want to spoil our fun. If you simply factor this in as one of the risks every sport involves you'll have a healthy attitude - and still have one helluva good time.

VII

HOW DO I KEEP FROM GETTING NAILED IN FREIGHTYARDS?

Once you've geared up, decided where you're going, gotten to, into and around the yards a bit the foremost consideration is **SAFETY**. The importance of this *most crucial aspect* of our sport cannot be overstressed.

The only equipment you need for safe and sane railroading is a good sturdy pair of gloves and boots and a good head on your shoulders - just good old *common sense* and some attention paid to what's going on around you.

Let's talk about safety techniques to use while walking around finding and getting on a train in the freightyards. To illustrate the degree of danger encountered if you're not careful in the yards, a little historical perspective sheds light on the risks we take riding the rails.

As the statistics for the years 1888 and 1898-1908 reveal, railroading used to be extremely dangerous - for passenger, employee and hobo alike. With fires, furnaces, boilers, hot water, pressurized steam, shovels, coal shutes, handbrakes, hand-couplers, inadequate signaling systems, "bad order" track and equipment people in America and Canada got snuffed and maimed on a daily basis.

Today much of the danger has been removed. Trains run on diesel or electricity, not wood, coal or oil. The risks of explosions, scaldings and asphyxiation have disappeared. In fact the largest cause of death on the railroad today is grade crossing accidents. There are roughly 180,000 unguarded grade crossings in America alone. Each year about 1500 people are killed and up to 3700 injured trying to beat trains across the tracks. Per annum trying to beat an approaching train across the grade represents two-

49

thirds of all deaths and injuries on the railroad. This is an engineer's greatest dread. In some areas railroads invite cops to ride up front and write tickets for people who play chicken with trains.

But on a day-to-day basis the biggest dangers for the *worker* were and still are operating locomotives, getting on and off trains, walking around in the yards and coupling freightcars together. According to the AAR in 1988 of the 28,253 employees and non-employees killed and injured by trains, 598 "trespassers" were killed and 920 were injured. In 1919 2,553 trespassers were killed and 2,658 injured; 1920 - 2,166 and 2,362. No statistics are available on how many of these trespassers were hobos as opposed to local residents crossing the tracks. From what I've seen the large majority must have been local residents based on the number of idiotic stunts and inattentiveness I've witnessed watching them wend their way through the yards.

We alluded earlier to the idea people lost fingers or worse working on the railroad. As an object lesson on why safety is paramount when riding the rails let's focus on why this happened.

In the 19th century the chief cause of injury among railroad workers was the primitive means used to couple cars together. The most dangerous method was the "link-and-pin" coupler, which in modified and safer form is still in use in much of the world today. Until 1888-98, instead of the solid metal drawbars and automatic couplings *now* used in North America and Russia, couplers consisted of primitive chains, then links and pins. The latter method was used for over 50 years.

Freightcars were equipped with a heavy metal link which hung down from a beam or draw-head jutting out each end of the car. One end of this link was fastened inside a slot in the draw-head with a large metal pin. To fasten the link the worker dropped the pin into a vertical hole through the draw-head, trapping the link inside. As the engineer pushed cars together the skill of the brakemen (ergo the danger) was in guiding the *other* end of the link into the slot of the approaching draw-head, then dropping a pin into that slot to complete the coupling.

The real art was in properly lining up the link, then *getting your hand out of there* before the two draw-heads smacked together and you got pinched. While some designs theoretically allowed brakemen to hold the link horizontal with a stick, or left room for the fingers when the draw-heads slammed together, in practice regardless of design the link-and-pin coupler was treacherous.

Brakemen planned ahead by readying the pin in the slot of the approaching car in a "cocked" position. Ordinarily the impact of the two draw-heads banging together shook the pin down into the slot, trapping the manually-inserted link in place. If the pin stuck however the brakeman had to pound it down with a spare pin or wooden mallet.

While guiding the link into the approaching slot or pounding one or both pins into position he had to stand *between* the cars where the engineer couldn't see him. This was a cramped, highly exposed and extremely dangerous position. The engineer might unexpectedly push one car against the other and crush the brakie's hands as he worked between the draw-heads. Or he'd get a finger or two stuck in the link when the engineer pulled the string taut. This operation was particularly dangerous on hills given the primitive brakes 19th century trains were equipped with.

Uncoupling cars was even more dangerous, especially if the cars were rolling during humping or switching. The brakeman had to run *between the rolling cars* to pull the pin. Or he could sit on one of the draw-heads (ride the bumpers) to pull it out. Can you imagine running or sitting between two enormous freightcars at night, in an unlit freightyard, over rails, switches and ties in the snow or rain, trying to pull a heavy metal pin out of a slot? Incredible, right? That's the way it was done.

Thousands of workers lost fingers or hands trying to wrestle with links and pins - or they'd get a foot stuck in a switch, either in the "frog" (the immovable part of a switch where two rails meet which allows the flanged wheels to cross from one rail to the other), or the "points" (the moveable part which switches back and forth from one track to the other).

Feet were crushed and severed. Some draw-heads didn't stick out very far. At times cars came close enough together to instantly crush a man to death.

Links and pins weren't the brakeman's only nightmare. Ladders and handholds ("grabirons" or "grabs") which workers used to ride cars during switching were also potential deathtraps. The walls and floors of old freightcars were made of wood. Oftentimes the bolts affixing grabirons and ladders were rotted out or stripped. Harried trainmen trying to hold a train to schedule often used nails or wire - whatever was at hand - to jerryrig broken "appliances" into place. A brakeman would grab the "repaired" hardware and it would suddenly snap off the car. He'd go flying - all-too-often under the wheels.

No railroad equipment inspections were required until well into the 20th century. Not until 1910 were railroads required to even *report* accidents, injuries and death. The Railroad Safety Act of 1970 was the first comprehensive law specifying inspections and penalties for violations.

Railroads were indifferent to the carnage. They considered disfigurement and death as ordinary hazards of a workingman's life. It was taken as a matter of course railroad men would be maimed and killed. Ready replacements were available. On rare occasions when confronted with the situation owners said accidents were "unfortunate" or "Acts of God." Only after a great hew and cry arose did legislation force the railroads to invest in safe equipment.

The degree of concern about railroad accidents is best reflected by the thousands of coupler designs patented between 1860 and 1890. Of these, Eli Hamilton Janney's "Automatic Coupler," invented in 1868 and refined by 1873 was ultimately selected for standardization and use.

Janney's coupler worked on the "clasped hand" principle. Two giant metal "hands" were attached to the ends of spring- or friction-loaded draft gears, instead of the more rigid draw-heads. To couple automatically one or both knuckles of the hands had to be open when the cars coupled. When the hands made contact the knuckle(s) swung to the closed position. A "lock" or modern-day pin dropped into place to hold the knuckles closed. Internal features prevented the lock from opening due to shock or vibration. To release couplers the cars were pushed together slightly to take the load off the coupler, called "taking in slack," "running in slack" or "cutting slack." The brakeman lifted up on the "cut" or uncoupler lever on the side of a car, neutralizing the lock and allowing one knuckle to open. The engineer could then separate the cars.

Janney tested his coupler exhaustively in 1874-76 and it was adopted by the Pennsylvania Railroad the latter year. Three patents later Janney's coupler was universally adopted in 1888 (the railroads forced Janney to waive patent rights on the shape of the coupler before adopting it). Even so 1888 was *five years* before the federal government "intervened." The coupling travesty was retroactively legislated away by the Federal Appliance Safety Act of 1893, which required only that coupling be somehow accomplished without the need to stand between cars.

Can you imagine the situation between 1873 and 1893 based on the killed-and-injured statistics for 1888? In fact, so memorable were the terrors of the link-and-pin system that to this day brakemen refer to themselves as "pin-pullers" and uncoupling cars as "pulling pins."

Through introduction of safety technology railroads have gradually minimized or eliminated the more glaring dangers in railroading. The employee injury figures remain high today because (as in other industries) even the most insignificant injury (i.e., a cut thumb) must be thoroughly documented. Government reluctantly intervened to ensure a minimum degree of safety was accorded all participants. In this century, persuaded by gradual realization train wrecks, workers' compensation claims and widow's benefits cut into profits, railroads have increasingly policed themselves safetywise.

Today *safety* is the thing railroads exhort their employees to keep uppermost in mind at all times. Safety meetings are frequent and safety reminders are plastered everywhere in the shops and yards. They say things like "One Moment of Carelessness Can Cause a Lifetime of Sorrow. **Work Safely**." You get the basic idea. Railroads have learned the hard way they're in a dangerous business. They rightfully encourage people to take things seriously out there. So should we.

As an adventurer you have to be physically and mentally prepared to walk around trains. But you shouldn't be *afraid* of them. Despite railroad-related killed-and-injured statistics national transportation studies show you're in more danger crossing a busy intersection than sitting on a freightcar - provided you're sitting on it *safely*. In fact the statistics indicate you run a greater chance of injuring yourself in your own *bathroom* than on the railroad.

Hearken back to the old railroad grade crossing signs painted with warnings like "Stop, Look, and Listen" or "Railroad Crossing - Look Out for the Cars." (My personal favorite is down in Mississippi - "Mississippi Law Says STOP.") Safetywise whenever you're on the railroad these time-honored maxims are in full force and effect. The fundamental rule here is to *always* stop, look and listen before putting yourself in a position where you could come into contact with a moving train or car. Follow the tips outlined below and you'll *be*, as well as feel, safe in the yards.

WALKING AROUND THE TRACKS

When walking along a track never, repeat *NEVER* walk, sit or lie on the rails or ties. Seriously - just never do it. Remember why they call freightcars "rolling stock." Because they roll.

Frequently in the yards a single car or string of cars will come rolling down a track, either coupled to an engine or not. At night or under certain atmospheric conditions like rain or fog you can't hear these cars approach until they're *right on top of you*. They appear out of nowhere, drifting silently along like huge ocean-going freighters. When vision or hearing are impaired moving freightcars can appear without warning - especially if the cars don't squeak. If you're on the track even if the cars are coupled to an engine the engineer can't see you and he won't know to stop.

Railroads go overboard to impress upon new workers the dangers of rolling cars. They teach them cars can roll silently day or night, regardless of the weather. They call rolling cars "Midnight creeps" - which gives us a good idea how serious the potential problem is.

We all know who wins in a collision between us and a 30 to 80 ton freightcar. We'll be dead meat. Railroad pizza. Do yourself a favor - never put yourself in a position where cars can sneak up on you. *Always walk and sit well to the side of all tracks.* Give yourself as much room as possible to the side so you don't even get nudged out of the way by a passing car. (Note: At times you'll see trackworkers walking on tracks. They do this because they have to and have been assured nothing's coming down the track. *We* never have this assurance. Do not follow their example.)

Also be on the lookout for things hanging off the sides of cars called "snags." Snags are often metal strapping, wood or wire used to hold down loads on cars. In general a snag can be anything sticking out from the vertical plane of the side of a car, even part of its load. If you're not careful you can get snagged with potentially serious consequences. Snags comprise a large portion of worker injuries and are one of a brakeman and switchman's greatest fears.

Your eyes and ears are your best friends in the yards - particularly your ears. Aside from good eyesight a keen alert sense of *hearing* is the greatest attribute we bring to a freightyard. Make a conscious effort to *listen* to what's going on around you. *EVERYTIME* you get ready to cross a track, and *before* crossing it, **stop, look both ways down the track** *and* *listen* **for approaching traffic.** This is rubric both in the yards and out over the road. After a short time this conscious effort will become second nature. You'll do it instinctively. Physically stop, or at least take a huge pause until you've developed the habit. Seriously folks. Always stop, look and listen to what's going on around you when playing this sport.

A couple of final points here: When you cross a track, *always step over the rail rather than on it,* particularly if it's highly polished. The railheads are more slippery than you think, especially if they're wet. They might have a fine sheen of dust or grease on them and away you'll go. Always step over them onto the ties.

Also be careful when you step on the ties. They're usually coated with engine or car oil and grease and have been treated with a coating such as creosote or a similar petroleum-based product which can become slippery when wet. Notice how water often beads up on the face of a tie. Even on a dry day if you're not looking where you're going you could take a nasty slip-and-fall.

Some hobos advise we ditch our pack before walking through the yards. This serves two purposes: (1) we look more like railroad employees; and (2) we can be safer in the yards looking for trains. I rarely do this and it's up to you.

In general be very careful crossing a track. Watch where you place your feet and move quickly. Don't tarry on a railroad track.

WALKING AROUND FREIGHTCARS

Aside from snags another dangerous situation arises when you have to get over to the other side of a standing string of cars. *If crossing a track only requires walking 10 or 20 cars always do this.* (The only exceptions are when you're in a hurry because something is leaving soon or there's a gung-ho bull you're staying between strings to avoid.) When there are lots of cars to walk around - like 30 or more - or you're in a hurry or have to stay out of sight, you'll have to climb over a car or up over the couplers to get across the track. There are two reasons it's dangerous to cross over or between cars - sudden takeoff/jerking and humping. Let's talk about sudden takeoff/jerking first.

SUDDEN TAKEOFF AND JERKING

Sudden takeoff occurs when a string of cars suddenly jerks into motion and starts rolling. This can happen in the yards or out over the road. Sudden takeoff occurs when either a switchengine ("billygoat" or "goat" in the business) or an over-the-road group of engines gets a signal to go and takes off. This is a gradual process up at the headend of a string. The first few cars don't jerk much as they start being pulled. But back down the string a car's commencement of travel can be sudden and at times extremely violent. This has to do with couplers.

As we mentioned automatic couplers are not rigidly affixed to the cars. Even before adoption of automatic couplers slack or "play" was built into link-and-pin couplers by use of a stout spring placed behind the draw-heads. This arrangement cushioned cars (but alas not brakemen).

After adoption of Janney's coupler freightcar designers found they could lessen the impact of starting, stopping and coupling cars by using friction between moving parts of the coupler system. A small amount of slack was built into the knuckles to assist single steam locomotives in starting to move a heavy train. Between closed knuckles of coupled cars there's still between 1/3" to 3/4" of "free slack." This slack allowed a single steam locomotive to start up pulling only the first few cars, then acquire more weight as it gathered speed and "stretched out" the string. Multiple diesel engines which generate far more tractive force than a single locomotive make this less of a problem today.

On older cars still in service a gigantic coiled spring is back-loaded behind each draft gear. Draft gears are flat metal bars housed in a "pocket" under the floor of the car at each end over the axles. They connect the coupler to the car by means of a "yoke." Although called gears they much more closely resemble long, flat metal plates. These gears slide in underneath the car in their pockets when "buff" or "run in" (compression) occurs in stopping or coupling. The gears slide out when "draft" or "stretch out" (pull) occurs in starting or uncoupling. The gear rubs against its metal pocket and creates friction as it moves in or out, easing the impact of buff or draft. You'll become familiar with the sound of draft gears grinding in or out underneath your car when your train starts or stops.

Draft gearing is the same idea incorporated into modern car bumpers. If you bang into something in a new car there's a small amount of give built into the bumper. The spring at the back of old draft gears and the pocket friction on newer ones provide the same kind of give. The distance (between 15 and 30 inches) a freightcar buffs in or drafts out is its "travel."

On older cars draft gears cushioned by springs absorb shock and provide for a smoother ride. Couplings can occur at speeds as high as 4 MPH before the risk of structural damage to the car arises. (Damage to freight is another matter, based on what the freight is and how it's been secured, called "dunnage" and "bracing.")

The further a gear and pocket extend in toward the center of a car the more pocket surface area is available to create cushioning friction for the gear. On modern cars draft gears extend into the center of the car by means of a "sliding center sill" which replaces a spring with a rubber or hydraulic "cushioning unit" under the center of the car. "Return springs" attached to sliding center sills re-center the gears after impact. Modern "cushion cars" provide structural integrity on impact at speeds as high as 13-14 MPH - depending on the number of inches of travel the sill provides. Today one-sixth of America's freightcars are cushion car-equipped, and are preferred by shippers of sensitive freight.

Thus no matter which type of draft gear/sliding center sill arrangement a train's various cars have, there's play in the string - especially in our situation where a string stands quietly on a yard track. Since the string isn't being pushed or pulled anywhere slack exists in the couplers and cushioning devices. Depending on the car models as much as 30 inches of slack exists per car. This slack adds up. A 150-car train of mixed loaded and empty cars extends for more than a mile and a half. The locomotives starting out move about 75 feet *before the last car even quivers.*

When an engine pushes or pulls on a string each coupler/draft gear/ sliding center sill down the line has its play buffed in or drafted out from front to back. Manipulating this play is a real challenge for an engineer when he begins moving his train. He has to draft out the play gently to avoid snapping a coupler and breaking his train in two (a "break-in-two"), or buffing it in too severely and shattering a coupler or damaging freight. His job gets complicated when the front half of his train is going uphill and the back half downhill or vice versa. Add in curves, braking and acceleration and his job becomes quite delicate. In fact it's fascinating how delicate thousands of tons of metal, wood and cargo become once in motion.

By the time the slack is drafted out or buffed in where you are say, back at the 57th car, the force and violence of the jerk can easily throw you down if you're standing on the car or toss you off its side if you're climbing around its exterior.

A subcategory of sudden takeoff is simple "jerking." Jerking occurs when the cars jolt violently but don't actually roll. The same dangers exist even though the cars don't move. The main cause of jerking is humping.

Fortunately our ears help out shortly before sudden takeoff or jerking occurs. Starting at the headend we hear a rolling "bo-bo-bo-bo-bo-Bo-Bo-Bo-Bo-**BO-BOOOOOM**" approaching. This enormous sound, like a series of artillery cannon discharging down a line in rapid-fire succession toward us or syncopated rolling thunder gives us from 1 to as many as 7 or 8 seconds to react - depending on how far away from the headend we are. *If you're standing on a car when the "Boom" approaches, crouch down as if getting ready to steal a base in baseball or grab hold of something.* If sudden takeoff or jerking occurs while climbing over couplers you're in a position of real danger. You could be thrown under the wheels. Using techniques we'll give you in a moment you can avoid this risk.

Humping

In the yards "humping" is the chief cause of sudden takeoff and jerking. Although you may *think* you know what humping is, chances are in railroad parlance you don't.

Humping a train is the means by which a railroad breaks up old trains to form new ones. This is the old-fashioned "marshaling" or "classification" of a train. There are two ways to hump a train - gravity-yard and flat-switch humping - depending on which kind of freightyard you're in.

In modern "gravity" yards a section of track toward the center of the yards is raised up in elevation. This is "The Hump." The hump has a tower or office located at its top or "apex." The idea is to push cars over the artificial hump then let gravity pull the cars onto the right track to couple with a train in the classification yards.

On the "receiving" or "arrival" side of the hump (where old trains are humped out of existence) each track leads through a switch onto a single track called a "switch leader." The switch leader leads toward one or two tracks which go over the hump. Down the other side the tracks fan out along switch leaders and through switches onto tracks in the classification, "departure" or "forwarding" yard to make up new trains. From an overhead view a hump yard is an hourglass configuration with the hump at the narrowest part of the glass. Here's how humping works in a gravity yard:

First the crew remove the old "road power" (and caboose if any) from the "dead string." Next a switchman "bleeds" the air out of each car's auxiliary air brake reservoir so the car can roll freely. To bleed a string he walks past each car and pushes on the "bleed rod" located underneath the floor near mid-car. This "vents" the reservoir's air into the atmosphere. You'll hear a small "poooooooofff" of air which slowly diminishes to nothing. He proceeds from car to car pushing bleed rods until all cars are bled.

While he's bleeding the old train the "Hump Master" and his assistants in the tower or office prepare orders governing which car goes to which track in the departure yards. These orders are printed on a "switchlist" which everyone gets before humping starts. (In computerized yards switchlists are no longer necessary. The computer does all the thinking.)

Once the string is ready a billygoat couples onto the "top end" of the string - the end away from the hump. With the help of switchmens' hand signals by day or lanterns by night (or signals in automated yards) the engineer pushes the train onto the switch leader and toward the hump. As the cars come up car inspectors in an "inspection pit" underneath the track survey the cars' "running gear" (wheels, springs, bearings, trucks, draft gears/sliding center sills, etc.). If they spot a problem they notify the tower, which humps the car onto a repair or "rip-track."

Every freightcar on a given railroad is assigned a 2- to 6-digit number such as 48, 5776 or 569022, usually in combination with a 2- to 4-letter initial, all of which comprises a system known as "reporting marks" (e.g., 778803 TTX). If the car is a private owner or lessee the alphabetical initial ends in an "X." The majority of tankcars, hopper cars and specialty cars are likely to be marked with an X.

At the top of the hump stands a switchman, switchlist of reporting marks in hand, reviewing the marks of each "cut" (one or more cars slated to go onto the same new train). He gets ready to pull pins at the cut lever, freeing the cut to roll down the other side. As the engineer pushes cars over the apex several things happen at once.

Because the cars were being pushed uphill their coupler, draft gear or sliding center sill slack is buffed in. Slack has to be cut so the switchman can pull the pin. When the cut reaches the apex the engineer is signaled to brake. He slows the string slightly but doesn't stop. At this precise moment the brakeman pulls the pin when neither buff nor draft pressure is extreme at the apex. The cut uncouples and rolls into the departure yards (also know as the "bowl" due to its hourglass shape).

To slow the cars to just the right speed (depending on their number, weight and distance needed to roll) the tower activates automatic brakes called "retarders" located on the downslope of the hump. Retarders are long, hydraulically-operated friction brakes on either side of the railhead which act as powerful jaws. They clamp onto the sides of the wheels a few inches above the railhead as the car rolls past.

Retarders do two things. First they slow the cars to the right speed to cover the distance to the new string. Second they ensure the cut collides solidly enough to couple securely, yet not too hard to damage freight or shatter couplers. Big yards have two sets of retarders - one at the foot of the hump called the "Master retarder" and another along the switch leader which leads to between five and nine bowl tracks called the "Group retarder." Retarder braking produces a high-pitched metallic squealing sound you'll learn to recognize.

Operating a retarder is a delicate procedure. A retarder operator watches the cut roll into the bowl. He applies and releases his brakes to keep the cut rolling at the right speed. He has to have an excellent eye for weight and distance of travel for each cut, called its "rollability." While he retards another operator throws switches to the right track. In state-of-the-art electronic classification yards all rollability, retarding and switching functions are performed by computer.

Once the "humped" cut has broken clean away the engineer is signaled to accelerate slightly then brake again. The switchman makes another cut which rolls down the hump, gets retarded, switched and coupled onto a new train. Optimally they proceed slow-start, slow-start until all cars are humped over to new trains.

Gravity humping makes sense when most cars on an old train are heading to different destinations than their neighbors. For the wayfarer however gravity humping has several independently important consequences.

First of all when walking around in the yards STAY AWAY FROM THE HUMP. It's a dangerous place. Even the workers won't like seeing you around. Switches are flying, brakes are clamping onto carwheels and cars are jolting and rolling around. If you stray into the action you could easily get flattened. And if management is in a bad mood or fears for your safety they may even call the bull. Humping is interesting to watch but *do so from a distance.*

If you wake up on a train in the yards that's going stop-go, stop-go in one direction GET OFF THAT TRAIN. You're being humped. It can be a scary experience. Boom-boom-boom-boom. If a worker finds you on a car being humped he'll ask you to get down before they continue. If you *wake up* on a train being humped don't feel stupid. Sometimes a train will die on us unexpectedly in the night and when we wake up it's being humped. The only time to feel stupid is if you know you're being humped and you still don't get off.

In older or smaller yards which don't have a gravity hump railroads hump trains another way. They "flat-switch" them in "flat switching yards." Rather than relying on gravity the billygoat itself has to get up the speed to push a cut off to where it's ordered.

As always the road power and caboose are removed and all air is bled out. The engineer couples at the top end. He pulls the entire string away from the yard along the switch leader, then onto an extension track which parallels the mainline. Out here the engineer pushes the train back toward the yard, carefully following his signals (radio signals if it's a long string). Once the string is at the right speed he gets the signal to stop and slams to a halt. When he brakes slack runs into the couplers. The switchman pulls up on the cut lever and makes the cut. The ordered cut uncouples and is "shoved," "kicked," "bunted" or "batted out" into the departure yard.

Next the engineer pulls forward to make room for another push. The switchman readies the next switch. When the engineer gets the go signal he pushes backward again then slams to a halt. More cars uncouple, etc., back-and-forth, back-and-forth.

Meanwhile at the front end the switchman is definitely earning his keep. He manually throws switches off the switch leader onto different marshaling tracks, following his switchlist. Once he's mentally squared away and has the switches aligned (called "lining track") he signals the engineer to push toward him. As the end cars approach he runs along the *side* of the cars (he doesn't have to get between them anymore), pulls up on the cut lever and signals stop. "Booooom." The cut rolls off toward its new train.

Flat-switch humping requires much more traincrew skill than gravity humping. The crew can't rely on others to retard or switch the cut to the right track. They themselves have to gauge rollability. Due to continued use of older cars impact speeds should not exceed 4 MPH. If the crew has a particularly sensitive carload, rather than humping it they push the whole string down the ordered track and nudge the car onto its new string. A top-notch crew bats out cuts quickly enough to have several rolling at the same time ready to "drop" onto a new train. Cars roll through the yards until the string is entirely humped.

The last act in either method of humping is the use of a "trimmer" engine. The trimmer is a billygoat which waits at the top end of the receiving bowl from the hump or hump engine. Trimmers nudge strings together to ensure all the couplers are securely locked. They also re-sort strings if humping alone can't get cars "blocked" in the right order.

If you're cruising around the yards during either gravity-yard or flat-switch humping you have two *major* safety risks. We've already mentioned one - rolling stock. This is the chief reason we NEVER sit or walk on the tracks. Loose cars can sneak up on us and "squash." We're history. Please stay off the tracks.

The other risk is when you're on a freightcar or climbing over cars or couplers in the departure yard. When humped cars collide with your's sudden takeoff or jerking occurs. "KABOOOOM." Here's where the risk lies when you climb over the floor of an open car or over couplings between enclosed cars:

Let's say they've humped 5 cars toward the 50 already on your track. The 5 are rolling along at a steady 4 MPH, about the speed of a brisk walk. They roll up to the 50 and "Kaboooom," they collide and couple. The other 50 will react to the collision. But how?

Visualize this in another setting. Suppose a high speed motorist rearends four or five cars stopped in the same lane. The fifth car plows into the fourth, the fourth less forcefully into the third, the third less forcefully into the second, etc. If you're on a freightcar near the collision or "drop-on point" of a string it's like being in the fifth car. The sudden takeoff will be much more violent than at the opposite end, 50 cars away. The sheer weight, inertia and slack in the cars diminishes the impact the further from the drop-on point you are. You might not even feel the impact 50 cars away.

Let's say you're crossing a car somewhere in the middle of the 50. Your car will takeoff about average. In fact 5 cars colliding with 50 might not create much takeoff at all. The 55 cars might only roll a matter of feet, depending on how much the cars weigh and the collision speed. Regardless whether the string actually takes off it will *always* jerk at 25 back. If caught unawares the jerk could be dangerous.

Now let's say the 5 cars going 4 MPH collide with only 5 others. Both the "Kabooooom" and no-doubt-about-it sudden takeoff will be *extremely* violent. All 10 will sudden takeoff and roll at under 2 MPH until they run out of momentum. This latter example of 5 on 5 is a very good reason why we don't want to cross over cars in the first place - unless we're crossing a long string. If you're on one of 4 cars which get hit by 20, we're talking MAJOR "Booooom" and MAJOR sudden takeoff. You may not be able to hang on with all your might. Always walk around strings of cars unless you don't have the option.

Despite the dangers of sudden takeoff and jerking there *are* times when we have to climb over cars. Before we can get you physically up on a car we need to talk about one more *very* important thing. Railroad air brakes. Before you ever lay a hand on a freightcar you'd better know exactly what its brakes are or aren't doing. This means being conversant with air brakes.

VIII

THE AIR BRAKE - A HOBO'S BEST FRIEND

As we've seen railroad trains are dangerous to play around with. One thing which makes them particularly dangerous aside from unpredictability is how hard they are to stop. Because of the tremendous weights involved a train is hard enough to get started but even harder to stop.

Take a freight train of any car length traveling 61 MPH. Its acquired energy if directed upward instead of forward would lift the entire train *130 feet into the air.* Since from a safety standpoint a train's starting and stopping have tremendous importance for us, let's talk about stopping. Let's talk brakes.

For early airplanes the biggest challenge was starting - getting the craft off the ground. Stopping was no problem. You've seen the old movies of the wacko contraptions inventors rigged up to effectuate heavier-than-air flight. *If* they got off the ground it was a success. Stopping was a mere formality - usually a simple crash-landing.

The opposite was true of early trains. Figuring out how to get them to go, while challenging, was basic steam and mechanical technology which had been around in stationary form for over 50 years. This is not to say incredible steam technology didn't evolve between say, 1800 and 1940. It did. The history of steam propulsion makes interesting reading. But the basic mechanics remained the same: Heat the water into steam and force it to push on things. This was the only game in town on the railroad until arrival of electric locomotives in the 1880s and diesel locomotives in the 1920-40s.

Beginning with the first experimental runs in England and America railroad inventors quickly realized they had *a lot* of drawing board work to do to ensure trains came to a halt *when* and *where* they were supposed to. Mechanical whizzes on each side of the Atlantic went to work on this perplexing problem.

It seems whenever Man tries to figure out how to do something mechanical his first instinct is to give the operator a hand lever to push or pull. Look for example at the Wright Brothers' airplane, early automobiles, trucks, tractors or other prototypical industrial equipment. All were equipped with lots of levers one manually exerted pressure on to get the thing to work - or stop working. Pioneer locomotive inventors were no exception. They were lever-happy - especially when it came to brakes.

The first railroad engine brake was little more than a big lever with a block of wood at the bottom end. The engineer pulled on the lever to press the wood against the iron drive wheel to slow the engine to a halt. This worked well for a time - at least during the experimental stage.

Inventors soon realized a locomotive in-and-of itself wasn't worth much. In order to impress governments, private investors and skeptics railroads were worth pursuing, railroad pioneers began hooking different kinds of *cars* onto locomotives - both passenger and freight. On Sunday afternoons they invited friends, family and local dignitaries out to the model stretch of track to watch the Iron Horse be put through its paces. Select individuals were cordially invited to have a seat in the new railroad "carriages" or "coaches" and come along for a ride. As the "train" (as the early combination locomotive-and-cars soon came to be called) huffed and puffed and banged its way into motion passengers good-naturedly picked themselves up off the floor, fanned sparks and ashes off their clothing and bemusedly rolled down the track at startling speeds of up to 15 MPH. Unfortunately on more than one embarrassing occasion they not-so-good-naturedly rolled *right off the end of the track* - engine, coaches and all - because the inventor hadn't figured out how to get the smoke and steam-belching beast to *stop*. In England several early prototypes ran on *circular* track, doubtless in part to avoid this type of embarrassment.

Railroads were little more than curiosity pieces until they developed the ability to travel faster than a galloping horse. After all for a long-distance voyage a good coach and four was more than sufficient (and oats much less expensive) than traveling on a huge, hot, noisy, sooty, greasy and dangerous metal contraption confined to wood, stone or iron tracks.

But railroad backers remained undaunted. Technology advanced as the races between trains and thoroughbreds continued. In time with bigger engines, better traction schemes and longer stretches of track trains became hands-down winners over our faithful four-legged friend. The most skeptical observers became persuaded railroads had a future. By the 1830s railroads were acknowledged to be a highly valuable industrial tool. There remained a long way to go however in solving the problems with brakes.

Simple mechanics suggested since the locomotive pulled the train from the front the locomotive could be relied upon to stop the train from the front as well. Railroad inventors went to work devising elaborate brake systems for locomotives. Within a short time they had some thoroughly decent steam brakes hooked up.

Next they extended the braking idea to include the caboose (which depending on which railroad on which continent you rode before the 1860s was known as the "cabin car," "conductor's van," "brakeman's cab," "accommodation car," "train car" and/or "way car"). With these improvements railroad development boomed.

A furious rush to lay track from Town A to B ensued in America and Canada. The Baltimore & Ohio Railroad (now part of CSX Transportation) began laying track through Maryland, Delaware and Virginia. Other railroads followed suit. Notable among pioneer railroads were the Mohawk & Hudson Railroad, the South Carolina Railroad, the Newcastle & Frenchtown Turnpike & Railway Company, the Allegheny Portage Railroad, the Pennsylvania Railroad and the New York & Erie. By 1850 the Eastern Seaboard was thoroughly connected by railroads.

But the Eastern Seaboard is essentially flat. Brakes worked fine on flat land with a locomotive only, then later a locomotive and caboose. When railroads made their first forays into the piedmont regions of the Appalachians, Alleghenies and Adirondacks the situation changed. As they extended upland, poking through the various gaps, hollers and passes, the question of braking equipment came vividly and annoyingly back into focus.

When these early trains were traveling uphill everything was fine - so long as the cars stayed coupled to the engine. But if for some reason one of the old chain, draw-head or link-and-pin couplings failed and a break-in-two occurred the caboose was too light to brake the cars uphill of it. Off the break-aways would go, back to town like a horse to the barn. And unlike their chief competitor the coaches of the Iron Horse very often never *made* it back to the barn. Rather they made it into a ravine or river some distance back down the track - often where the first pronounced curve could be found.

We've all seen runaway train movies so we won't elaborate on this too much. Interestingly though the problem still persists in less-developed countries. In 1991 for example 96 people were killed and over 300 injured in Nampula Mozambique when cars broke away from the engine, rolled *six miles* downhill to the station, jumped the rails and crashed. You can imagine what an adventure railroading was for those passengers for about 10 minutes or so (at least they made it back to the barn).

Suffice it to say this typical occurrence was not heartening to passenger, shipper or railroader. The mechanical engineers went back to the drawing board to figure out how to brake the coaches themselves independent of the locomotive. They seized upon the admirable idea of putting - you guessed it - *hand* brakes on each of the coaches.

After initially experimenting with simple levers they came up with a brake operated by hand-turning a wheel. The wheel was attached to a chain and the chain to a brake. Turn the wheel one way to pull up the chain and set the brake, then turn it the other way to release the chain and brake.

These handbrakes weren't geared. The brakeman simply wound a chain around a vertical "brake staff." A major factor in this arrangement was a brakeman's strength in applying enough brake to provide stopping power. A commonly-used equalizer was a stout oak staff called a "brakeman's club" or "brake staff" which you stuck in the spokes of the brakewheel to turn it tight. An entirely new profession was created by stroke of compass and straightedge - the Railroad Brakeman.

Here's how it worked: A brakeman was assigned to ride each coach of a passenger train. These brakemen had a cushy job. They could ride inside in bad weather where their only obligation was to keep the wood stoves properly stoked. On freights in good weather the men rode the deck. In foul weather they rode up in the cab with the engineer and fireman or back in the caboose with the conductor.

When the engineer "whistled down" (blew his whistle in a certain cadence of short bursts signaling to brake) brakemen ran to their positions and madly spun the brakewheels. There was a real art to applying *just enough* brake to slow the individual coaches in unison. If one guy cranked down too hard he could lock his carriage's wheels and jackknife his car out of line. At minimum over-application of brakes caused wheels to lock up

and slide down the rail, grinding flat. Flatwheels were an annoying problem. (Unbelievably, railroads charged the cost of repairing flat wheels to
the responsible brakeman - if they could prove who'd done the dastardly
deed.)

In an emergency all the engineer could do was set the steam brake
on the locomotive drivers (*or* put the drivers in reverse), whistle down-
brakes to wind 'em up and start praying. (To this day when an engineer is
confronted with a fast-stop situation he refers to it as "dragging his foot on
the ground.") Cars at the rear of the train would slam into cars up front.
Although the primitive spring-loaded draw-heads usually kept cars from
jackknifing, all-in-all it was not a pretty proposition.

If everything went smoothly however and the train slowed or stopped
as desired, the engineer would "whistle up" with a different cadence, the
brakemen would unwind and away they'd go. The real benefit of the system
came during break-in-twos. Assuming the brakemen were in position or
could get there in time, they'd stay with the escaping cars, brake (with more
than a bit of self-preservation in mind) and *usually* save the day.

All this worked well for a time - at least in the opinion of the
railroads - except using handbrakes severely limited the length and weight
of trains. The longest freight trains were perhaps 50 cars in length. The
problem during inclimate weather was getting the brakemen into position
on the brakewheels at the right time. On passenger trains at whistle-down
brakies threw open the doors and ran down the aisles of each car, hurdling
baggage and sleeping children to get from brakewheel to brakewheel. Freight
trains had no aisles. In the old days they were made up exclusively of
boxcars and flatcars. Weather permitting when the engineer whistled up or
down brakies had to run along the roofs or floors of each car to get from
wheel to wheel, jumping couplers, scrabbling over loads and climbing or
descending ladders en route.

Freight braking was even less satisfactory if the brakies were riding
in the cab and caboose. Up front they'd have to crawl over the contents of
the tender to get to the first car. At the rear they'd climb up ladders to get to
boxcar height. A prescient engineer had to anticipate these positioning
limitations in timing his whistle-downs. After a time car manufacturers
magnanimously added wooden "roofwalks" along the tops of boxcars.

Of course this new job of being a brakeman was lots of fun. On
hilly or curvy stretches of track or during inclimate weather, oftentimes one
or two *fewer* brakies made it into the next station as had left the last. Many

were the embarrassed brakies who had to hoof it home after being bucked off - if they could hoof it at all.

Moreover, brakewheels and chains suffered from the same neglect as grabirons and ladders - poor maintenance and no inspection. Many times a man would crank down on a wheel only to feel the chain snap or the wheel's fasteners tear out of the car. When this happened chances were 50-50 of being thrown onto the tracks - perhaps with appliance in hand. In the early days railroads were liable for injuries to *passengers* caused by their negligence but were completely exempt from damages for negligent injury to *employees,* under legal theories such as Master-Servant, contributory negligence and assumption of risk. The gruesome death and injury statistics mounted year after bloody year.

Aside from the danger of this braking method it was also labor-intensive. At first a brakeman was assigned to every car to ensure brakes were applied or released quickly enough to guide the train safely. Later it became *practically* every car. Later still when the technique was "refined" a bit railroads assigned a brakie to every third car. Over the years railroad executives (incessantly preoccupied with the bottom line) concluded they could use fewer and fewer brakemen and make them cover more and more cars. This meant being a brakeman was not unlike being a 200-yard hurdle man. Depending on terrain a man would have to set brakes for 5, then 7, then as many as 8 or 10 cars. You can imagine how athletic this was. While railroads solved their labor overhead problem they increased the risk of injury by requiring too few brakemen to cover too many cars. Brakemen disappeared from cars with increasing regularity.

What bothered the railroad companies was not carnage but the continued inability to run longer trains. Regardless of the number of brakemen required for a 10- or 50-car train at least three employees - engineer, fireman and conductor - were always necessary. The owners deduced the longer the train the fewer crew members would have to be paid. Brakemen could simply run farther. Result? In the 19th century North American railroads *never sought out a better brake.*

In the 1860s an entirely new braking idea surfaced - using *mechanical* pressure instead of manual to set train brakes. The use of pressure to do mechanical things of course was nothing new. Since the English Industrial Revolution of the 1760s people had used steam, water, oil, air and wind pressure to push and pull all sorts of things. Water and steam were the most popular hydraulics. But with the advent of more sophisticated steam engines air, or "pneumatic" pressure came into use as a mechanical motivator. Invention of the air compressor running off a steam engine allowed manufacturers to use forced air to perform tasks previously reserved for humans.

Railroad inventors in particular were intrigued with air in deciding which type of pressure could replace human in braking trains. They were looking for a means of providing "continuous brakes" for an entire train - brakes which would mechanically set and release at or near the same time from front to back. American inventors concluded air pressure was the way to go.

Here's where a fellow named George C. Westinghouse came into the picture. In 1866 Westinghouse was a 19-year old Union Army veteran with a genius for invention. He was toying with ways to brake trains and came up with a fascinating idea.

First install an air compressor on your locomotive. The air compressor could be run by the same process which drove the train - fire, heat, water, steam, pressure, cylinder, push the drive rods - and also activate the compressor. Next rig up a system of pipes and hoses under your coaches as a conduit for sending the compressed air back through the train. Underneath each coach (soon known as a car) install a metal pipe to convey the pressurized air. Between the cars install flexible rubber hoses connected together with nozzles - much the same as the clasped-hand coupling system Eli Janney devised to couple up cars - with a configuration called "glad hands." Flexible so the hoses could be easily coupled and uncoupled and round curves. When workers couple cars together they can also couple up air hoses as well. Also include an air cylinder underneath each car which opens or closes depending on the amount of pressure in the system. Connect the cylinder to the brakes, again by chains. Push on the cylinder with air pressure and pull the chains tight setting brakes (which are otherwise held off the wheels with springs). Release the pressure, loosen the chains and let the springs push the brakes off. Westinghouse came up with an internal air system available to set and release the brakes for every kind of train, governed by a "brake throttle" in the cab of the locomotive.

His first air system, the "Straight Air System" worked like this: When the engineer wanted to slow or stop he'd activate the air compressor with his brake throttle. The compressor pumped air into the train's hose-pipe-cylinder system. The increase in air pressure pushed on the cylinders, which pulled back on the chains and set the brakes. *Voila.* When the engineer wanted to release the brakes he simply vented the air out of the system and the springs pushed the brakes off. Everything worked fine.

Railroads however quickly discovered a problem with the Westinghouse Straight Air System. It was the same problem as the original. If cars broke away from the train the hoses at the break-in-two point snapped apart and the *whole train* (except the locomotive) lost its air and brakes. Away the cars went back to the barn again. Same thing if the locomotive's air compressor failed or a brake hose burst.

Another problem was the *time* it took to set all the cars' brakes. Before the brakes at the rear of a longer train even *began* taking hold the forward brakes were completely set. The train's slack would draft in, often too quickly. With the addition of improved locomotive steam brakes the result could be quite violent - often buckling the train or shattering couplers.

Just in the nick of time Westinghouse returned in 1869 with a patented "Automatic Air Brake" and founded the Westinghouse Air Brake Company. He had a brilliantly simple idea - reverse the original straight-air principle.

Instead of applying air pressure to set the brakes, apply it to *release* them. Pump air into the system to push off the brakes, which in the absence of air pressure were now spring-loaded to rest *on* rather than *off* the brakes. To slow or stop, release air pressure. When braking was required the engineer would move his "automatic brake valve throttle" to a position within the "service range," depending on the amount of braking needed. This reduced pressure in the brake pipes and hoses. The reduction in pipe pressure caused the air valve on each car to open, releasing the air from the brake cylinder. Reserve air stored in an auxiliary air reservoir (when the air valve was closed) now traveled into the brake cylinder which, designed to recognize the difference, now *applied* the brakes.

The engineer controlled how much air flowed from the reservoir into the cylinder by governing how much pressure dropped in the pipes. If the compressor failed, a hose burst or coupler failed, the pipes, hoses and cylinders lost all pressure. The reservoir then forced all its reserve air into the cylinder and all brakes automatically set. Any runaway cars ground to a halt. The engine could come back to retrieve its charges, the crew replace the hose, fix the compressor or coupler and the train could then proceed.

This solved both manpower and length/weight problems. Westinghouse continued to work on and refine the process and had something to talk about as early as 1873 - the year in which further refinement made the "Westinghouse Continuous Automatic Air Brake" workable.

With prototypical patented automatic couplers and air brakes in existence by 1873, the following 25-year period can only be viewed as the railroads' most sinister hour. Except for a handful of enlightened Northern railroads owners refused to spend money to incorporate these designs into their equipment. In their view it was simply cheaper to pay paltry settlements for killed and injured passengers and find new workers than to revamp rolling stock. Perhaps they were right. And without question no one told the railroads what to do during this era. For 20 years only a few passenger train systems used air brakes and automatic couplings - and *no freight trains!*

Had it not been for the near-lifelong commitment of a man with a messianic mission to hound the railroads into accepting the new brakes and couplers, we might still have brakemen riding atop railroad cars and guiding links into slots with two fingers per hand. After a career spent being thrown out of railroad executives' offices, being listened to with silent disdain and derided as "The Air Brake Fanatic," Lorenzo Coffin finally succeeded in forcing the railroads to adopt Janney's coupler and Westinghouse's brake - primarily through harnessing public opinion against the railroads.

As we've noted, Janney's automatic coupler while adopted as early as 1876 wasn't made mandatory until 1893 by the Federal Safety Appliance Act. It took a separate but related Act of Congress popularly known as the "Coffin Bill" to mandate continuous air brakes as well - with compliance delayed until January 1, 1898. By 1894 employee accidents dropped a staggering 60%. However one cannot honestly say the modern era of railroading arrived much before 1900.

To be completely fair to the railroads the bugs were not entirely ironed out of the air brake until 1887. It seems in the 1870s and early 1880s Westinghouse lost interest in pursuing utilization of his brake. One supposes this is an all-too common characteristic of genius. The mind races on to other things. In fact in 1883 he went on record with the belief only an electrically-controlled air brake would stop long trains (he was right - electric brakes are used on today's passenger trains in conjunction with his air brake). One also suspects that well-knowing the predilection of railroads for holding down costs Westinghouse concluded it was futile to fight their resistance.

Westinghouse was himself partially responsible for the delay.

He insisted on rigorous standardization in order to ensure air hoses of Westinghouse-fitted stock could be coupled together on any railroad (as they are today). He also invented switching and signaling equipment and founded the Union Switch & Signal Company in 1881.

Comprehensive testing of the air brake didn't occur until 1886-87 with less than satisfactory results. During the first two tests the brakes came on too slowly at the rear. The back cars again slammed into the front ones. The owners and railroad commissioners walked away snorting and smirking. Coffin continued his campaign however while Westinghouse, never one to be laughed at, regained interest in his brake.

During a third test late in the Summer of 1887 (with Messrs. Westinghouse and Coffin in attendance) a 50-car freight train traveling 40 MPH was air-braked to a halt in 500 feet with "hardly a jar." Coffin wept with joy. And Mr. Westinghouse, sensing with this deceptively simple yet brilliant invention that perhaps he'd outdone himself in the brake department, went on to dabble in household appliances (the Westinghouse Electric Company - 1886). To this day when it comes to braking a freight train to a halt, "You can be sure, 'cause it's Westinghouse."

The key to the modern Westinghouse brake is its "serial action" feature. Through a sensitive negative feedback system air is transferred between the pipes, hoses, valves, cylinders and reservoirs, thereby speeding up brake application and release times. Today in an emergency brake application (the "big hole position" or dragging your foot), the rate of application back through the train is as fast as 900 ft. per second (near the speed of sound [1,100 ft./sec.], or about 8.8 seconds along the length of our hypothetical 150-car train). Don't get overconfident though at grade crossings.

The Westinghouse braking system is in use on freight trains throughout North America and on many railroads in Europe. There have been several modifications, begun in the 1930s. The "AB" pneumatic brake further refined the original Westinghouse design, as have the later "ABD" and "ABDW" freight brake systems. New locomotives are equipped with the "26L" brake, which further speeds set and release times. But the original Westinghouse principles remain the same.

On passenger trains a newer electropneumatic brake is used. The engineer can control the brakes either electronically or by use of the air system. Electrically-controlled air brakes are used on all multiple-engine electric trains in passenger train and rapid-transit service. At first development of the "HSC Electro-Pneumatic Brake" for high-speed passenger trains meant different engines were required for freight and passenger service. Since the 1950s however all diesel locomotives have been equipped with electropneumatic braking capacity and can haul either freight or passenger trains. That's why we see freight engines hauling Amtrak trains when Amtrak's engines die or are too scarce to find.

The above stories of the automatic coupler and air brake illustrate how dangerous railroading is. These systems have been responsible for saving the lives and limbs of *hundreds of thousands* of working and traveling Americans - including the wandering wayfarer.

Let's return now to see how this information assists us when we're about to climb over a string of cars. *As you get ready to mount the car, stop and take a good long listen to what the air is doing.* Every pressurized air system has leaks. Wherever there's a leak air hisses out. This hissing sound - or its absence - is what we listen for. Take a healthy listen to the air BEFORE CLIMBING ON.

The way to do this is simple. Just *lean down and cock your ear underneath the floor of the car.* Listen for air leaking out of the pipes, reservoir or cylinder. Or take a *good long listen from a safe distance away from the hoses underneath the couplers.* Or step in *very* briefly and kick the hoses. If they're stiff they're "aired up." When you check the air one of four situations will present itself. The first is when you can't hear any air at all.

No Air:

If the air isn't hissing this *almost* always means there's no power connected to the string. If there *is* power it's probably a billygoat waiting to do something with the string like hump or switch it. Hearing no air says a couple of conflicting things.

Number one there's a lessened chance the string will jerk or take off since the odds are good there's nothing to push or pull it. That's good. Number Two however there's nothing to prevent a crew from dropping their engine or a cut onto it, which *could* cause a jerk or sudden takeoff. Thus when there's no air as you climb over there's little risk on one hand and greater risk on the other.

With no air *theoretically* the cars' brakes are set - just as a runaway train's brakes would be set so the cars stop rolling. But recall how switchmen bleed the air out of brake reservoirs before humping a train to release the brakes. Since we never know on arrival whether the air has been bled or not (the reservoirs don't leak - or at least aren't legally supposed to), it's anybody's guess whether the string's brakes are set or not. Nevertheless it's safer to cross an airless string than one which has air.

However, **well-note the following**: Today's freightcar brakes can still be set and released *manually*. Manual brakewheels still exist on all freightcars to serve as a backup for the air (brakewheels are found at the "B" end; the brakewheelless end being "A"; some cars have wheels at either end). Manual brakes are also used when workers "spot" (park) a free-rolling car at a particular location, and to eliminate the risk of wind or other disturbance from setting a car rolling where no one expects it to go.

(Incredible though it may seem a strong steady wind can set even a string of loaded *coalcars* rolling if their brakes aren't properly set. On March 26th, 1884 a gale wind ("Chinook") ripped the roof off a roundhouse at the Chicago, Burlington & Quincy's ("CB&Q," "Quincy," or "Q" - today part of the Burlington Northern system) Akron yards east of Denver, setting eight loaded coalcars on the move. They ran onto the mainline where the wind drove them along at speeds varying between 40 and 70 MPH for *100 miles*. Finally a freight locomotive gave chase, coupled onto the cars and saved the day. The cars covered the 100 miles in well under 3 hours.)

Workers also use brakewheels to spot cars during humping. The wheels are placed as *low down* as practicable so if the brakeman happens to slip or fall off his platform, grabiron, or footboard more likely he'll fall to the side of the track rather than on it. But brakewheels are also placed *high* enough up so passersby are deterred from monkeying with them.

Just as in the old days these wheels are connected to the brakes with a chain. Today's wheels are geared, so brakemen needn't play King Kong with brake staffs to set brakes. Spin the wheel one way and the brake sets. Pull a lever which extracts a pin and the wheel spins the other way to release. *Don't EVER pull a brakewheel's lever.* Not only can you release its brakes *if* they're set (with potentially dangerous consequences), the wheel can spin so violently if you're holding on you can be catapulted off the car.

You'll see switchmen and brakemen spotting cars in the yards and out over the road. Say for example during humping a billygoat bats out a 4-car cut onto an empty yardtrack. The cut drifts through the yards with a switchman hanging on the side of a car. As the cut approaches the spot where the crew want it to stop, the switchman reaches up and spins the brakewheel to set his car's brakes. His car brakes the other three and the cut stops where desired. The same procedure is followed spotting cars on a customer's siding. The sound a brakewheel makes as it clicks through its gears and locking teeth is not unlike the sound made by an uninspired washboard renditionist.

All of which means *please* don't get cocky just because you can't hear any air. If the cars' brakes have been bled the string can still roll. Moreover regardless whether the brakes are set or not standing cars will move if pushed or pulled hard enough. In this regard freightcars are just like automobiles. Even if you're stopped in your car with the brake pedal pushed down as hard as possible if someone crashes into you hard enough you'll move. So *even though your string doesn't have air treat it as if it did, the brakes were off and it could move at any moment.*

STEADY AIR:

The next situation is where the air is hissing steadily. Long and steady but somewhat softly. This *almost* always means the string has power coupled on and could move at any moment. (There's one exception where the system hisses without power. This occurs when the workers ready a string for departure [when the train is "hosed-up"] and connect air to an end of it. "Yard air" has greater pressure than a diesel locomotive and can fill an air system more quickly. The power can come out, couple on and quickly depart - without having to pump its own air all the way back. This saves time *ergo* wages. A locomotive takes up to 20 or 30 minutes to fill a long train's air system.)

In the usual situation steady air means you already have power coupled on. What you *can't* tell is whether enough pressure has been pumped into the system to release the brakes. You can look at the brakeshoes between the wheels, but often this won't tell you much. When brakes release they move such a small distance off the wheel treads (the flat shiny part of the wheel which rolls over the railhead) that it's impossible to tell if they're set or not.

Here the probabilities and risks are reversed from where there's no air. Since 90 times out of 100 with a steady hiss you have power and you don't know if the brakes are on or off, you could be subject to sudden takeoff at any moment. The crew could "get the bell" and go at any time. Conversely since power is never left on a train which is being "humped-up" (the collisions could knock an engine out of kilter) you're not threatened with sudden takeoff or jerking. In the steady-air situation your odds of movement are slightly greater than with no air.

AIR INCREASES:

A third situation is when you either don't hear air hissing or it's hissing soft and steadily. Then it increases and the brakes release off the wheels. You can't mistake this event because you'll hear very loud and distinctive sounds coming from underneath the cars.

When a crew pump air into a string they're releasing its brakes. The air makes a higher more intense hissing sound, rising in pitch and intensity. The dead giveaway is when the brakes come off the wheels. They make distinctive clanking, popping, compressing-metal sounds. You'll hear a rapid "Chunk-chunk-chunk-chunk," pings, groanings, whincings and all manner of metallic racket - the sounds of metal readjusting as it comes off other metal. The sound of compressing brake springs is as easy to recognize as retarded humped cars.

In this situation the crew's getting ready to move the string. If you're going to take a chance - and it's a big one - you'd better move fast. If a train already has "operating" air pressure, it takes at least 1 to 3 minutes to get up enough additional air to ensure all brakes are released. The longer the train the longer it takes to get "legal" air, which is required to be between 70 and 90 psi depending on the weight of the train and the terrain to be crossed.

Once the air stabilizes at the legal rate the engineer conducts an "air test." The air test makes a sound like, "Tiiiist-tiiiist," like letting air out of a bicycle tire. The engineer tests the air one, two or three times. The brakes have to be tested because if there's more than 15 psi difference between the headend and rearend of the train (due to system-wide leakage) by law the train can't leave. When the engineer finishes testing he's happy with the pressure and could take off at any moment.

Here you're clearly in the sudden takeoff zone. This is the most dangerous situation. If at all feasible I'd advise walking *around* the string or climbing *over* the floor of an open-air car rather than climbing over couplers. You ultimately will be the judge. You can always climb over the floor of an open car, but in this situation do it with care and speed.

AIR RELEASES:

Finally there's the situation where the air is hissing steadily away then suddenly goes "Poooooooofff." All the air releases out of the system and the brakes come whincing onto the wheels. You'll hear a *very* rapid "Chu-chu-chu-chu-chu-chu-chu-chu" as air transfers from the reservoir to the cylinder, forcing the brakes to clamp on the wheels. The power has just uncoupled, "breaking the air" or "dynamiting."

Broken air is by far the safest of the four situations since the power has just left and the crew are no longer interested in moving the string. Even with a hotshot the likelihood of cars being humped on or off the string is small for a number of minutes. Without full pressure the workers can't move the string until they bleed all reservoirs and it's unlikely new cars will be humped onto the string. So go for it, using the same precautions we use even if the air had just come up and the brakes released. (NOTE: If you're rolling along out over the road and hear the air go "Pooooof" get ready for a grinding fast stop. A hose has burst and the Westinghouse system will rapidly come to the rescue. The car whose hose has burst is called a "dynamite car." All the train's brakes will clamp on within 8 to 10 seconds and it will grind to a halt *tout de suite*. Get into a safe position on the car.)

In general *no matter which* of the four air situations presents itself, **ALWAYS CROSS OVER A TRAIN EXPECTING IT TO MOVE AT ANY MOMENT.** Err here on the side of caution. This is the *most dangerous* thing to learn riding the rails.

One final thing to do ears and eyes-wise before crossing over cars is to stop, look and listen to what's happening in the yards in general. If it's dead quiet - no locomotives pounding away, no "Boooooms," squeakings or movement to be heard - chances are greatly diminished the string of cars you want to cross will move. If on the other hand there's lots of activity - trains being humped, power moving around, cars gliding by, "Boooooms," hump retarders squealing, etc. , then no matter what the air's doing on your string the risk in crossing is increased. Govern all movements accordingly.

Above all remember: *Never* take anything for granted. Play it as if the worst could happen. The tips provided now on how to climb around on freightcars should be followed at all times; and please, I mean AT ALL TIMES.

IX

HOW DO I SAFELY CLIMB AROUND ON STANDING CARS AND TRAINS IN THE YARDS?

The first and foremost rule is **NEVER climb under a car or coupler to get across a track**. This is high folly, extremely dangerous and just downright dumb. No matter how quiet the yards or isolated a string appears to be we never know when a sudden takeoff might occur. If it does and you're trapped under the car you could get knocked unconscious by bracings on the undercarriage, the axles, the air cylinder, reservoir or the air hoses hanging down. So *please*, no matter how short or agile you think you are or how tempting it might seem, *never climb under freightcars*.

To go over a string always try to *find an open car to jump up on, walk across and jump back off*. An "open car" means a *unwalled* car - flatcars, some auto racks, piggybacks, or any other car which isn't walled shut. If such a car is close by *always* choose it to climb over. Climbing over couplers at the ends of "closed cars" (i.e., boxcars, hoppers, gondolas, most auto racks, reefers, tankcars and anything else with a wall on the side) should be done *only if no open cars are available*. There are three reasons why:

First it's much *safer* to climb over an open car. You get up onto the *floor* of the car itself. You can do this at a spot midway down the car - well-away from the couplers and wheels. Then no matter what happens if you fall you won't get caught on the track. Even if you manage to accomplish the almost unbelievable gymnastic feat of winding up *underneath* the car, you'll have time (assuming you're conscious) to climb out before any harm results.

Second it's much *easier* to go over the floor of a car than hoisting yourself and your gear over the couplers. Try the two techniques to make your own comparison. It's a lot easier to jump up on a car floor than climb around an end wall. The latter is like climbing around on a jungle gym. Footboards and grabirons crossing the front and back of tankcars also offer a convenient and safe way to get over.

Third workers don't like to see us near the brakewheels. If someone fools with a brakewheel and causes a mess the worker could look very bad. For all these reasons *go over a car before going over its couplers.*

If you're stuck and have to go over the couplers here's what to do: Notice how a walled-shut freightcar has ladders on either side of each end. Brakemen and switchmen use these ladders to ride on cars so the engineer can see their signals and they can manually set and release brakes. *We* can use these same ladders to get up and over the ends of cars.

Before climbing the ladder *throw your gear onto the other side of the track.* Get rid of all gear before swinging around on the ends of cars like an Industrial Tarzan (recall Tarzan was never burdened with a backpack). This is one reason your pack and its contents should be relatively indestructible - so you can throw it places without damaging anything. After chucking the gear *put your gloves on.* This is a time when they come in mighty handy.

Below each ladder you'll find a rectangular U-shaped piece of metal called the "stirrup." It looks like a larger version of a saddle stirrup and provides additional insight into why trains were call Iron Horses. For a person of average height standing by a freightcar the bottom of the stirrup is at belt level while the foot of the ladder is at chest level.

After stopping, looking and listening to the air *and* any activity in the yards *and* getting rid of your gear, *step up and put a foot into the stirrup, grab hold of the ladder and hoist yourself up.* This is simple enough. The tough part comes next.

Once in the stirrup take a look around the end of the car. *Climb up a couple of rungs until your feet are level with the top of the couplers.* The height from the railhead to the top of couplers is closely standardized so couplers don't "slip-by" each other when the train is moving. Coupler heights range between 31.5 and 34.5 inches from railhead to top of coupler, whether the car is loaded or empty. The knuckles themselves have 11 vertical inches of metal so there will always be at least 8 inches of engagement to prevent slip-bys.

Once up 30 to 35 inches above railhead *swing around to the back of the car.* You'll have to reach around for something to grab onto. You'll also need to find some footing to cross in to the coupler. There are several different types of rather tenuous footholds to step onto - depending on your car.

The worst foothold to use is the *metal bar* which connects the cut lever to the pin (part of the "coupler fixtures"). It's a narrow metal bar which runs from the side of the car to the coupler. Choose each step carefully. *Swing onto the bar then sidle along it while hanging onto a grabiron up above* **with both hands** until you step onto the draft gear.

If possible find another car nearby which has a better foothold than the cut lever bar. *Find a car with a flange of metal or footboard sticking out the bottom of the end walls.* On newer cars you'll find a narrow footboard running over the coupler. On hoppers and open-ended auto racks with siding you can use the floor of the car itself. On many tankcars there's a wide footboard with grabs to hold onto. Whatever's available to step on, use it. The distance from the ladder to the coupler is much too great to step directly onto.

As for *handholds* for worker safety there's a grabiron running across the ends of all cars except open-ended auto racks. While it's rare a railroad employee climbs over couplers it does happen. I suppose grabs also come in handy when workers perform shop maintenance on cars.

Grabirons are an example of continuing efforts to improve safety conditions on the railroad. In fact on cars manufactured since 1970 these safely appliances must be placed in standardized locations, regardless of car ownership, so day or night workers can count on a foot or handhold where expected.

Take advantage of the grabs and grip them WITH BOTH HANDS. Same thing on ladders. Whether on the ladder *or* crossing the end of the car make sure at ALL TIMES BOTH HANDS ARE FIRMLY HOLDING SOMETHING. You never know when the car might move - perhaps violently. Also *move quickly.* Don't tarry in this vulnerable position.

To get down on the other side reverse the process. *Step on or over the coupler then onto the cut lever bar, flange or footboard to the other side,* **while holding onto something with each hand every step of the way.** Using one hand after the other swing out onto the ladder, climb down into the stirrup and step off. You're across.

In bigger yards you might have to cross five or more tracks to get where you want to be. This becomes energetic. You'll be glad to have gloves along for these little climbing/swinging excursions. Boots, too.

No matter how many strings you have to cross follow the procedure laid out here. *Walk around strings of cars before crossing over them.* If for some *good* reason you can't walk around, *stop, look and listen.* Don't touch a car until you're reasonably confident its string won't move, based on what the air is doing and what's going on around you. If *and only if* you're reasonably confident the string won't move, try to find an *open car to climb over.* Failing that and *only in a pinch, find a closed car with a good footboard or other foothold available. Hang onto whatever grabirons are available with both hands.* Then go for it. And do it *as quickly as possible.*

X

HOW DO I SELECT MY PERSONAL PULLMAN?

What governs the decision on the kind of car we choose? There are *lots* of things involved in choosing an enjoyable car to ride and at least *seven* rides to choose from. While walking a train think about whether the car you'd prefer is likely to be on as well as the weather, time of day, how advisable it is to stay out of sight, how many miles you're going, how much scenery you want to see, how much and how soundly you want to sleep, etc.

Here are our basic freightcar-riding requirements: By far the most important concern is to *find a car which is safe to ride either awake or asleep* - one on which you can't fall, roll off or get squashed by its load. Find a car which *keeps you out of the wind* as much as possible. Find one which affords *some type of overhead protection* from the elements - especially if the weather's lousy. Also find one which has some *room to move around* in or on the car, and one which affords an *opportunity to see what's out there* - to see America first.

Let's discuss the different kinds of cars available with a view to what you ultimately select as your own, personal Pullman. (This chapter is dedicated to George M. Pullman and the Pullman Car Company, the man responsible in 1894 for the deaths of more striking employees than any other capitalist in North American history.)

The Boxcar

The boxcar is the cadillac of commercial carriers. Far and away its biggest advantage is the ability to get inside - behind walls and under a roof. Here's a typical example of a cadillac waiting to be boarded, courtesy of the national railroad run by our friends South of the Border - *Nacional de Mexico* ("N de M").

If you're lucky *both* doors will be open. Hobos call boxcars "Side Door Pullmans." I divide boxcar Pullmans into two subcategories, calling both-doors-open ones "Scenic Cruisers" and one-door-open ones "One-Eyed Bandits."

Let's begin with the actual *doors* themselves - the side doors of this Pullman. There is a wide range of different boxcar door configurations which don't have much direct impact on the wayfarer. The only important question is whether a door is open and whether it will *stay* open.

What can we conclude if the doors are shut? Two things: Either the car is loaded or it's empty but both doors have been purposely shut.

When looking at a boxcar with both doors shut there's a neat way to tell if the car is loaded. If it is a warehouseman at the loading dock puts a small strip of stainless steel through the doorlatches or "hasps," forming a loop through each latch. Then he seals its ends with a small piece of crushed lead - the same technique used to seal a letter or scroll in the old days. The absence of a strip is a strong indication the car is unloaded. Warehousemen snap off the metal strip to open the latch so it's missing.

Visualize for a moment how boxcars are loaded. The railroad spots the car alongside a factory loading dock, which ordinarily means only one side of the car faces the dock. The workers open the door on their side, load the car then latch the door shut and seal it with a metal tag. They never open the other door.

I mention this because while walking one side of a train looking for a Pullman, if a boxcar has a closed and tagged door the door on the other side could be wide open and the car actually empty. You have to *check both sides of a boxcar to be sure it's unavailable*, which means to find a rideable boxcar you might have to walk both sides of a train.

The second both-doors-closed situation means although the boxcar's not loaded somebody at the loading dock was inconsiderate enough to close the door. Try as one might there's almost no way to slide a boxcar door open from the outside. Don't try to open a tagless door from the outside without some help from a buddy or two - even if you fancy yourself the Big Bad Wolf. (An exception to the usual door opening arrangement is the "Singleton" door opener. Note some boxcars have a wheel adjacent to the doors to make them easy to open manually. You can use this wheel as easily as anyone else *if* the door isn't tagged shut.)

The main reason you don't want to try opening doors from ground-level is you don't want to *herniate* yourself in the middle of a freightyard. It would take one helluva strong person to slide open a boxcar door while standing on the ground below it - superhumanly strong in fact. The door itself weighs at least a ton and its runners are usually poorly lubricated - if at all. Years of accumulated rust and railroad grime make boxcar doors manually immobile. At the warehouse for example the workers often open the door by hooking a forklift to the latch and taking off.

Ninety-five times out of 100 if you find one or two doors open the car's empty. Shippers *almost* always shut the doors on loaded cars. Sometimes however a boxcar is loaded with relatively indestructible freight (like wood, sheetrock or industrial paper products) and it doesn't matter if the load gets a bit wet or a wayfarer rides with it. Then too at times boxcars are loaded with doors shut but the doors aren't tagged. The car probably has freight of little value or else the workers forgot to tag the door. But if the door is shut that's probably the end of the question. If a door is open but the car's loaded there's always the danger of riding with a load (see within).

When walking a string you'll often find *all* boxcar doors shut. Don't despair. You've only seen one side of the train. Let's assume you have a few minutes to canvass the train. How long will it take?

An average freight train has anywhere from 30 to 150 cars - often more in the West. The AAR says the average train-length in America is 69 cars. To get a handle on the *outside* time limits in walking a train, let's use our 150-car train example. You can cover one side of a 150-car train within

30 to 40 minutes allowing for stops and walking on ballast with gear.

Let's say after walking one side no boxcar doors are open. You're best bet for a boxcar is a one-eyed bandit. Do you really want one? Here an appraisal of the weather, time of day, bull danger, scenery, sleep requirements, etc, comes into play, because you'll miss 50% of the scenery.

Ask yourself "O.K., which 50%?" Sometimes the scenery out one side is more interesting than the other. Mountains are a good example. Which side will have the big view and which only the cut in the mountain? Bodies of water are another example. Nobody wants to miss the Columbia River. A quick appraisal of the countryside you'll be traveling helps you decide whether to ride a one-eyed bandit.

If the weather is hot or cold which side of the car will the sun be on? Do you have a particular preference for north, south, east or west? Do you have a favorite shoulder to hang out the door with to look ahead or behind? Is it a nighttime journey and you'll be sleeping? Is rain blowing in from one direction?

Once up inside a one-eyed bandit you can always try to open the other door. Good luck. Before heaving-ho make sure the metal tag has been removed from the outside latch and the latch is unfastened. You'll have to exit the car and cross over the track to do this. Metal tags are easy to remove. Find a good sturdy stick, a small bar of metal or a pulled-up spike, stick it in the tag and twist. It will pop right off. Then throw the latch, get back in and try to slide the door open.

Unfortunately freightcar manufacturers don't put handles on the insides of doors. There's usually only a flat surface and it's tough getting a handhold on anything to pull open with. Inside however you have better leverage on the door. You might succeed, even if just getting it open a crack.

Alas, newer boxcars require the shipper to close and latch both doors before the railroad moves the car. Otherwise I suppose a door might fall off. Every now and again you'll see a boxcar door lying alongside the right-of-way so they do fall off. Moreover open doors create a wind suction situation. Believe it or not *wind resistance* is a major fuel consumption concern on the railroad. They prefer doors be shut even if the boxcar's empty. Newer boxcars have an admonishment spray-painted inside and outside the doors which goes something like "Doors must be closed and bulkheads locked before moving car." Thus even if a newer boxcar is empty there's no way to get in. I'd counsel against opening a door if it should be closed. You might get someone in trouble - probably yourself. Just say somebody else must have left it open - they have no proof.

Once you've chosen a boxcar you have to figure out how to get up inside. Jumping onto any type of freightcar gives one a good idea of personal stature. It's roughly analogous to jumping up onto a chest-high wall.

To jump up on any kind of freightcar first throw on your gear and put on your gloves. Put both hands palms down on the floor. Spring up and throw a leg onto the floor of the car then roll in and scramble on.

You can also use the doorlatch and *swing* up inside. This is an old pro trick. If a hobo's too short to vault into a boxcar or the train's already moving, first he'll throw in his gear. Then he draws even with the doorlatch, grabs onto it and swings himself legs-first into the car. This works especially well when a train's moving. You can harness the train's momentum to swing up and in. Maybe you've seen this in the movies. Using a doorlatch takes practice like any advanced sporting technique.

Once inside the boxcar **make sure at least one door can't slide shut.** Freightcars get banged around a lot - both in the yards and out over the road. When a boxcar gets slammed the impact can jar a door loose and slide it open or shut. If a door slides open, great. But if the only one open slides shut you could be in a real fix.

I've sought to avoid anecdotes in this primer. But this one is so delightful - and illustrative of the problems which arise if a boxcar door slams shut - I can't resist. I don't know where this story took place but it's a hobo favorite.

Legend has it two little boys were kicking around the freightyards one day. While walking they came upon a boxcar with one door open but the car was loaded. Guess what was inside? A fresh batch of hundreds of cases of beer. Of course out of natural curiosity the kids climbed in to sniff around a bit.

Well, the train took off while the kids were in the process of examining matters. They either couldn't or wouldn't get off in time. Soon the train was moving too fast and they had to go along for the ride.

I'll bet you can guess what happened next. That's right - somewhere along the line the kids' car got banged rather forcefully - as they are wont to do - and the door slid shut. And literally for the life of them the kids couldn't get that door back open.

It seems their parents were a bit on the negligent side and didn't miss the tots for some time. The kids were stuck in this car for *two weeks*. They tried everything: Beating on the walls, yelling, you-name-it. Nobody heard their cries. You see how isolated one can be in the freightyards.

Anyhow, when the kids were finally rescued at the other end of the continent, miraculously they had no noticeable signs of dehydration or malnutrition. Found with them in the boxcar were about four empty cases of beer. Well, happily the kids got reshipped back home to Mom and Dad and that was that.

This little saga illustrates an important point. You need to keep an open boxcar door *open*. Find a healthy piece of wood lying around, or better yet a loose railroad spike. Plenty of either commodity are found in the yards. Sometimes there'll be something in the car itself to use. Take this item and jam it into the bottom runner of the door or between the door and the wall to keep it open. This way the door won't slide shut and force you to drink and yell. The pros will show you this one. Use it religiously.

Tragedies occur when doors slide shut. Whether closed on purpose - as wetbacks do - or by sheer accident, there have been cases of people (not beer) who got trapped in boxcars out in the desert sun and asphyxiated or permanently boiled over. Don't let this happen to you.

So much for boxcar doors. Let's talk about boxcar floors. If you're lucky enough to *have* a choice of empty boxcars, get picky about the one to ride in. Boxcar floors come in two varieties - wood and metal. The older ones are generally wood; the newer metal. Metal floors are cleaner than wood but harder to sleep on. If it's cold outside give some thought to whether it will be fun to sleep on a cold metal floor. That chill can suck the heat right out of even a Himalaya-proof designer bag. Wouldn't wood be a lot nicer?

But then if fully prepared you've found that nice chunk of 1000-mile paper. Floors won't be as much of an issue. No matter how hard, cold or dirty a floor is you have shielding, cushioning and insulation.

Then too you could always bring along a "tokay blanket" (aka "canned heat"). Although drinking fortified wine might not be the most imaginative way to get to sleep it gets the job done. "Tokay blanket" means any type of intoxicant, liquid or otherwise, which knocks you out and blots out all sense of hot or cold. Although not necessarily recommended tokay blankets work. Oftentimes if a pro knows it's going to get cold he'll bring along a bottle of Night Train Express, Red or White Rocket, La Boheme, Gallo Red or White Port, Thunderbird, Muscatel ("white puke"), Manishewitz or some similar kick-ass fortified (18-22%) wine (aka *inter alia* "sneaky pete"). After consuming enough to be oblivious to distraction he'll roll out in 1000-mile paper or a blanket or two and ride out the cold. No kidding. It works.

This is an especially handy technique when going over a "Hump." Not a freightyard hump mind you. A high mountain pass. Hobos call it "going over the hump." Get the old antifreeze in the radiator before bedding down and you'll sleep like a baby. Make sure you wake up on the other side. Don't catch that "Westbound" to the "Big Hole in the Sky" before your time.

Getting further acquainted with the boxcar, notice how much larger one feels inside than outside. Take a little stroll around the car and get familiar with its features, preferably when it's light out so you can note any obstacles or stumbling blocks it might contain. Although many different boxcar designs are in current service, generally the inside walls are either vertical wall struts covered with exterior siding or plywood paneling lining the inside.

The plainest unequipped boxcar for general service (merchandise and machinery of all types) is called the "XM" "free-running" boxcar. These are simply big metal boxes on wheels with two sliding doors. Free runners are the oldest boxcar design (although still made) and the ones you'll find open most often. A less-numerous cousin has the same design but a regular sliding door which is wider and a "plug" door next to it which jacks into the wall. These "combination-door" "XMs" won't be open as often because shippers are advised to shut the doors.

Some boxcars have sliding panels inside called "load restraining devices" which cut the boxcar into lateral sections. These panels slide up and down the car and fasten into holes along the sidewalls in the floor and roof. They provide dunnage and bracing for loads like pulp, paper, newsprint, glass and clay products and prevent freight damage during impacts. They also allow "less-then-full-car" shippers to double-up and fill a boxcar. On the outside wall you'll see the letters "DF" or "XL." Even with a door shut we can often identify a load-restraining boxcar by the shape of its external walls. The walls have a waffle pattern or other corrugated appearance.

A "food service" boxcar for processed and packaged foods has inside walls made of seamless plastic lining. You'll probably never see a door on a foodcar open because they have a special plug design. The doors are forced inward when closed. This provides a flat wall for the stacks of food and prevents contamination of the car's interior. These boxcars have an "XF" painted outside. All told in 1989 there were 104,185 "plain" boxcars and 103,495 "equipped" boxcars - plenty for everyone.

THE CLOSED HOPPER CAR

After boxcars the next most desirable car is the closed "Hopper" car (aka "bulk loader" or "grainer"). Closed hoppers are bulk commodities cars. They carry products in bulk which need protection from the elements, like corn, wheat, sorghum, malt, beans, salt, phosphate, ground limestone, cement, feldspar, granulated plastics and soda ash.

There are two types of closed hoppers - one which is rideable and one which isn't. The most commonly encountered rideable hopper is the "Ace Centerflow" hopper. Look for Ace Centerflows when scoping out a train. The name is usually painted somewhere near midcar.

Notice how the hopper is unique from a side view. Its end-walls cut in at the bottom, forming one side of a V-shape over the wheels. Rideable closed hoppers are easy to spot. If you look at one end-on it has rounded walls instead of flat, vertical walls. Their unusual non-angular design, like big sausages set down on wheels and clipped at each end, distinguishes them from non-rideable hoppers. Notice the difference from a straight-walled hopper.

The difference between an "open" and "closed" hopper is the latter has a roof and hatches on top. You can't see this standing on the ground except from a distance. Open hoppers are roofless and carry commodities like coal, crushed rock, gravel, sand, asphalt, mineral ores, woodchips and sugarbeets. It doesn't matter whether these commodities get wet. While open hoppers are not safe to ride, closed or "covered" hoppers (known in formal industry parlance as the "LO Small Cube Covered Hopper Car") are safe and a great ride.

What you *can* see from the ground on any hopper are two, three or four chutes extending down from the car's underside. These chutes are variously called "doors," "bays," "outlet gates" or "bottoms." On a closed hopper (which we'll refer to simply as a "hopper" since open hoppers don't concern us) workers open the top hatches to pour the bulk commodity in from above. At the receiving end workers open the "bottoms" to pour the load out from below. Gravity does the work at both ends. Some hoppers are unloaded by vacuum tube, especially those used for plastic granule ladings and other light commodities which would stick inside the car without suction.

Open hoppers also work with gravity but don't have a top hatch to aim for in loading. They're often loaded while rolling and are extremely efficient. State-of-the-art coal and other mineral hoppers have rotating couplers so the car can be tipped over on its side to "roll-dump" the load while rolling, then aright so the next car can roll-dump.

Hoppers are used extensively throughout the country (1989 - 284,566 covered hoppers and 237,116 open hoppers). Most "regular" freight trains or "consists" (the most common type of train, see within) include at least one of them and usually several. ("Consist" is railroadspeak for the cars and engines a freight train is made up of - or consists of - pronounced CON-sist.) Hoppers are often coupled together in strings of 5, 10 or more.

Next time you see a freight train take a look at the round-sided rideable hopper. At each end where the body of the car cuts in there's a platform over the wheels. Sometimes these platforms are made of thick metal grating, much like a subway ventilator or sewer grate. These are tough to lie on and not recommended if you plan to sleep. More often the platforms are made of solid metal plate. In the industry they're called the "body bolster top shear plate." We'll call them platforms. This is where we ride. (Note: Flat-walled closed hoppers which have rideable platforms have made a recent appearance. Although rare keep a lookout for them.)

We might otherwise be able to ride on either platform, but because of the bottoms there's no room for the air system's piping, cylinder and reservoir (which on other cars are affixed underneath the floor). Instead the air system is located atop the B-end platform of the car because the brakewheel is located here. Notice the air system consists of a brake chain, bleeder rod, air brake valve, release valve, auxiliary-emergency air reservoir, brake cylinder, the brake cylinder push rod which sets and releases the brakes and lots of curved metal piping. The system takes up most of the platform. But the *other* platform is empty and affords an excellent ride.

Since this is an open-air riding accommodation the question of aerodynamics arises. Riding outside it's *much* more fun to be out of the wind. Prolonged exposure to a strong steady wind can make you crazy riding freights.

Always ride on the *back* platform out of the wind. Once you know which end of the train is the back end, take a look at the back platform of a hopper you're interested in. Is it the empty platform? If not, find another hopper. The air system takes up all the platform space. You can stand up easily enough or sit on the pipes, valves and cylinders. But you can't lie down.

Luck will usually be with you however. Most regular consists have several hoppers in a row. The odds of finding one facing the right direction are 50-50 for each hopper. If one has the air at the back check the next hopper and the next until you find one with the empty platform in back. Always eyeball *any* kind of hopper because car manufacturers keep coming out with new designs which might have rideable platforms.

Put on your gloves, throw your gear on, climb up the stirrup and ladder of your hopper, swing onto the platform and take a look around. You'll notice several things. First you can walk across the platform from one side of the car to the other. Second you can see out both sides of the train. This bodes well for sightseeing. Third the platform has a neat set of grabirons around its perimeter at about chest level. Use them as handholds while the train's in motion or during sudden takeoffs or jerks. Fourth most platforms have a fairly high lip ("apron" or "combing") sticking up around the edges. This prevents you or your gear from rolling off at high speeds or on curves and hills.

As a matter of fact you might think railcar manufacturers had the *hobo in mind* in designing hoppers (or at least used to). One could plausibly argue since hopper cars have largely agricultural uses manufacturers put platforms on them to allow farmworkers to follow the harvest. Not actually likely being called body bolster top shear plates, but an interesting idea. The result of course is great for us.

Even more interesting is the big hole cut out of the body of the car at the inside edge of the platforms midway along the width of the car (the "cubbyhole," see ADMX 85247 photo above). The crawl space afforded inside is a perfect hideout for you or your gear when paranoia gets the better of you - or when a real need for concealment arises. You can climb inside this compartment and sit there. It's quite confining but practically impossible to be seen. This hole is great for caching your gear if you want to walk around.

Returning to railroad aerodynamics, no matter what speed the train is traveling two spots on the hopper's back platform provide dead air - to the right and left of the center hole up against the back wall. Here you can light a match and it burns freely. The back platform provides a good space for riding without the discomfort of interminable maddening wind.

Even though *technically* you're outside you stay dry - even in the pouring rain. The overhead hatch design provides a roof. Wind and temperature allowing this roof makes the hopper perfect for all-weather wayfaring. The only time problems arise is when you're stopped and the wind blows rain or snow onto the platform. In general you get a great view from the back platform of a hopper and all basic requirements are met.

Hoppers tend to be a bit *loud*. You're sitting right over your wheels with the wheels of the following car staring you right in the face. Also note on some hoppers the solid metal platforms aren't completely flat. They have upward bulges over the tops of the wheels. These bulges make lying down uncomfortable. If you have a choice of several hoppers choose one which doesn't have bulges in the floors.

Some newer hoppers are hobo-proof. They've done one of two things to spoil the platform arrangement. Either they've sealed off the platforms with a big metal box so we can't get inside, or they've discontinued putting the platform over the wheels (like most straight-walled covered hoppers and all open hoppers). Even if you come across a new access-proof car however keep looking. There's something to ride 90% of the time. It will be years before they modify, "redline" or "condemn" (scrap) the older accessible models. Happy Highball!

The Piggyback

If your train doesn't have any accessible boxcars or hoppers, the next best bet is to ride a "Piggyback" (aka "piggies" and "pigs"). As the name implies this is a setup whereby something rides on the back of something else - in our case a flatcar with one or two semi-truck trailers on top.

Piggybacks are long flat freightcars which often have a metal ridge or depression running down the center of the floor. Railroads variously refer to a piggyback as "Intermodal Freight" or "Trailer-on-Flatcar" (TOFC) if it hauls one or two truck trailers, or "Container-on-Flatcar" (COFC) if it hauls big boxes. Many piggybacks can carry both.

Piggybacks are a hot innovation on the railroad, which is constantly seeking back business lost to trucks. Weather permitting the piggyback is a very respectable ride; one we should always keep an eye out for. Let's talk about truck-trailer piggies first.

We want to *ride a piggyback only when it's got a piggy on its back - that is, a trailer or box on it.* Without a trailer or box there's no protection from wind, rain or the bull. Unloaded piggies are like riding an empty flatcar.

(But Note: There's a small exception to the only-ride-a-loaded-piggy rule. Notice at one end of *some* piggybacks is a flat metal plate which is hinged to the floor of the car. This plate snaps up into a vertical position - even if the piggy is empty. It's called the "bridge plate" or "apron."

In older loading operations trailers are driven up a ramp onto a piggy. The plates snap down forming a bridge, so trailers can roll from one piggy to the next. Once the trailers are on, the bridge plate snaps back up. If it's a nice day and you're reasonably confident your presence is inoffensive you can ride behind one of these plates if it's at the front end of the car. The plate breaks the wind enough to make the ride enjoyable and prevents us from sliding off during a sudden stop. Although an exposed and not highly recommended ride it's an empty piggyback option.

The ramp or "circus loading" (circuses still travel by train) method of driving trailers onto piggies has largely been replace by "gantry" and "side" loading. In gantry loading a traveling overhead gantry crane straddling the track lifts the trailer or box on and off the piggyback. In side loading a giant forklift-type machine called a "Piggybacker" bodily lifts the trailer or box on and off the piggyback. As a result many bridge plates have been removed. In general look for piggybacks with trailers and boxes on them.)

Let's talk about trailer piggies first. The piggyback itself is little more than a longer, specialized version of a flatcar. A "standard flat" piggyback is 89 feet long and handles two 40-ft. trailers. 70,000 standard flats were in service in 1990. Since passage of the Surface Transportation Act of 1982 however trailers have increased in length from 40 to 45, 48 and even 53 feet. Railroads have had to scramble to augment their standard flat fleet to accommodate longer trailers.

Let's talk about truck trailers. When you get an opportunity do some piggyback research in your spare time. Cruise down to the local truck stop and take a closer look at a standard North American truck trailer. Notice these trailers have two axles with four 20 to 22-inch tires on each axle for a total of 8 tires (or even three axles with 12 tires). Also notice if you climb in underneath the axles it's hard to see you from the side of the trailer - unless someone's specifically looking. Keep this in mind if the bull is a consideration in your yard. It's a little greasy under there and has low overhead clearance.

Under ordinary circumstances *ride a piggyback sitting down on the leeward (away from the wind) side of the tires facing backwards. Sit with your back against the tires for support.* The question becomes *which side* of the tires will be leeward.

During your pre-voyage trailer inspection tour notice all properly-maintained trailers have mudflaps on the backdoor side of the tires. These mudflaps prevent the duals from showering motorists with water, mud or rocks flung out at high rpm's. Unfortunately they also prevent us from sitting behind the tires on the backdoor side of the trailer. They're in the way like air equipment at the B-end of a hopper.

The trailer you want to ride has to have its backdoors and mudflaps facing *forward* so the flapless side of the duals is in back. From here we have a near 360-degree view. There's an even better view if we crawl down the car away from the tires toward the folding-down "single-point hitch" the front of the trailer rests on without a tractor.

You do in fact have to crawl on a loaded piggyback because you're under a trailer. You won't be able to stand up unless you're so short riding freight trains wouldn't be advisable (like well under five feet tall). You can get on your knees with your head bent down but that's about it. Taking a leak for either sex can be a real challenge on a piggyback. You can easily piss your leg or foot. The only place you *can* stand up is at the ends or the middle of the car, behind or between the trailers. The trailer and tires provide good wind and rain protection but not nearly as good as a boxcar or hopper. Like a hopper you watch the country glide by behind you because you're facing backwards.

It seems the old two-trailers-to-a-standard-flat-piggy arrangement isn't good enough anymore. The latest piggyback innovation is a mini-piggyback which has been out 6 or 7 years. The most popular model is the "Front Runner." Front runners are 53'-10" in length and hold only one trailer. I call mini-piggies "Piggly-Wigglies" and you'll understand why in a minute.

The ever-increasing length of truck trailers has rendered the 89-ft. standard flat largely obsolete. With trailer lengths taken beyond the traditional 40-ft. it's impossible to fit two longer trailers on one standard flat. Railroads have been forced to either use standards with only one trailer on top (or a trailer and a short box) or to re-equip their fleet using shorter single-trailer flats.

To accommodate the longer trailers railroads have come up with a variety of new designs and renovations such as the Front Runner. One new idea pioneered by AT&SF has been to connect four or five cars together by articulation and solid drawbars. Santa Fe's new design is called the "Fuel Foiler." Other four-car designs are called "Four Runners." The whole set of cars are considered as one as is reflected in their reporting marks.

Some railroads (Southern for example, now Norfolk Southern Railway Company) saw off 50-ft. boxcars and convert them to single piggies. The shorter a freightcar the easier it is on track. The longer the car the more its wheels grind the rails. You'll constantly hear this grinding on the railroad. Pigglie-wigglies don't grind track as badly as a standard flat. Pigglie-wigglies are also much lighter than standards so the train hauls less excess floor tonnage, saving fuel and equipment. And with less-rigid construction the mini-piggie torsions more easily on curves. Their wheels are articulated like bending buses. They have only 4 wheels instead of 8 per car, which saves even more on track. They wiggle down the track, hence "Piggly-Wigglies."

But thank goodness there's still plenty of room on a piggly-wiggly to sit or lie down on the wide part of the floor behind the duals. Unlike hoppers I can't think of any practicable way of hobo-proofing piggybacks.

One final observation with any piggyback is the same as with hoppers. Find one which has a metal apron running along the edges of the floor to keep you and your gear on board.

The TOFC's brother, COFC (container-on-flatcar) carries intermodal containers (let's use the word "box"). "Intermodal" means the box can be shipped by ocean freighter, truck or flatcar. These boxes come in various lengths and are placed either end-to-end on a "platform" or "double-stacked" on top of each other - the latest box craze. 24,000 double-stack piggies were in service in 1988.

An even more recent piggyback innovation is the "well car" for double-stack box loading. Rather than having a flat floor the floor surface is dropped close down to the railhead forming a long rectangular sandbox shape. The lower box rides down close to minimize upper box tunnel and bridge clearance restrictions. Keep an eye out for well cars whose floors are basically missing however. They have only a lip to set the edges of the container on. Well cars with complete floors are spottable because they have corrugated designs on their exterior walls.

Well cars often come in units of four or five and are articulated like piggly-wigglies. If you find one empty it's a great ride because the well provides a safe yet scenic space to ride. If one's loaded we have to ride on the ends, which may or may not be spacious. You also have to stand up to see anything or sit on the platform over the wheels. These cars are the wave of the future so look for them.

Here's a freebee on freightcars in general. If properly maintained a freightcar has an average 22-year lifespan. Every car says on its side when and where it was "new" or "rebuilt." There's additional information on a car's ownership (more of its reporting marks), including its height ("In Height," or "IH"), width ("IW"), length ("IL"), load limit ("LD LMT" or "LD LT"), freight weight capacity ("CAPY"), cubic feet of load available ("CU FT") and unloaded or "light" weight ("LT WT").

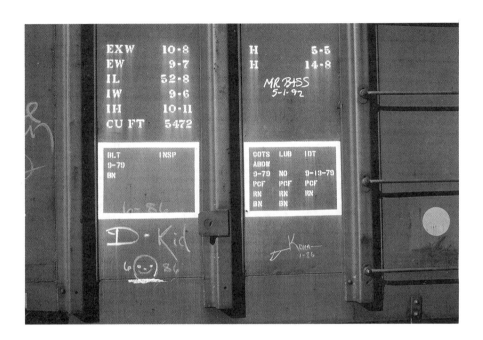

THE GONDOLA

When you say "gondola" most people think of those funny boats tourists float around in when they visit Venice; the ones where the boatman has to wear a funny hat and striped shirt or else the locals throw fruit at him. A *real* gondola is found no where else but - you guessed it - on the railroad.

Real gondolas are freightcars which look like doorless boxcars cut off halfway up. They're nothing more than short roofless rectangular boxes on wheels. (There's a new fibreglass-covered variant which we can't access but they're few and far between. They carry mineral ores.)

Gondolas have a flat metal floor and shouldn't be confused with open hoppers, which although taller look much the same from the side. Notice any hopper is distinguishable by its slope-sheet floors leading to the gravity chutes underneath.

Gondolas or "gons" generally carry steel pipe, waste products or recyclable junk metal. Some in the 52 to 65-ft. range called open-top "mill gons" carry structural shapes, pipe and other long or extremely heavy products. If a gon has one of its ends painted a different color than its normal color scheme it's a "rotary coupler gon," which can carry coal to generating plants and is roll-dumped like a rotary hopper. Beware of trying to ride in a coal gon. They're higher sided and you may not be able to climb back out at the end of the line. Coal gons are mainly built by Thrall Car Company and are commonly referred to as "bathtub gons."

Even taller gons are called "woodchip gons" and haul chips for reconstituted wood products (i.e., plywood and fiberboard).

Other gondolas have end-walls which fold down to ship extra long structural shapes or ribbon rail.

    The best thing to say about a gondola is it's the most bull-proof car we can ride. The only person who can see you in the yards has to be up in a tower. Tower operators could care less about us being on a train. The bull's never going to get out of his car, climb up the ladder and check inside a gondola, so we're safe.

    The bad thing about gondolas is if *we* want to see anything beyond the clouds overhead we have to remain standing up or bring along a very tall stool. Depending on the height of the walls we can only see over the sides if we're somewhat over six feet tall.

    Gondolas are easy to get into. Climb up the stirrup and ladder, go over the wall or "top sill" and jump down to the floor. The problem is getting back *out*. You have to scale the wall and there are no footholds inside.

    Never ride the top sill of a gon. There's nothing to hang onto and you could easily be catapulted onto the track during a sudden takeoff or jerk.

Professional hobos like gondolas. For many the scenery isn't particularly interesting anymore. They're simply trying to get where they want to go. If you're taking a more leisurely sightseeing trip the gondola will be rough on your feet. You'll be on your feet the *entire journey* peering over the top of the car, as in a well car. Gondolas are not glorious or romantic but they get the job done - except when it's raining.

REFRIGERATION CARS

Speaking of boxes in railroading, let's take a trip down hobo memory lane. I throw this in as a comparison of the sport today with the way it was played in the old days and because we're talking about riding in boxes.

Railroads have freightcars called refrigerator cars (or "reefers" for short.) Reefers are insulated, mechanically-refrigerated cars used to ship perishable products like fruit, meat, dairy, floral and other produce items, or less frequently photographic film.

Reefers can be heated as well as cooled so they're an all-tempera-ture car. They have the exact same look and design as a boxcar with a plug door on either side. They're usually painted orange or less-often white and are often coupled together in long strings. Over the last four decades they've been cooled by diesel-powered compressors like the 'fridge at home (only yours probably runs on electricity - or kerosene if you're Amish).

In the old days reefers were different. They were still designed like boxcars and painted orange. But from their debut in 1872 they were cooled by placing large blocks of ice into compartments called "ice-bunkers" or "end-bunkers" at each end of the car. Ice factories were built next to yards where growers brought in perishables to be shipped. Loading crews "iced" the reefers by top-loading ice into the end-bunkers. They'd shut the top bunker doors, load the shipment and try to get it wherever it was going before the ice melted. When feasible the shipment was insulated by packing sawdust around it. All-reefer trains were fast freight in the old days. If it was a long haul - say 6 to 10 days from California to Pennsylvania - "reefer trains" had to stop along the way to "re-ice" the cars.

Initially reefers were slow to catch on. It took people a while to believe the produce they saw in stores during a mid-January blizzard. Produce like California winter artichokes and asparagus began appearing in New York City in the late 19th century. Once people recovered from their initial skepticism about the quality of the produce they started snapping it up. By the 1880s (rich) folks were sipping fresh orange juice in February in Boston. If the railroad didn't drag its feet the ice system worked well and lasted into the 1960s.

The old ice-bunker reefers had to be shipped back empty, since in January NYC had no produce to ship back to California or Florida (come to think of it - it still doesn't in August either). The ice-bunkers of course were empty. When reefer trains left heading west or south hobos climbed up the ladders to the roof, then down into the "bunkhouse." They'd "bunk down" by shutting the hatches over their head so bulls couldn't find them.

You talk about being in a box! These guys were in pitch blackness as the train left out of the yards. Once out over the road however they opened the hatches and - weather permitting - climbed onto the roof to ride the deck. I don't know *how* they got back out of the bunkhouse but some-how they managed it. Traincrews could see them riding the deck. They didn't care if a few ticketless passengers were along for the ride. But hobos had to bunk down and shut the hatches when coming into a yard. While bunked down they ran the risk of being trapped inside if a trainman acciden-tally (or intentionally) slipped a locking pin through the latch fastener. Many hobos were found inside. Due to the bull factor however the ice reefer was a popular ride for upwards of 90 years.

Today diesel compressor-cooled or heated reefers can't be accessed like the old ice reefers. The end-bunker is a thing of the past. Old reefers were redlined or refitted for other uses long ago. Every now and then you'll see them off on a dead siding, rusting in the sun and rain. Before transit shippers close and lock the plug doors with diesel reefers whether loaded or empty. Otherwise the doors are so heavy (insulated like the walls with thick layers of wood or polyethylene) they fall off their runners when the car gets knocked around.

Modern reefers have additional problems. Perishable freight rates were deregulated in the 1960s when trucks made inroads into the market. Today railroads have a tough task competing in this time-sensitive market. Unlike a trucker who has the refrigeration unit right behind his cab, a compressor failure on a reefer often isn't discovered until a train's ICC mandatory "1000-mile inspection" - usually too late to save the freight.

The average reefer can make only about 10 "revenue trips" a year because it's shipped back empty. Profitability no longer justifies the ex-pense. While built in the 1960s many were retired in the 1970s and 80s when their AAR-mandated "15-year overhaul" came due. Today reefer truck trailers are shipped by piggyback but have the same driverless com-pressor failure problems.

The latest refrigeration innovations are big reefer *boxes* with refrigeration units which run off engine electricity and "RBL" boxcars which are heavily insulated and able to maintain a certain temperature for days. Lots of beer is shipped in RBL boxcars. Thus a bit of perspective on the changing nature of the freight train world.

Back to gondolas. One thing about open gondolas is that like boxcars and reefers they're slowly falling into disuse. We don't find as many of them as we used to. Each takes too much manpower to load.

One has to admit boxcars *are* inefficient to load and unload. At each end of the line repeated trips are required by forklift operators in and out of the boxcar. The operator has a tough time seeing where he's going. Merchandise gets crushed against the walls or door of the car or in picking it up and setting it down. At times the operator wipes out making turns and smashes fellow workers. Anybody who's worked around a forklift knows how dangerous they can be.

Gondolas have similar loading and unloading limitations. Shippers can't use gravity to unload them like a chute-equipped hopper or rotary coupler roll-dump car. They have to be loaded from the top and off-loaded from the top. That's why gondolas are often used to ship metal products. Electromagnet cranes dump the metal in then pluck it out again. Open gondolas are also disappearing because the kind of freight they can handle is limited. Gondolas and boxcars are going the way of the reefer, caboose and fireman - into railroad ashcans and annals.

Today shippers prefer piggyback trailers and intermodal boxes. I don't know why loading a trailer or a box is any easier than loading a boxcar, but apparently it is. Perhaps it's because they don't have to make the turn at the boxcar door. Pig trailers and containers are clearly more economical because the shipper loads it at one end and the receiver unloads it at the other. Intermediate loading and unloading at the freightyard is eliminated. Shippers have found it takes roughly 1/6th the time to load and unload trailers and containers compared to boxcars and gondolas.

We won't miss gondolas nearly as much as boxcars. They're rigorous to ride and we can't see much. But on hot railroads their bull-proof quality will be missed. They won't entirely disappear either. They're still the best way to ship freight which can't be handled any other way. 134,769 of them were rolling in 1989.

THE FLATCAR

Flatcars (or "general-service" flatcars in industry parlance) as the name implies are just flat cars. No walls of any kind. They have wood or nailable metal floors or "decks" to nail down "load blocking" to prevent shift, and "stake pockets" on the sides if vertical staking is necessary.

The only distinguishing feature newer flatcars have (apart from piggybacks, platforms and well cars) is end-walls or "bulkheads" at each end of the car. These flatcars are called "bulkhead flats." The bulkheads keep a load from sliding off during humping or stops. Bulkhead flats are great for two reasons: The front bulkhead provides a solid windbreak like the folded-up bridge plate on an empty standard piggyback. We can also sit up against it for comfort - and to stay on the car.

Flatcars are used primarily for building materials like pipe, lumber, re-bar, brick, prefabricated rock and sheetrock. Less frequently they're used to ship big farm or road building equipment or military hardware like harvesters, bulldozers and tanks. Sometimes we find huge coils of metal strapped to them but more often these coils are shipped in gondolas.

I've ridden lots of flatcars. Under favorable conditions they're an excellent ride. Before riding one however it's worth taking a moment to consider some of their plusses and minuses.

The good news is if you want to see the sights a flatcar can't be beat. It's nothing short of 3-D panoramic. You see the great country flow past like a tableau in a geodesic dome theater with a wrap-around screen. It's like having a different movie rolling on either side of the car. You can watch one or the other - or split the difference and watch a little of each. A flatcar absolutely cannot be beat for high summer riding out in the country. Without doubt we also get that California tan we crave. There's nothing to prevent the elements from paying a prolonged visit. In point of fact we're extremely exposed on a flatcar. You might feel quite naked for the first few miles. The bad news is there's a constant risk of falling off. Flatcars rarely have lips or aprons.

There's a brilliant new flatcar coming into use on the big Northwestern railroads (Burlington Northern, Union Pacific, Southern Pacific, British Columbia Railway, Canadian National and Canadian Pacific) which carries finished lumber products. Its full name is the "Center-Beam Bulkhead Flat Car." This car is like a bulkhead flat with a twist. Through the center of the car from end to end runs a metal center beam at the same height as the bulkheads, splitting the car into two halves. This car is popular with lumbermen because the center beam allows for easy forklift loading and load "strap-down." The car is popular with wayfarers because there's an additional wall on the car which breaks the wind and doubles as protection from rock throwing and bull trouble on the other side of the train. Look for these center-beam bulkhead flats.

Another encouraging innovation is the popular modular/intermodal/COFC platform. These flatcars are just as rideable as any other, with all the attendant advantages and disadvantages of older models. More of them are available as railroads go modular so keep an eye out for them.

The great thing about modular flatcar platforms is if they're *loaded* the boxes provide a valuable windbreak. They're almost as good as a hopper at blocking the wind. You can also play hide-and-seek with kids and bulls by using the boxes as cover. Many times a modular platform has two non-stacked boxes on it and the boxes don't take up all the floorspace. There's room to lie down between them or behind the back one. The boxes are securely bolted to the floor so there's little risk of being crushed or shoved off the car. The best position to take is *between* the boxes for safety, wind and detection protection.

Unfortunately I've noticed a recent trend where the boxes *do* cover all the floorspace and leave no room to sit or lie down. There's also the new "big box" - one box which covers the entire floorspace. The current double-stacking rage sometimes leaves little floorspace available.

All different types of modular flats and platforms are out there. Take a look at what's available.

In general while terrific for sightseeing the flatcar is windy, danger-ous and affords little protection from the elements, kids or bulls. Ninety percent of the time I'd counsel against one. The only three exceptions are if the flatcar has bulkheads, *or* if it's one of the newer modular units with boxes on it yet also space for you, *or* has a load you feel confident won't shift which you can hop on behind *and keep an eye on* (see within).

It bears mention at this juncture there are two other commonly-used cars we *can't* ride because there's nowhere to sit or lie down. The first is the tankcar.

Tankcars are big long tanks set down on the wheel trucks. Unlike hoppers they have no platforms at each end. Rather they *might* have a footboard at each end, or one which goes all the way around the car made out of heavy metal mesh. These footboards aren't designed with us in mind. Footboards are for workers to stand on to fill, empty, switch or maintain the car. They're much too narrow to ride without hanging onto a grabiron. Remember however they are a convenient way of getting across a standing train. In fact because of the grabs and footboards a tankcar is the easiest kind of car to cross over. In a pinch you can also ride one a short distance - but don't get stuck on one for more than 50-80 miles.

Another thing to keep in mind about tankcars is what they're loaded with. They carry some strange and dangerous cargoes, as was vividly illustrated in the Southern Pacific freight derailment of July 14th 1991. Nineteen thousand gallons of herbicide from a punctured tankcar were dumped into the Sacramento River near Dunsmuir in Northern California, virtually eliminating aquatic life for 45 miles downstream and polluting Lake Shasta. The only positive result the pundits noted was that the surviving fish no longer bore fleas.

The problem with tankcars is government has suddenly discovered it has practically *no regulations* concerning rail shipment of hazardous materials (this shouldn't be too awfully surprising given the *laisse faire* attitude government has taken toward railroads over the past 150 years).   Until the situation changes I'd give tankcars a wide berth.   They're safe enough to walk next to I suppose.   But I wouldn't want to ride one or even brush up against it.   Many have painted on their sides what they carry (i.e., "chlorine") or have placards with numbers that mean something to someone.   In case of doubt I'd say keep walking.

Almost 180,000 tankcars roll around America carrying over one million loads of hazardous materials each year.   Many of them out-and-out *smell* bad.   Some trains consist of nothing but tankcars and are known as "oilcan" or "tank" trains.

The second unrideable car is the open or uncovered hopper mentioned earlier.   Although cut in at each end there's no platform over the wheels.   Unlike a gondola open hoppers are too deep to climb back out of, much less see anything from.   Moreover their floors aren't flat.   The slope-sheet floors drop into the chutes.

Coal train consists of all-open hoppers move to power plants and docks continent-wide out of the Powder River Basin in Wyoming as well as Appalachian and British Columbia coal regions. Tankcars and open hoppers bear little direct impact on our sport. Simply be aware most trains have them along and some are nothing but.

A variety of specialty cars also roll on America's railroads. Their number and complexity exceed the scope of this book. I mention them so you don't feel betrayed if you see a strange car every now and then. The military has some unique rolling stock (one supposes they have some unique cargoes as well). Speciality cars have non-standard configurations and are generally unrideable, but given the ride requirements mentioned at the beginning of the chapter you ultimately will be the judge of this.

One further note: Railroads aren't the only show in town in terms of freightcar ownership. A number of companies which are *not* railroads own, lease or operate freightcars. Some own many more cars than most railroads. Of the 1,250,000 freightcars operating in North America in 1989, 412,000 (or 30%) were owned by private car companies and shippers. Many owners deal in a certain kind of car such as piggy-backs, reefers, hoppers, tankcars or specialty cars. Sixty non-railroad companies own 1,000 cars or more. The largest, Trailer Train Co. ("TTX," well cars and piggybacks) owns over 90,000 cars (although it in turn is owned by a conglomerate of railroads).

In fact freightcar ownership is coming full-circle. Before the 1870s nearly all freightcars were privately owned by non-railroads. Railroads didn't get into the ownership picture much before the 1880s. From the 1880s until after World War II the percentage of railroad-owned rolling stock steadily increased.

Now the railroad ownership percentage is shrinking again. Who owns what percentage of cars will have an impact on what's available to ride in the future, although just what that impact will be isn't clear. (You also may see privately-owned passenger cars tacked onto a freight train or Amtrak train. Hobos call these cars "private varnish." They're used by large corporations to reward successful employees or woo prospective customers, or by rich individuals who like trains. These cars are absolutely deluxe inside with sleeping, dining and leisure facilities.)

On an even brighter note I have a rather embarrassing confession to make. I *dissembled* when I said boxcars are the cadillac of railroad cruising. They *are* in fact the cadillac of regular railroading. What we'll talk about next is something you shouldn't try the first times out. If you want to earn a high-degree black belt in freight training however there are two *even better* rides than a boxcar. Here's one.

The Auto Rack

Here is a closely-guarded adventure secret. I want to make it clear *I am not encouraging, much less recommending* anyone do what I now describe.

We've all seen car manufacturers ship new cars and trucks on trains. New vehicles are shipped on what railroads call the "Bi- or Tri-Level Auto Rack" which we'll call collectively the "Auto Rack."

It has been known to occur in the annals of freight train ridership that hobos ship themselves *right along with the cars and trucks* on an auto rack. With a little luck *it has been occasioned* a hobo finds a car or truck which is **unlocked.** *It has come to pass* people *get in* a brand-new vehicle. *Rumor has it* this is the cadillac of railroading.

In the old days *so the story goes* auto manufacturers thought they'd be clever by driving autos onto auto racks, locking them and hiding the key in the tailpipe. Folks at the receiving end could fish the key out, unlock the car and drive it to its ultimate destination. A later variant was to tape the key inside the little door which hid the gas cap - either behind the fold-down license plate or the little door on the side panel of the vehicle. Manufacturers however became even *more* clever. They always left *a second ignition key in the ignition* of the locked cars.

Alert hobos picked up on these techniques quickly. They regularly fished the door key out of its hiding place and took a nice ride - often through sub-zero or 100°-plus temperatures. The temptation was practically irresistible. You could start the car with the key and turn on the heater or air conditioning - and check out all the options.

The *problem* was car dealers were receiving trashed cars. Industry giants slowly realized they had a problem. They thought they'd solve it by sending the door keys directly to the dealer separate from the vehicle. Although foulups occur and keys get mixed up, this is the procedure today. Alas no more golden key to ferret out from the vehicle. Perhaps some shippers do it "the old-fashioned way," but I haven't *heard of* this since the early 1980s. Today *according to the grapevine* one has to get lucky and find a vehicle they *forgot to lock*. *They say* it's not hard to do.

Perhaps some of you alert readers already know how to get into a locked car without a key (assuming you're alert enough to read). From a quick perusal of national crime statistics I'd say there are many of you out there. But for those not wise to the ways of auto boosting here's how *legend has it* one goes about finding an unlocked new car/truck.

Usually a train has 2, 3, 7, 10 or more auto racks coupled together. Sometimes a whole train is loaded auto racks. *Tales abound* of people climbing onto each auto rack *during nighttime only* and going from deck to deck, car to car, gently lifting up on the *driver's* doorhandle. *According to conventional wisdom* forget the passenger door. It comes out locked at the factory. With any luck however a driver's doors will be open. *This is risky business - one experts say should not be engaged in during broad daylight.*

Once one finds that magically unlocked door *they tell me* people open it up and climb in. Usually there is a key in the ignition. Most new vehicles have about 1/4th tank of gas - to see if they actually work and to drive them onto the auto racks, trucks and onto the dealer's lot or showroom. *I am told* new vehicles have big new batteries in them - and nicer radios, tape decks and CDs each year.

People suggest another exciting possibility is to get in the small vans which are later customized - the vans Detroit cranks out which have a driver's compartment but nothing yet in the way of a body or shipping compartment in back. People convert these half-builts into RVs, catering trucks, plumbers' vans, etc. Many military vans come this way. Detroit seals the back of the driver's compartment with stiff cardboard or fiber-board. But *it has been known to occur* one can easily dislodge this backing and climb in. *I've heard* this is another excellent ride.

Once inside *sportsmen say* one can take a test drive without moving an inch. They check the interior upholstery and dome lights.

A couple of other notes of caution: When people riding in new vehicles come into yards and stations *I've heard* they slouch down below the window level. *Nobody* wants to see them in the new cars/trucks. People get *very mad* at hobos if they find them inside a new vehicle. Moreover at night they recommend one keep one's foot off the brake pedal. It's a dead giveaway if the bull sees brakelights going on-and-off as someone tries to avoid a railroad fender bender. A suggested solution: Sit in the front *passenger's* seat.

All-in-all *I've been told* it's good clean fun. If the shipper paid the schome who drives the vehicle a decent wage *maybe* he'd remember to lock every car. Until this occurs people will continue to climb in and enjoy new-car ambiance.

One final note about getting caught: *They tell me* in many states to prove auto theft one element of the crime is the *car was locked* when the owner parked it and relinquished control. Since auto rack autos are sometimes unlocked nobody gets nailed for GTA - or even joyriding. After all you never move an inch, eh? Rather the cops go with a trespassing, misappropriation of property or reckless disregard of property type of offense. In short don't sweat it.

Let's talk about the auto rack as a freightcar. We can ride the freightcar itself whether loaded or empty.

The older auto racks are sideless except for the upright struts which support the second and third decks. The problem was sideless auto racks offered no protection from rock-throwing kids or luckless hunters with auto-payment blues. The solution was to retrofit old auto racks and build new ones with metal siding. Almost no sideless auto racks are still on the road.

As we've seen more and more of today's railcar manufacturers make their rollingstock hobo, kid, railroad hunter and vandal/thief-proof. In addition to siding they've also put large metal *doors* at each end of the car. These newer auto racks are called "Enclosed Bi- and Tri-Level Auto Racks." When these doors are shut *folks say* it ranges from hard to nearly-impossible to get in and take a test-drive - or even simply ride the auto rack. We can get over the top of some "end-door" configurations but it's gymnastic to say the least.

These end-doors come in two varieties. Some (as in the photo) are large, hinged double doors which open outward. Other doors have two- or three-piece designs, one for each deck which slide down into place. After schmoe drives the cars/trucks onto the decks he shuts and locks the doors. For all intents and purposes siding plus end-doors make auto racks inaccessible to the sportman. *Except for the top deck.*

Detroit et al. are more worried about rocks and thieves than test-drives. For example *it's been related to me* professional thieves climb on during stops in the country. They promptly go to work removing batteries while the train is rolling and stack them at car-end. Then like clockwork the next time the train stops a pickup truck is waiting out in the middle of nowhere. The crooks off-load the batteries and make good their get-away.

I've never figured out *how* crooks know where a train stops - unless they or their accomplices work for the railroad. If *you're* on an auto rack when a professional thief gets on and goes to work *crawl under one of the cars and stay put.* These guys won't like witnesses.

You remember the "wilding" incidents in Central Park in the late 1980s? Peppering a train with rocks is a current fad called "rocking." Many more railroad rockers abound across the land than thieves or hobos. Thus since railroads are most concerned with what's coming up at the auto rack from the ground *they often neglect to put a roof* over the upper deck. *If there's a ladder up to the top deck and this deck doesn't have a roof over it, climb up and ride there.*

Now for an additional bit of bull advice regarding riding an auto rack . *Stay off the bottom deck.* Always climb up to the second or third deck. When the bull drives around he can't *see* you. Bulls are terrestrial creatures - very much affixed to the earth. They're conditioned to look for action at chest-high level or lower (like legs under cars). It's also never a good idea to show off in the yards. Experienced hobos will tell you to never poke your nose out of a car while the train is still in the yards. Keep back and don't move. *In yards and stations get away from the sides of the auto rack and down on the floor.* You'll be even harder to spot. This is also a good idea if you want to sleep and the deck doesn't have an apron or siding. Be careful.

Things were great when they started putting siding on in the 1970s. We could still see the sights yet were protected from bulls and rock-throwing kids - two nuisances of roughly equal caliber.

The only drawback to riding an auto rack is wind. If you're on an old one with no siding or doors hang onto your hat. There's no windbreak. Even on the newer ones with siding but no end-doors there's nothing to stop the wind from tunneling through the car. The only good thing to say about end-doors is they provide great windblock. No matter how or where one rides on an auto rack it's a thoroughly respectable ride. There are 30,000 available in America. Highball!

THE REAR UNIT

Here again I'll stick my neck out and say if you're *really* clever you can find *yet another* ride which puts even boxcars and auto racks to shame. We're talking about getting into the *back engine* of the units pulling a train - and play engineer like we've always dreamed. This time the railroads themselves will commence a search-and-destroy mission. But what's life about if not to stir up a little excitement?

Why will the railroads kneecap me? Because diesel locomotives are sophisticated, highly-specialized and expensive pieces of equipment. The last thing railroads want is for us to climb inside. Most are either "Special Duty" 3-axle ("SD") or "General Purpose" 2-axle ("GP" or "Geeps") "Electro-Motives" manufactured by the Electro-Motive Division of General Motors ("EMD") in McCook, Illinois (just west of Chicago - LaGrange is only a mailing address). They have arcane model numbers such as SD9E, SD40-2, SD40M-2, SD40-R, SD45, SDFP45, SD60, SD60MAC, GP7, GP9, GP10, GP18, GP20, GP30, GP38, GP38-2, GP38AC, GP40, GP40-2, GP49, GP60 and GP60M.

Other popular models are manufactured by General Electric at its Erie Pennsylvania plant and known generally through the mid-1980s as "U-boats," such as the U28-B, U28-C, U30-B, U30-C, U33-C, B23-7, B32-8, B39-8, BW, C, C32-8, C39-8, CM, CW and Dash 8-40 B.

Before going any further I want to emphasize the idea **you should never mess with company equipment**. *Please* don't mess around with the equipment or they'll hire so many bulls none of us will be able to get *close* to the yards. Look at equipment to your heart's content. But please **don't touch the equipment**. The Number One Unwritten Hobo Rule is: Don't mess with a good thing.

Yes friends, we can ride in the back unit. First off what is meant by this term "unit?" Unlike railroading's more descriptive monikers a "unit" is railroad parlance for a diesel-electric locomotive. In the old days of steam which ended in the 1950s locomotives were called locomotives.

Before the age of diesel-electrics all freight was pulled by steam engines. Several passenger routes went electric beginning in the 1880s.

Even a couple of railroads electrified freight routes in the early 20th century. I'm told Milwaukee Road has also abandoned its electric system. Steam for locomotives was the thing for 120 years.

Steam locomotives worked great individually. But when railroads wanted longer heavier consists they needed more than one engine to pull the train. The desire to couple up steam locomotives to pull in unison (called "double-heading") revealed the inherent weakness of steam-driven motive power - its unmanageability.

Steam is indeed a powerful motive force. How long can we hold the lid down on a pot of boiling water? Trying to do so demonstrates how extremely *fickle* steam is. It makes a break out one side of the lid, then another and a third.

An invention by Englishman and self-taught inventor Richard Trevithick in 1803 made steam powerful enough to push a locomotive with enough power left over to haul a load. Trevithick is the father of the steam locomotive. As a young man in Cornwall he watched the operation of Newcomen and Watt atmospheric pressure condensing steam engines at work in the Cornish tin mines. Rather than the Newcomen and Watt system of exhausting steam from an engine's cylinders after it finished pushing whatever it pushed (in our case the locomotive's cylinders after pushing the drivers), Trevithick routed the exhausted steam up the smokestack through a nozzle. The intermittent puffing action of steam forced through the stack nozzle made the machine into a "choo choo." Trevithick's arrangement sucked air through the firebox so rapidly the boiler could generate steam at a rate many times greater than a stationary engine of the same size and weight. Trevithick's invention was also self-regulating; the harder the locomotive worked the more steam went out the stack, the faster the fuel burned and the more steam became available. For 125 years the reciprocating steam locomotive with its exhaust-stimulated white-hot fire was the most effective way to get horsepower out of a (relatively) small motive vehicle.

The diesel engine (which ignites fuel by compression alone - no spark is needed) was invented in 1901. It quickly became clear diesel power could convert fossil fuel into motive power much more efficiently than wood, coal or oil. Only in the late 1920s however was the diesel engine's size reduced to the point where a diesel-electric locomotive could navigate curvy track and still compete with steam.

    The first diesel-electric was put into service by Canadian National Railways in 1928. During the 1930s the New York Central Railroad ("NYC") toyed with diesels for freight but never got serious about them. The first GM Electro-Motive appeared in 1939. Although the American Locomotive Company ("Alco"), Montreal Locomotive Works ("MLW"), Baldwin Locomotive Works ("BLW"), Fairbanks-Morse ("FM") and General Electric ("GE") also manufactured diesels, they were not as well-received as the Electro-Motive.

    In 1940 the Santa Fe Railway used diesel-electrics in regular freight service. A 1,000,000 lb. steam locomotive proved no match for a series of four synchronized Electro-Motive units. During a one-year demonstration in 1939-40, a four-unit Electro-Motive generating 5,400 HP hauled 83,000 miles of freight on 21 railroads in 37 states in temperatures ranging from minus 40 to 110°F, at altitudes from below sea level to Colorado's 10,148-ft. Monarch Pass. In 1.5 hours the four units hauled 1800 tons of freight from Mojave California up the Southern Pacific/Santa Fe's Tehachapi Pass (a 2.5% grade) toward Bakersfield, completely outclassing the biggest steam locomotives. From this date forward the fate of the steam locomotive was sealed.

    By the early 1960s the era of steam had passed. In 1961 America had 110 steam engines in service, 480 electrics and *28,150* diesels. In 1983 GE passed EMD as the diesel-electric manufacturer of choice. Today GM and GE are in neck-and-neck competition in the diesel-electric market. American railroads rely equally on the 2-cycle EMD and the 4-cycle "Cummings Diesel" GE unit to haul freights (some old Alcos and BLWs are also out there). In Canada in addition to GM and GE the 4-cycle Bombardier Inc. (MLW) locomotive is popular. A variety of makes and models is the hallmark of the North American railroad. In America a little under 20,000 diesel-electrics are in service. Fewer are needed today because they are more powerful. Railroads also "power-share" their equipment with each other.

    To get an idea of the power of a diesel-electric at work just listen to one. They make a *tremendous* amount of noise and generate an even more tremendous amount of motive power. The largest engines generate 1,300,000,000,000 HP (actually it's more like 6600 HP) and about 2 zillion volts of electricity. Most new units are in the 3900 to 4000 HP range. Earlier 1750 to 3000 HP models are being cannibalized or scrapped. The majority of freight locomotives follow two basic types - four- and six-axle "line-haul units" or "road switchers" (one electric motor for each axle) coupled together into "Multiple Units" ("MUs").

The diesel engine in the core of the locomotive (the "long end" of the unit behind the cab area and inside the panels or "long hood" lining the body of the beast) is comprised of between 8 and 20 large cylinders (the longer the engine head the more likelihood of heat warping). Also inside the long hood is a powerful electric generator for the "electric traction motors" (the electric motor components which actually drive each axle of wheels), air compressors for the brakes, "blowers" which cool the traction motors, "coolers" for lubricating oil and "dynamic" brakes. Inside the "nose," "short end " or "short hood" in front of the cab is a bathroom and air equipment (except on some GE units where the very short nose is reserved for the sanding tank; the electrical cabinet is under the cab itself and the toilet is on the back wall). (Note: Occasionally you may find an over-the-road unit without a bathroom. These are switch engines which are used as trailing units.)

Billygoats or "yard switching units" generally have less horse-power, less-complicated wheel designs not suitable for road speeds, a lower shorter long hood for 360 degree visibility and no short hood (*ergo* no toilet). Often they have no equipment for MU linkage. The most widely used billys today are the "Type 5" unit.

Some railroads also use cableless "slug" or "Tractive Effort Booster Units" (TEBUs) which are all engine for backup power. They're cut-down versions of an over-the-road unit, standing only about three feet high off their platform. Their use is generally limited to the yards for switching and humping.

Another rideless engine you might encounter is the "B-unit." B-units were popular in the early age of diesel. They were the back units attached to a streamlined headend which had no cab and were tag-on powerplants for the engineer. They've become popular again with the large western railroads and we can expect to see more of them in the future.

Thus diesel-electric locomotives are gigantic powerplants on wheels with brakes. Even so interestingly the average diesel engine and attached main generator represent less than 15% of total locomotive weight. Diesels are "ballasted" (weighted down) with thicker steel plate than necessary to harness gravity's help in applying more tractive force. When an engine is too light for its load it becomes "slippery" and its wheels spin. Along for the ride also are an average 300 gallons of engine-cooling water, 250 gallons of engine lube oil, 3,000 gallons of diesel fuel and 2 tons of sand for sanding wet or icy track - to prevent "wheel slippage" in inclement weather.

Speaking of motive power, people in some regions of America - notably the Northeast Corridor - see railroads running on *electricity*. The units pick up power from an overhead high-tension wire called a "catenary" by means of a sliding "shoe" held against the wire by an overhead trolley or "pantograph" - or else from a shoe held down against an electrified "third rail." Electric units are gigantic electric motors on wheels with brakes which run on utility company power.

Why you may ask don't we see more of this in North America? Europe and Japan are steadily approaching complete electrification of their passenger and freight "trunk" (main) routes. Texas recently bought the French electric "TGV" (Train à Grande Vitesse - "High Speed Train") for a pioneer route connecting Houston, Dallas-Ft. Worth and San Antonio. Since 1964 Japan has enjoyed electrical powering of its "Shinkansen" or Bullet Train. The current American Administration has proposed similar innovations. Where is North America in all this today?

The advantages of electric motive power over diesel-electric are numerous. Using electricity rather than fossil fuels limits the area where energy production results in pollution (i.e., no smoke and fuel everywhere). Electricity generates faster, cleaner and much quieter power. Electric locomotives draw almost unlimited power from the pantograph or third rail while accelerating a train with 7,000 HP *per unit*. Electric engines sit quietly turned off when not in use. Maintenance is much less frequent, expensive or time-consuming. A safely designed electric system is less dangerous than an internal combustion system. Why don't we see more electric trains?

The problem stems from the fact North America is a vast area. Mile-per-mile passenger and freight traffic is relatively sparse compared to Western Europe and Japan. Therefore it's prohibitively expensive (at least with current technology) to keep the wires or third rail filled with enough juice all day to run trains.

Take for example an average mainline in the middle of the wide-open spaces of say, Oklahoma - a representative state. We might see a train pass by between six and sixteen times a day. In fact according to the AAR the average mainline in America carries 8.1 trains per mile of track a day. With electricity you'd have to keep the whole system cranked up 24 hours a day - and it's a long way across Oklahoma. Compare this with high-volume European or Far Eastern systems where trains pass over shorter distances a minimum of several times each hour.

Physicists and electrical engineers have yet to overcome metal wire's resistance to electricity, which over distance diminishes the flow of current. Although at the high voltages electric railroads use (25 or 50 KV and 60 Hz) electricity can be transmitted over long distances without significant current loss, the system still has to be used intensively to make it worthwhile to build and maintain.

Apparently whatever their overall ecological, congestion-relief and other social benefits, introduction of electric trains in North America must first be proven financially feasible. Ideas on the table like nuclear fusion, space age electromagnetics (magnetic levitation), steel-wheel and tilting train technology and super-cooling when commercially viable will someday change the entire way the world runs trains.

Instead North America puts together long heavy trains and runs them on diesel. The longer the train the less wages. Only along a handful of eastern routes has it remained economically feasible to electrify the rail system. It's capital-intensive to electrify a railroad, but with technological advances *hopefully* someday railroads will see the light and make the investment. After all - if they can afford to abandon and tear up track or weld joint rail together (see within) they can afford to erect towers with high-tension wires or third-rails and run trains the 21st century way.

Back to diesel-electric units. Railroads today couple 5 and even 6 diesel engines to the headend of a train. The only limitation is the amount of stress placed on the couplers. The more power pulling a train and the greater the number of slows or stops, the greater the likelihood of a break-in-two caused by a "pulled" coupler. (The knuckle of the coupler is purposely designed to be the weak link or most "failure prone" part of the coupling system. If one fails it can be quickly replaced by the crew. In a radical compression situation such as a big hole stop the knuckle fails before something more serious occurs such as a buckled draft gear or jack-knifed car.)

Assuming the correct amount of power is on the consist each unit runs harmoniously by means of electronics. Thus it makes sense calling diesel-electrics "units." Some railroads call trailing units "helper" or "pusher" units. Helper units are cut in for power or braking purposes separate from the headend when the train consists of over 5000 tons of freight. In Canada they're called "slave" units (no crew and completely remote operation) which illustrates their conceptual purpose. One or more helpers prevent the train from "string-lining" on curves to keep it on the track (the problem encountered in the SP's Dunsmuir accident).

Oftentimes a train needs more power than one freightcar coupler can handle. Companies split up the units among two or more parts of the train to prevent break-in-twos. In the Canadian Rockies, on heavy Appalachian and Western coal trains and on drag freights going over humps railroads tack on or "cut in" helper, pusher or slave units at the middle to back of a train. Another reason to segment power is to keep the cars safely buffed in or drafted out on grades.

Each unit in an MU consist runs in unison by means of electronic synchronization. A 27-pin electric connector wire passes from unit to unit to relay electrical signals. Four or five air hoses connect up between each unit as well so their combined air fills the system and applies and releases brakes as quickly as possible. To run slave units the engineer at the headend transmits radio control signals similar to those passed by the 27-pin wires. If a foulup occurs in transmission or reception of signals slave units automatically go to idle.

In general we should have a very healthy degree of respect for the diesel locomotive. But without showing any disrespect we can also get in one and ride.

O.K. This sport provides thrills. One of them is psyching yourself up for getting in a back unit. It's scary but if you pull it off it's a *gas*.

Here's how it works: First of all just like riding in new cars/trucks *do this only at night* - at least as far as initially *getting in* the unit is concerned. I've never had the nerve to get in a back unit in broad daylight except during a couple of really severe storms (when everyone's distracted and vision is poor). If you've got the moxie be my guest. But I'd recommend confining this stunt to nighttime - at least the first few times out.

At the headend ride in the very backmost unit. Stay as far away from the crew in the "on-the-point" unit as possible. Don't bug them. Don't do anything which might implicate them in your audacity. You don't want to get them sent to the principal for your shenanigans. On crewless slave units at the middle or end of the train you can ride any unit which catches your fancy.

To get on the back unit at the headend *position yourself close to the headend before the train pulls out. Don't get on until the very last possible moment.* Find a place somewhere out of sight nearby for a last-minute rush into the unit. Keep your weathereye open and be listening to that air. When the engineer, brakeman-engineman-conductor (enginemen) are all aboard, get the signal to go and ready for departure they'll pump air into the train to release the brakes. When you hear the air start hissing and the brakes coming off it's time to make your move.

There's a door at the front and back of every diesel cab. *With great stealth and aplomb wend your way warily toward the steps up to the cab of the back unit. Climb up quickly, open the door and get in.*

NOTE: These doors allow maintenance workers and traincrews to pass through MU's hassle-free. They can be locked but rarely are. If yours is you're out of luck. Climb back down and find a freightcar quickly. Locked cab doors are rare because at some point during the journey a brakeman usually cruises through the units to check their well-being. To check the units he needs to physically get into each cab. He quickly trucks from unit to unit making sure the gauges, dials and levers are operating properly. He can't be bothered carrying keys around for the two doors to each unit. He'd have to unlock and relock each door going back and forth through the cabs. His hands are often full of things like lanterns, tools, etc. At least until the time geniuses down at the "railroad police force" catch wind of this book it's been rare to come across a locked unit door.

Once inside the door shut it behind you and head for cover. Don't fiddle with the gadgets or sit in the crewmembers' seats. Head for cover *pronto.* Cover is found in most noses of engines. The railroad's name or insignia is painted on the nose (called the "nose herald"). Down inside is a cramped crew bathroom. The company doesn't want the crew hanging out down there instead of keeping an eye on the train so the bathroom is as confining and bare-bones as can be. If the bathroom isn't in the nose it's somewhere opposite it in the cab. Look for the door.

The nose is separated from the cab by a metal door. *Once in the cab, find and open the door to the nose, lower yourself into the bathroom, shut the door behind you and sit on the throne.* Then pray you haven't been seen.

This is one of those great secret agent activities which really gets the blood pumping. While sitting there for the first few moments you'll have no idea whether you've been seen - or if so whether anyone cares. Your answer will come quickly because *if* the crew wants you out of there they'll waste no time coming to get you. They'll make their move before the train departs. Thus you're only at risk until the train starts moving.

Here's the way getting busted cowering on the porcelain throne (actually it's metal) works: While keeping your fingers crossed and praying for takeoff you'll hear one of the doors to the cab open and shut. Then there'll be about a 3-10 second interval. Someone will open the bathroom door and say something like "Hi. Wanna come on outta there?" You're busted. This will happen within the first 3-5 minutes you're down inside. The more time passes the better your chances nobody has seen you - or cares.

If you get busted it's always by a crewmember. If you're nice and sort of sheepish about it (the attitude test) he'll tell you not to ride there and send you on your way. If there's still time go find a car down the line. Ask him when the train's leaving so you'll know whether you have to run.

I've never heard of anyone getting turned over to the bull for trying to ride a back unit. If anything crewmembers think we're rather enterprising - or at least we have some experience - both of which they respect. They must figure we have some cheek and probably wouldn't appreciate having to deal with the bull. Remember - railroad people *like* us to ride their trains. And they don't like bulls. The most they'll ever do is tell us to go away and only because it might make them look bad.

However, **NOTE WELL:** If you're a jerk when you get caught, guaranteed the crewmember will turn you over to the yardmaster or bull. A hobo fiddling around with a unit's equipment can result in an entire crew being killed in a wreck. If you give the worker the impression of being even the least bit untrustworthy *no way* he'll risk his life just so you can get where you're going. You're miles ahead of the game if you act decently and forthrightly on the railroad.

Once the train starts moving it's a good sign no one will pay you a visit. The moment you take off you're practically guaranteed to be home free. And what a cause for celebration you have at this joyous moment! When you pull off getting into a unit and head out you've earned another blackbelt in railroading. *Don't get cocky* however as the train picks up speed. Stay in the john. You're not over all the hurdles yet.

While yet ascendant on the throne amuse yourself by listening to the immense power generated by a diesel-electric locomotive. As the train moves out listen to and *feel* the extraordinary expenditure of raw energy being harnessed to pull those thousands of tons of cars and freight. You're literally in the belly of the beast listening to the engines convert diesel fuel into traction, electricity and pressurized air.

While listening to the power accelerate the train your unit will start slowly rocking back and forth. It's hitting the joints and switches in the old yard rails and switch leaders which bring it out onto the mainline. As the train picks up speed you'll hear a variety of creakings, groanings and air rushing through the pipes near your head.

Then suddenly the rocking and creaking will stop. You're on smooth track. There's a distinct difference in the way the wheels roll over the rails. You're on the mainline. Once the units pull the rest of the train up onto it *you're outta there.*

Nevertheless stay in the john. Be *patient.* Don't emerge until you're positive the train's on the mainline *and* has covered enough distance to put the yard and everyone in it far behind. Stay in the john a minimum ten minutes from the time the train starts moving. Be cautious. In case of doubt, wait. More than once trains have been stopped heading out because some yo-yo saw a hobo in a back unit and sicked the bull on him.

The first thing to do back up in the cab is to see if a crewmember from the headend is on his way back to your unit. It's doubtful anyone will be but you never know. The crew usually conduct checkups on back units only when something's amiss or else a good deal later on during the trip.

In the daytime we can see these guys approaching down the footboards past the long hoods of the units because, well, we can see. Same thing at night because the crewmember carries a lighted brakeman's lantern. You'll easily spot the light as he makes his way along the footboards and through the various cabs. The more units on your train the better. He has more units to check, footboards to travel and doors to get through before getting to your unit. This increases your lead time to scramble into the john. It's like hide-and-seek when they count to 100 instead of 50.

Even if someone's coming back you don't *have* to hide. This is an intuition-based judgment call only you can make. Most crewmembers *couldn't care less* if someone's in a back unit - as long as he's not damaging anything, pissing the floor or threatening either their job or safety.

If you don't want to hide when the guy or gal gets to your unit make sure to present yourself in the least surprising or threatening manner possible. As in the yards they'll be surprised to see you. Help lessen the surprise by being passive and nice. Say something about the weather. Put them at ease.

The second thing to NOT do is turn on any cab lights. If you do you might as well turn a 1000-watt spotlight on yourself and say "Here I am - come get me."

Where should we sit in the cab? We have at least two and often three choices. The standard seating arrangement is one chair for the engineer to the right of the door to the john and one or two to his left against the opposite wall for the other enginemen. It's impossible to confuse which chair is the engineer's (known in the industry as his "control stand" or "console") because it's in front of all the train-driving equipment. Choose a seat other than the engineer's until you have more confidence and brashness up.

I say this because for us train nuts there's a certain aura of mystery and power surrounding the job of engineer. He's the high priest in our sport. To sit in his chair straightaway would be like climbing into the pulpit of a church we're paying our first visit to. Wouldn't that be a bit presumptuous - at least until we've said a few prayers, dropped a little money into the alms plate or bought some candles? In other words until we've paid our dues? At any rate it's up to you.

You most surely can *stand* behind the engineer's chair and check out all the gauges, dials and levers he gets to play with. He has a speedometer, an air pressure gauge and other little gismos he keeps his eye on over the road. He has an "ammeter" (which shows the current going through the traction motors indicating how hot they're getting), a "reverse/ selector handle" (which determines the direction of travel and selects engine power or braking action) and a "wheel slip" light (warning of wheel slippage on the rail). He has a lever for his left hand which governs his speed called the "throttle handle." He also has a switch which throws the engines into reverse for big hole position stops and the automatic brake valve handle and/or dynamic brake mentioned earlier which uses the engines' power to brake (*if* the engines are equipped with dynamic brakes). On modern equipment he has a telephone to reach out and touch someone when decisions need to be made. And overhead he has a cord which blows the whistle (or "airhorn" as modern railroaders call it - but I hate that). DON'T BLOW THE WHISTLE or you'll literally be blowing it on yourself.

I'd like to reemphasize you not mess around with or even touch any engine equipment - especially the throttle and reverse. You could very easily make a wreck. MUs are hooked up to each other to run at the same number of rpms, brake at the same time with the same force, etc. Don't throw your unit out of kilter by fiddling with any of the things in front of you. Just take a look at all of it.

Check out the mystery panel of hidden things located against the long hood wall of the cab. Inside the metal doors are the electrical components of the apparatus - the brains of the beast. Don't open these doors or mess with what's inside. You could get yourself electrocuted.

Notice however the funny clicking sounds inside. I don't know what's going on in there. It's obviously circuitry - switches, relays and fuses. Be content to know everything in there is doing what it's designed to do and don't fiddle with it. The door panels usually say something like "Caution! 5 zillion volts!" Respect this. Railroads are not kidding. To play with the circuitry is about as bright as playing in the back of a turned-on TV set only with many many more volts.

Railroads are dangerous to begin with. If they had to put a danger sign everywhere danger is encountered they'd have wall-to-wall signs (thank god lawyers haven't looked into this). So when they *do* say "Danger" take their word for it.

One of the more interesting pieces of equipment on older units is the "deadman's pedal." Sounds interesting doesn't it? It's located on the floor at the engineer's feet. *Don't touch it.* Just look at it with great respect.

On older units whenever the train is moving the engineer has to keep his foot on the deadman's pedal. If he lifts his foot the train immediately brakes and stops. If he suffers a heart attack or some other incapacitating event and keels out of his chair or slumps into unconsciousness, *theoretically* his foot slips off the pedal and the train automatically sets its brakes. Neat, huh?

Engineers developed bad habits with the deadman's pedal however. If they wanted to get up and stretch or pee they'd lay a brick or a heavy wrench on the pedal and abandon the helm. Thus on modern diesels railroads install a device known as the "alertor." If the engineer removes his hands from the throttle *and* brake for more than 10 seconds a red light and loud buzzer go off. If 8 more seconds elapse the alertor automatically sets the train's brakes. Same thing if the engineer holds onto the throttle and brake too long - as if asleep, unconscious, drunk or dead. He has to hold onto and let go of the throttle and brake in a certain pattern to convince the equipment he's alert.

These vigilance methods have been taken even a step further. On all Amtrak passenger diesels the engineer's *seat* is now the deadman's pedal. Not only does he have to play patty-cake, patty-cake with the throttle and brake (which somebody else could do in his absence), his seat is wired to detect if he gets up. The very second he does while the train is moving alarms inside the cab and in a traffic control center go off. The guy's busted. Amtrak also keeps the engineer alert by playing other unpredictable alarm games with him - games he has to stay seated to beat.

There are two or more heaters in the cab. One's usually to the right and behind where the engineer sits. The other's against the opposite wall where the crew sit. These heaters have dials which go from "Off" to "Max." *These* you can play with. They're safe and harmless. Create your own weather system by adjusting the heaters and sliding glass windows on each side of the cab. Many units also have a water dispenser, often designed like a "Days of Steam" water tower which we can use to refill water containers. There also might be a small refrigerator on board for lunches. Check to see if there's any purified water inside. The 'fridge is great for perishables like cheese or fruit which coolness could preserve longer.

Always keep both cab doors and the door to the john shut. Even if you try to keep a cab door open it's hinged to swing shut with the slightest motion. Unless you prop it open it will close - but maybe not hard enough to latch shut. Unlatched doors bang against the wall of the cab or the hood and get annoying. You also attract attention to yourself if you prop open a door. The main idea is to ride the unit just the way you find it. You're a temporary and very fortunate guest. Please comport yourself accordingly.

Settle into one of the crew chairs and get comfortable. Be sure to position yourself to see if anyone's coming back from the headend. Notice the cab has four long oblong windows facing front and back, two in the doors and two built into the walls. They enable the crew to keep an eye on what's happening on the track up ahead and back down the train. These and the side windows provide a great view. But they also enable alert engineers and crew to see *you*, which you might not want.

One game to learn is called "hide-and-seek-with-the-engineer." No matter what the other crewmembers are doing the engineer is *always* up there sitting on the righthand side of the "point unit." He has to keep his foot on the deadman's pedal, or is wired to his throttle, brake or even seat. He's co-pilotless. If he leaves his seat he violates every safety rule in the Book.

If you're sitting on the right side of the cab when the train is on straight track there's enough grime on the 6 to 10 windows between you and the engineer to obscure you from view. But going around a right-hand curve he can look back and see you. Thus whenever you're rounding a right-hand curve lean into the center of the car - out of sight of the oblong window - to avoid detection.

The only reason you *might* want to avoid being seen by the engineer is arguably he's the only guy on the train with a proprietary interest in it - or who feels responsible enough to create a hassle for you (assuming anyone does). "What's that SOB doing on my train?" But I seriously doubt it. Most engineers are brakemen with seniority who went to engineer school. At bottom they're no different than any other working stiff on the railroad.

The same sort of hide-and-seek technique is in order if you're afraid of being seen by *anyone* up at the headend. Whichever side of the cab you're sitting on, when you round a curve in that direction lean into the center of the cab. Some hobos prefer to sit or lie down on the floor when riding a back unit. When the train is coming into any type of station or yard get into the john to prevent the bull from seeing you.

There's a special timing situation in exiting a back unit. Let's address the idea here while covering how to get off freight trains generally in a following chapter. When you've arrived at your destination get off as quickly as possible - preferably before the train stops. Jump ship off a back unit quicker than any other car.

That's all the advice to offer on riding back units. Summing up on personal pullmans, by preference look for: Back unit (at night), car/ truck (at night *I've heard*), scenic cruiser, one-eyed bandit, hopper facing the right way, loaded piggyback, loaded auto rack, flatcar or wellcar with boxes, center-beam bulkhead flatcar, empty auto rack, hopper facing the wrong way, empty flatcar with bulkheads, loaded flatcar with bulkheads, gondola, empty piggyback, and lastly, plain empty flatcar.

XI

HOW DO I SIZE UP MY TRAIN?

Once you've selected the perfect personal Pullman and are ready to hit the road it's nice to know what kind of *performance* to expect out of your train. By "performance" we mean whether it will be fast or slow, make a lot of stops or only a few and on single-track mainline whether it or other trains will go into the hole on a meet. The best source of information as always will be someone in the yards. Whenever possible ask workers or other adventurers what kind of train you'll be riding - Peddlar, Regular or Hotshot - the subject of this chapter.

Workers have a good idea what to expect out of a train - especially if they've helped hump it together. Experienced hobos know a lot about trains having ridden through the area frequently. But if there's nobody around to ask you can "suss" what type of performance to expect by using the following information.

First off individual tastes differ. I like freight trains which *haul ass*. We're talking rattle the hocks off her. The kind of train that takes off with engines at "full shout," goes 65-75 MPH and doesn't stop for 150 miles. When it does stop it's only long enough to let me get down and skirmish around a bit. Then it takes off again and goes *another* 150 miles. I like to cover ground rather than wait around. It's not that I'm impatient mind you. I just like to get the show on the road riding the rails.

If you have to figure out your train's likely status yourself, first make a mental note of the different kinds of cars it consists of. The consist of a train says many things about likely performance. Although it's hard to pinpoint the kind of train you're looking at based *solely* on consist, some broad generalities indicate the probabilities of performance based on consist.

143

An initial note of caution about consist is warranted. Even if you're slated to catch out on one of the clunkiest, funkiest looking trains in America, once out over the road it might take off and rattle the dentures right out of your head. On the other hand no matter how sheik, svelte and sexy a train looks on first blush it could turn into a real dragass bummer. You never know without asking in advance. Use the tips here to verify what you're told or when there's no-one to ask.

PEDDLAR FREIGHTS

The "Peddlar," "Work Train," "Drag," "Local Switcher," "Turn," "Junk Train" "Bull Local" or "Way" freight is a work train - the local business train. Hobos call these trains peddlars or drags so we will too. On peddlar trains local crews handle "industry switching" as they work their way down the line from customer to customer. One or two crews handle a day's work down a given line with occasional overtime.

The local train's various names illustrate what it does. It stops at lots of factories and grain elevators, etc. out on the mainline. It "cuts out" or "sets out" (I prefer "cut out" and use it here) and "picks up" or "cuts in" (let's use "pick up" for clarity) cars along the way. This is its *peddlar* aspect. It performs a railroad's basic work - handling local business. These trains stop and go all the time. This is the *drag* or *junk train* aspect. They drag along from customer to customer. This can get very wearing on one's nerves. *Local switcher* and *bull local* are clear - they switch cars to and from local customers. The *turn* denomination reflects the fact a peddlar conducts business out a certain distance then turns back toward home. The *way* aspect reflects service in a particular locality, e.g. "They send a train out our *way* twice a week."

Not only do peddlars often stop to do business, they have low priority. They have to get out of the way for other over-the-road traffic. On single-track mainline they go into the hole to clear track for hotter trains. Add these things together and a drag freight can get to be just that - a drag.

Moreover on a peddlar there's always the risk your car will be cut out in front of say, the Uniroyal plant. When this happens you have to scramble to find a new pullman - or find another way home (i.e., walk or hitchhike). If not awake and on your toes you can get cut out high and dry somewhere you'd rather not be - like in the complete middle of nowhere.

The question becomes: How do we recognize peddlars? There are several ways. First *take a look at the cars themselves.* Are most of them *empty?* If the consist is auto racks, flatcars, boxcars with one or both doors open, piggybacks, open hoppers or gondolas a quick glance answers this question. If so likely you have a peddlar. These empties will be dropped off along the way.

It's not easy though to calculate how many cars are empty when you can't see inside them. If your train has boxcars with both doors shut, or hoppers, tankcars or reefers, how do you know if they're empty or not? When fully loaded from the outside these cars look no different than when empty. They don't ride much lower on the track to prevent coupler slip-bys.

Remember the dogtags they squash around boxcar door latches and bottoms? The corporate-American way of announcing the car's loaded? Dogtags are used on boxcars, hoppers, tankcars, piggyback trailers and reefers alike, looped through the latch of a bay, door or hatch. Or you can take a rock or stick and tap the side of a hopper. You'll learn to recognize the hollow echoing sound of an empty.

On reefers there's a more obvious giveaway. When loaded their diesel-powered compressors are running. These compressors make quite a racket and crank out foul smelling exhaust. Check the percentage of empties.

Another extremely important technique is to *figure out what kinds of cars agro-industry uses in your neck of the woods.* Say there are lots of empties on the train. Are they cars agro-industry uses around here? If so you're probably looking at a drag freight. Say for example you're in Nebraska and the train has lots of empty grain hoppers. That's exactly the kind of car needed in The *Corn* Husker State. Odds are it's a drag freight. This train will stop at grain elevator after grain elevator cutting out hoppers. Conversely if a train in the woods of Montana consists mainly of empty auto racks it won't be dropping them off. Who would they be for? If eastbound it's a *regular* freight of empties going from Western auto dealers back to Detroit. If westbound it's going to Portland or Seattle to pick up Asian imports. And it will likely be a pretty fast train.

The same agro-industry evaluation applies to *loaded* cars. Say you have a train which is 50% loaded boxcars which say "Auto Parts Lading Only" and you know of a large auto assembly plant 40 miles down the track. You know where these boxcars are going. And you can extrapolate the rest of the train won't go much farther. You have a peddlar.

Another characteristic of peddlars is they tend to be shorter than other trains (except hotshots). *Evaluate the number of cars on the train.* If it's 50 cars or fewer this points to a peddlar. As we've seen to hold down wages most (but not all) railroads try to run the longest trains possible. With a comparatively short train (50 cars or less) the cars probably won't go far. The crew will parcel them out down the line - at most 30 to 40 miles out from the yards - then turn and come home.

Also *note the overall quality of the cars.* Does the train have lots of older, rusty, beat-up looking cars? If so odds are it's a peddlar. Railroads tend to give local shippers their older cars. Of course they will vehemently deny this but it's true. Many smaller shippers are steady local customers tied to the only railroad around since time immemorial. With today's railroad mergers it's not as if shippers can shop for a railroad.

Smaller, single-plant outfits don't ship their products throughout the nation. They don't use multi-million dollar ad campaigns and don't own their own freightcars. They don't need to dress up the product with fancy packaging schemes or freightcars. They don't need razzle-dazzle sexiness from the railroad. And you can be sure if they don't ask *and pay* for razzle-dazzle the railroad won't deliver it. The average shipper expects a reasonably load-worthy car and dependable service at a competitive price. Optimally that's what he gets. If your train is made up of ugly locally-used agro-industry cars, whether loaded or empty it's probably a peddlar.

Look for the consistency of cars coupled together. If your train has 2 of this kind of car, 3 of that then 1 of the other jumbled together this further indicates a peddlar. Greater uniformity in the consist, or how cars are blocked together suggests a long-haul train rather than a local.

Don't forget to *take a look at the type of power they put on the train.* Are the units great big modern ones, newly painted or washed? Or are they old, beat-up, exhaust-befouled clunkers with funny designs which look like they should have been redlined years ago? If the latter you're looking at a peddlar. Railroads use their worn-out power for local trains and switching. They prefer to limit breakdowns to slower local trains rather than big-revenue over-the-roaders. The average life-expectancy of a diesel-electric is 20 to 25 years. The older an engine gets the more localized its service area becomes.

Railroads also have less incentive to sell an image to local businesses than their big customers. As long as the power can pull the customer's cars at the right price and time the railroad gets the business.

How much power are they putting on anyway? If it's four or more fairly decent looking units you have a regular to hot train on your hands. If it's only one, two or three clunkers you're probably looking at a peddlar.

Do they put a caboose on the tailend? If so in America it's not a hot train. They'll use it for additional seating for crewmembers at the rearend. The train is slated to do significant backing up onto sidings. The additional crew in the caboose can get off and switch, cut out or pick up cars without having to make "the long walk" to the headend after finishing each piece of business. A caboose means a peddlar.

Lastly, *where is the train slated to go*? If it's heading down a short spur line of 50 miles or less instead of a mainline this is a clear indication of a drag freight.

REGULAR FREIGHTS

"Regular" or "mixed" freights, being in the middle area of equipment and overall sexiness are harder to generalize about than peddlars. Nevertheless here are some tips in deciding whether or not you're looking at a regular.

The regular freight (known in railroad parlance as either "Advertised Freight Service," "Symbol," "Manifest," "Section" or "Extra") is the bread-and-butter workhorse on the railroad. Seventy to 75% of all over-the-road freight trains are regulars. They go farther than drag freights and do less cut-out or pick-up work. On a good day a regular goes from 150-300 miles before making its first stop, usually to change crews.

A regular freight is comprised of any and all types of cars, regardless of the region you're in. Most regular trains are 70-80% loaded. That's what railroads shoot for anyway - but the loaded/empty ratio varies widely. If an important customer needs cars in a hurry or the railroad's worried about demurrage charges on "foreign" (non-owned) cars, a regular can be all empties. An *empty* regular (called a "rattler" by hobos) is distinguishable from a peddlar by its greater number of cars, since it's possible to move many cars with one crew and fewer units - which railroads love.

An "extra" regular runs when an overflow of business has built up and one train can't haul all the cars. They split the train in two. A "section" regular is one of two or three scheduled regulars which has the same designation but is divided into a separate train.

To figure out whether you're looking at a peddlar or regular freight, it helps to know something about the railroad and territory you're set to ride through. *Always* ask yourself what agro-industry is up to where you're going. Compare what's around and what's up ahead against your train's consist. If the consist is something *other* than what's done here at your bend in the river, odds are it's a regular freight. For example if you're in the middle of Florida orange juice country and have a train made up primarily of woodcars chances are it won't do much peddling.

Unless a railroad is short on equipment regular freights have *more, sexier units* than peddlars. The average Class I Line Haul railroad's regular freight (except one which is all empties) will have 3 to 10 units tacked on - either at the headend, or with some cut in at the middle or rearend. In contrast a regular *empty* train will have two or at most three units. Regulars have *more cars* too - anywhere from 70 up to 180+ cars - and 180 cars is a big, big train.

Regulars have *far more consistency* in blocking than peddlars. If your train has 24 hoppers blocked, then 8 auto racks, 47 boxcars and 77 reefers, chances are it's a regular freight - unless you know of two big grain elevators, an auto manufacturer or port, myriad small manufacturers and some dedicated orange juice drinkers down the line. Otherwise this train will cover a respectable distance before it turns peddlar - if at all. Even when there's a wide variety of cars on a train if they're not jumbled and you have some moderately sexy power, odds are you have a regular freight. (The only exception is a rattler, whose empties are often jumbled together.)

Once you've been told or surmise you're looking at a regular the main concern is it's *priority* in comparison to other trains it meets (see within).

HOTSHOTS

Finally we have the hotshot. "Hotshot" to the railroad means "Expedited Freight" or "First Class Train." The old term was "Red Ball Manifest." Nobody in the yards refers to a hotshot as an expedited freight or red ball manifest. They call them hotshots. In fact everybody but the bigshots calls a hotshot a hotshot. To a railroad man hotshot means he has a deadline to meet in readying a train for departure. As a matter of fact hotshots are the only freight trains which run on anything resembling a timetable. Hotshot to the hobo means *hang on.*

Hotshots carry cargo such as perishables (flowers, film, fruit, Aunt Hilda), big ticket items like autos and appliances, mail or anything else a shipper will pay a premium rate to move quickly. The more business a railroad has the more specialized its hotshots are - made up entirely of one or two types of products requiring only one or two types of cars. Piggyback trains and well car trains with trailers or intermodal boxes are the railroad's hottest. Hotshots are the cadillac of freight consists. When you latch onto one hold onto your hat. You're "ticketed" for a rocket ride.

The kinds of cars hotshots are made up of are easier to recognize than peddlars or regulars. You can spot a hotshot a mile away by looking at its consist. If a train has only *loaded auto racks, reefers, modular freight or piggybacks* or some combination thereof, chances are it's hot. If it has only *25-65 cars* it's getting hotter. And if they put *4-6 big, sexy units on it* get out the chapstick.

Another way to identify a hotshot is to *watch the workers*. If they're paying attention to one string of cars - as if *hurrying* to make up the train - chances are that string is hot. A flurry of activity around a train is a strong indication a hotshot is being readied for us.

Hotshots as the name implies cook out over the road. Here's a good 'fer instance. If you want to take one rock 'n roll ride catch out on the Santa Fe's hotshot 198 and 199 westbounds or 891/991 eastbounds (all formerly known as the "Super C") anywhere they stop between Chicago and St. Louis then along Route 66 to L.A. The Santa Fe shoots these babies out of the cannon from each end and they go from the City of Big Shoulders to the City of Angels (or vice versa) in *under 36 hours*. No truck driver can beat the 198-991s no matter what pills he eats. Out over the road they average 65-80 MPH on well-maintained, primarily double-track ribbon rail. You never go into the hole - even for the Amtrak Super Chief (O.K. - now they call it the "Southwest Chief." What marketing genius!). On the Santa Fe's mainline freight and passenger trains boom past each other. What a ride!

On hotshots crews often change on the run. Hotshots never stop for long except to slap on refueled units along the way. The Santa Fe for example has straight track except through the Southwest. But even across the deserts and mountains of Arizona and New Mexico the 198-991s really smoke.

Heading eastbound you take off from L.A. at 318 feet. After San Bernadino you hit Cajon Pass at 3822 ft., then slide down to Cadiz at 789 ft.

Then it's up over Goff's Pass at 2585 ft. and down to the Colorado at Needles - 476 ft. Next you rise steadily past Kingman to the Arizona Divide at 7313 ft. near Flagstaff, loop down to Winslow at 4843 ft. and run back up to the Continental Divide east of Gallup at 7247 ft. After the divide it's down to Belen on the Rio Grande at 4785 ft. up to Mountainair at 6470 ft., then a long, slow descent to Chicago at 593 feet. See what I mean about ascent and descent?

But AT&SF puts so much power on its hotshots it almost *doesn't matter* what the terrain is like. Out across the Great Plains you really get rolling. Hotshots are a must for the avid adventurer. They're the hallmark of fast freight training. (But watch out for bulls on the Santa Fe. They like their work.)

Every Class I railroad has hotshot service through at least part of its system. Most schedules provide overnight service. Let's say you're the Editor-in-Chief of the *Baltimore Sun*. One late afternoon you decide to put a special section in tomorrow's paper using green-colored newsprint. The closest green newsprint manufacturer is in western North Carolina. You order the paper and make arrangements for a Norfolk Southern Railway Company hotshot to pick up the paper and deliver it to your printing plant by 5 a.m.

NS runs a hotshot every night from Atlanta to Washington D.C. and lines up a standard flat piggyback for two trailers to accommodate you. The papermill loads the trailers and shoots them by tractor to the freightyards at Charlotte. NS loads the trailers onto the piggyback at 7 p.m. The hotshot stops and picks up the piggy at 9 p.m. at the division, then it's off to the races all night up through the Piedmont Region of the Southeast, arriving in D.C. at 3:45 a.m. Tractors hook up to the trailers, the paper arrives in Baltimore at 4:45 a.m. and is waiting for the presses at press time. As an unintended third-party beneficiary we're in D.C. for a nice predawn cup of coffee.

Ask around to find out when hotshots leave. Of course if you're riding the Moscow, Camden and San Augustine's ("MC&SA") 7 miles of track out of Camden Texas, maybe there won't be a hotshot available. When you plan to catch out on one of the Big 14 railroads however you'll have the option to ride the pride of their system - the hotshot.

This is not to say regular freights never roll like a hotshot. Fast regulars have few empties and usually run around 90 cars in length.

Sometimes on a regular you'll get a latter-day Casey Jones for an engineer. You'll know this guy is at the throttle when the train reaches speeds which make you think your Pullman is taking tap-dance lessons under you. There's a certain thrill in sitting on a huge piece of steel passing cars and trucks, rattling along with a momentum which couldn't be stopped in two miles. If like me you derive greatest sporting pleasure from going fast on the railroad, ask around or keep you eyelids peeled for hotshots. Once they straighten out on the mainline and get the bell *they put everything behind them.* Hang on. And Happy Highball!

UNIT TRAINS, DEDICATED PIGGYBACK TRAINS AND LAND BRIDGE TRAINS

Three additional types of trains should be mentioned. The first is the "Unit Train." A unit train consists of only one kind of car - all coalcars or piggybacks, modular flatcars, reefers, hoppers, autoparts boxcars or auto racks. Units trains are becoming increasingly common as railroads struggle to streamline.

These trains run back and forth over the same route between the same shipping and receiving customers. Specialized loading facilities load and unload the train by gantry crane, rotary dumping or gravity chute. Bleeding, humping, switching, coupling and connecting air hoses is eliminated. Unit trains can cover over 1,500 miles without any change in consist.

Unfortunately the most common unit train is the unrideable (except the units) all-coalcar train, which shunts from coal mine to power plant and back. Other common consists ship orange juice, hot liquid sulfur, semi-finished steel, autoparts, grain, crude oil, fertilizer, double-stacked intermodal boxes - even salt water! Unit trains aren't necessarily hotshots or regulars. They could be either. Obviously they're never peddlars. Their importance to the wayfarer is they consist of cars which are either entirely rideable or entirely unrideable. Keep a lookout for them.

"Dedicated Piggyback Trains" follow the same concept as the unit train but consist of only 25 to 50 cars. Although 75% of all freight shipped by rail in America travels over two or more railroads, dedicated piggyback trains *always* travel long distances over several railroads in hand-off fashion. Ironically the driving ambition of the rail barons - to build a coast-to-coast railroad - has to date never been realized. There exists no one wholly-owned transcontinental railroad in America. In Canada of course two exist - the Canadian National and Canadian Pacific.

Nevertheless with power sharing and "run through" trains dedicateds make as few stops as possible even though they cross into different railroads' territory. When they do stop it's to cut out or pick up large blocks of cars at major terminals. These trains provide a long-distance ride and should be inquired into.

Another exciting development for the adventurer is establishment of "Land Bridge Trains" across the continent. Today large shipments of ocean-going intermodal boxes which used to travel by boat from Europe to Asia or vice versa cross our continent by train. The original vessel no longer sails through the Panama Canal. The economy in this type of arrangement is the reduced turnaround time for the vessel. The containers travel cross-country in unit trains on fairly fast schedules.

The result is transcontinental trains from the four major West Coast ports (Seattle, Portland, Oakland and Long Beach) to the four major East Coast ports (Savannah, Norfolk, Baltimore and New York) or vice versa. A "mini" land bridge extends from Los Angeles to Galveston and various "micro" land bridges - say from Norfolk to St. Louis - also exist. If you're near one of these port cities hang out until the railroad assembles an all-intermodal box train. You can glide all the way across country without changing cars once. And that's cadillac railroading.

Alright. So far we've confined our discussion to catching a train out of the yards - a train which has just been made up. This situation covers about *half* the trains available for sports ridership. The other half are made up somewhere else and are headed our way over the road. As you read on bear in mind the previous information about picking out your Pullman and sizing up a train. Now let's make some general comments about how railroads run trains. Then we'll talk about catching out over-the-road.

XII

HOW DO RAILROADS RUN FREIGHT TRAINS?

TRAIN PRIORITY

We've alluded to priority, "preference," or "superiority" of trains before. Let's round out the concept now.

Train priority comes into play when a railroad relies upon all or mainly single-track mainline. Over 65% of the 155,000 miles of mainline track in America is single-track and unbelievably the percentage is growing each year. When two trains meet one has to get out of the other's way. This is expensive (starting and stopping trains guzzles diesel), time-consuming and increases safety hazards. But going into the hole for a higher priority train happens all the time riding the rails. If you're on a train with low priority it's frustrating to get "knocked" into the "pocket."

The question becomes: What determines priority of approaching trains? Aside from asking some well-tailored questions in the yards there are few guidelines here. You can get on a freight which goes like gang-busters for 50 miles then peters out into a peddlar for the next 50, then rattles the hocks off it again - or the opposite. The inability to figure out what a train's priority is puts more mystique and adventure into the sport, and can surprise and delight - or sicken and dismay (maybe scanners are a result of this).

In the company's mind priority is based on a combination of factors. The most important is the *freight* a train is carrying. The more important the freight (i.e., more profitable) the higher the train's priority. Profitability of freight bears direct relationship to how often a train has to go into the hole. If a train has high-revenue cargo railroads knock out other trains to deliver it quickly.   From a business perspective this makes sense.   Everyone services his most important (i.e., most profitable) customer fastest.   But from a sporting perspective it's a bit of a piss off riding along with unimportant freight.

Railroads claim to have logical reasons for how they prioritize freight. On steeper grades some railroads stop uphill trains because downhill trains are too hard to stop.   Some stop downhill trains because uphill trains are too expensive to restart or might break-in-two.   But to a large extent any logic employed in setting priorities remains a mystery to the wayfarer.

Apart from bottom-line considerations each railroad has devised its own general priority scheme, often rather arbitrarily.   All other things being equal one method of prioritizing trains is whether it's daytime or nighttime. Railroads need to be fair to traffic in both directions so everything moves at roughly the same speed.   Otherwise all the equipment winds up at one end of the line.   This is particularly true of engines.

If a railroad has a poorly distributed directional balance of loaded vs. unloaded traffic it often has too many units stacked up at one end of the line (because more units pull in the loaded direction).   For example much of the boxcar traffic from east to west is either high-bulk (appliances or furniture) or heavy (paper).   Railroads find it tough to find this tonnage coming back the other direction.   To balance things they either tack extra units onto unloaded or underloaded trains coming east or run units back "light" (several units run back together without cars).

To minimize the frequency of these situations, let's say we're rolling westbound on a railroad which says: "Eastbound traffic priority daylight.   Westbound traffic night."   During the day our westbound train might clunk along on single-track, going into hole after hole for eastbound trains.   But then it picks up at night.

Some railroads prioritize by day of the week.   Eastbound might have priority during a 24-hour Monday, Wednesday and Friday, while westbound takes priority Tuesday, Thursday, Saturday and Sunday. Ask a worker how his railroad runs things.   Or else ride the railroad a few times and figure it out for yourself.

Priority on the large railroads therefore is governed by (1) the perceived profitability of freight, (2) the direction of travel (eastbound or westbound), and, to a lesser extent, (3) whether it's daytime or nighttime, (4) the day of the week and/or (5) uphill vs. downhill.

For example even if it's nighttime and westbound traffic has priority if your eastbound train has important enough freight you'll knock a few "opposing" westbounds into the hole. On the other hand simply because you have the right time of the day on your side you'll fly by *slightly* more profitable trains opposing you. But you will *always* go into the hole for a hotshot unless you're on one too. When two hotshots meet factors (2) through (5) govern who wins.

Remember, priority is only an issue on single-track mainline. If you're on double-track you can expect to make very decent progress regardless of what's coming or going around you. The beauty of double-track is we don't get knocked into the hole all the time. Far in advance of a meet traffic is carefully routed around other traffic by "cross-over" tracks so everybody can keep moving at high speed. Even peddlars whip along from customer to customer.

One final note about priority on regulars. Sometimes a fast freight sneaks up behind a slow one. If you're on the slow one you'll get knocked into the hole to make way. This has more to do with profitability than time of day, etc. For us speed freaks it's tough to accept being passed by a following train. But if you're in no hurry take a walk and get to know the part of the country you're visiting until the track clears and you can proceed.

RAILROAD NORTH, SOUTH, EAST AND WEST

Let's talk about railroad north, south, east and west. The main thrust of expansion on the railroad, as with the countries themselves was from east to west. This mentality has stuck with most railroads. It seems the impact of the Transcontinental Railroads permanently affected the railroads' headset. If you go from Washington D.C. to Miami for example - that's westbound. Or from Portland Oregon to Los Angeles - that's eastbound. In other words railroads are funny when it comes to the points of the compass. East-to-west or west-to-east is very roughly defined as being the point from which a railroad started building to where it finally went. Some examples:

The old Chicago, Rock Island & Pacific ("CRI&P," "Rock Island Line" or "The Rock") began in Chicago and made it to Rock Island all right but never went past New Mexico and Colorado. Same thing with the old St. Louis-San Francisco ("SL-SF" or "Frisco Line"). The Frisco never made it to Frisco but did get as far west as Oklahoma City and *east* to *Florida*.

Often the directors were long on vision but short on cash. Some were smart and simply said "X, Y, Z and Western," like "Atlantic and Western," "New York, Susquehanna & Western" or "Grand Trunk Western." Then they'd roll the dice. Others kept it extremely vague - undoubtedly because they were extremely vague on where they would actually wind up - like "Western Pacific," "Great Western" or "Great Northern." Others were "So-and-So Northern, Southern or Eastern."

Other railroads left little doubt as to their ultimate ambitions. Take for example the two railroads driving to meet each other to form the first transcontinental - "Union Pacific" ("UP") and "Central Pacific" ("CP," now part of "Southern Pacific" - "SP"). The Union Pacific sought to unite the Atlantic and Pacific Oceans, which it did. The Central Pacific sought the same thing along the central route of the California Trail, which it did.

Some railroads made it right where their names indicated they were headed. The old Chicago, Milwaukee, St. Paul and Pacific ("CMSP&P," or "The Milwaukee Road") made it to these towns *and* out to Seattle. Still other railroads overshot their mark, like the AT&SF. Cyrus Holliday set out for Santa Fe and hit Atchison and Topeka along the way. Due to topography however he narrowly missed Santa Fe (he got close, to Lamy N.M., 18 miles away, then built a spur line up to Santa Fe). After several railroad "wars" over mountain passes and rivers with the Denver & Rio Grande (today's "Denver and Rio Grande Western," or "D&RGW" - a subsidiary of Southern Pacific), and later with the Southern Pacific itself, the Santa Fe fought and won its way out to Los Angeles, San Diego and San Francisco - without ever saying "Western" or "Pacific."

Despite their names railroads went off in whichever direction promised most profit. Today it's hard to tell where the original railroad companies went or intended to go because railroad mergers are slowly erasing the colorful names.

RAILROAD SPEED LIMITS

Ostensibly railroads set their own speed limits over different stretches of track. Usually they have two limits: One for freight and another for passenger (if any). Because of the weight and length of a freight train its speed limits are slower. Track speeds must be validated by the FRA based on grade, curvature and quality of track. A typical stretch of straight, well-maintained track will have a 65/55 MPH limit - 65 passenger/ 55 freight.

Railroads post speed limit signs on both sides of the track. These are small signs, black-on-white or white-on-black, with numbers like "65-55." Other times on curves, bad track or near yards they'll have a one-speed-limit-fits-all, like "40." As you travel along watch for the little sign facing you on the right. It's *supposed* to control the engineer.

Many diesels have tapes which record speeds, like a black box on jets and the modern equivalent of the Dutch Clock (see below). These tapes help maintenance people determine what causes the problems a particular diesel develops. The company can also use the tapes to get on the ass of an engineer who likes to Highball excessively.

Excessive highballing has long been a problem for railroads. Like motorists a significant percentage of railroad engineers have always loved to rattle the hocks off their trains - all-too-often with disastrous consequences. To combat the problem in the old days the companies put "Dutch clocks" in cabooses to monitor speeds. More often than not the conductor used to tamper with the tape and saw to it his Casey Jones wasn't found out.

PRESENT DAY FREIGHT RAILROAD PROBLEMS

The chief problem confronting North American freight railroads is themselves. I'm not making any friends in the railroad industry writing this book. I might as well tell it like it is.

If you want to find out what's wrong with our freight train system just try shipping something with them. Then compare it with a trucker. All your questions will be answered. The time it takes to get your shipment to its destination is the worst comparison. For most trucking companies a shipment which arrives more than 30 minutes late is considered a failure. On the railroad shippers cross their fingers and hope the freight arrives within a few days on either side of the promise. As the demands of the business world continue to intensify and speed up, shippers happily pay a premium to ensure they keep their commitments. To do so they call a truck.

Believe it or not, multi-million dollar railroads' business offices are only open from 9 to 5, Monday through Friday. In comparison you can deliver flowers 24 hours a day. If you want to know what happened to your shipment on the railroad other than from 9 to 5, forget it. You'll get a recorded message. The computerized "Shipper Assist Message" (SAM) system which monitors freightcar movement by subscribing railroads, while highly-touted by the AAR hasn't wooed many shippers back to the railroad. What's even more incredible is on holidays many railroads shut down their entire system (wages) and stop trains wherever they happen to be.

Railroads have learned next to nothing about service in the past 13 years of deregulation. Rather than designing their service to dovetail with shippers' traffic requirements they expect shippers to fit into their existing service. Unfortunately today despite the ardent pleas of agro-industry railroads perform their services in a time and manner which suits *them* rather than the customer. Railroads are slow, often late, deaf, and all-too-often arrive with smashed freight. Apropos of smashed freight, if executives could see their way to making the working environment more rewarding for the individual employee, the employee wouldn't shove cars around like sweeping the floor. Middle management's hands are tied when decisions need to be made and are rarely expected to make them. Other than a paycheck and a safety meeting the guy or gal in the yards or over the road gets no encouragement to work with pride (exception - the employee-owned Chicago & North Western). Thus shippers avoid railroads whenever serious business needs doing. As a result the railroads don't make much money and are caught in a vicious cycle of their own making.

Not only is railroading a disappointing industry profit-wise; it's also a highly vulnerable one. A mere sneeze in the economy gives the railroads pneumonia. Many years railroads show little or no profit. Twenty-four percent of their operating revenue goes to federal, state and local taxes compared to between 4 and 5% for trucks. During recessions railroads hang on for dear life, go belly up or merge.

XIII

HOW DO I CATCH A FREIGHT TRAIN OVER THE ROAD?

WHERE TO GO TO CATCH OUT - THE DIVISION

In addition to catching out from a yard where a train originates or "comes out of" there's another time-honored way to catch a freight - on one which is en route. These freights are on the move all across the country every day of the week (except holidays).

An over-the-road freight train looks pretty inaccessible rolling down the track. Pretty unstoppable. But the magical thing is they *have* to stop every so often even if they're getting green lights all the way down the line. We've already mentioned the fact freights stop to change crews at predesignated intervals. The beauty of this is if you find out *where* they do this you can grab one en route and take a ride.

First off here's more railroadspeak: The stations or yards where railroads change crews are called "division points," "divisions," "crew divisions" or "the division." Divisions are located at predetermined intervals which correspond to roughly 8 or 10 hours of work. By law after 12 hours a crew goes "dead on the clock" and have to stop working their train. Seventy percent of the towns listed state-by-state or province in the Appendix are divisions. A little walk through history gives us a good idea where divisions are located along a given route.

Railroads have gradually shut down and eliminated nearly half their division points - many more in the sparsely-populated West than back East. It's been a piecemeal process over the last 25 years and continues today. Hotshots can now go up to 500 miles in an 8-hour shift. On a normal day the average regular freight can cover 200 to 300 miles in 8 hours. Elimination of divisions speeds things up for the *official* participants but makes things trickier for us. Today we have to travel farther to find the division and catch out.

Here's one way to find the nearest division: Wherever you are, go down to the nearest freightyard - even a tiny one. Ask a worker where the divisions are out in each direction along the route. All workers know the two or three closest divisions in each direction. Or get as current a railroad atlas as possible and show it to a worker. Ask him which towns are still divisions - or which ones he hears about the most during shoptalk. Divisions will change after this book is printed so in places you'll have to do your own research for up-to-the-minute information.

POSITIONING YOURSELF TO CATCH OUT AT THE DIVISION

The fine art in hopping a freight at a division is knowing where to position yourself at the optimum spot. Two basic considerations are involved: First we need to position ourselves so we can *see* what the train consists of as it comes in to quickly select a Pullman. Second we need to be in a position to then get to and get on this car as quickly as possible.

New over-the-road traincrews wait at a predesignated spot to make the change. When you see a new crew make their move it's a safe bet your train is not far away. The crew get the word the train is approaching and only then make their move. There are two ways new crews get to where the headend will stop.

In smaller yards the headend usually stops in front of the depot. A couple of minutes before arrival you'll see the new crew walk out in front of the depot with black travel bags in hand (their "grips"). The headend comes in, slows to a stop (usually) in front of the depot and the change is made.

In larger yards the crew get driven in a "crewcar" from the office to where the headend will stop. Most crewcars are white or off-white Chevrolet Suburbans - or always some other American-made passenger van. Crewcars are painted a light color so the old crew can see them from a distance and so yard engines don't run them over. The new crew sit in the crewcar until their train's arrival.

In big yards the headend often stops at the opposite end of the yard from the end it enters so the whole train's in the yard during the change. The train slows down coming through the yard, then (usually) stops next to the crewcar.

One thing which lights a legal fire under a traincrew's butt is when their train cuts off a town's major thoroughfares. Federal law says a railroad can't cut a town in half with a *fully*-stopped train longer than 10 minutes for *any* reason - short of emergency. The policy reason: What if the town's cut in half and somebody has a heart attack or there's a burglary or fire in progress, etc.? This is a good law.

In a town where streets cross through the yards instead of overhead on bridges the crew have three options: One, they can take all the time they want by "sawing" the train in half at each crossing to let cars through. This is labor-intensive and time-consuming - and therefore costly. Crews don't like doing this either. Two, they can stop, make the change and get the train moving again within 10 minutes. Or three they can change crews "on the fly" or "on the run" (I use "on the run").

Regardless whether we're in a small or large yard if we want to hop an over-the-road train we need to position ourselves back down the track from where the headend stops to change crews. This way we can watch the train roll slowly by until it stops, giving us a good preview of what cars are available.

Whether it's crewmembers inspecting a passing train or hobos checking it out for Pullmans, sizing up a moving train is called "rolling a train." Brakemen on over-the-road trains are required to roll their trains on curves and watch for equipment problems. This is usually how they notice hobos are aboard.

For us the idea is to let the train's fingers do the walking while we select a Pullman. It's the same idea as picking a convenient, well-situated spot where we can watch a yardcrew hump up a newly-made train on a yard track.

First get your directional bearings. If you're headed eastbound figure out which way is east and west in the yard. Next figure out which track the train will stop on. In smaller yards an over-the-road train usually stops on the mainline - but not always. It might come off the mainline onto a secondary track - especially if another train with priority is approaching, power needs to be fueled, added or taken off, or the crew has pick-up or cut-out business to do. In larger yards they stop on the mainline or another track close to it. If you're familiar with the division you'll know where to wait. If it's your first visit ask which track your train will stop on to change crews - or just sit and watch.

Assuming you've got your bearings as to *where* and on *which track* the headend will stop, find a place to wait on the *other side of the track* from the depot or crewcar. When the train comes in you can't be seen when you hop on a car. This minimizes the chances the odd pantywaist will see you and play tattle-tale. Figure out the sightlines so the train blocks you from view.

Once determining where the train stops and where you'll be blocked from view, position yourself back down the tracks a goodly distance in the direction the train will come from. Get an idea of how many cars the average train on this road has. Are trains generally 70 cars long or 170? If you want to take a siesta one clever trick is to lie near a remote-controlled switch. When you hear them throw the switch it's train time (the "hobo alarm clock").

Here's where artfulness and adventure combine. Get far enough down the track so that 2/3rds to 3/4ths of the train rolls past you before stopping. When it comes in, roll it for scenic cruisers, one-eyed bandits, hoppers, etc. as it slows to a halt. Once it's stopped and you see a car you absolutely must have, grab your gear and go for it. You'll have to hurry if the Pullman's up toward the front of the train - where generally we don't want to ride anyway (see below). If nothing attractive passes check out the cars which haven't passed. If you're positioned far enough away from the train to see 20 or 30 cars in either direction, check out the last 1/4th to 1/3rd - also without moving. See whether there are any sexy, enticing cars back there which warrant further inquiry. After spotting the perfect Pullman, jog along merrily and **nail that sucker**.

Besides rolling your train from 2/3rds to 3/4ths of the way back there are other reasons to ride the back part of a freight train. These reasons are best grouped under the idea that it's *best* to ride the back half of a freight train. With car choices toward the front and back choose a car toward the back. This is important so let's develop it.

The main reason to ride the back of a train is we're not up there bugging the crew. If we're in the first car behind the units and a hassle develops with the bull or some other yo-yo, the crew might be called upon to explain why they didn't see us and tell us to leave. Don't place trainmen in a situation where they couldn't possibly overlook you on their train. With elimination of cabooses we're the only show in town on the back end of a freight train. We can even ride the back car right next to the EOT ("End of Train" device, aka FRED "Fucking Rear End Device"), a flashing red light which replaces the caboose and monitors speeds, air pressure and other functions at the end of the train). FRED doesn't have a sensor for us. Moreover when we get off we're far away from the depot, crewcar, etc. We can easily lowline.

Another reason to ride toward the back is diesel smoke. The farther back from the units the less smoke we inhale. When a freight train takes off the units can belch out clouds of gray-black smoke - especially if one or more isn't well tuned.

The smoke factor gets significant in tunnel country. If we're up near the headend and go through a long tunnel we *chew* diesel exhaust. It can also get rather warm inside the tunnel - sometimes *fucking* hot. At the front end after a short time in a long tunnel we have to breathe through our clothing, like the arm of our shirt or jacket. If it gets really bad pour water on a piece of fabric and breathe through it.

In the days of steam hobos asphyxiated from coal smoke in long tunnels. In the West the Southern Pacific ordered "cab-forward" locomotives ahead of the smokestack so crews wouldn't choke out passing through tunnels and snowsheds on Donner Pass or across Lake Shasta. There are several tunnels to watch out for in North America.

Most notable in the U.S. is the Burlington Northern's Cascade Tunnel, 92 miles east of Seattle's Interbay Yards and about 50 miles west of Wenatchee. This tunnel blasts through a wall of the Cascades. It goes on and on for just short of 8 miles of continuous, non-stop, no-break-in-the-action tunnel.

BN built a giant fan at the west end to blow air through the tunnel after a train passes. They even slam shut a huge door over the western mouth of the tunnel to facilitate the process. But when you're going eastbound up the grade through this tunnel get ready for *air pollution*. Even toward the backend of the train it's a different kind of experience.

Another big tunnel to watch out for is BN's Flathead or Libby Dam Tunnel up in western Montana, west of Whitefish and 50-odd miles east of Libby, passing under Elk Mountain for almost 8 miles. Don't forget the Denver and Rio Grande Western Railroad's ("D-Rye-o Grandee's") Moffat Tunnel under James Peak, about 60 miles west of Denver heading toward Glenwood Springs. Westbound look for Winter Park. This tunnel is over 6 miles long. Back east keep a lookout for the Hoosac Tunnel up in Massachusetts. It's on the Boston & Maine Railroad's

("B&M," now part of the Guilford System or "GTI") mainline from Boston to Albany 10 miles east of North Adams and 30-odd miles west of Greenfield, and runs nearly 5 miles long (and took 24 years of blasting to build). Also ask around about the Big Bend Tunnel on C&O's (CSX Transportation Co.'s) mainline back east.

Up in British Columbia be on the alert for two parallel tunnels on CP Rail's Beaver Hill, west of Field and east of Revelstoke. The newer and longer Mount Macdonald Tunnels are reserved for westbound trains. One is a 1-mile bore while the other is a 9-mile bore. The 9-miler has a super ventilation system but CP still has to wait 30 minutes between trains to blow out the smoke. Eastbound you pass through the older 5-mile long Connaught Tunnel.

Smoke is truly a problem in long tunnels. Railroads drill down from the top or in from the sides to install ventilator shafts with big fans. While the train's moving through the tunnel however they don't help much. Even in a shorter tunnel if you're up near the power you won't like it. (In fact the railroad "accident" which resulted in the world's second-highest number of deaths occurred in a tunnel. And it wasn't really an accident at all. In wartime Italy on March 2nd, 1944, 509 hobos died from coal smoke poisoning while riding a freight train which stalled in Armi Tunnel near Salerno.) Plus the roar of the engines can drive you to near-distraction. In short stay to the back of a freight train in tunnel country.

The third reason to ride the back part of a train is to minimize the likelihood of your car being cut out. On a regular train cars slated to be cut out tend to be blocked toward the front. Get to the back where the odds of being cut out are *somewhat* (never entirely) lessened.

A fourth reason to wait for a train toward its rear is that if you don't see a car you like on the first side of the train you can run around the last car, say "hello" to FRED and check out the other side. You won't have to climb over the cars, which as we've seen is the most dangerous aspect of the sport - especially on an over-the-road train which could sudden takeoff at any moment.

Finally there are sudden stops which we'll cover later. All other things being equal wait for and ride a freight train toward its back end.

Let's take the situation where you've found a car but have a hunch you might find something better. If you continue looking up *ahead* of this car but hear the air come up and the brakes start releasing, definitely run back to the car and grab it. Your train is close to departure. If you simply stand there and wait for the car to come to you the train could pick up too much speed to climb on. You take a larger risk of being left behind the farther ahead of this car you walk without finding something else. Remember the *common sense* notion that you can pass many more cars running against the direction of a train's travel than with it. And if you're looking for something *behind* this car you'd better not stray too far behind it. Catching up to it when the train takes off will be even tougher.

From the moment a train first moves I'd estimate a runner of average-speed (10 to 12 MPH) with an average load (20 lbs.) could reasonably expect to catch a car as many as 6 or 8 cars ahead. Remember on take off freight trains are huge lumbering beasts - especially if they're heading up-hill. Once slack in the couplers and draft gears has been drafted out the average freight train (say 90 cars with four units) on level ground accelerates at a rate of 0.2 to 0.3 MPH per second. Thus if the engineer pulls out as quickly as possible the train will be moving between 12 and 18 MPH within a minute. You have roughly one minute to nail a Pullman.

Fifteen to 18 MPH is the fastest speed we can climb on a car, depending on how fast and how tall we are and whether we're using a stirrup and ladder or vaulting onto a floor. Hotshots however bolt out of there *muy pronto*. A hotshot can get going too fast in much less than a minute. Under normal circumstances don't panic if the train takes off. Simply be aware that time is now *extremely* short and your options are limited. Get on something quickly.

Also bear in mind which track the train is on. If it's on the mainline there's nothing to prevent the engineer from leaning on the throttle and getting up speed as quickly as possible. If however the train's on another track it has to pass through one or more switches to return to the main. A train has to go slow through switches in yards, drifting until it clears all switches before getting up a good head of steam.

But NOTE CAREFULLY: If the train is leaving and you haven't found anything which would do, even in a pinch, *no matter how badly you want to get on* DON'T COMPROMISE YOUR SAFETY AND WELLBEING *by climbing on an unsafe or exposed car. Don't* climb onto something dangerous. Since we never know for sure *when* a train will stop next common sense counsels if we decide to hang onto a ladder, footboard, coupling or roof we might have to stay there for the next *72 miles*. We don't want this to happen. After a while a bad ride is like the old Harold-Lloyd-on-the-Clock routine.

In other words if you've tried your best to nail something decent - or *at least safe* - and failed, have the patience and maturity to recognize you did everything possible. Let the train go. Sometimes it just doesn't work out. Get ready to catch the next train. I know how missing a train can be disheartening. Nobody wins every match in any sport. **REMEMBER** however: **It's *better to be delayed than dead.***

CATCHING OUT ON THE RUN

At times catching out on an *en route* train at the division gets trickier. Sometimes especially with hotshots railroads change crews on the run. This saves time and fuel even though it's a bit dangerous for the crew - and more so for us. The tips provided here will make it safe and easy for you to catch out on the run.

Here's how crews change on the run: Visualize the old crew slowing the train down as it comes into the division. There they are up in the point unit. They've packed their gear into their grips. The engineer's braking down and approaching the depot or crewcar. Since the train is moving he has to stay seated, or at least keep his hands on the throttles or his foot on the deadman's pedal. The new crew stands ready at trackside. The old engineer slows it down to between 3 and 4 MPH to make the switch (crews *will not run* to make the switch).

When the headend meets the new crew the engineers switch first. The new engineer climbs in and goes over to the control stand. With the old engineer he either puts his foot down on the deadman's pedal and the old one slides out of the seat, or they exchange handholds on the throttles or with the new wiring arrangement the new engineer slides into the old one's seat. Whichever way it works it's a gymnastic, contortionist little dance they do with each other.

But the train keeps rolling. While the engineers switch the other crewmembers climb down and the new ones climb on. *Voila.* The change is complete. The new engineer gets the bell and it's Highball.

During this time we have to be quick and we have to be moderately lucky. Quick because in terms of timing there's only a brief window of opportunity to latch onto something rideable. Lucky because a rideable car has to be fairly close by. This is during either side of the 3 to 4 MPH range the crew make their change at. Realistically we have a decent shot at about

30 cars, the 15 which approach as the train slows down enough to climb on, through the time the switch is made, and continues through the next 10 cars which pass before the train is moving too fast again. If those 30-odd cars are unrideable that's the breaks. But 80% of the time we have a good shot at something.

Always throw your gear on first unless you're doubtful whether you can actually get on the car you've selected. This lessens your weight and enhances your agility. With a boxcar you'll have to vault or swing up into the car. Throw your gear on first then go for it. With a hopper throw your gear on the platform then mount the stirrup and ladder, swing onto the platform and go. Same thing with an accessible auto rack. If it has end-doors I wouldn't mess with it on the run. You'd have to climb all the way up the ladder with your gear on, then climb in over the doors while hanging directly over the track. If you can tell it doesn't have a roof however climb up and go.

With a pig use the stirrup-ladder or grabiron or if you're tall enough vault directly onto the floor. This can be tough if the piggyback has the apron we prefer because the height up onto the floor is increased. A flatcar with bulkheads will have a ladder going up the side of the bulkhead. Use it. A straight or modular flatcar will only have a stirrup and grabiron. Unless very agile you'll have to vault bulkheadless flatcars. With a gondola throw your gear over the top sill and climb the ladder. Be careful for a sudden jerk while going over the top sill and get down into the car quickly. Going over the top of a moving gondola is a critical moment; you're off-balance and have only the wall to hang onto.

Most trains hot enough to change crews on the run won't have many empties - if any - unless the whole railroad's hot. Our chances of finding a scenic cruiser or one-eyed bandit are slim. And trains which change crews on the run generally won't have gondolas or non-modular flatcars. There are exceptions of course but don't count on them. Hotshots have their share of tankcars and unrideable hoppers but these don't concern us. If anything they're a nuisance because they cut down on the percentage of cars we have to choose from during the window of opportunity.

The main idea is knowing what your individual requirements are in terms of weather, scenery and general ambiance. In time you'll learn whether you can nail a particular type of car on the run or not. Make a snap decision whether the car you're shooting for is attainable and will fill the bill.

Perhaps you remember watching those great 1920s to 40s train movies where the hobos pile out of the jungle and grab onto cars as the train rumbles by. They run alongside a car, throw their bindle up to their buddy who's just climbed on then climb up the ladder or swing into the car with the door latch and take off. Usually the big bad bull is hot on their tail, hurling threats, firing his gun in the air and being left in the dust.

Catching out on the run today isn't far off from that great old scenario - except there won't be a bull on your tail. You get a *real sense of accomplishment* once you've pulled it off.

If you have true grit and it's nighttime you can do exactly what the crew does and clamber onto a back or slave unit like they clamber onto the point. This is actually much easier than vaulting or climbing a freightcar because you can use the *steps* up to the cab.

With a little luck and some arrows in your quiver you'll learn how to catch out over the road even on the run. It's just as easy - and at times *much* easier and quicker - than catching out on a new train. You don't have to wait for them to make it up, call the power and Highball. You don't have to walk around looking for a Pullman. You either know the approximate arrival time from asking someone or you watch for the crew and read the signals to see when the train is coming down. You don't subject yourself to the risks attendant in traipsing around the yards. Often the bull is asleep at a division - *if* the railroad even has one. At smaller divisions they rarely do. Jump on and take a ride.

XIV

OVER THE ROAD DO'S AND DON'TS

LYING DOWN AND SITTING DOWN FOR A SAFE RIDE

Once you've settled upon a car I have some recommendations based on two fundamental notions of physics - gravity and inertia. Let's talk about inertia first.

As with any mode of conveyance which moves on wheels a freight train will stop faster than it ever starts (unless you're rear-ended which today on the railroad is *extremely* rare). Sudden railroad stops occur on that rare yet ever-woeful day when the engineer chokes and slams the train into something big (i.e., another train) or the train "climbs the rails" (i.e., derails). If this happens we *might* go flying. Assuming we fly the questions become: (1) how far do we want to fly; (2) what do we want to land on or up against; and (3) in what position?

Objects in motion tend to stay in motion. This is the physical law of Inertia - the "tendency of matter to remain at rest if at rest, or, if moving, to keep moving in the same direction, unless affected by some outside force." In a sudden freight train stop this outside force is something solid on the train (i.e., a wall) or the ground if we're thrown from the train. Our body seeks to conserve its momentum; a function of its mass and velocity. Before getting completely paranoid however I'd like to reemphasize the chances of getting into a train wreck are *remote*.

The damage resulting from a freight train wreck is minimized by the fact most derailments begin *and end* at the headend. The units are the heaviest equipment. If there's a track problem odds are they'll find it first. Closely examine freight derailment photos in your newspaper. Notice very

169

few cars behind the front units leave the track - at most maybe 20 or so. The cars that *do* climb the rails usually roll on their sides. A few cars at the front of the train might twist, burrow and stack up. The great majority down the line however slam to a halt but stay on the track. In the most common collision - the head-on - the front of the train bears the brunt of impact.

Derailments and head-ons are two additional reasons to choose a Pullman toward the back of a train. Of course in a high-speed wreck cars get flung around like matchsticks. But these wrecks are rare. If you're toward the back you further narrow the chance of injury. If unlucky enough to be in a wreck you'll have to be *even more* unlucky to be in one of the cars involved. As mentioned wrecks are far less common than 100 years ago. In the heyday of the hobo between 1890 and 1910 they say 32,276 travelers were killed on American railroads.

Let's talk for a moment about what happens in a crash. What are things people commonly slam into when they crash? On a freight train it's some type of wall (on boxcars, hoppers, gondolas, flatcars with bulkheads, intermodal flatcars and back units), or something other than a wall (on piggybacks [tires and axles], loaded auto racks [tires and bumpers] and in new cars [steering wheels, windshields, doors or dashboards]). Sometimes there isn't much to break our flight (like empty auto racks, empty piggybacks and straight empty flatcars). Our inertia and momentum are conserved as we fly or slide. Same thing on sudden takeoffs and jerking. On all but the most exposed cars how far and where we fly or slide, what we hit and how we hit it can be *largely determined in advance by us.*

Think of yourself as a friend of mine does, "The Human Slingshot." Plan ahead where you'll land - like the circus clown who gets shot out of the cannon. Make a conscious pre-disaster decision which part of your body makes contact with whatever's in front of it. Always think about whether "the big stop" will cause you a concussion and broken neck or a bruised right shoulder and bloodied finger. If the train stops suddenly you'll go in the last - known direction of travel - forward. Don't let your head make first contact with whatever you hit.

LYING DOWN

Let's begin with the prone, lying down or kicked-back position. The first consideration is to minimize the distance you'd slide in a sudden stop.

Stay close to a wall, tire or anything immediately in front of you in the direction of travel.

For example on a boxcar, gondola, hopper or flatcar with bulkheads lie down close to and *parallel* to the front wall. On a sudden stop you won't travel far. You'll simply roll against the wall. Your whole body is available to cushion the impact. Better yet on boxcars, gondolas and hoppers (space allowing) lie with your *feet* facing the front wall. Your feet and legs will absorb initial impact. (Although I've never seen this I've been told you can rig up a hammock from the walls of a boxcar and have a thoroughly enjoyable ride. Just find something to hook either end up and take a siesta.) On a loaded auto rack or TOFC piggyback lie down close to something relatively flat, like a tire (no pun intended) or bridgeplate which will break your slide.

Piggybacks present an interesting positioning conflict. While it's best to be close to the edge of the car where the trailer's duals are (to have something to sit against, break the wind *and* break a slide on a fast stop) it's also best to be in the center of the car to keep from rolling off (if there's no apron) or getting thrown or bounced off in a wreck. Conversely in the center of the car you could slide off forward under the trailer's axles during a fast stop. So it's a tossup.

I get behind the tires head-first but place my backpack between my head and the tires to cushion a blow. I sleep head-first toward the point of impact *only* on piggybacks for two reasons: First because I'd only hit a tire instead of an unforgiving wall (with my backpack in between). Second because I like to keep my head out of the wind as much as possible while sleeping. These are personal choices. On a piggyback use your own intuition in deciding where to lie down.

On *loaded* auto racks position yourself feet forward behind the back tire of the back car or truck. This way you hit the car instead of the other way around. As mentioned this goes by way of saying always ride on the back of the auto rack - loaded or unloaded, siding or no siding. During minor wrecks on a loaded auto rack the cars/trucks stay in place. Their axles are chained to the floor of the car. Even if it's a severe accident when you're behind everything you lessen the risk of getting hit by axleless vehicles flying like toys. Thus not only do you have less wind to contend with, you also avoid being squashed like a bug.

On *loaded* straight flatcars *if* you're reasonably confident the load won't shift (a dubious proposition at best) always ride *behind the load.* If the load breaks loose you won't get pushed off the front with it. This is very important.

Recall most non-modular flatcar loads are construction materials or large machinery. Also remember physical properties apply to loads as well as people. On sudden stops loads also keep going forward. On any loaded flatcar stay behind the load to break the wind and let the load break your flight.

On *empty* straight flatcars there's nothing but a rough wooden floor to break a slide forward. You have no choice on positioning - another drawback to riding one. Of all the personal Pullmans on an empty bulkheadless flatcar whether straight, TOFC or COFC you're at greatest risk of being flung off the car in a wreck (*except* in "sandbox" well cars). An empty flatcar is roughly analogous to riding on the bed of a flatbed truck in a wreck - without a passenger compartment to stop forward progress. To minimize the risk stay in the center of an empty flatcar's floor toward the back.

In back units at the headend or cut in somewhere down the string we're safe - except for the fact at the headend we're on the part of the train most likely to leave the tracks or get creamed. The guys on the point are the big losers if the train piles into something. With all that weight and inertia/ momentum behind them they're sitting ducks.

In a simple derailment the crew have an excellent chance of survival. Due to the engines' weight and ballast they often simply tip over on their sides and burrow to a halt. The walls of the cab prevent people from flying. Unlike the crew's on-the-point unit we're back two or more units. Odds are our unit won't get nearly as beat up regardless whether it's a collision or derailment. Chances are we'll slide to a halt or get spit out the side. Riding in units cut in at the middle or back of the train is even safer. Nevertheless lie down parallel to the front wall. If they make a wreck you'll roll up against the door to the john.

The main idea is to minimize the distance of flight or slide. The corollary is to make contact with something relatively benign (i.e., flat) with a part of the body which is harder to hurt (i.e., back, sides, butt, legs or feet). The human body is built to withstand a lot of physical punishment so capitalize on all parts of your body which can cushion blows.

SITTING DOWN

The same principles for lying down hold true for sitting down. In a wreck or ultra-fast stop we're much safer sitting down than lying down since the odds of hitting our head are greatly diminished. Sitting down it's best to back yourself up firmly against something. The best analogy is riding in the back of a pickup. We always want our back against the front wall of the bed. On trains we also want to avoid any chance of getting catapulted off if we hit a bad rail or the Pullman jumps somehow. Always stay as far away from the open sides of a freightcar as practicable.

Boxcars have an interesting sitting-down angle. You might be tempted to sit in the middle of the floor in front of the open door(s). I do not recommend this. During a wreck you're in the same position as on an open car. If you go straight forward no problem. The three front walls will stop you. But if you go sideways you'll go right out the door.

On scenic cruisers I recommend sitting with your back against the side wall *opposite* the door you're looking out of and in front of the other door you're next to. This way if you're thrown forward no problem. The three front walls protect you. If you're thrown to the side the walls will also protect you.

On one-eyed bandits we're safer - assuming the closed door stays on and stays shut. Sit in the same position as on a scenic cruiser. Moreover never sit with your back against the closed door of a boxcar. Treat the door as if it could open or fall off anytime. In general confine all activities to the front half of a boxcar for best wind and wreck protection. You can walk around in the back of the car if you like. But reside primarily in front of the open door(s).

Here's one last sitting up safety tip: No matter what kind of car you're riding at times you'll be tempted to sit with your legs dangling over the side. This is practically irresistible because it's a really nice free feeling. You'll see photos of hobos doing this in other books about hoboing. Be forewarned: **NEVER HANG YOUR LEGS OFF THE SIDE OF A MOVING FREIGHTCAR**. This is one of the Cardinal Sins after walking on tracks and climbing under freightcars. It's one of the *dumbest* things you can do on the railroad. A switching block, "dwarf" signal or other low obstacle near the track can come by and rip your legs off.

I'm being gruesome here for effect: One moment you'll be sitting there feeling like Tom Sawyer, drowsing away a lazy summer's day dangling your feet off the raft and fishing on the Mississippi. The next moment you'll be a writhing, legless stump. Don't *ever* hang your legs over the side of a moving freightcar.

In general keep all body parts as well inside the car as possible when it's moving. Unless you're in the desert there's no telling when a tree branch or other impediment hangs down close to the tracks - particularly in the Deep South and New England where at times dense foliage actually forms a tunnel around the train. If you have an arm or leg hanging outside the vertical plane of the Pullman "Whack," and you have a problem. Always remain inside the imaginary boundaries of a freightcar. It's no brighter to do otherwise than in a moving auto or bus.

STANDING UP AND WALKING AROUND SAFELY ON A MOVING FREIGHTCAR

Even though the same physical forces are at work, standing and walking on a moving train present completely different circumstances and concerns. The main rule is if there's any chance of falling or getting thrown off the train when standing up or walking always, repeat ALWAYS HANG ONTO SOMETHING FOR SAFETY. This rule cannot be overstressed. Whether it's your first time out or your thousandth never get so cocksure as to think you don't need to hang onto something AT ALL TIMES standing up on a Pullman (with noted exceptions). When veteran railroadmen stand up on moving equipment they always hang onto something. That's how they become veterans.

As with lying and sitting down the risks taken standing up and walking around bear direct relationship to the kind of car you're on. You should **never** let go of something when standing or walking on piggybacks, hoppers, sideless auto racks and all flatcars - even if this means being on all fours or on hands and knees. One false move by you or the car and you'll be the man who lost hold of the flying trapeze. In boxcars, gondolas, sided auto racks and back units the risk is considerably less. And if you can walk around in a new vehicle *immediately buy it*.

You can get thrown to the floor on any kind of car if the train comes to a sudden halt or buffs in slack severely. But you have your hands and body to break the fall. It's not a bad idea to wear your gloves at all times practicable for this very occurrence. The key concern is getting thrown off the car. Let's go Pullman-by-Pullman and describe how to hang on when you stand or move.

On boxcars you're in danger only near the open door(s). Never get anywhere near an open door on your feet without holding onto something. The observance of safety when standing next to an open boxcar door is important because it's very tempting - again one might say irresistible - to linger next to the door for long periods. There's nothing quite like standing at the door watching America enter, perform, curtsy and bow out. But while watching the show keep your hands on something secure. If you want to lean out of the car *for a very brief moment*, always use both hands to hang onto something.

Your face can sustain a good bashing if it's partway out the door when the train stops or jerks suddenly. Bang. Your head will hit the side of the door or wall. There's a special way to use your hands and body to protect your face while *briefly* hanging out the door. *Place your hands on the side of the door or wall at face level.* This way your face will hit your hands instead of the hard surface. Also tip your head away from the vertical surface. Your chest or shoulder will hit first.

In fact use this technique whenever you're peering around anything hard while holding on in transit. Protect your face with your hands from truck trailers, intermodal boxes, auto rack siding or the wall of a hopper - anything your head could suddenly be thrown against.

Away from open boxcar doors there's not much to worry about. You can dance, pace, practice other sports or move about as you wish. But please confine most activity to the front end of the car.

On hoppers we have those made-to-order grabirons surrounding the A-end platform at chest level. Always hang onto the grabs and/or the body of the car when standing or walking on a hopper. You might be tempted to think the grabs will break your fall. They will if you're tall enough and standing upright. Sometimes though you'll be in a bent-over position arranging bedding or getting things out of your pack. In a bent-over position you could fall off *under* the grabs on a sudden stop or jerk. These grabs play no structural support role for the hopper. They're included only for safety. Always keep a hand on them when on your feet.

On piggybacks we have another interesting situation. As indicated due to restricted overhead clearance it's impossible to walk under the trailers on most of the car. After sitting for a long time however it's nice to stretch the legs. If you want to get up and stretch on a piggyback crawl carefully to the *back end* or *middle* of the car - preferably the middle - and stand up there. *Never stand at the front end of a piggyback or any other open car.* Whenever you stand up on an open car you're in a highly-vulnerable position. Protect yourself by clinging to whatever's available - which on a piggyback is usually nothing more than the side of the trailer (which isn't exactly designed to be held). Often trailers' sides are corrugated however and give you at least a little something to hang onto. Or you can hold onto the underside of the trailer. They often have a lip or apron underneath.

If you're on a standard flat piggyback with only one trailer you might foolishly be tempted to walk around the empty part of the car. I strongly recommend that you never, **never** do this. It's as risky as walking on an empty flatcar. You place yourself in an extremely untenable position. There's *nothing* to grab onto if the car lurches, jumps or stops quickly. If you simply *must* move around for some stupid reason on the open-air part of a flatcar do it by crawling or on hands and knees.

Empty flatcars are *even worse* than piggybacks for standing or walking around. You may be tempted to try your luck at some kind of highwire act standing or walking on the car. Resist the temptation. You'll see what I mean once you're out on one. It's not unusual to get a mild case of the totters standing on top of an empty wall-less car. It's the hypnotic 3-D effect mentioned earlier which can disorient you in unexpected ways at unexpected times. Unanticipated lurches and shifts make this a *very stupid* activity to engage in.

Don't stand or walk around on an empty wall-less flatcar unless you enjoy courting disaster or tempting the devil. There's plenty of thrill and adventure in this sport and no need to inject more into it. Stay down on the car and reach over to grab the side of the floor if the need arises. On empty bulkhead flats or center-beam bulkhead flats always keep a hand - and preferably both hands - on the front bulkhead wall when standing or walking.

On *loaded* flatcars where you're *always behind the load* you can stand up and stretch if you keep firm hold of the load or back bulkhead. The ability to hold onto the load depends on the load itself. Most often we have lumber coming from the Northwest. Sometimes the lumber is neatly stacked and packaged resembling a box with nothing prominent to hold onto except the sides of the load. Nevertheless always keep both hands on the load or bulkhead when you're on your feet.

Other times the boards *appear* to be different lengths. Some stick out from the rest of the stack. (Query whether the load was set down in this haphazard fashion or whether it's *shifted* in transit.) With this kind of load we have individual boards to get a handhold on. Use your gloves and make sure the board you're holding can't slide out any further. If the flatcar has another type of load (e.g., machinery, etc.) hold onto whatever's available.

On flatcars with intermodal box freight *if* there's any area remaining for us to ride it will be limited. The boxes are the same width as the car itself leaving no room to walk along their sides. This is good because trying to creep along the side of a box in transit would be the height of folly.

Thus you're confined to standing or walking on the narrow floorstrip between or at the *back* end of the boxes. If you simply must perambulate take firm hold of the box anytime you get near the edge of the car. Freight trains can be maddening and sometimes frightening beasts. Don't risk being overconfident when walking around on an open car.

At the other end of the scale in gondolas, deeper well cars and back units we have to be someone *very special* to fall off. Like getting an "F" in school we'd have to work at it. All three Pullmans completely wall us in so we'd have to purposefully vault out of one to fall from it. As we've mentioned however never sit on the top sill of a gondola. This is as dangerous as hanging your legs off the side of a car. There's nothing to hang onto up there. If you leave the cab of a back unit, always use the handrails of the long or short hood just as you use the grabs of a hopper or the lifelines at the gunwales of a ship.

As with sailing in time you'll get your "sea legs." You'll develop a feel for the motion of the train and will factor this in when choosing your steps. It's the same skill the conductor or waiter on a passenger train has, or a flight attendant. You'll walk with your feet tracing a wider path than normal. You'll learn to walk with your legs ever-so-slightly bent and separated to enhance balance and be prepared for jolts. You'll take slower surer steps. You'll learn to chart where you're going in advance.

Charting where you're going has a sliding scale of importance depending on the Pullman you're riding. The easier it is to fall off the more advanced planning is required. If the danger is great visualize where you're going and how to do it before setting out.

Please, *please* remember - it's easier than you think to get thrown off a train. Even if you don't get thrown off you can always take a good tumble if the train suddenly slows, stops or jerks. A train is constantly subject to the same violent jolts over the road as it is in the yards. Factor this in and rely on common sense to tell you whether it's smart to move around on your car.

Two final observations. First in a wreck there will be a split second warning before your car does anything radical. You'll hear the slack in the couplers and draft gears buff in with the rolling "Booooom" sound. Or worse you'll hear the rolling sound of units and freightcars stacking up ahead of you. Perhaps you'll have a 2 or 3 second warning - perhaps more. Pure reflex will determine how you react under the circumstances and no advice can be given. You won't have time to reflect back on these techniques. **That's why pre-positioning is crucial riding the rails.**

The second observation is *economy of motion*. If you're on an open car don't move around without good reason. Curiosity isn't a good reason. Neither is daring yourself. Don't climb around just for the halibut. With the exception of boxcars, gondolas, back units and hoppers every time you move the odds increase something unfortunate will happen. Be *conservative* in your choice of movement. Stay put in your safest position. Don't roam around on exposed cars. Minimize and plan movement carefully. And above all **hang on**.

Riding Loaded Cars

Whether you've had the luxury of canvassing the cars available on a train or not there's always a question whether to ride on a loaded car. It's a crucial safety question - one we've alluded to earlier.

Let's start with the sobering proposition the majority of hobos who bought the farm were asleep, inattentive or drunk and were crushed to death by shifting loads. Many are the gruesome warehouseman's tales of finding someone pancaked in a freightcar. The basic idea riding with a load is "Do you feel lucky punk? Well, do you?"

Therefore the general rule is: *Stay off loaded freightcars* - as always with notable exceptions.

The only good thing to say about riding with a load is it takes some of the roughness out of the ride and provides wind block. Not many cars are rough to begin with. Loaded cars minimize lurching and rolling however.

We know a freight train will always stop faster than it starts. Therefore a load will shift forward on a car more often than backward. Let's talk about backwards and forwards for a minute, then side-to-side.

Never, repeat **NEVER** get between the load of a car and its front wall or edge. If the train slows or stops quickly the load can crush you or shove you right off under the wheels. **ON ALL LOADED CARS ALWAYS GET BEHIND OR ON TOP OF THE LOAD.** When you're behind the load it will go the other direction from you if the train slams to a halt and you can rely on it to stop you rather than the other way around.

BAD ORDER TRACK AND EQUIPMENT ON THE RAILROAD

"Bad order" for a freightcar means the car is not roadworthy. It's in bad order. Many things can go wrong with a freightcar.

First of all the only thing which keeps a freightcar in one piece is *gravity*. The chassis or carriage (floor, walls, etc.) rests on top of the wheel trucks only by its weight. Same thing for the trucks resting on top of the wheel axles. In the absence of gravity the various components of a freightcar would float away separately. Because of the weights involved freightcar components constantly rub against each other.

One bad order problem which results from this friction is when a "journalbox" develops lubrication problems. The journalbox is the wheel assembly which connects the axles to the car trucks. The trucks serve as the intermediaries between the axles and the undercarriage and connect to the latter by means of swivel bearings.

All freightcars have 4 axles numbered (1) through (4) except for articulated piggly-wigglies and COFC well cars. Numbers (3) and (4) are at the A-end of the car while numbers (1) and (2) are at the B-end of the car. The four axles connect to the two trucks at each side by a journalbox. Thus we have 8 journalboxes per car. When one overheats it's called a "hotbox" or "smoker." Hotboxes are a big problem with older cars which have a more primitive lubrication system.

Given a freightcar's weight spinning steel axles rolling against the bearings in the journalbox generate an incredible amount of friction heat. To prevent over-heating freightcars have one of two types of journal lubrication - friction-bearing or roller-bearing.

The older friction-bearing method disperses heat by the use of grease. Journalboxes are packed with oil-saturated wool fibers called "waste." The greased waste provides a thin film of oil around the axle and bearing, allowing them to turn without burning up. The bearing is a babbit-faced brass design which sits on top of the axle by the weight of the car. Older journalboxes are unbeatable with just 2 lbs. of friction per ton of weight pulled.

But just like an automobile engine if a journalbox loses its lubrication it overheats. If the problem isn't caught in time the wheel seizes up. When a journalbox heats up it starts to smoke - or worse, melt and snap.

To prevent friction-bearing journalboxes from overheating carmen pull open the "hinged-lid" journalbox door with a metal hook, then pour industrial-strength gearlube (~120-weight) into the boxes. The axle overheats if they forget to oil a box at required intervals or the box leaks. If not caught in time a hotbox can heat up the entire wheel to a nasty dayglow orange. The journalbox can get so hot the axle softens and snaps under the weight of the car. Overheated journalboxes are a chief cause of fires and derailments.

After World War II hotboxes became more frequent when increased loads and speeds became common. Delays caused in cutting out cars with hotboxes increased exponentially. In part the problem was solved by replacing the loose waste packing with "spring-loaded wick-fed lubricator pads" but the problem has remained.

We can quickly detect a hotbox on an older car in front of us. Railcar manufacturers put a "hotbox alarm" inside journalboxes. Two capsules filled with different liquids melt as the heat rises in the journalbox. One liquid vaporizes and puts off a foul odor while the other sends off a dense blue smoke. Ahead or behind during daylight we can easily spot the problem because bluish smoke starts pouring out of the afflicted journalbox. And if we're behind it it stinks as if a pungent blue-smoke torch has been lit under the afflicted car.

This alarm system is only half as effective in America since cabooses are almost a thing of the past. No one is at the tailend to smell the vapor. FRED can't smell. The headend crew can't see the smoke at night. This means they have to be doubly alert and roll the train frequently. The unions argued eliminating cabooses would exacerbate the threat of hotbox fires and derailments - especially at night. No soap. America's 19,000-odd cabooses remain idle. Cabooses are still used in Canada.

Instead railroads place "infrared heat sensors" at various intervals along the track to detect hotboxes. The sensors are placed low between the ties outside the rails roughly every 8 to 50 miles. Each bearing rolls over the sensors as the train passes. If a hot bearing is detected a readout device in the cab alerts the crew. These sensors aren't infallible however and often aren't located where the problem develops. The cheaper the railroad the fewer the number of sensors placed along the track.

Hotbox detectors are the white boxes outside rails.

The hotbox problem has been greatly reduced on newer cars which have closed journalboxes with self-lubricating bearings called "journal roller bearings." This new bearing is similar to bearings in our autos. A group of self-lubricating bearings encircle the axle. These bearings supposedly stay lubricated until legally-mandated maintenance is performed. The latest model roller bearings ("NFL" or "No Field Lubrication") are certified to run 10 years before servicing.

NFLs are a great improvement over the old hinge-lidded gearlube-and-particle-waste boxes. All cars since 1963 have been built with roller bearings. Today 90-95% of the larger railroads' rolling stock is so equipped. Even many of the older hinged-lid journalboxes have roller bearing replacements inside. Although hotboxes are less of a bad order problem they still exist.

The minute a crewmember detects, sees or perhaps smells a hotbox the engineer stops that train so fast you'll think you're in a big hole situation. The crew know the minute a box overheats they run the risk of a very ugly fire or derailment. For a first-hand demonstration of railroad heroism in action watch what happens when a hotbox starts a car on fire. Marvel at how fast the crew moves to cut the car out and get it isolated before the fire spreads.

Another common problem is dragging equipment, usually brake rigging. Railroads have installed dragging equipment detectors for this problem. When activated the detector tells the crew to stop and approximates which axle back from the front (give or take four or five cars) has the problem. Load shift detectors use electronic sensors to notify the crew of loads that are outside the car's spacial limits or cars that are too tall to pass through an approaching tunnel.

Dragging equipment detector is the trip wire inside rails

With or without an elevated hump, car inspectors, carmen or carknockers are *supposed* to spot bad order problems before they turn into tragedies. *If* they spot a problem before a car goes out they hang a blue sign on it saying "Bad Order" and shunt it onto the rip-track. In many yards you'll see strings of bad order cars on deadend sidings waiting to be serviced or scrapped.

The hell of it is these inspection people *don't ride along* with the cars over the road. Unless there's something palpably wrong with the car - something a person can quickly eyeball - bad orders get sent out again and again without servicing. Very often problems aren't visible - problems which make cars jump around and smash freight.

Hotboxes for example are nearly impossible to visually detect until *after* they've occurred. As mentioned if a box gets hot enough the heat will turn the wheel orange. Afterwards when cool again the wheel is permanently discolored. If a worker spots such a wheel the car is immediately removed from service. Sometimes however railroads just aren't lucky and problems continue to occur.

Because the workers don't ride with the cars they're not there when freight arrives damaged at the loading dock. Railroads don't get wind of a problem until a shipper complains of receiving a shipment which is F-U-B-A-R ("Fucked-Up Beyond All Recognition"). Perhaps a warehouse complains about receiving a load of dented washing machines. The railroad eventually gets around to flagging the car for inspection and servicing. Not always. The odds get better each time we ride of catching out on a bad order car. In my experience roughly 5% of America's rolling stock is bad order, so our odds of catching out on a serious bad order run about 1 in 20. I've noticed in particular a recent increase in flatwheelers (see below). I'd say 1 in 8 cars has one, although most are not severe enough to cause discomfort (beyond the aural annoyance of a constant thudding sound).

Another bad order = shifting load problem is the "flatwheeler." A flatwheeler is a car which has a flat wheel on it. Simple enough eh? The wheel is not entirely round anymore. Part of its wheeltread has been ground down or out of round either by a brake or the rails themselves. We talked a bit about flatwheelers during the old brakeman-on-the-roof days. Today wheels are flattened differently. A flatwheeler is literally a pain in the ass.

Railroad wheels range in diameter from 28 to 38 inches and are made of either cast or forged steel. The most common way a wheel goes flat is by sliding instead of rolling down the railhead. Recall how brakemen in the 19th century caused flatwheelers by winding 'em up too tightly.

Today a wheel slides because its automatic brakes are badly aligned. When the engineer sets the brakes the badly-aligned brake clamps too hard on the tread. Instead of slowing, the wheel stops turning, slides down the rail and is ground flat. When the car rolls again each time the flat tread hits the rail it bangs on it and the car bounces. (One funny thing is a given flat wheel usually has only *one* flat spot on it. You'd think they'd have several if the brakes were oversetting all the time - the wheel would stop just any-old-place and get flattened in several spots. This doesn't seem to happen. My guess is when the flat part of the wheel hits the rail it provides just enough pause in the wheel's spin for the bad brake to clamp down and freeze further rotation.)

Railroads have tried to prevent flatwheels by installing sensing devices in the air brake system. One system, the Westinghouse Air Brake Company's "Decelostat" automatically changes the air pressure in the brake cylinder for an instant if the wheel hesitates. Then it applies pressure again when the wheel frees up.

But sometimes the sensor is out of whack, a wheel locks, slides and gets flat. Once you have an ear for flatwheelers you'll discover even the most modern equipment suffers from them. New hi-tech passenger cars, subways and light rail systems have them. This problem is far from licked.

The other wheel problem is the "out-of-round" wheel. The average service life of a railroad wheel is 200,000 to 350,000 miles. Sometimes along the way the punishment the rail metes out to the tread grinds it unevenly and the tread loses its roundness. The net effect of an out-of-round wheel is the same as a flatwheeler but not quite as pronounced.

The tough thing about flatwheelers and out-of-rounders is we can't know we're on one until just about the time the train is going too fast to get off. You know you're on a flatwheeler or out-of-rounder when you start hearing a continuous drumming sound underneath you, like "Dun-dun-dun-dun-dun-dun-dun-dun" which accelerates as the train picks up speed. When the train reaches normal cruising speed this constant thudding sound can make you crazy.

What's worse either type of wheel can make it practically impossible to remain standing upright, seated or lying down. And a loaded flatwheeler or out-of-rounder can bounce a load around in ways we'd never dream possible.

Similarly at times a suspension system on a car is bad order by being substandard or shot. Freightcar suspension systems are little more than giant coiled springs and/or leaf springs which cushion the carriage from the truck. You can see a car's suspension system sticking out the sides of the trucks on each side of the bearings. The system has to be quite stiff so cars don't sag or bounce to prevent slip-bys.

When a suspension system isn't operating properly we get the same feeling as in the old auto. Our auto bounces and sways around even at moderate speeds on decently-paved roads. Anything riding on a freightcar with bum cushioning gets the shit severely shaken out of it in no time at all - including us. We're in another bad situation. As with bum wheels we have no hint of the problem until the train is moving too fast to bail. Bad suspension systems further counsel against riding with a load.

When we're along for the ride with a load on *any* type of bad order car we have the old bull-in-the-china-shop dilemma. Where's the load headed next? Is it a rumba dancer, fox-trotter, waltzer, bunny-hugger, clogger, two-stepper, jerker, roger-rabbiter or what? Probably The Locomotion. Who will it ask to dance with next? We don't want to be on the dancefloor with a load when "The Bumwheelers" strike up the band.

The hell of it is since we never know whether we're *on* a bad-order car until the train gets up some speed, we have no opportunity to change cars until it stops. These are some of the potential risks we run riding with a load. Think long and hard before doing so.

Some railroads also have a lot of bad order *track*. They haven't put money into the road and their track is beat to shit. In this regard at least American railroads *admit* they operate over some pretty rough track.

Railroad track is much more complicated than a highway. With a highway assuming no one's cheating on materials and everything's done according to specification, a construction outfit grades, paves or pours it once and that's it. All one has to do is come back and patch the potholes - or repave the whole thing.

On the railroad each joint, spike, tie-plate, fish-plate, rail, tie and stretch of ballast requires regular massage and inspection. When it comes to physical plant there's no other commercial enterprise where so much depends on so little (except maybe cranes). Knock over just one rail at high speed and everything goes flying like a deck of cards tossed to the wind.

A loaded freightcar weighs up to four times its light weight. On joint rail the reduced stiffness of the rail at the joint causes greater weight to be exerted on the ties and supporting ballast underneath. This results in "low joints" which create resonant "rock and roll" for certain types and lengths of freightcars. If the railroad doesn't put money into the road by frequent ballast tamping, tie replacement and joint tightening the track definitely goes bad order. On bad order track *every* car on *every* train bobs, bounces, boogies and bows like a holy roller on Saturday night. Imagine what it's like on a *loaded* car under these circumstances.

When a railroad's fiscal sheet starts looking grim the first thing it cuts back on is maintenance. A euphemistic term of art exists for this grim reality - "deferred maintenance," which is corporate doublespeak for saying "Not today. Maybe tomorrow." At times the ICC steps in and requires a railroad's petitioned rate increase be linked to a reduction in its percentage of deferred maintenance track. Whether and to what extent deferred maintenance track exists is a lively topic in railroad corporate boardrooms. At minimum bad order track will continue to be a problem until neglectful railroads decide it's time to take care of Job One.

Rather than fix track lazy or poor railroads content themselves to send track inspection equipment over a stretch - as infrequently as possible. An even cheaper solution is to put a track inspector in the point unit to see how much it rocks and rolls over the road. In my opinion they ought to put these folks on a loaded freightcar. They'd get an *extremely* accurate idea of the state of the roadway. On cheap or poor railroads the general idea is: "Check to see how much more mileage we can get out of the track before we're forced to throw some money at it." Put another way the orientation is: "How long can we use the track before we make a wreck?"

As a last-ditch effort when truly cheap or broke, railroads run trains on failure prone track by issuing "slow orders" to all crews for the afflicted stretch. Engineers obey slow-orders out of self-preservation. The better an engineer knows management the more he obeys. Slow orders are taken much more seriously than speed limits.

To be fair not all railroads simply live with bad order track. The Santa Fe, Union Pacific and Southern lines have been historically conscientious about maintaining track. Notably bad lines include most northeastern roads (chiefly PennCentral, now Conrail), most "regionals" and "short lines," the Burlington Northern and the Southern Pacific. Investment in infrastructure tells us a lot about a country's long-range perspective - or lack thereof. Equipment and track maintenance tell us *a lot* about the attitude a railroad takes toward its work. Some railroads like railroading. Others obviously don't - or can't afford to.

If you've been bopping along at a good clip over the road then suddenly slow down and mope along at 30-40 MPH for a long spell while still on the mainline you'll know why - slow order.

Happily unlike other bad order equipment we can detect bad order track in advance. Take a look down a representative stretch of mainline or travel over it once. Unlike a bad order car, bad order/slow order track is there every time we travel it. You can make your *own* inspection beforehand. If you're on a highway paralleling a mainline you plan to travel take a look at the mainline. Is it nice and straight or is it bowed out at every joint, uneven and crooked as you scan the span? If the latter it *doesn't matter* whether the cars are bad order or not. You're in for a rough ride.

Bad order cars and track make riding a loaded car ultra-hazardous - particularly if you plan to sleep. What's more sometimes even with well-maintained cars and track ordinary car motion will cause a load to shift - backwards, forwards or side-to-side. This is especially true of freight which due to its sheer weight has simply been set down on the car in the hope it will stay stationary. Lumber, sheetrock and pipes are often relied upon to provide enough weight to compensate for sub-standard dunnage and bracing.

This is another *gravity* aspect of riding freights. Shippers all too often plop a load down on a car, maybe tack a few blocks around the foot of it or strap a few strips of restraining metal over it and hope everything works out. But as they say "Shit Happens." Loads can and do shift and we're at risk riding with them.

Gondolas, straight flatcars and flatcars with bulkheads present the biggest risk because there's NO EXIT. If a load waltzes our way we have to climb up and *stay* up on a wall or bulkhead or climb onto the coupler of a straight flatcar or climb up on top of the load, whatever it is. **NEVER, NEVER, NEVER ride in a loaded gondola.** A loaded gondola is the A-No. 1 cause of death for negligent hobos. Never ride a loaded boxcar unless you can climb on top of the load if it starts shifting. With any loaded car **think seriously about staying awake.**

Other types of freight such as cars/trucks, trailers, modular freight or heavy equipment are usually more than adequately chained, strapped or bolted down to the car. Loads won't move unless there's a full-scale wreck. The load may bounce but it won't *move*. Freight can bounce all it wants and that's fine. We get worried when it starts moving.

None of this shifting load danger applies to hoppers. We're never physically exposed to the load. It's all inside the metal walls of the car.

If we expose ourselves to a load it's safer to ride loaded auto racks, piggybacks and flatcars with modular boxes or heavy equipment. Of course there's still some risk. But life really is six-of-one-and-half-dozen-of-another isn't it? Unless you're an exceptionally secure, cloistered person (which to the adventurer is tantamount to boring) you never know which shoe will fall next. One can minimize risk in any sport but never entirely eliminate it.

To summarize: Always get on an empty car before getting on a loaded one. If you do decide to get on a loaded one, get *behind* the load, not in front of it or to its side. If it isn't securely fastened to the floor of the car keep your fingers crossed. Seriously consider not going to sleep, particularly under bad order circumstances. Keep your eyes closely glued to a load *regardless* whether it's moving or not. Check to make sure things aren't moving - even ever-so-slightly. A load moving ever-so-slightly covers an amazing amount of distance in an amazingly short amount of time. Be extra-careful around loads.

XV

WHAT'S THE DEAL WITH RAILROAD TRACK?

Now that we know what to ride and where to ride it this is a good time to talk about railroad track. Railroad track will become a very close friend riding the rails. We've mentioned a few ideas but many more are involved. The basic tasks railroad track perform are two-fold: 1) keep the train on the track; and 2) spread the train's weight over a large enough area to minimize damage to the rails, their hardware and the ties and ballast below. Let's look at how track is laid, why, what it's components are and how it's maintained.

To lay a track first a roadbed is graded. A perfectly flat grade is ideal but often unattainable. A track's grade is a function of its rise in feet per 100 linear feet of track. Thus a 2% grade of track rises two feet for every 100 feet of rail. Railroad grades rarely exceed 3%.

Once the grade is established "sub-ballast" of pit-run gravel is poured over the grade. Above it "top ballast" of crushed rock or mining slag is poured. Ballast is brought to the site in railroad-owned open hopper cars. During the ballast-laying process giant hydraulic "tamping" machines pack the ballast to maximum density. Ballast depth is a function of track usage (frequency and weight), curvature and grade. The more demanding the use the deeper ballast must be. Depths range between 6 and 30 inches off the grade.

Before dumping the last carloads of top ballast wooden railroad ties are laid down. A standard North American tie is 8 feet, 6 inches long, 7 inches deep and 9 inches across ("face" thickness). Lengths vary widely depending on track configuration and weight transfer requirements onto the ballast. A standard-sized tie weighs approximately 200 pounds.

190

Railroad ties in North America are made of wood due to our abundance of forests (except along high-speed, curvy or heavily-used track in the Northeast Corridor, the Rockies and Appalachians where cement or steel ties are used). Wooden ties need preservatives and fire retardents to prolong life. Tie manufacturers bore small holes into ties and inject up to 25 lbs. of preservative (usually creosote-based) into the holes. Ties are brought out on flatcars and laid down approximately 21 inches apart or about 3,000 ties per mile. The heavier the track use the closer ties are laid together. Once laid out ballast is tamped between them to cement them into position.

Next tie-plates (or "steel chairs") are laid down on top of the ties. Tie-plates are the intermediaries between the rails and ties and are the key component in the fastening system. They keep the rails from shifting sideways and distribute the train's weight over as large a surface of tie and ballast as necessary.

Tie-plates cover the face of the tie but vary in length according to weight-distribution requirements. On heavily-used mainlines tie-plates are as long as 18 inches. Each has a series of holes - from 4 to 12 - to spike down the plate to the tie and the rail to the plate. More holes than spikes leave "unholed" portions of tie available to allow maintenance crews to respike into a fresh portion of tie after a spike has worked out. More spikes are driven on curves where centrifugal force places added stress on the rail apparata. Once ballast, ties and tie-plates are in place the rail is laid down.

Early rail was made of stone - dating back to Roman times. Next came hard woods (too soft for a train's weight) then hard woods with iron strips fastened on top ("strap-rail" whose strips often peeled upward and ripped through car floors), then cast iron (hard but brittle) or wrought iron (not brittle but too soft) and finally steel. Refinement of the Bessemer and open-hearth means of rolling steel in the late 19th century brought steel's cost within the railroads' reach. In 1881 one-third of all rail was steel; by 1900 all mainlines had steel rail.

Viewed in cross-section rail is an upside-down "T" shape. The rail "foot" or bottom horizontal is wider than the railhead. This "flat-bottomed" design, invented by American Robert Livingston Stevens in 1830, provides great stability and has been adopted world-wide.

Interestingly the *weight* of a train keeps the wheels on the track rather than the spikes or rails themselves. Assuming the track is properly aligned and maintained the train's weight on the flat-bottomed rail keeps the rail upright.

The more steel per yard the stronger the rail. In North America new rail weighs between 112 and 145 pounds per yard and is 6 to 8 inches high. Higher speeds, frequent use, curves and heavy trains require use of heavier "poundage" rail. In freightyards where slow straight movement is the norm 70 to 90 lb. rail is adequate.

New rail is used on mainlines whereas yard, branch and secondary track is commonly laid with used or "relay" rail. On curves wear patterns differ and occur much more quickly on the "high" or outside rail. To prolong rail life railroads "transpose" rail from one side of the track to the other or to another location. Rail life can exceed 60 years and the date a rail was rolled is always noted along its length.

Two types of rail are used in North America. "Bolted-rail track" (commonly known as "joint rail") comes in standard lengths of 39, 45, 60 and now 78-foot sections. The original 39-ft. length corresponded to the standard 40-ft. freightcar to minimize "rock and roll." New rails are longer to accommodate longer freightcars. Joints (where two rails meet) are staggered down the line. Only one side of the wheels hits a joint at one time to further diminish rock and roll.

Joint rail is brought out on flatcars. Workers remove the rail from the end of the flatcar and lay it down on tie-plates. Once aligned into the proper gauge the rails and tie-plates are spiked down into the ties with hydraulic spikedrivers. The spikes used are called "claw spikes," also invented by Mr. Stevens in 1830. In industry parlance they're called "track fasteners." The "claw" at the top pins the rail to the tie-plate and the tie-plate to the tie.

Once spiked down rail joints are fastened together with "joint bars" or "fish-plates" - another Stevens invention. Fish-plates are long strips of thick metal bolted together as a clamp on the inside and outside of the rail to brace each joint. Four to six lockwasher bolts inserted through the rail and fish-plate brace up the joint. The head-ends of the bolts are inserted alternately on the inside and outside of the rail to prevent a derailed wheel from slicing off all the nut-ends of the bolts in a joint.

Joint rail has inherent problems. We've mentioned joints banging up and down and wearing out the underlying ties and weakening the ballast, resulting in low-joints. Another problem is temperature change which causes rail to expand and contract. This is a real challenge in the desert for example where a normal day's temperature fluctuation might reach as much as 45-50° F. To compensate for expansion and contraction rail is laid so each joint barely closes on the hottest days. During average to low temperatures the gap created by the shortened rail produces the clickety-clack, "din-din din-din, dun-dun dun-dun" sound we adore.

Another problem is "rail creep" which occurs where temperature changes or braking on steep grades (particularly with loaded traffic in one direction) causes rail to move lengthwise or "creep," forcing ties and switches out of alignment and making track buckle sideways. To combat creep heavy-duty track is equipped with "rail anchors" or "anti-creepers" - spring clips which snap onto the rail's foot and the tie to restrain motion. In extreme situations as many as four anchors per tie are used.

The chief problem with joint rail is maintenance. The larger the number of moveable parts in a track the more possibility something can go wrong. To avoid disaster railroads send out maintenance crews to retighten fish-plate bolts, redrive spikes and retamp ballast. This is labor-intensive - anathema to railroads.

Scouting parties are sent out to survey track. The old fashioned version of track surveillance equipment is a little gasoline-propelled track "motor car" on flanged wheels, usually painted orange. One or two workers go put-put-putting down the track looking for problems and making repairs as necessary. (Track workers also watch for approaching trains and at times have to hustle to lift the buggy off the track in front of one.) You'll often see motor cars off to the side of the track or stored in sheds at trackside. Today company pickup trucks are dually equipped with railroad wheels to roll down the line. "Track Geometry Cars" also roll over the track to check alignment.

To hold down on labor overhead and provide greater track durability railroads are adopting the use of "ribbon rail," or what executives call "continuous-welded rail." Ribbon rail is made from welded-together sections of joint rail, usually 1,500 ft. in length but at times up to one-half mile.

Rails are welded together at a central facility then loaded onto permanently-coupled "rail-trains" and hauled to the installation point. Steel though hard is also amazingly resilient. The welded-together rails bend around curves on the rail-train en route to the installation site.

At the site the train pulls out from under each pair of rails, which are spiked down after alignment. The few remaining joints can be replaced by on-site "field" welding with portable equipment. Between 0 and 100° F a 1,500-ft. section of ribbon rail contracts or expands *over 11 inches*. Thus to lay ribbon rail the ambient temperature must be near the hot end of the average fluctuation or the rail must be heated in advance. When temperatures change the steel stretches or contracts, slightly lessening its height and width. Each weld must be solid enough to avoid "pull-aparts" on cold days.

Another way to "ribbonize" rail is to remove the fish-plates from joint rail and field weld each joint together. When you see a guy bent over a rail welding he's turning joint rail into ribbon rail. Both new and relay rail can be ribbonized by field welding. Today close to 100,000 miles of track are ribbon rail. Although initially capital-intensive the savings in maintenance pay off over the life of the rail.

One problem all types of rail develop is "transverse fissures." These are fatigue cracks inside the railhead which begin where impurities in the steel exist. These fissures grow gradually under heavy prolonged use. If not detected in time the rail breaks under a train.

In the old days the only defense against transverse fissures was to keep a record of which mill produced which batch or "heat" of rail and where that rail was laid. When a failure occurred an entire heat would be removed. In 1926 the "Sperry Detector Car" was developed using a magnetic (now ultrasonic) process to detect and pinpoint flaws as it rolls over the rails. Moreover back at the steel mill new technologies such as inert-gas stirring and continuous- or vacuum-casting produce cleaner rail. Remember however rail life can exceed 60 years. Some of the old rail is still out there.

We mentioned the fact rails dish out a real pounding to freightcar wheels. This works both ways. On close inspection you'll notice a railhead develops pits and marrings. To combat pitting the "Speno Rail-Grinding Train" travels down the track grinding the railhead into a new smooth surface. Along the way it emits rail-grinding debris, "grind-wheel" smoke and an ear-shattering screech.

Another aspect of railroad track is alignment or gauge. A railroad's gauge is the distance from the inside edge of one railhead to the inside edge of the other. The North American gauge is 4-feet, 8-1/2-inches (1435 mm.). Thus the same freightcar can run from

Alaska to Central America on three countries' track. 4'-8-1/2" is "standard gauge" used throughout the world.

As you can imagine standardization of gauge facilitates transfer of freight from one railroad or country to another. Non-standardization causes traffic snarls. During the 19th century countries with unfriendly neighbors tended to select different gauges, either through nationalist pigheadedness or to prevent use of their railroads during an invasion - like Spain under Franco, France and Poland near Bismark and Finland next to the Czars.

In Europe today the end of the Cold War and reunion of east and west make standardization of track gauges imperative - particularly in light of the EC's projected union this year. Ireland, Spain, Portugal, Finland, Poland, Bulgaria, Rumania and the former USSR have non-standard gauges. International rail traffic remains a real headache.

At borders crews have to stop and readjust the gauge of the wheels on an entire train. Some countries with frequent international traffic (France [standard] and Spain [5 ft., 6 in.]) have these readjustments down fairly well. It takes about an hour on an average-length train to change wheel gauges. At other borders however freightcars must be off-loaded and freight placed in new cars at "break-of-gauge" points. This dulls railroading's competitive edge.

Differences in gauge were by no means unknown in North America. While 4'-8-1/2" was standard it was by no means nationwide. Through the 1870s at least half a dozen gauges existed. The Erie Railroad used a whopping 6-foot gauge, the Pennsylvania a 4'-9" gauge and many Southern roads a 5' gauge. In the South nonstandard gauges were employed primarily to prevent *ante-bellum* Northern railroad dominance. Several mountain roads like the Denver & Rio Grande used gauges as narrow as 3 feet. This plethora of gauges was a constant challenge in early American railroading, tangling domestic passenger and freight transport right through Reconstruction.

One early solution for railroads with close yet different gauges was to employ "compromise cars." As with most compromises these cars never pleased anyone. One railroad running on standard gauge for example would meet another running on 4'-10" track. Compromise cars had wide wheeltreads which completely covered the standard-gauge railhead, but were too narrow to cover all the railhead on the wider gauge. Under normal operations everything went smoothly. But any motion which threw the wheels too far off-center on the wider gauge could result in a derailment.

After a number of spectacular compromise car wrecks the compromise was abandoned in the 1880s. Although President Lincoln designated 4'-8-1/2" as the gauge for the first transcontinental railroad in 1863, variances persisted until 1887 - mainly in the South. That year 3,000 miles of track were changed to standard gauge *in a single weekend.*

The laying of rail in the last century was the stuff of tale and legend - and intense competition. Even today kids learn the story of John Henry and his race against the steamdrill. John Henry won the race, but lay down his hammer "all painted red" saying to his Captain "Please tell 'em I'm gone. Won't you tell 'em I'm gone?" ("John Henry" - Mississippi John Hurt.)

While building the transcontinental railroad the "Big Four" of the Central Pacific, Charles Crocker, Mark Hopkins, Collis P. Huntington and Leland Stanford bet the Union Pacific's Henry Farnum and T.C. Durant their "gandydancers" (tracklayers) could lay more track in a day. These bets were based on the following track-laying realities:

Cantonese laborers in the West (who sailed the Pacific to "Old Gold Mountain") and European immigrants in the East prepared the grading, ballasting, laying of ties and positioning of tie-plates. Some distance behind them mainly Irish gandys loaded 39-ft. rail onto 40-ft. flatcars. A locomotive pushed the loaded cars to "end-of-track." Here the gandies lifted the rails two-by-two off the flatcar with hand-held tongs and pulled them out ahead. They'd ease the rails onto the tie-plates, drop the tongs, pick up hammers, spike the rails down and bolt them together. On the Great Plains they were often obliged to drop hammer and pick up rifles when buffalo or hostile Indians came calling. Once a flatcar was emptied they'd tip it over off the track, roll up the next one and recommence.

The big men's track-laying bets weren't entirely fair. From Omaha to Wyoming the UP was coming across essentially straight flat prairie while the CP was blasting, digging, filling and trestling its way across the western mountains and deserts. UP won the early races.

Yet the Central Pacific eventually won the bet. On April 28, 1869 the laborers and gandys laid down TEN miles and 56 feet of track - and still had time for lunch. This was just shy of a mile of track an hour - no small feat considering the antiquated methods used to lay track 120 years ago. This record still stands.

XVI

WHAT WILL THIS TRAIN DO NEXT?

Let's move to the next important aspect of the sport: Figuring out what your train will do next. We begin by focusing on two common situations: Either you're on a train poised to leave the yards or you've been rolling along over the road but have stopped for some reason.

PHYSICAL POSITIONING OF TRAINS AS A CLUE TO DEPARTURE

Develop a sense of where your train is located right now. Two examples: In the yards is it among the group of tracks in the departure yard where trains get sent out to where you're going? Or are you over the road but in the hole with power coupled up waiting on a red signal?

CLUES IN THE YARDS

The numbered tracks in larger yards are divided into different functions. There's a distinct logic to the way yards are laid out. Let's suppose one set of tracks is used to hump up trains while a second set is used to hump others out of existence.

Suppose you're in hypothetical Yard X in Town Y of State or Province Z. Yard is a small flat-switching yard. It has a single-track mainline running east-west on its north side. South of it branching off along switch leaders are 20 tracks.

FREIGHTYARD

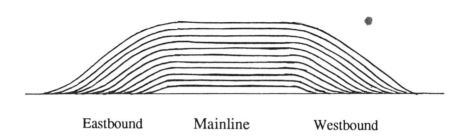

Eastbound   Mainline   Westbound

(Illustration by Bruce Miller)

The first two tracks are reserved for trains going into the hole either for approaching trains on the mainline with priority or to wait while the crew conduct business. The third track is reserved for switch engines so yardcrews can run up and down the yards. This is called the "run-around" or "thoroughfare" track. Tracks 4, 5 and 6 are reserved for humping up eastbound trains which wait for power to go out. Some trains are too long for the yard and are "doubled over" on two or more tracks. Tracks 7 through 14 are separated from the north six by an access road. These seven tracks are used to sideline dead but unhumped trains or to sidetrack various blocks of cars with low priority. Further south is another access road. Tracks 15 through 17 are used to hump up westbound trains. Finally tracks 18, 19 and 20 are used for track maintenance and wreck equipment, rip-track, bad order and condemned cars. Let's further posit today you're going eastbound.

1. Two strings catch your eye on tracks 4 and 6. Because you know the layout of the yard you know they're slated to go east. If one has power, air up and a "red plaque" or FRED on the last car find a Pullman quickly. The train is ready to go.

2. Same situation but neither string has power. You have more time to canvass the train, find some 1000-mile paper, etc.

3. Same situation but you know when power's called and it's not time yet.

4. A train has power and is standing on the single-track *main*line. You know it's eastbound because either the power or the red plaque/EOT/ FRED tell you so. It's blocking other over-the-road traffic and won't be there long. Find something to ride quickly.

5. Your train's on the mainline but has no power. It could sit for a while.

6. The train's on double-track mainline with power. Find a Pullman quickly.

7. The train's on double-track mainline but doesn't have power. Same situation as No. 5 above.

8. Your train's off the mainline and the yardcrew's still humping cuts onto it. You have at least an hour. The carman or carknocker hasn't hooked up the hoses and rolled the train for bad orders.

9. If only 20 cars are on the eastbound track you have more time than if there are 90. A 90-car train is nearing over-the-road readiness while a 20-car train isn't - unless it's very hot or a peddlar.

Another question is *where* a train will go. In smaller yards with only one mainline the answer is clear when they put power on. It's on an eastbound yard track with power on the east end = eastbound. Same thing on the mainline. Power on the east end of one mainline = eastbound. Same thing with the red plaque or FRED on the west side of the string. Use your atlas to confirm your surmise.

In larger yards things get more complicated. Often mainlines split at the yard limits into two directions - say, north and east at one end; south and west at the other. Find somebody to ask which way a train you're interested in will go. If you can see bills of lading like auto stickers check their destinations.

If there's no-one to ask or shipping instructions to read play the percentages. Say you're in Houston and want to get up to Dallas. The mainline you're looking at runs east-west but you know this railroad goes to Dallas and New Orleans. If Dallas or further north is where this railroad does most of its business you can take an odds-on gamble. Most of the time you'll cut north to Dallas.

Let's say you've never ridden this road before but you have an atlas. One track goes to Large Metropolis; the other to Small Metropolis. Chances are the train will go to Large Metropolis. Same thing if one track is the company's mainline while the other is a spur line. Stroll out to the yard limits and see if the diverging tracks tell you anything about frequency of use. Then climb on and keep your fingers crossed.

Over the Road

Over-the-road trains often stop to pick up or cut out cars.

1. If it's a brief cut-out or pick-up the traincrew does the work (but they're paid extra to do it). Whether the cut is from the front, middle or back of the train, the power goes off into the yards, drops off cut-outs and/or picks up add-ons. When finished they come back on the mainline to recouple and proceed. This can take anywhere from 10 minutes to an hour or more.

2. If it's an extensive reshuffling the traincrew turn the job over to a yardcrew. The power uncouples and goes off somewhere to wait (usually the roundhouse or depot). A yard billy knocks the train around until they have it right. The power comes back (perhaps with a new crew) and off you go. This takes longer and you have more time to make your decisions.

3. If unsure whether the train itself or your car will continue find somebody to ask or wait to see what the final consist is.

4. Your train is rolling over single-track mainline but stops on the mainline with the power coupled. Guaranteed you won't be there long. Nine times out of 10 you're waiting for something up ahead to clear into the hole. Stick with your car.

5. You stop on the mainline but the power uncouples. This usually means the crew's leaving to do business with customers. You have at least 5 or 10 minutes to do something - usually longer.

6. Get a general idea how long you'll block the mainline by noting how many trains you've passed today. If you pass lots of trains you won't block traffic long. But if you haven't seen much traffic today you could be there awhile.

Also factor in the *kind* of train you're on. If you're on *single-track* **mainline**:

1. Peddlars by definition do lots of business. They stop and fool around everywhere.

2. Regular trains vary widely. We never know with regulars unless we ask in advance. Stop-and-go or straight shooters - it's always a tossup.

3. Hotshots, unit trains, dedicated piggybacks and land-bridgers rarely do business along the way. They keep moving unless something gets in their way.

Double-track mainline: With double-track it's unlikely anything's in the way. Opposing or slower trains are switched to the other track on a cross-over track so you can pass. Either in yards or out over the road it's hard to tell what will happen when a train stops on double-track. We could be there 1-2 minutes or sit for an hour. In general when in doubt play it safe and stick with the train.

What *kind of siding* are you on?

1. If you go onto a "dead-end siding" it's unlikely you'll do any business. The headend is trapped. Your train probably has to clear the mainline for something else and this siding is the only thing available. You back out to continue onward.

If a deadend siding comes off the mainline in the headend direction it's called a "facing-point" siding. If it comes off in the tailend direction so the train would have to back up to get onto it it's called a "trailing-point" siding. Most sidings come off the main then re-attach, called "double-ended" sidings. Others do the same but branch out along a switch leader into additional sidings (like in the yards) then branch back on along another switch leader. Some go off to a factory's loading dock or under a grain elevator. Some like spur lines go off who-knows-where into the distance.

2. Take note of the sidings along the right-of-way. In the hole you can put 2+2 together with other information to figure out how long you'll be there.

3. Look at the *rails* on sidings you're passing.

a. Are the railheads shiny (used often) or rusty, bowed out and abandoned-looking? On single-track mainline if your siding is shiny and its switches automatic the less time you'll be on it. Your railroad uses it as part of a system-wide traffic-routing scheme. Hopefully your train will stay in the hole just long enough for the higher priority train(s) to clear your siding. If you're on a rusty old rarely-used siding one of three things could be happening: Your train is (i) doing business with a relatively infrequent customer; (ii) something unusual has happened on the mainline ahead of you; or (iii) there's something wrong with your train. Odds are you'll be there longer.

b. Are the sidings long in distance like two or three miles or more, or fairly short? The longer the siding chances are the shorter time you'll be there.

c. Are there lots of sidings along the way or only

one every 10 or 20 miles? Greater frequency points to customer service while less to traffic routing.

     d. Do the switches on and off the sidings operate with automatic switching equipment or are they manual? Automatic means traffic routing while manual means customer service.

    4. Check to see which siding you're taking when you pull onto a siding in a yard.

     a. If you go only one track off the mainline you probably still have a viable train.

     b. If you get buried 9 tracks over between other strings and the power dynamites your train is history. It's definitely history if a worker comes along and bleeds the air. Time to find another freight unless you're where you want to be.

Moreover there are lots of physically-inhibiting things to take into account. Switches have to be thrown, tracks crossed, other trains cleared, hoses hooked up, air pumped back, signals changed, crews changed, business done over the road, etc., etc., etc.

LISTENING TO THE AIR, OR, WHAT IS THE POWER UP TO?

Whenever you've been traveling over the road and come to a halt, *check to see what the power's doing.* Being able to actually *watch* what it's doing works best, but often isn't possible if trees, land, curves or buildings block the view. If you can't see out one side try the other.

If you can't see the headend *immediately after the train stops listen closely to the air.* Every time a freight train stops it does one of two things:

1. As or right after it stops you'll hear the crew break the air - or you won't. If the air breaks you know the power has uncoupled. The engines are headed somewhere. You have an automatic 5 minutes to do whatever you want because even if the power immediately recouples (which is unlikely - why would they have uncoupled to begin with?) it takes time to recouple, hook up the air hoses, pump legal air all the way back, get everyone in the cab, get the bell, get the throttle and go. You're safe enough to at least jump down and take a look at what's going on.

2. You stop but the air stays up. You may only be waiting for something to clear before going. Listen closely to the air before making any moves. Is it making that steady, low hissing sound? If so the power is still on. The train's ready to go and could pump up air and take off at any minute.

3. You stop and the air keeps hissing steady and low. Then it's pumped back up and the brakes release. *Do not leave your car.* The train's readying for departure.

Here's a **very important** note of caution on leaving a train in the hole. If the power stays coupled and you're waiting for something to clear and *if* you cross to the *other* side of the mainline there's a risk of getting cut off by the passing train. Your crew might start out of the hole *before* the passing train clears. By the time the passing train clears *your* train might be moving at a good little clip. Your car definitely won't be in the same spot you left it. To avoid this unpleasant surprise:

1. Take note of what your train does with passing trains on prior sidings. If the engineer recommences travel at the earliest possible moment (before the other train clears) forget crossing the mainline. You run the risk of being cut off.

2. Keep listening to the air. If you don't hear anything you're fine. The power's not back on and you can calmly reattain your Pullman. If the air comes up turn back. The train's getting ready to leave. If you've rambled a distance from your car start jogging *if not flat-out running* back to your Pullman.

LET THE CREW HELP YOU TO KNOW WHAT TO DO

You'll notice traincrews are a distant and curious bunch. They're way up there at the headend - small bodies doing nondescript things the effect of which we can only watch and guess at. But watching a crew provides additional clues as to what a stopped train will do.

A yardcrew will *never* take a train out over the road farther than the distance they have to retrace or turn to get back in one shift (perhaps with some overtime). A traincrew will *never* do any significant amount of switching in the yards. Perhaps a yardcrew will take a peddlar out a few miles and cut out or pick up cars here and there. And maybe a traincrew will cut out or pick up a few cars in the odd yard or out at a few customers' sidings over the road, but never anything intensive. Keep in mind *which kind of crew* are working your train.

If you can see power or hear air but don't know if anyone's up at the headend, while looking for a Pullman take a walk up there to figure this out. When a crew come out on the power you're probably out of there pretty soon. Figure out whether the over-the-road crew have come out. Get up close to the headend to see if someone's elbow is sticking out the on-the-point unit's window, or if someone is visible in the cab.

Over the road we have a different set of circumstances. The only time we'll see *anybody* from the traincrew is when the train's stopping or stopped (unless somebody visits us in the back unit). When a train is slowing down it's a good idea not only to figure out whether you're going into the hole but also *take a look up ahead to see if anybody is getting down from the headend.* Whether in the hole or still on the mainline if a crewmember gets down from the cab it's business time, or they're rolling a passing train, or there's a track or equipment problem. We may be there awhile.

Going into the hole has lots of safety and commercial implications so it deserves a bit more development. This is so because for the sportsman the procedure is a dear friend - and at times a hated adversary.

When a train gets a signal to go into the hole with manual switches a brakeman at the headend jumps down and *runs* out ahead of the train. He manually throws the switch before the train "hits" the siding. The engineer "drifts" the train down to around 5 MPH behind the brakeman. This is a closely-timed operation.

The brakeman unlocks the switch padlock with his railroad-issued key, pulls up the switch lever, leans on it with all his might, turns it around to "throw the points," pushes the lever down again and re-padlocks it. All the while the train is slowly bearing down on him. If he doesn't make it around in time the train passes on the mainline then has to stop, back up and come at it again. If the train hits the switch when he's halfway around the points are halfway between tracks. The engines' wheels can split the difference and the engines will likely derail.

In the old days if a switch needed to be thrown often enough railroads hired a special guy - a real bonafide Switchman - to sit in a little shed by the switch for 8, 10 or 12 hours waiting to do his thing. Especially during slow periods this was not an exciting job. Presumably the expression "Asleep at the switch" originated here.

Assume you're on a peddlar with a caboose. After the headend brakeman throws the switch he climbs back into the cab as the train slides into the hole until the caboose clears the mainline. But the mainline is still blocked by the open siding switch. As soon as the caboose clears a brakeman at the rear throws the switch back over to the mainline, following in reverse the same procedure as the headend brakie.

Once the passing train clears the on-the-point brakie throws the headend siding switch open to the mainline. He climbs into the cab and the train pulls onto the mainline. Now the mainline is blocked *again* by the open siding switch. The caboose-end brakie jumps down as the caboose clears onto the mainline to close and lock the siding. He has to *run* after the departing caboose to catch on as the engineer drifts the train before they take off.

Fellows can tell how good buddies they are with the engineer by how hard he makes them run. In the old days if a train was running behind time friendship didn't enter in the picture. Not only is this procedure labor-intensive, it's dangerous. Automatic switches do away with the process.

On today's cabooseless trains at a manual switch, instead of having guys at the tailend to close switches a guy from the headend has to do everything. He drops off, opens the first switch onto the siding then closes it for the mainline. Then he has to walk all the way up to the headend - the long walk. After the passing train clears or they're done with business he opens the headend switch and waits for the train to clear onto the mainline. Then he has to walk the whole train *a second time* to get back to the engines. You can imagine what fun this gets to be after the third siding on a 160-car train. But using the old switches saves on overhead (except in protest over having eliminated cabooses [jobs] engineers often back up the whole train to pick up the stranded brakeman, costing the company many additional gallons of fuel). As a time consideration manual switching requires our considerable patience.

In the interest of saving money many smaller railroads haven't automated their switches. As a general rule on any railroad the only automated ones are on sidings which are used to route traffic. Customers' switches are still largely manual and require the switchman's waltz described above.

What does all this mean in terms of keeping an eye on the over-the-road crew when slowing to a halt? Since *most* routing-around switching is done automatically on the big railroads, when a brakeman *does* climb down out of the cab it means business, or he's required to roll a passing train or there's a problem. Make sure they're not about to cut your car out.

Which raises an interesting point. What do we do if it looks like they want to cut out our car? A brakeman has climbed down and is approaching you. Better get your gear together. You may have to take quick action.

Keep an eye on the brakeman while throwing your stuff together. Maybe you'll pass him. He'll probably step up to a car behind yours and pull the cut lever. Then he'll lean back with the lever up and signal "go" to the headend. The cars he's standing by uncouple and your half of the train pulls ahead. You're being taken somewhere which is a sure sign you're at least *at risk* of being cut out. Here's where thoroughly canvassing your train pays off in advance. It's your judgment call what to do.

All is not lost in this situation. Unless you're riding a peddlar where *all* cars will be cut out (otherwise why bring them along?) railroads try to block cut outs toward the headend. This makes for less uncoupling and coupling and less walking for the crew. It's also easier to see the brakeman's signals since he's not far away.

Often a train can't be blocked perfectly. A train made up of empties in front and loads in back can be unmanageable. Tonnage has to be carefully balanced. Thus your train can have cars in the middle or back to be cut out. Or the crew may have orders to pick up cars to be blocked at the middle or backend. Much also depends on the variety of tracks and switches a crew have at their disposal.

Let's say the cut outs are toward the back. The power has to uncouple, use another track (maybe the mainline) to go around the train, get back on your track, couple up, uncouple the cut outs and everything between them then head to the drop off. By comparison if the cut outs are toward the middle the crew can pull the front half of the train to the far end of the customer's siding (length of siding permitting) then back the ordered cars onto the siding, pull forward and return. Same thing if the cars are at the front of the train.

One fun type of switching to watch for is called the "running" or "flying" switch. Assume the headend faces a deadend facing-point siding. Obviously the cut it needs to drop is behind the engines. There's no way to get behind the cut to push it onto the siding because the rest of the train holds the back door shut. If the engines pull the cut onto the siding they can't get back off.

Some distance before reaching the siding switch the train stops. The cut is made and the engines and cut accelerate rapidly. The engines brake briefly to cut slack into the cars' couplers. A brakeman riding at the cut pulls up on the cut lever and loosens the knuckles. Then the engines accelerate and break away from the cut. The engines pass the switch ahead of the free-rolling cut but stay on the mainline. Before the cut itself reaches the switch a second brakeman throws the switch over to the siding. The cut rolls onto the siding and the first brakeman uses the brakewheel to spot it. Timing is crucial in fly-switching. Many things can go wrong and the flying switching is increasingly limited, discouraged or forbidden - but lots of fun to watch.

Another reason it's best to ride toward the back of a train is the ideally-blocked freight has cars 1 through 5 blocked for Customer One, 6 through 18 blocked for Customer Two, etc. In the quite common less-than-ideal blocking situation however a great deal of shifting and fiddling must be performed by the over-the-road crew. Here are some typical options we have when they might cut out our car:

1. Where is the cut in relation to your car? The closer the cut the more likely you'll be cut out.

2. What's around you where you're stopped. If it's a business which uses your kind of car the more likely you'll be cut out.

3. Can you speak with the brakeman to find out what their intentions are? If so do so. They'll tell you if your car is slated for cut-out. The information might save you a lot of hassle.

4. Perhaps they're just picking cars up. Are cars standing nearby which look loaded (tough to tell with enclosed cars - check dogtags)? Example - sawmill with no empty woodcars on your train but five loaded ones sitting on the mill's siding.

5. Do you know of another safe Pullman on your train you can reach?

In general if you're way up from the cut I'd say take a wait-and-see attitude. If you're the last car I'd say jump. If you're within 8 or so cars of the cut I'd also say jump - especially if it's a big plant which looks hungry for your car and you know of a rideable car on the rest of the train.

When confronted with a cut-out possibility the rules are as follows: The smaller the customer the less likely you'll be cut out - unless you're very close to the cut in the train. Odds are stay put. A big customer can gobble up half a train. If you're not sure whether it will be you or not *and* if you know of a rideable car on the rest of the train, jump down and go for it. If you don't know of such a car or you know there isn't one *and* you're not sure if you'll get cut out I'd say stick with your Pullman and keep your fingers crossed. If it's pretty clear you will be cut out because you don't see anything to be picked up, you're near the cut or riding the kind of car needed, get down and find something rideable behind you or wait for something rideable to come back. If you're not sure and ride along to discover it's not you who gets cut out, no harm no foul. But what if you *do* get cut out?

If you ride out to customerland and they cut out your car be ready to move quickly. You have five options:

1. Walk or run back to the rest of the train and grab a new Pullman before the units beat you back. This is the most likely scenario.

2. If you're too far away to walk or run back to the train find a car to ride back on but *make it safe.* Don't hang onto a ladder if you might lose your grip. DO NOT ride couplers.

3. If they take you a long way away and there's no safe car to ride back on, get into one of the back units to get back to the train then find another Pullman as quickly as possible.

4. Hitchhike away, chalk it up to bad luck and let the train go - if you're near a road.

5. If there's no road around get back on that train *any fucking way you can.* Throw yourself on the mercy and good offices of the crew. They'll never leave you high and dry out there miles from nowhere. In fact it's one of *their* chief concerns as well. They'll always help us out rather than leave us high and dry. Leaving a hobo in the dust could border on criminal negligence or worse.

Of course all this assumes we're awake. If you sleep soundly you could wake up to a real surprise someday. Don't worry about this too much because if you sleep soundly while the train is making all its racket you'll likely wake up when it falls silent. You might want to consider sleeping in your clothes and even leaving your boots on. If the crew find you asleep they'll awaken you rather than leave you behind. If they don't find you all I can say is it will be very nice to have a map, a good pair of boots, a compass and some water on this sad day.

We have yet another aid in the quest to figure out what our train will do next. It's called the signals. The Block Signal System.

XVII

RED-YELLOW-GREEN—LET THE SIGNALS DO THE TALKING

The railroad signaling system is a big deal in our sport. It gives us lots of information about what to expect next. Let's talk about signals - how the system developed, which signals to read and what they mean.

We've all seen old photographs of steam locomotives stacked on top of each other like toys after a head-on collision, with little men standing by looking important for the newspapers. As the volume of rail traffic increased between 1830 and 1895 railroad accidents increased proportionally. The problem reached scandalous proportions as early as the 1850s. Gory pictures and details of collapsed bridges, derailments, head-ons, rear-ons, side-ons, break-away trains, mangled cars and bodies filled newspapers, tabloids and magazines. For over 60 years among the most popular illustrations and photographs in America were those depicting grisly railroad accidents.

Although braking and coupling problems were eventually solved another major problem remained unsolved - the signaling of trains to make engineers aware of other trains' whereabouts. It was a major problem which needed a major solution.

The railroad signaling system developed over the course of many years, lots of trial and *plenty* of error. The first signal system was no signal system - the "Smoke and Headlight Rule." If an engineer saw the smoke of an approaching train by day or its headlight by night he was required to stop until everyone sorted out what to do next. This proved unsatisfactory, particularly during spats of bad weather. All too often a run-of-the-mill prairie meet turned into a "cornfield meet" (a head-on collision). Creative minds set to work resolving these annoying occurrences.

213

The challenge stemmed from the speeds involved. Railroading was the first transportation system where stopping distance exceeded sighting distance. Thus some means beyond an alert engineer was needed to assure a train ran on clear track. Taking their cue from maritime lighthouses and buoys railroaders decided they needed a system of *signals* to help crews figure out what was happening around them.

Railroads tried pretty much everything in the book to use for signaling. Before the days of bright oil-burning lamps they built fires and sent up smoke signals (I'm not making this up), or put a flatcar in front of the locomotive with a bonfire blazing away, or had guys on horses with signs, or used variously-configured lights, colors, balls, flags, kites, yardarms, discs, crossbars, semaphore, telegraph, miniature trackside explosives, horns, whistles and bells. They even strung up orders to grab as the train rolled by. Early signals were enormous. They loomed against the sky to be seen far enough away to safely apply handbrakes. Try as signal inventors might however nothing worked the way railroads wished things would. Trains kept piling into each other and climbing the rails in more or less direct ratio to the increase in traffic. The Las Vegas (N.M.) *Optic* commented in November, 1883 there hadn't been a collision on the Santa Fe in Northern New Mexico for *over a month*.

As a comparison early automobile motorists had the same problems - especially at intersections. Ever hear the one about how there were two automobiles in the whole state of Ohio in 1902 and one day they *ran into each other!* The handwriting was on the wall. Something had to be done.

Horses were in complete accord. Did you know there were more horses than people in America until the 1920 Census? Horses did not like cars - or trains. And neither did their owners.

Early motoring signal solutions were as bizarre as the railroads' - and as ineffective. State laws required for example that you climb down from your car before crossing an intersection, walk forthrightly into the middle with a big brass horn and honk a couple of times - to warn horse-propelled travelers of your intention to cross. Buggy drivers didn't want anyone sneaking up in a tin lizzy.

Finally railroad and automobile geniuses arrived upon the red/yellow/green signaling system which is known, used, loved and ignored the world over. It took a lot of death and injury and a lot of head-scratching before today's railroad signaling system was perfected.

The first truly *technological* signaling innovation in America came in 1844 when the Baltimore & Ohio Railroad (always a farsighted road) introduced the use of telegraphy for maintaining communication. The first use of a telegraph for *dispatching* a train from a station came in 1851 at Turner (today Harriman) New York. Erie Railroad Superintendent Charles Minot used his recently-installed telegraph line to issue a train order - a message changing the prairie meet point between two trains. Minot had to get out and run the train himself - the engineer wasn't about to disobey his preordained timetable.

The safety aspect of using telegraphy was its ability to confirm whether engineers actually *got* the message. Telegraphic "timetable and train orders" ("T&TO") came into vogue. In telegraph dispatching an operator signaled orders ahead to the next station as a train passed by or pulled out. This helped immensely from station to station but left over-the-road crews in the dark as to the approach of other trains. Conductors often had to stop their trains, climb a pole to hook up to the telegraph wires with a portable key and wire to find out what was going on or to notify others of a problem.

Out on the treeless plains those big old buffalo *loved* to scratch themselves on telegraph poles. This often resulted in temporary gaps in communication. Believe it or not buffalo interference with telegraphy was a major justification for blowing them away to near-extinction. Severe weather was another daunting problem. Ice storms, blizzards, high winds, floods, fires and locust consistently knocked out large stretches of communication. Simply locating where the line was out was a major challenge. Getting someone out there to fix it was something else again.

The telegraph's contribution to railroad safety should not be diminished however. Its use to signal a train's whereabouts represented an enormous improvement over earlier methods. (As recently as February 1992 for example Albania's national railroad abandoned all passenger service when citizens began stealing the copper wire from railroad telephone lines.)

Nevertheless telegraphy left much to be desired. By the 1860s railroads had grown quite fond of their arms, balls, bells and whistles, etc. (especially the Highball). "Automatic" signals were in use as early as the 1840s - automatic only in the sense a train would run over a piece of wood or metal or pull a string and a signal would change mechanically. The human element was never far away. Humans had to reset the signals which increased their unreliability. Confusion among signalmen was common. After one too many wrecks owners decided to give colored lights a try.

The English were way ahead of us in signaling. The first non-automatic telegraphic block system came from England to America in 1865. Next automatic block signals by telegraphy arrived in 1866. We invented electric track circuiting in 1870. A "lock and block" system was introduced in 1882. After a series of patent duels and modifications the track circuiting automatic block system was adopted in North America. Trainwrecks diminished dramatically.

The "Track Circuiting Automatic Block System" is used today along with its more-sophisticated little brother, "Centralized Traffic Control" (CTC). Keep in mind however the way railroads use red/yellow/green is completely different from the automobile traffic engineer. The railroad system bears almost no relationship to the motoring message of the medium.

The first light signaling system wasn't red/yellow/green but red/yellow/*white*. White meant "go." As electric lights became common in the 1890s however and engineers' confusion mounted railroads were forced to change to green for "go." The FRA made use of a white light illegal in 1918 since a missing or stuck lens could give a false clear signal. Interestingly even the use of red/yellow/*green* didn't solve all problems - at least not at first.

One problem railroaders quickly discovered was some people are red-green *colorblind*. One in 100 men can't tell the difference. Nobody knew what a common affliction this was until railroad engineers were forced to decide whether to stop or start their trains by colored flags or signals. Red-green color-blindness is quite prevalent among Native American males. Not only were Navajo and Sioux languages used for secret radio transmissions during World War II (the enemy couldn't decipher them because they had no written form), but the Allies brought Native American males along on aerial reconnaissance missions because they could *see right through* camouflage. Native Americans definitely did their part during the war. Fortunately or not depending on your perspective few Native Americans became engineers.

On the railroad engineers with this peculiar affliction regularly roared past flags and signals, much to the chagrin of passenger and passersby alike. On many railroads you couldn't work if you were colorblind. One effort to solve the problem was standardizing the positioning of signals - red on top, yellow in the middle and green on the bottom. This way even if you didn't know which *color* it was you knew what to do by the *position* of the signal. The large majority of automobile traffic signals worldwide are arranged this way for the same reason.

Surprisingly according to the railroads the primary purpose of a signal system is not to increase safety. It's to increase the capacity of a track to handle traffic. At least that's what railroads say as they blithely rip up double-track and rely on signaling to carry the day. Before addressing how train signals work let's talk about their shapes and positioning.

Railroads call their signaling equipment "wayside signals." We'll simply call them "signals" for short. Signals are attached to the top of what a motorist would call a light standard but which (due to signaling's nautical origins) on the railroad is known as a "signal mast."

The most common railroad signal has only one light called the "searchlight" signal with a round black "bull's-eye" or "target" backing which provides contrast to the light and the daytime sky.

On a minority of roads signals are still designed with three light positions - red on top, yellow in the middle and green at bottom with black backing, called the "position light" signal.

On still fewer roads the older "semaphore" or "upper quadrant" system remains where a moveable arm coupled with lights for nighttime signaling controls the action. A straight up arm means go, 45 degrees means caution and horizontal means stop.

A tiny minority use "colored position" signals which are too complicated to explain easily. In regions with a rigorous winter railroads put a "visor" around the signal so it isn't blotted out by snow.

On railroads which have come into line with the standard target signal, signals have *one* (instead of three) white high-intensity bulb with a super-directional lens. Instead of issuing diffused light like an ordinary lightbulb the lens channels or "polarizes" the light waves into one direction so a signal is visible from a much greater distance. Signals no longer have to be enormously tall as in the old days. Since World War I when electric lamp and lens systems were developed which were bright enough to see against the sun, most railroads have adopted colored light systems and abandoned mechanical semaphore systems. With the searchlight design one of three colored lenses, red, green or yellow, snaps into place in front of the white light to signal orders. With the less common position light signal the lenses of the three lights also polarize the light. Like on the highway the signal changes color by illuminating one color's bulb and extinguishing the others.

Another important concern is *which* signal governs our train. Please bear with me through the following description. Railroad signals aren't as simple as first meets the eye. To read them right their operation must be developed meticulously.

The question which signal is which is best illustrated in a big yard. Looking toward the end of yard you might see 2, 3, 6, 8 or more signals staring back at you. Usually each has its own mast. Other times a series of signals cross the tracks on an overhead span called a "signal bridge."

Which signal applies to us?

The Mother of all signaling rules is: *The signal immediately to the right of the track your train is on in your direction of travel controls your train.* To illustrate this point imagine for a moment you're an engineer.

Where are you sitting? On the right-hand side of the train in its direction of travel. This is opposite the left-hand side most of the world's motorists sit on. One sees how England got the jump on us in railroading. Think like the English. Signal-wise get on the right-hand side and look out ahead to understand what's going on.

Remember our description of the physical layout of a diesel loco-motive? The cab is located toward one end of the unit (except on a few old billygoats where it's in the middle). On a road switcher the short hood of the on-the-point unit always faces forward for maximum visibility. Optimal vision is important for an engineer with all the goofy stunts people pull around moving trains. Back, slave or helper units can face either direction (the reverse/selector handle lines them up to pull in the right direction).

In the on-the-point unit with its cab forward the engineer sits on the right side of the train. The only signal facing him of consequence to him is the one *directly to the right of his track.* This is the signal *we* also want to keep an eye on.

Maybe I'm a bit of a slow learner but it took me a good deal of time to figure this out. Before English railroad engineers would agree to design a developing country's railroad (which we were at the time) they insisted things be done their way. One example of this is that English trains like their cars pass each other on the left. We kicked this habit and today on double-track in North America (where it still exists) trains normally pass on the right, just like driving. Our engineers however sit on the outside of the action as would an English driver on an American road. Due to English insistence other railroads run backassward in countries all over the world. (Paris is a good example. Whereas French-designed Paris "Metropolitan" {"Metro"} subway trains pass on the right, British-designed Parisian-subur-ban "RER" {"Reseau Express Regional"} trains pass on the *left*. People constantly reach for the wrong door on the RER.)

Of course there's an exception to the signal-to-the-right rule. In a big yard or out over the road some railroads use signal bridges instead of trackside masts to post signals. With a signal bridge the signal controlling your train is directly overhead.

YARD SIGNALS

Don't be overly concerned with signals in the yards. They tell us what's coming or going on main tracks but have little bearing on when a new train will leave. Individual yard tracks don't have searchlight signals. Yardmasters usually give the final "Highball" by radio. Crews rely on dwarf lights or semaphore indicators on switches. Watch where the power is vis-a-vis your train coupled with information gleaned from passersby, listening to the air and watching which crew are doing what. More than signals, people call the shots in the yards. Put another way the main benefit derived from knowing how to read signals comes once we're over the road.

OVER THE ROAD SIGNALS

Over the road signals are our close friends. They help us figure out what our train will do next. Keep an eye on the signal to your right as you roll. If you're on straight track or track curving to the right you can see signals far in advance. In hill country, dense forests, a mile back from the headend or tracing a big slow curve to the left your view of signals is limited (for example going southbound around Lake Ponchartrain north of New Orleans or northbound around it on the Norfolk Southern - the longest continuous railroad curves in North America).

The color of a signal is known as its "aspect." As a *general* proposition red means "stop," yellow means "approach" with caution and green means "clear" or go for it. On the railroad however there are many situations where the same colored signal means different things. We'll use illustrations to flesh out these situations one at a time. First let's look at the big picture. Let's talk about the system itself - the "Automatic Block System."

The Automatic Block System ("ABS," "track section system," or "block system" [which I use]) is railroad lingo for the most common signaling system. Think of a mainline as being divided into sections or "blocks" of about two miles in length. The length of a given block is determined by the distance a train needs to stop. A block must be as long as the longest stopping distance for the heaviest train on the route, traveling at maximum *authorized* speed. Block lengths increase where heavily loaded trains run at high speeds. Blocks are less than two miles long through hilly or curvy country where trains move slowly, or longer than two miles through straight flat terrain where they roll.

Generally speaking each block has two signals at each end - one facing each direction and *roughly* two miles from the next pair. The track between the four signals is the block. Each time you pass a pair of signals you've moved onto a new block.

Each pair of signals is wired to the track. Along the wire is an electronic sensor called a "track relay." Each block of rails has a low current of electricity running through it emanating from trackside batteries. This current passes through the track relay to the signal. The circuit remains complete across rail joints by "electric bond wires" which run from one rail-end to the next. When the wheels of the on-the-point unit hit a new block the wheels interrupt or "shunt" the current. Instead of flowing in a circuit through the rails, relay and signal the steel wheels draw the current up into the train itself. The track relay senses the interruption and tells the signal you've hit its block. The signal changes from green to red. As you roll along you'll see your green signal flip to red up ahead within a few seconds after the headend shunts the new block.

The block system is "fail safe" in the sense that as long as *any* of the train's wheels are on *any* portion of the block, or the battery fails or a rail breaks, the track relay can't pick up current and a clear signal won't display. The presence of the train itself on the block protects it from approaching traffic. "Track circuiting" was invented by American Dr. William Robinson in 1872.

Some block systems are more complex than others. Each railroad establishes a blocking sequence which best suits its needs. The standard arrangement is the "two-block, three-indication" system. But "three-block, four-indication" and "four-block, five indication" systems also exist. Blocking sequences concern the engineer, not us, so their subtleties are not developed here.

Let's say you're stopped on a single-track mainline facing a green signal on the right on a standard block system. When an opposing train approaches, your signal first reacts when that train hits the rails two blocks (about 4 miles) away. Your green light turns yellow. When that train hits the rail on the next block closer (2 miles away) your light turns red. Thus even if your engineer can't see the approaching train the signal gives him an excellent idea how far away it is and how quickly it's approaching.

Some signals are "absolute" in the sense a red light means "stop and stay" stopped. The signal can only be passed by a train order overriding the signal. In contrast a "permissive" red signal allows the engineer to "stop and proceed." He has to come to a full stop but then may proceed - usually at 15 MPH maximum - but be ready to stop short of another train or other obstruction. Permissive signals are identified by a number plate on the mast or a second signal light in a lower, staggered position from the upper. If your train stops then immediately starts again but rolls slowly look for a permissive red on your right.

On less heavily-traveled routes a "manual block" system is used. Instead of running current through the track human operators set the signals. Before signaling a block is clear the operator must verify by radio or telephone that any train which was on the block is now clear of it and keep written records for the next operator. Although relatively primitive this system is quite satisfactory. The FRA allows a maximum speed of 79 MPH for freight and passenger trains on either an automatic or manual block system.

Surprisingly about half of America's track mileage is "dark" or has *no* signal system. On this track usually only one train at a time is moving. On dark track speed limits are 49 freight and 59 passenger. We rarely find ourselves on dark track, which generally serves marginally-profitable parts of the country (e.g., Midwestern grain belts) and is quickly being abandoned by the big roads when they get ICC approval to do so. New "Short Line" railroads (generally 150 miles or less) acquire much of this track and make it profitable.

A recent innovation is "cab signaling" where approaching signals are brought up from the track into the cab of the point unit. The signal can't be obscured by snow or fog and is backed up with an audible alarm to alert the crew of track status changes.

The big signaling innovation is Centralized Traffic Control. CTC is a system first implemented in the 1930s. It's used in all big yards and on roughly 50,000 of America's 155,000 miles of mainline. CTC extends the idea of the block system over a much larger area - say 200 miles or more. As a train approaches instead of each block controlling its signals independently all signals and switches are wired into a "communications center" where traffic operators set switches and signals. The communications center directs traffic in either direction, allowing for centralized control of priority. Each center has a big board of winking lights showing the color of every signal, set of every switch and the location of every train in its territory (or "division"). Traffic controllers keep engineers radio- or telephone-advised about traffic in the vicinity miles in advance. (Note: Railroads use the terms "division" and "district" differently than workers and wayfarers. Railroads and railfans talk about this "district" or that "subdivision" of this "division." To avoid confusion for purposes of this book a "division" is where trains change crews, as the term has meant for workers and hobos for decades.)

We know we're in CTC country because railroads are proud of having it on line. They put up signs saying "Start CTC" or "End CTC" so everyone relaxes in the knowledge Big Brother is handling things.

Even though railroads are cheap and CTC-ing track is expensive its use allows railroads to tear up double-track. More track is more expensive. Recently CTC communication has begun moving by microwave transmission. With CTC or cab signaling trains can exceed 79 MPH - track and equipment allowing. The latest advances in signaling technology represent a big improvement, but something better is sure to come along.

The important thing is no matter whether you have the most primitive block system or CTC, modern signaling equipment lets an over the road engineer know when someone else is nearby. "Nearby" on the railroad is like the Navy - within 10 miles.

(If the Illinois Central had the block system on April 30, 1900 near Vaughn Mississippi, Casey Jones would never have died with his "hand upon the throttle." Casey would have known a freight train ahead of him which was too long for its siding had its caboose hanging out on the mainline. He wouldn't have piled into it. The story of Casey Jones is illustrative of the dangers involved in relying upon single-track with sidings for trains to pass each other. Casey was running a passenger train "behind time." He passed the headend of an opposing freight which was in the process of executing a "saw-by." A saw-by is where a train which is too long for its siding lets a passing train roll by its headend, then curls out onto the mainline and clears the rearend before the passing train gets there. Casey was going too fast for the freight to get its caboose out of his way. With signals he would have known the freight hadn't finished its saw-by and would have stopped.)

Now for some illustrations of the types of situations which different signal configurations represent. "WB" means westbound and "EB" eastbound (since most North American railroads run east and west). "SR" means signal red, "SY" yellow and "SG" green. "D" means dark signal. "S1" means the higher signal on a mast and "S2" the lower. ⊃ means train and its direction of travel.

WAITING FOR A TRAIN

1. WB ———— S-G/R ————————————— S-R ⊂ EB
You

WB train approaching. SG/R tells engineer track is clear WB until he hits the block and it turns red behind him, while SR tells EB train (if any) to stop.

2.

WB ___C___ S-R ⎯⎯⎯⎯⎯⎯⎯⎯⎯⎯⎯⎯⎯⎯⎯ S-G/D ⎯⎯⎯⎯⎯ EB
                        You

WB train has passed. SR tells following WB train (if any) to stop. SG/D says no such WB train exists.

3. WB ⎯⎯ S-G/D ⎯⎯⎯⎯⎯⎯⎯⎯⎯⎯⎯⎯⎯⎯ S-R ⎯⎯⎯⎯⎯ EB
                        You

EB train has passed. SR tells following EB train (if any) to stop. SG/D says no such EB train exists.

4. WB ⎯⎯ S-G/D ⎯⎯⎯⎯⎯⎯⎯⎯⎯⎯⎯⎯⎯⎯ S-G/D ⎯⎯⎯⎯⎯ EB
                        You

No train approaching from either direction. If both Ss are G, "constant-lit" RR. If both Ss are D, "non-constant-lit" RR.

5. WB ⊃ S-R ⎯⎯⎯⎯⎯⎯⎯⎯⎯⎯⎯⎯⎯⎯⎯ S-G/R ⎯⎯⎯⎯⎯ EB
                        You

EB train approaching. SG/R says track clear EB and SR tells WB train (if any) to stop.

6. WB ___C___ S-Y ⎯⎯⎯⎯⎯⎯⎯⎯⎯⎯⎯⎯⎯⎯ S-G/D ⎯⎯⎯⎯⎯ EB
                        You

WB train has passed but two or more blocks away. SY says caution to approaching WB train (if any). SG/D says no such train exists.

7. WB ___C___ S-Y ⎯⎯⎯⎯⎯⎯⎯⎯⎯⎯⎯⎯⎯⎯ S-R ⎯⎯⎯⎯⎯ EB
                        You

WB train has passed but is now two or more blocks away. Second WB train approaching. SY says caution to approaching WB train of first's location. SR tells EB train (if any) to stop.

8. WB ————————— S-G/D —————————————————————— S-Y ⊃ EB
      |
          You

EB train has passed but is now two or more blocks away. SY says caution to following EB train (if any). SG/D says no such train exists (opposite of No. 6).

9. WB ⊃ ————— S-R ——————————————————————— S-Y ⊃ EB
          |
              You

EB train has passed but is now two or more blocks away. Second EB train approaching. SY says caution to approaching EB train of first's location. SR tells WB train (if any) to stop.

10. WB ⊂ ——— S-Y ——————————————————————— S-Y ⊃ EB
          | |
              You

WB and EB trains have passed & are now distancing themselves from you. SYs say caution to approaching WB or EB trains (if any) of trains' locations.

11. WB ⊃ ——— S-Y ——————————————————————— S-Y ⊃ EB
          | |
              You

EB train has passed but is now two or more blocks away. Second EB train is approaching, but is two or more blocks away. WB SY says caution to approaching WB train (if any). EB SY says caution to approaching EB of first's location.

12. WB ⊃ ——— S-Y ——————————————————————— S-G/D ——— EB
          | |
              You

EB train is approaching but is two or more blocks away. SG/D says track clear EB and SY says caution to approaching WB train (if any).

13. WB ⊃ ——— S-R ——————————————————————— S-R ⊂ EB
          | |
              You

EB and WB trains bearing down on each other, each within a block (rare). SRs in either direction tell each to stop immediately. Prairie meet could become a cornfield meet.

RIDING A TRAIN

1. WB   S-G/R ⊂ S-G/R ⊂ S-G/R ⊂ S-G/R ⊂ S-G/R ⊂ EB

WB train has clear track as it hits each block. SG/R signifies all clear WB, then for a following WB train (if any) to stop when the first train's headend shunts the current and the G flips to R.

stop
2. WB ⊂⊃   S-R   S-R ∪ S-Y/R⊂ slow S-G/R ⊂   S-G/R ⊂   EB

WB train has clear track until the third block. SG/R signifies all clear WB, then stop for following WB train (if any)(see No. 1 above). SY/R signifies caution and slow at third block- other train ahead WB but two or more blocks away (Y signals also flip to red after being passed). SR means stop. Another train (either WB or EB) is blocking track less than two blocks away. Train must stay stopped (unless a permissive stop-and-proceed signal, ordered to proceed or block turns SG or SY).

slow   slow
3. WB   S-G/R   ⊂ S-G/R   ⊂S-Y/R ⊂ S-Y/R   ⊂ S-G/R   ⊂ EB

WB train has clear track until second block. SY/R signifies caution and slow at second block - other train ahead EB or WB but two or more blocks away. SY/R caution continues on third block, usually meaning you're trailing a slower WB. SG/R at fourth block signifies leading WB has cleared mainline. Whatever was blocking track ahead - WB or EB has cleared - probably into the hole. SG/R signals proceed again.

S-R   stop   slow   slow
4. WB   S-G/R ⊂ S-G/R ∪ S-Y/R ⊂   S-Y/R ⊂ S-G/R ⊂ EB

WB train has clear track etc. SY/R signifies caution/slow through second and third blocks. SR means stop - track ahead blocked. SR changes to S-G/R and train is free again WB. You probably had to wait for something to go into the hole.

GOING INTO AND COMING OUT OF THE HOLE

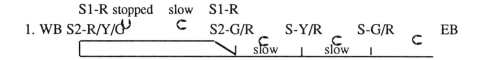

WB train has clear track until block two. Block three's top signal S1 is R. Bottom signal S2 is G, signifying main line is blocked but siding is open. Train slows and goes into the hole. S2 flips R to signify WB train has blocked siding, leaving both eastern S1 and S2 R. At western S1R/S2R your WB waits until the approaching train (WB or EB) clears the siding. S2 turns Y or G to return to mainline while S1 stays R so you're not rearended by another WB.

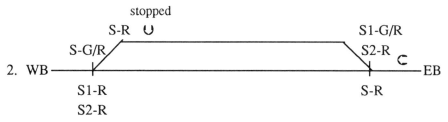

WB train passes your train in the hole. Eastern WB S1G/R for approaching train. WB S2R tells approaching train of your WB in the hole. Western WB SR on siding tells your train to stay put. Western WB SG/R beckons approaching train to clear siding. Western EB S1R and S2R tells EB train to stop immediately, as does eastern SR.

WB train now past your train in the hole. Eastern WB S2R stops third WB train (if any) from entering siding and rearending you. Eastern WB S1R stops any third train from hitting you as you return to the mainline. Eastern EB SR stops EB trains (if any). Western siding SG/R allows you to return to mainline. Western EB S1R stops any mainline EB train. Western EB S2R stops any EB train from trying to enter your siding.

As you can see the more signals surrounding you the more confusing it gets. The solution is to watch every signal you can see. By watching the way the signals change in relation to each other you can deduce what's coming or going from each direction.

There's only one more trick to rounding out your railroad repertoire: How to get off a moving train without getting mangled. We'll cover this in detail because the technique changes depending on what kind of car you're riding.

XVIII

HOW DO I GET OFF A FREIGHT TRAIN?

We know trains sometimes slow way down but don't stop. First let's mention one thing to keep in mind when they do stop. Then we'll talk about how to get off when they don't.

Many times trains stop exactly where we want them to. On *rare* occasions this can be truer than we could ever imagine. Then too at times trains stop in places we'd very much rather they hadn't.

Obviously to get off you have to wait until your train slows way down. If you've planned your trip carefully by consulting a railroad atlas you'll be lucky. The train will slow or stop where you want to get off. But railroad atlas or not, trains slow down or stop wherever they want to.

In any event ready yourself and your gear several miles before your destination. If it's your first time over this road you won't know whether the railroad stops to change crews or does it on the run. Be ready for either procedure. When approaching a town you'd like to visit get ready in case the train slows down enough to bail. Maybe it will stop for some reason even though you're not at a division. The key idea is to be ready so you're flexible.

The fastest speed a person can get off a freight train without eating it is around 20 MPH. For folks like you and me with normal appendages and strength it's considerably slower - like around 15 MPH max. The key question is *why* you're getting off before the train stops. How *compelling* is your reason to bail beforehand? The higher the speed the more compelling your reason should be.

There are two ways to get off a moving train. The first is to literally jump off. The second is to use the ladder/grabs and stirrup to lower yourself down as you would on any ladder. The first technique is rather primitive;

231

the second highly sophisticated. Knowledge of each is necessary and let's take them in order.

JUMPING OFF A MOVING FREIGHTCAR

This is a technique we use about half the time - either because of our car's logistics or because time is short. The logistical reasons for jumping off a train are simple: (1) you don't have time to get back to the ladder/stirrup to climb down; or (2) you can't *get* to the ladder and stirrup (like on a boxcar or modular freight flatcar) because a wall or box blocks your path.

The first thing to do is summons up your courage. It looks rather scary staring at the ballast passing by underneath. It seems farther down and sharper than it's looked before. An analogy is sitting on the bed of a high-up flatbed truck driving over ballast and contemplating jumping off. Regardless you have to jump.

The first thing to do is PUT ON YOUR GLOVES. *This* is the situation where they're most needed. Protect your hands if you tumble. You will be *so happy* to have gloves along. They provide confidence as you psych yourself up for the lunge.

Next look out ahead to make sure no signalblocks, switching equipment, dwarf signals, sidings or other obstacles are approaching. Be particularly on the lookout for dwarf signals along yardtracks. If you hit one you'll go for a cartwheel.

Likewise with sidings coming off the track. Don't jump down where you run the risk of having to fast-foot your way around rails, switches, frogs and ties. Look for clean clear ballast as your landing strip.

Once assured you have a clear runway *toss your gear off before you get off.* Nine times out of 10 you don't want to jump holding any gear. Its added weight can make you lose your footing.

The only exception is if the train is going fast and you think you'll dump when you jump. In this case consider keeping your backpack on. When you jump you can do a somersault and land on your gear, butt and the back of your legs. This is like the gymnast's floor-ex stunt of running down the mat, diving head-first and rolling over in a somersault - except he springs back onto his feet and does a couple more fancy rolls and flips. You'll wind up on your back.

If you know you'll roll plan ahead visually how to do it. It goes without saying the best way to make first contact is on your feet. Once on the ground when your momentum pushes your torso ahead faster than your legs can follow, quickly curl forward, hit the ground with a shoulder, flip over and wind up on your back - or even your feet again. Curl up into as tiny a ball as possible and roll, being careful to protect your head as you go over. Once on your back kip your legs out flat to keep from rolling more than once. It's helpful to wear a jacket for cushioning. A hat's not a bad idea either. Your backpack helps soften the impact and stop the roll. A variation is to land quickly, turn around backwards and land on your back with the pack on then skid a few feet.

In the ordinary situation where you're reasonably confident of keeping your footing, get rid of the gear first. There's a special way to throw gear off a moving train. Take hold of it in one hand while keeping firm hold of something on the car with the other. Then *lob the gear backward off the car.* By "backward" I mean against the direction of travel. Use an underhand toss. Hang the arm holding the gear as low to the ground as possible. Then swing it underhand behind you the same way you slowpitch a softball. Tossing your stuff off backward reduces its landing impact. If the train is going 13 MPH but you lob the gear backwards at 8 it hits the ground at 5. If properly packed with soft contents it easily survives.

If it's light you can throw your gear far enough away from the track so it doesn't hit the ballast - assuming the ballast only goes a few feet out to the side of the track. This is great for two reasons. First if the bag lands on dirt its fabric and contents stand a better chance of escaping damage. Second you eliminate the possibility of the bag rolling up onto the track.

Limber up your legs if you've been seated for a long time. Then sit down on the side of the car. Make sure no obstacles have snuck up since you lobbed the gear off. Turn facing as far forward as you safely can and hang your legs over the edge. This is the ONLY time you hang your legs over the edge of a moving freightcar and ONLY because you've checked in advance for clearance. Next place your hands at the sides of your hips. Push yourself off the floor and *away you go*. While in the air turn the rest of the way forward so when you land you're facing the direction of travel. Make sure your legs and mind are running before you hit the ground.

When you hit the strength in your legs will slow you down. To stabilize yourself keep hold of the car if possible for the first few steps. Always try to do this. As soon as you're sure you won't tumble let go of the car and get away. Make tracks turning out away from the train. Depending on speed it takes anywhere from 8 to 15 strides to break your inertia and come to a halt. Collect yourself, shake it out, reflect on a mission well accomplished, get your gear and lowline.

One final note of caution: No matter how badly you want to get off a train for whatever reason, **don't risk your personal well-being any more than *you* think is warranted.** In other words don't get off a fast-moving freight unless you have to. If there's *any* chance it will slow down further give yourself more time until it does. Resign yourself to walking a bit farther or being more devious exiting the yards. If your concern is the bull, remember he rarely stops us on the way *out* of the yards. His job is to keep us off trains and out of the yards. Once off a train and leaving the yards his job is done. It's the bull's favorite job, too. He doesn't have to lift a finger.

All this is chalked up to common sense. You be the judge of whether the risk is worth the reward. In case of doubt I'd suggest: (1) wait; or (2) get ready to roll.

CLIMBING DOWN THE LADDER/STIRRUP

Using a ladder and stirrup to disembark is more sophisticated than simply jumping off a car. It's also a lot safer. *Whenever you have a choice -particularly when the train's moving in the 10-20 MPH range- use the ladder.* You can access the ladders on any freightcar except a boxcar or a COFC flatcar with a box in the way. Straight flatcars and most piggybacks only have a grabiron - no ladder. Nevertheless whenever possible avail yourself of this handy technique.

Before climbing on the ladder and stepping into the stirrup make the preliminary check up ahead for obstacles. Limber up and put on the gloves, jacket and hat. Lob the gear off backwards in advance.

Next swing onto the ladder. The most important thing on the ladder is to keep both hands firmly holding onto a rung AT ALL TIMES. It's the same idea as climbing over couplers. Never hang there one-handed. Trains can jolt at any moment. Once securely on the ladder climb down into the stirrup. Get both feet in it and keep both hands on a rung of the ladder.

Here's where the real art comes in. While standing in the stirrup you're facing the side of the car, 90 degrees to the direction of travel. You have one foot in back of the other (closer to the tailend of the train). It could be your left or right foot depending on which side of the car you're on.

Keep both feet in the stirrup while rechecking your landing strip. Next lower your hands one at a time to the rung which is at waist or fly level. The lower the better. This way your hands are low enough to keep hold of the ladder for support when your feet hit the ground. Then to lower your center of gravity stick your butt out and down from the car. Make a final clearance check.

In this position many hobos use a traditional technique to determine whether the train's moving too fast to get off. They stick their back foot down until it grazes the ballast. If their leg kicks up and they boot themselves in the ass the train's moving too fast.

When you take your first step off the stirrup to the ground do it with your **BACK FOOT FIRST**. This runs counter to instinct but is a brilliant nexus between momentum and human physiology. Step down with the *back foot first*. You'll feel awkward the first couple of times doing this but it works.

Once your back foot hits the ground your front foot will follow it out of the stirrup. Hang onto a low rung of the ladder with your inside hand as your legs slow you down. When you're confident you won't tumble let go of the ladder and get away from the train, get your bearings, take a deep breath and retrieve your gear.

The best way to learn this technique is to watch switchmen use it in the yards. Watch as they ride around humping and switching cars. The man hangs on the ladder. When he gets to where he wants off he sticks his ass down and out and steps out of the stirrup with his back foot first. Then light as a feather he alights from the train and walks off to do his thing. It's pretty to watch - much like a ballet movement. Switchmen make it look effortless. And in no time at all it is. Back-foot-first makes getting off freightcars a breeze compared to *jumping* off them.

The same principles apply getting off a back unit. Instead of a stirrup however we have a bottom step which is lower to the ground than a stirrup and makes things even easier. Instead of rungs or grabirons we have a white or yellow handrail on either side of the stairs. This makes quick disembarkment a piece of cake. Once ready, face the unit with your heels hanging off the bottom step. Step off with the back foot just like stepping out of a stirrup and hang onto the railing until you've got your balance. You're home free.

One final note. While watching workers get off stirrups and ladders also watch how they get *up* on them as cars roll by. If the car they want to mount is rolling slowly they might step up with either foot. But if the train's got up some speed, *every time* they step up with their back foot first. If you put your front foot into the stirrup first it can slide backward and block the space for your back foot. If you slip using your back foot first you'll spin out away from the train. Watch for this neat little trick. It helps us catch out on the run.

XIX

PATIENCE IS A VIRTUE ON THE RAILROAD

Patience is the most important virtue we can develop riding freight trains. Its concomitant, impatience, is railroading's greatest vice. It takes patience to wait for the railroad to perform. Patience comes into play not only waiting for a train but also once it's underway. Patience keeps us from blowing a gasket or busting a gut riding the rails.

Just when everything is rolling along sweetly your train can go into the hole. Boom-boom-boom down into the hole. Then you sit there. You sit there long enough to start getting *real* curious about what's going on. You climb around the car and check the signals. None of them changes to answer the question. Neither does the air. It makes its maddeningly steady hissing sound. The headend doesn't uncouple. No crewmember is down doing anything. Everything is dead stop and for the life of you you can't figure out *why*.

O.K. Now you have to fall back on other traveling aids to figure out what's up. By knowing the territory (or checking your atlas or map) you can figure out where you are. Let's suppose however you don't know where you are or when you'll next get under way. It's not like you can stroll to the headend and holler up at the crew, "Hey, whenner you guys gonna move this thing?" No. Definitely not an option.

If you approach riding freights with the firm expectation there will be long time outs you can enjoy them - and learn something about yourself in the process. You'll learn to resist the driving forces of ordinary life. Ordinary life generates impatience - impatience for any delay or unforeseen eventuality.

When downtimes occur riding the rails - and they will - there's a whole range of things do to with your time. One of my favorite pastimes riding freights (and one I'd happily recommend if you don't already enjoy it) is admiring the natural surroundings. Just stay put in one place. After a while you'll notice you're surrounded by little bits of nature here and there which fascinate and amuse, even in the middle of North America's premiere bombed-out cities. Birds, insects, flowers, plants and yes, even the earth itself are available to admire.

North America is a beautiful place. We've been blessed with a veritable cornucopia of natural beauty. Revel in it riding the rails. Take time out to admire the reasons why we have so much to be thankful for. It's been an incredible gift, America. Savor it.

Admire the unfathomable precision with which nature works her handicraft. Watch the sun race its course across the sky on a frosty winter's day. Ponder how man has added to and diminished nature's wonders. Despite the crush and hassle we endure take a minute to simply stop out there in the heartlands and heal yourself with some good old-fashioned country peace. Without becoming transcendental let's just say you should do yourself a favor and take a brief moment - or respite if you will - of relaxation.

You'll find each time you hit out over the highline your patience for life in general as well as for your sport increases. You'll find yourself more tolerant of delays, missed opportunities, missed trains, no trains, late people and those inevitable, incomprehensible foulups life is so full of. In the process you'll grow more appreciative of your surroundings both natural and manmade (assuming you believe man is something apart from nature).

After all not only is patience a virtue - it's a blessing. Don't you admire people who never let things rattle them? People who take things one day at a time, confident at some point they'll get what they want or where they want to be? People who exude that elusive mellowness the rest of us crave? I know I do. And although it's foolhardy to make blanket promises you probably can't practice another sport which teaches patience like riding freight trains.

XX

THE RAILROADS' IMPACT ON THE AMERICAN EXPERIENCE

Railroads have been of bedrock importance to the North American way of life for over a century and a half. Soon after 1800 rumors began crossing the Atlantic from England of strange technological beasts called "locomotives." These beasts had curious names like "Catch me who can," "Puffing Billy" and "Grasshopper." Nevertheless the first thirty years of our 19th century transportation reality were dominated by horse drawn, river-ferried and ocean-steamered conveyance. Once the economic value of a railroad became clear however we wasted little time in following England's lead. In fact England and America were truly the world's railroad pioneers.

The opening shot in railroad viability was sounded in England in 1829 when a locomotive named the "Rocket" won the first of many races with a galloping horse. Another locomotive pulling a coal train, the "Active," won a race that year against a stagecoach between Darlington and Stockton.

America's first experiment was with the "Stourbridge Lion," which was shipped here in pieces from England, reassembled and test run on August 8th, 1829. The first American-built locomotive, the "Tom Thumb," took her first trip on August 25th, 1830. Neither engine pulled a train however and was regarded as little more than an interesting toy. On December 14th, 1830 the Charleston & Hamburg Railway's "Best Friend of Charleston" was the first American-built locomotive to pull a string of cars. Other notable early American locomotives were the "De Witt Clinton" and the "West Point."

The first railroad chartered by the U.S. Government was the Pennsylvania Railroad in 1823 (technically America's "oldest" railroad). However the first *successful* railroad venture was the Baltimore & Ohio chartered in 1827. Construction on the B&O began in 1828. The first passenger and freight traffic - between Baltimore and Ellicott's Mills Maryland - began on May 24th, 1830 (with an English locomotive).

Through the 1830s and 40s railroads quickly traversed the Eastern Seaboard. United States Mail was first carried by rail on the South Carolina Railroad in November, 1831. Washington D.C. was connected to Baltimore on August 24th, 1835 and was linked to New York in January, 1838. Despite pronounced economic contraction following the Panic of 1837 by 1840, 3,000 miles of track had been laid - more than in all of Europe. The Great Lakes were reached at Buffalo in 1842. The first train out of Chicago (shipped by boat from Buffalo) pulled out in 1848.

By 1850 trackage had trebled to 9,000 miles but was still confined to the eastern states. Chicago was reached by rail on January 24th, 1854. The Chicago & Rock Island Railroad reached the Mississippi on February 22nd, 1854. The first railroad on the Pacific Coast opened on November 13th, 1855, eventually running 18 miles from Sacramento to Folsom California. The equipment for the tiny Sacramento Valley Railroad was shipped around Cape Horn by steamer. The first southern railroad to reach the Mississippi at Memphis was completed on April 1st, 1857. By 1860 trackage had trebled again to well over 30,000 miles, out to and across the great Mississippi.

Bridging the Mississippi was a formidable task. On April 21st, 1856 the first bridge was opened between Rock Island Illinois and Davenport Iowa - the biggest event in the first 40 years of American railroading (and undoubtedly the most controversial). Riverboatmen were not happy with the railroad's arrival. They and many other Americans believed railroads should be limited to providing overland transport between water ports.

In fact this first bridge built by the Mississippi and Missouri River Railroad was closed on May 6th, two weeks after opening, when a river steamer "accidentally" crashed into one of its piers, exploded and burned an entire span. Riverboatmen brought suit claiming the bridge was a nuisance and should be torn down. An Illinois lawyer hired by the railroad, Abraham Lincoln, armed with river current information provided by U.S. Army Lieutenant of Engineers Robert E. Lee, disproved the nuisance theory before the Supreme Court, securing beyond question the right of railroads to bridge navigable rivers.

By the mid-1850s railroads were positioned to explode across the "Great American Desert." Tracks fanned out across Minnesota, Iowa, Missouri, Arkansas and Texas. Protracted bridge litigation, the Panic of 1857 and the Civil War however stymied westward railroad expansion for the better part of a decade.

Binding the nation together from sea to shining sea with bands of steel was a 40-year national obsession during the 1830s-60s, the scale of which dwarfs even our dream of putting a man on the moon in the 1960s. The passionate fires for a rail link were stoked by events such as the treaty settlement with Britain of the "Oregon Question" in 1846 (establishing the Canadian border at the 49th Parallel), the world-renowned California Gold Rush of 1849-51, the wild scramble for silver in Nevada's Comstock lode in 1859-60 and similar though smaller mineral booms in Colorado and Utah. The flame was further fueled by the early statehoods of Texas (1845), California (1850), Oregon (1861) and Nevada (1864), the inclusion of Arizona, Utah and New Mexico as territories after the Mexican War of 1846-48 and the Gadsden Purchase of southern Arizona and New Mexico in 1853 (bought to complete a southern transcontinental route).

The tensions of pre-war America had a direct impact on railroad development. The Missouri Compromise of 1854 contemplated the creation of a railroad to the Pacific through Northern, non-slave states. In the early 1850s Secretary of War Jefferson Davis chartered surveys for five western rail routes, two paralleling our new borders and three through the nation's interior (his preference of course was for a southern route). Each route would be a transcontinental railroad within 30 years.

As an incentive to push the tracks further west the Pacific Railway Act of 1862 granted railroads extensive land holdings in the form of "land grants." In addition to free mile-square "sections" of land granted on alternate sides of a right-of-way, the government paid railroads $16,000 per mile of track laid across the plains, $32,000 across the deserts and plateaus and $48,000 over the mountains. States and territories also granted large tracts of land, some as wide as *50 miles* on either side of laid track. Early western railroads received an average of 10 square miles of land for each mile of track laid.

But for the dominance of Northern railroads the Confederacy may well have won the Civil War, or sued for much better terms on surrender. In fact the Civil War was the world's *first* modern war - fought with air reconnaissance, sustained artillery bombardments, submarines, metal warships, machine guns, mortars and most importantly, heavy reliance on railroads.

The four year slaughter (over one-half million casualties in a nation of 31 to 33 million) would have been impossible without rail shipments of fresh troops and weaponry to the battlefield. The South's railroad network, grossly inferior to the North's in 1861, was systematically destroyed as the war intensified (e.g., General William Tecumsah Sherman's "March to the Sea"). Nevertheless as late as 1864 railroads were still helping Confederate armies slip back and forth for lightning raids on Union troops. The North's railroad superiority coupled with the passage of time and industrial might resulted in victory *only* by prolonging the slaughter and slowly bringing the South to its knees.

During the war railroad expansion ground to a halt. The little railroad in Sacramento continued east toward the Sierras, while enfeebled attempts to cross the eastern prairies sputtered, stalled and were finally abandoned. Despite the lull the dreams and planning continued.

With the war finally behind them railroad men recommenced the drive to complete an overland railroad. Small armies of men were hired to drive iron, rock and wood together. The Golden Spike Ceremony at Promontory Point Utah Territory on May 10th, 1869 occasioned a national holiday of unprecedented proportions, punctuated by victory marches, thanksgiving services, the ringing of the Liberty Bell and outpourings of oration and verse. The celebrants out on the Great Salt Desert hooked up the Golden Spike to a hastily-erected telegraph line. People east and west listened via telegraph to the first blow of the hammer driving the spike home (delivered by California's Governor Leland Stanford - which missed). Witnessing dignitaries' speeches were telegraphed and read to spellbound listeners at railroad depots nationwide, much the same way we watched Neil Armstrong's "One Small Step" in front of our televisions a century later.

Although railroads played a leading role in the carnage of the Civil War, after the war they were indispensable in "Bind[ing] up the Nation's wounds." A large portion of Reconstruction energy was devoted to restoring the South's devastated railroad network. In the late 1860s western railroad construction revived with an enormous infusion of cash, men and materials lasting until the Panic of 1873. Armies of former soldiers and slaves joined new immigrants in laying down rails. By 1870 American trackage totaled 60,000 miles. The stall of 1873 however lasted the rest of the decade.

The greatest decade of railroad building followed. In the 1880s 70,000 miles of new track were laid. By 1889 five transcontinental railroads had reached the Pacific - the Great Northern, the Northern Pacific, the Union-Central Pacific, the Santa Fe and the Southern Pacific. The Canadian transcontinental was completed on November 7th, 1885. Bound together by peace and transcontinental railroads the twin North American giants embarked upon an era of economic expansion the likes of which the world had neither seen before, nor has seen since except post-WWII Japan.

Even before 1869 railroads had proven their importance in the emerging American experience. Like vine runners setting out ever-longer stems and shoots, tracks spread across the far-flung expanses of the continent. Overland treks which once took weeks were reduced to a matter of hours. Farms, factories and mines sprang up where desolation had once reigned. Railroads connected rich farmlands with river and seaports making American agricultural exports dirt cheap in world markets. Mail and telegraph communication facilitated growth. Our ability to communicate speeded up immensely.

Without question however there was a downside to railroad expansion. As early as 1860 generations of Americans were already mortgaged to the railroad and knew it. For immigrants the mortgage began before ever setting foot on New World soil. Across both sides of the Atlantic railroads employed gaudy posters, full-page advertisements, gaffers, bilko artists, bogus weather reports, forwarding agents, con artists, grifters and hawkers to entice immigrants to climb aboard ocean-going vessels and come to America. Railroad agents fanned out across Europe to stimulate immigration. Immigrants were counseled on how to secure passports, purchase tickets and find their way to the right boat. On arrival railroad promoters greeted them with high pressure sales pitches and outlandish offers of cheap land and ready riches. Once through the gates at Ellis Island immigrants were directed to the "right" train.

After the railroads staked out and connected towns together they populated them by use of outrageous regional reports, even more outrageous land offers and fabulously cheap tickets. In addition to advertising in Europe they placed full-page ads in major ethnic or Eastern newspapers enticing immigrant and native son alike to "Go West Young Man." Once the railroads got people Out West much of the fertile western bottomland granted them along the rivers was sold for a matter of $25 to $50 an acre. Marginal dryland tracts (of which they had plenty) could be had for as little as $2. Either way each dollar made was more than the railroads ever paid for the land.

Early on the Federal government jumped on the western expansion bandwagon. Before the Civil War federal land cost as little as $1.25 an acre (about a day's wage for an unskilled worker). Even though that $1.25 was equivalent to about $50 today it was a small price to pay for a full acre of land. Later under the Homestead Act of 1862 the government *gave* away land. All a settler needed to do to perfect title to his 160 acres (a quarter section) was stake it out, be over 21, live on it for five years and erect one structure on it with a wall and a window.

The railroads and other large land speculators (i.e., cattlemen, timber barons and miners) jumped on the wagon and gobbled up additional territory. They wiggled in under the terms of the Act by dummying up non-existent persons and placing a stick in the ground with a piece of glass stuck to it. Corrupt federal agents looked the other way when railroads registered these bogus claims. Through this ruse railroads gained title to thousands of additional acres of public domain. Much of this land was later sold to European interests - particularly British cattle speculators.

One exciting aspect of "peopling" the West was the introduction of incredible passenger fare reductions - the likes of which make today's airline fare reductions seem rather chinzy. Railroads quickly realized the best way to establish longterm profitability was to *people* their right-of-ways, especially along feeder lines branching onto their mainlines. Passenger rate wars ensued the likes of which have never been equaled. During the most heated period of settler competition during the 1880s a traveler could ride from St. Louis or Chicago to San Francisco or Los Angeles for *one dollar*!

The claims railroads made regarding soil fertility and availability of water were equally incredible. In the 1870s in the midst of a severe drought eastern Colorado, Wyoming and Montana were billed as the "Rain Belt of America." Utah miraculously metamorphosed from desert into a "Land of Milk and Honey." After the turn of the century railroads advertised Southern California tobogganing in the morning in the San Bernadino Mountains (once they decided it was O.K. to admit it snowed in California), ocean bathing in the afternoon in Santa Monica Bay and sipping orange juice at sunset by an Anaheim orange grove.

Sure enough the people came West - in droves. So did the freight needed to sustain them. And profits came rolling in on the railroad.

First came the Irish and Germans in the 1840s and 50s, fleeing the Potato Famine in Ireland and successive political and religious crises in

Germany. After the Civil War they were joined by Scots, Swedes, Norwegians, Danes, Poles, Russians, Italians and Greeks. Often a young member of an Old World community called a "runner" was sent ahead to verify an agent's high-flying claims.

True, false or somewhere in the middle people poured into the West. A cogent historical argument could be made that even more than America's religious or political freedom or economic opportunity, the driving force behind immigration was the railroads' voracious appetite for workers and settlers. Once the immigrants arrived what they did, where they went and what became of their children remain a matter of intense pride and legend in Canada and America.

But the impact of North American railroading goes much farther than this. Railroad builders and financiers, second to none politically and economically between 1870 and 1900, literally ran the country. In the commercial realm their brain children - the "pooling agreement," "monopoly," "subsidiary ownership," "rate rebate" and "trust" - became dizzyingly successful means of maintaining economic control over the citizenry. Other industries imitated railroads, banding together through similar business arrangements to dominate, intimidate and where possible strangulate competition. The Standard Oil Trust, the copper trust, the steel, coal, iron, sugar, meat and paper trusts followed the railroads' lead in corroding free and open competition. Never forget however the kernel for the idea of unfair business practices was cultivated, nurtured and brought into flower by the railroads.

Railroads rode roughshod over their regional economic fiefdoms with dedicated fury, extracting maximum profit at minimum expense. Railroad track was built so quickly and badly west of the Mississippi it had to be entirely rebuilt by the end of the century. Thousands of miles of track surveyed and built were entirely abandoned and rebuilt elsewhere (especially on the Santa Fe in Arizona and the Denver & Rio Grande in Colorado).

Nevertheless railroads reaped *enormous* profits from their facilities. More than any western boomtown - thrown up one year and deserted the next - railroads wrote the book on the terms "boom" *and* "bust."

The political concomitants of corruption, influence peddling and outright intimidation of the ordinary citizen were never far behind. Railroads played lead roles at all levels of wholesale governmental corruption, from City Council to Congress. They had entire state legislatures in their back pocket between 1860 and the early 1900s.

When the railroads desired a certain piece of legislation or an important judicial ruling they mounted intense and expensive lobbying efforts until their wishes were met - usually by the method as old as man. In fact the railroads *invented* state and congressional "lobbying" as we know and love it today. Today's Political Action Committees (PACs) are little more than sophisticated versions of 19th century railroads' (and later other industrialists') permanent lobbyists stationed in Washington D.C. and state capitals. Collis P. Huntington of the Central-Southern Pacific (unquestionably the most tenacious of railroad lobbyists) summed it up best in writing from Washington to a close associate that: "It costs money to fix things, [but] with $200,000 I can pass our bill." Free lifetime rail passes for legislators were an efficacious means of getting the job done.

Legislators themselves often took the initiative. A bill would be brought to the floor of such-and-such a legislative body which would be costly or awkward for a railroad. After talking long and loud about the merits of the bill its sponsor would retire to chambers and await the inevitable railroad hireling's visit to make him an offer he couldn't refuse. The bill would be withdrawn. At times as many as 35 railroad bills were pending within a legislative session. Railroad corruption of government was a free-for-all only a handful of legislators missed.

Finally the public lost patience. First Grange, Populist and then Progressive candidates began winning elections. In time and in conjunction with America's cycles of recession-depression-deflation the people slowly broke the back of the railroads and their political patrons. The origins of state electoral processes, specifically the Initiative, Referendum and Recall, are directly attributable to the people's desire to take power back from the railroads and their cronies. It was a great ultimate victory for democracy - but borne of even greater pain. Until railroads lost the power they made it pay - for themselves and many duly-elected/duly-corrupted legislators.

On the other hand one must remember railroad speculators took great financial risks in building their empires. Beyond question the country ultimately derived immense benefit from the development made possible by railroads. At times they overshot their targets and went bust.

But a lopsided amount of the country's wealth wound up in the hands of a few select families. The largest fortunes the world had ever known were made during the Gilded Age by greedy, self-serving railroad executives. Their mansions still bedeck our cities - legacies of unbridled acquisitiveness. Their fortunes came in large part from wholesale bartering off of the public domain.

Railroad executives' greed seemed to exceed even their egomaniacal quest for personal empire. They became known collectively as the "Robber Barons" and school children were taught to refer to railroads as "The Octopus." During their heyday railroads were continually in court (alongside Rockefeller's Standard Oil) either creating or defending pooling agreements, trusts and monopolies. By the time Americans woke up and realized how thoroughly the Robber Barons had them by the throat the basic railroad infrastructure was in place. Everyone - farmer, miner, manufacturer, miller, midwife and middleman - was *beholden* to the railroads for everything he or she needed or made.

How did railroads put the choke hold on America? In the typical scenario they'd build a railroad and entice small farmers and merchants out onto previously untilled soil. The people went to work, crops were harvested, products sold and goods shipped east and west. On Year One a railroad would set the price of shipping a bushel of wheat or barrel of salt at say 2 cents a mile. On Year Two the rate unannounced would rise to 7 cents, then on Year Three to 18 cents. Although repeated rate wars ensued between competing railroads between 1870 and 1900 (which brought temporary relief in different regions at different times), in general freight rates bore no relation to railroad overhead.

Result? Coupled with droughts and depressions in the 40 years between 1875 and 1915 American farmers enjoyed only *11 years of profit*. Small merchants fared little better. The net effect was people were lured out into the western territories then promptly ground into the dust. Southern sharecroppers suffered the same fate. To get an idea of the enormity of the situation consider that in 1890 there was one mortgage for every two people (including children) in Kansas and North Dakota, and one for every three in Nebraska, South Dakota and Minnesota. By 1900 *one-third* of all American farmers were tenants on their own land. They continued to feed the world while losing title to their tillage.

Legislative bodies sprang into existence to curb railroad rip-offs. The ICC (1887) and the FTC (1914) were founded in an attempt to curtail the combined excesses of the railroad, oil and other robber barons. The principal concern of the ICC was to prevent railroads from giving illegal rebates to subsidiaries. The State Railroad Commissions, precursors of our various state Commerce Commissions, came into existence to supposedly "regulate" freight rates by means of rate bureaus. Massachusetts, Illinois and Wisconsin led the way soon after the Panic of 1873. Other states followed their lead (Iowa 1878, California 1880, Kansas 1883, Minnesota, Nebraska, Colorado and Oregon, 1885, Missouri 1887 and Texas 1891). Each new state - North Dakota, South Dakota, Washington, Wyoming, Montana, Idaho and Utah - included restrictive railroad provisions in its constitution.

However like many of today's state Insurance Commissions railroad commissioners were quickly bought off by the industry. Until McKinley's assassination in 1901 and the rise of Teddy Roosevelt, Hiram Johnson and the "Trust Busters" few politicians were immune to the corrupting influence of railroad money.

The nation began to scream bloody murder about corporate business methods in response to economic hardship back-to-back with incredible private wealth. In fact along with the oil industry - which *continues* to demonstrate a dogged determination to profit at the expense of everyone else - railroads were primarily responsible (much to their chagrin) for enactment of laws curbing antitrust, pooling agreements, monopolies, mergers, price-fixing and other unfair business practices.

The twin pillars of legislation were the blockbuster Sherman Antitrust Act of 1890 and the Clayton Antitrust Act of 1914. These two acts, emasculated though they were by hostile courts and Republican Administrations (and reemasculated after 12 years of recent Republican Administrations) continue to constitute the backbone of business legislation in America today. (Interestingly, railroads quickly evaded application of the Sherman Act by ducking behind the skirts of the industry-friendly ICC, which continued to regulate them until *1980*. The Staggers Act finally subjected railroads to antitrust scrutiny [pitiful though it is today] and removed the last vestige of railroad dominance over industry-related legislation.)

Another reason railroads rode roughshod over America was that in the 19th century the central government was *extremely* weak. It didn't collect an income tax until 1913. The Feds were basically broke. National revenue came almost exclusively from trade tariffs, bartering off the public domain to private interests and service charges (sounds familiar, doesn't it?). The federal government was preoccupied with Reconstruction, the "Indian

Problem," monetary imbalance, recurrent depressions and nascent Imperialism.

In other words during the halcyon days of American "Federalism" the federal government little understood and therefore gladly acceded responsibility to state and local legislatures for overseeing railroad expansion. These bodies in turn were for the most part in the railroads' pocket.

Who were the men responsible for railroad dominance of America? Financial tycoons the likes of Jay Gould, Edward L. Harriman, Jay Cooke, James J. Hill, Collis P. Huntington, Jim Fisk, Jr., J.P. Morgan, George M. Pullman and "Commodore" Cornelius Vanderbilt - men who stopped at little in their quest for Private Empire. The ethics of these masters in the "Age of Bare Knuckles" were succinctly summed up by Commodore Vanderbilt with the infamous quote: "The public be damned."

By the 1870s these men's names were household words. Their callous disregard for anything beyond amassing gargantuan personal fortune enraged America's working men and women. Americans grew to regard the Robber Barons collectively as Public Enemy Number One. Their financial machinations, infighting and speculative combinations were the chief cause of radical economic upturns and downturns. Between 1870 and 1905 economic trauma was the hallmark of American life. Reform movements were in large part the direct result of railroad avarice. Railroad and oil excesses finally prompted government's acceptance of a need to play a role in the marketplace.

Whereas railroads became far and away the nation's biggest economic force before the fateful rendezvous at Appomattox, after the war they burst onto the economic stage as the *world's* first "Big Business." They remained North America's biggest business until supplanted by the automobile and steel industries in the 1920s. In 1880 for example while there were just over 300,000 textile mill workers and 230,000 miners there were well over 400,000 railroad workers. In the 1890s the Pennsylvania Railroad alone employed 15,000 more workers than the Post Office, our then-largest federal agency. Several other roads each engaged as many men as were enlisted in all the U.S. armed services. The reasons perhaps were inevitable.

When it came to developing natural resources America was perennially short of capital and manpower. Many ambitious railroad projects floundered for lack of cash. As a result railroad ownership concentrated increasingly in the hands of a small group of eastern banking houses. Only they had the ways and means to assemble the enormous sums of money required to build and run a railroad. These banking houses soon became popularly reviled for making decisions which suited only their financial ends rather than the needs of the nation. They were primarily responsible for the deep antipathy which developed between Western and Southern interests and those of the East. To a certain degree these antipathies continue to daunt us.

Banking houses consolidated disparate railroad systems into enormous networks and in the process invented and refined the corporate form of business used worldwide today. Current business phenomena - chief executive officers, vice-presidents, managing directors, budget officers, cost-benefit appraisals, shareholders, limited liability and division of responsibility - were unheard of before 1870. The sheer size and complexity of a railroad required creation of new organizational forms, replacing traditional family-owned business methods.

Railroads attracted the bulk of foreign investment drawn to these shores - mainly from England. Sensing a good thing in North American railroading billions of dollars poured in from eastern mercantilist and European dynasty alike, financing and furthering our railroad rambunctiousness. These investors were paid handsomely for their foresight (except during the periods of economic contraction in the 1870s and 1890s). They greased the wheel of industrial development from cottage industry to steel mill. And as became painfully obvious to the man on the street they greased their own pockets quite handsomely as well.

The very building of a railroad became gigantic industry. Insatiable demands for timber, iron, steel, coal, dynamite, engines, rolling stock, bridging and tunneling materials and thousands of laborers catapulted the fledgling industry into a behemoth, megamillion-dollar monolith. The substitution of steel rails for iron alone between 1870 and 1900 represented a staggering expenditure of national resources. Nothing like this simple change in metals would so tax the nation's energy and mineral wealth until the World Wars.

As we've seen whole armies of laborers were wooed to the new land - not to farm or even permanently settle - but to build railroads. Most notable were the illiterate Irish in the East and the Chinese in the West. Nobody - least of all the railroads - expected these workers to stay. But stay they did. Newly-freed slaves found railroads a ready employer throughout the South, Midwest and West (for unskilled jobs only such as warehouseman, flagman, messenger, coal shoveler - and yes, janitor). Japanese immigrants and Indians in the Southwest, mainly Navajo, Pueblo and Mojave, also lent a hand in lower skilled positions. Italian immigrants took many lower skilled jobs. Except during depressions anyone looking for a job needed look no farther than the nearest railroad.

Railroads even changed the way Americans tell time. During the 18th and 19th centuries North Americans devised a mishmash "system" of over fifty different time zones (known as "sun times") established by major towns and adhered to by local communities, and over 100 "local times" observed by railroads. Making connections was practically impossible. After a series of railroad time conventions, at noon on November 18th, 1883 American and Canadian railroads set their clocks to four standard times: Eastern, Central, Mountain and Pacific.

Parochial hostility immediately arose to "time standardization." A vocal minority viewed the zones as un-American and un-Godly - the basic idea being the sun shone only on them. Others disputed where the lines were drawn. Despite initially rancorous discord however standard time came as a welcome relief to Americans, and was soon accepted throughout the nation. The federal government took *25 years* to make it official with the Standard Time Act of March 19th, 1918 (which also created "Daylight Savings Time" - a war economy measure reinstituted permanently after Pearl Harbor on February 9th, 1942). This 25-year gap between reality and official decree further illustrates how far ahead of government the railroads were - and everybody else for that matter - in the latter 19th century. It also illustrates how often railroad activity or inactivity eventually prompted governmental action.

Today by comparison although largely unobtrusive railroads play a vital role in American life. Despite all the trucks we see everywhere according to the AAR railroads carry roughly 70% of American coal, 74% of canned and frozen foods, 46% of meat and dairy products, 71% of household appliances, 76% of automobiles, 86% of pulp and paper, 78% of lumber products, 63% of chemicals, 68% of primary metal products and roughly 60% of all mail. If the railroads shut down for *one week* our GDP would fall 6%; after eight weeks 24% - with 22% additional unemployment. Railroads truly are "The Arteries of America."

The pervasive role railroads played in the American experience goes far beyond their material usefulness. Railroads symbolized the hopes and dreams of tomorrow through 11 decades of the North American saga (1850-1950). Long before the social and economic liberation afforded by the automobile and airplane the railroad represented the way to a new and better life for countless millions. The impact railroads had on the lives of our predecessors is largely lost upon younger generations. It seems our grand-parents forgot to tell us how much day-to-day life depended on the railroads.

For example in the period between 1840 and 1916 when a railroad came to town you *counted* for something. You were connected to all parts of the nation if you lived in a town staked out or reached by the railroad. You could come and go as whim or economic circumstance dictated. If your town lost its crew division or repair shops it probably didn't exist a year later.

As we've seen railroading was plagued early on by a number of daunting obstacles - lack of bridges, lack of connecting lines, lack of safety devices, lack of brakes and signaling, lack of cohesive scheduling and an appalling diversity of track gauges. Once the initial bugs were ironed out however people grew to rely on railroads to take them and their freight *where* they wanted, *when* they wanted and in *whatever fashion* they could afford (including a boxcar!).

Between 1850 and World War II railroads saturated American popu-lar culture in song, saga and scene, as well as its social, and yes *even religious* activities. Take for example enormously popular books such as *The Octopus* by Frank Norris, *The Road* by Jack London and *The Roaring UP Trail* by Zane Grey. Consider the sheaves of lithographs depicting railroad tableaux published for over 50 years by Currier and Ives. Think back on songs such as "The Wabash Canonball," "Pennsylvania 6-5000," "The Orange Blossom Special," "The Big Rock Candy Mountain," "All Around The Water Tower" and "The Chattanooga Choo-Choo." Recall performing artists such as Woody Guthrie, Mississippi John Hurt, Hank Williams, Bob Wills, Johnny Cash, Pete Seeger and Jimmy Rodgers, "The Singing Brakeman." Myriad Tin Pan Alley ditties, nickelodeon dramas and dime novels proliferated on the subject of working for or riding the railroad. Countless railroad traveling themes sprang up from bluegrass and country-western composers, Wobblies, hobos and blues art-ists from the Delta to Chicago. American photography was greatly influ-enced by railroads (again - perhaps the singlemost popular photographic subject of the 19th century). Painters from Whistler and Homer to Rockwell turned their canvases toward the tracks. A blizzard of "Blue Laws" swept the land attempting to keep people in church rather than on the rail-road each Sunday. American folk heroes like Casey Jones and John Henry were lionized by the railroad experience of North America.

Railroad workers themselves played a large part in the continent's cultural composition. They were a highly mobile workforce. Often a worker and family would move 10 to 20 times over the course of a career to learn the road and acquire promotions. They were often shunned by other townsfolk because of their nomadic nature and hard-living reputation (except in towns with a large percentage of railroad workers). To lessen their sense of isolation and exclusion railroaders formed hundreds of fraternal organizations, as did their wives. These organizations provided reading rooms, balls, teas, sewing circles, alcohol and temperance counseling, potlucks, self-insurance and a host of self-improvement courses which otherwise would have been unavailable to the itinerant railroad individual or family.

In short practically all forms of the nation's cultural development *and* imagination became inextricably bound up with the bands of steel. Moreover from their very beginning railroads sparked an intense desire on the part of the individual American to make like the Bear Who Went Over the Mountain "To see what he could see." This and the seasonal nature of North American economic reality played a fundamental part in the advent of the phenomenon called hoboing.

Before the Civil War hopping freights wasn't popular. Railroads were fragmented and long distance track didn't exist. It was easier to drive a horse and wagon. The first wave of rail vagabonds broke just after the war's end. Soldiers returning home found little permanent work available as wartime industries shut down. They'd learned how to live outdoors from the war. They strapped on their satchel and headed to the depot with nothing to tie them down and "Go West Young Man" ringing in their ears.

Many ex-soldiers worked for the railroad but usually only long enough to get up a grubstake. In the process they learned their skill at anywhere from one to four dollars a day. Since they often blew their wages soon after discharge riding the rails became the natural way to get around.

Thousands of workers were discharged after the collapse of 1873. Those remaining suffered between 25 and 30 percent wage reductions. Men let go felt they were owed something more than a "thank-you" and a few dollars. They climbed on railroads built with their own hands and set off in search of work.

Other factors contributed to the post-1873 waves of non-paying patronage. Railroad builders heralded their systems as the national panacea. Taken at their word people believed it would be forever up-up-and-away with railroad expansion. After the crash however stories of rail baron machinations spread quickly. People who had once attributed God-like qualities to railroad entrepreneurs turned venomous. Patrons of Husbandry movements in the Midwest and South quickly identified railroads as their chief source of discontent.

The first major strike in America, The Great Railroad Strike of 1877, was caused by draconian railroad wage reductions and layoffs. This strike was brutally suppressed by state and federal troops assisted by thuggish Pinkerton Agency employees. Meanwhile on the prairie and in the Deep South drought drove thousands of farmers into bankruptcy, debt and despair.

Result? Emergence of both a *need* to move on and a sense of *entitlement* to ride trains free of charge. The ranks of the hobo swelled again.

In the 1880's the economy revived and a speculative boom developed. Industry soared, railroads expanded rapidly and favorable weather patterns heralded successive years of bumper crops. Americans stopped riding the rails *en masse* and came back home.

In the decade from 1887 to 1897 however a severe drought set in across the South and Midwest. Farmers went bankrupt in unprecedented numbers. With slack traffic railroads infuriated everyone by raising rates without notice while slashing wages. The Panic of 1893 arrived in the midst of this hardship. This depression (second in severity only to the Great Depression) caused a sharp rise in unemployment. People banded together in groups of 50 to 100 people and traveled in search of work. In the spring of 1894 Jacob Coxey and "Coxey's Army" of 500 unemployed men descended on Washington to demand an audience with the government. They were ignored, Coxey was arrested and his followers forcibly dispersed. The same fate awaited other armies arriving later that year. As the ranks of the dispossessed multiplied settlement houses and churches serving the poor proliferated. In stark, ominous contrast governments built armories - often paid for by private railroad subscriptions.

The steady, grinding devaluation of the gold standard dollar was one cause of migration. Total currency in circulation per person had been $30 in 1865. By 1889 this figure had declined nearly 24% to $23. Linear devaluation resulted in more expensive loan and mortgage repayments. The dollar you borrowed last year had to be repaid with a more expensive dollar this year. Recall William Jennings Bryan's "Cross of Gold" speech of 1896: "You shall not press down upon the brow of labor this crown of thorns. You shall not crucify mankind on a cross of gold." Farm overproduction also depressed world commodity prices which, coupled with exorbitant and unpredictable freight rates, bankrupted farmers by the tens of thousands. The only escape was to mortgage farm equipment, homes and future crops.

It was understood in those days when times got tough you hit the road. The ranks of the hobo swelled for the third time. Unlike the post-Civil War period and the 1870s however these hobos were thoroughly radicalized. No longer content to simply jump trains, they often blocked tracks with railroad ties and commandeered them. Train crews usually surrendered out of sympathy (and not being much better off themselves). Railroads were still the only way to travel. In short riding trains free of charge was hardly unusual - especially if you were a card-carrying member of a railroad Brotherhood. Few of today's misconceptions about riding the rails existed one hundred years ago.

In fact during the 20 years between 1891 and 1910 the unemployed vagabond was brought home to Americans as a fanciful, glorious character. Hobos termed themselves "Knights of the Road." Cartoons of the sometimes comical, ofttimes pathetic exploits of "Weary Willie" and "Happy Hooligan" drawn by Zim and Opper were published nationwide. (Probably the American and Russian word "hooliganism" originated here.)

Hobos infused the American language with a wealth of popular lingo. Much of it remains in current North American parlance although a particular meaning may have changed. Most but not all of the following were invented by hobos. All were used by them.

"Main drag" or "stem," "jackroller" or "shifty" (thief), "town clown" or "dick" (policeman), "hijack" (robbery), "frisk," "flophouse" (cheap housing), "ditch" a train (get off), "freeloader" (hobo), "cinder trail" (path hobo walks), "crowbar hotel/bluebar hotel/pokey" (jail), "front" (personal appearance), "getting by," "putting over" (deceiving someone), "white collar" (businessman), "touching hearts," "panhandling," "putting the rigging on" or "putting the touch on someone" (begging), "carry the banner" (walk the streets broke), "rum-dum" (drunk), "sneaky pete" (cheap wine), "roll" (wad of money), "jack roll" (rob), "stake" (earned wages), "go broke," "blow in" (arrive somewhere), "backdoor bumming" (seeking food at back door to limit embarrassment), "snipes" (other people's cigarette butts [O.P.C.]), "hand-out" (hobo credo to never enter house of person when seeking food - food was handed out the backdoor), "set-down" (being invited in to eat), "turned down" (refused a meal), "moocher," "gladhander" or "ballyhooer" (beggar), "bouncer" (mission employee who keeps men awake during services), "benny" (winter overcoat), "down-and-out," "blind pig" (white liquor salesman), "coke head" or "snow bird" (cocaine user), "dope" or "hop head" (drug user), "junkie" (heroin addict), "Hobohemia" (part of town inhabited by transients), "bindle stiff" (hobo), "mission stiff" (mission habitué), "mushfaker" (repairman), "scissor bill" (knife and scissors sharpener or thief), "crip" (cripple), "ding bat" (down-and-out hobo), "shine" or "dingy" (black hobo), "punk" (young boy discarded after a sexual relation with an older hobo; also bread), "fairie" or "fag," "dummy" (dumb or deaf and dumb person), "bad actor" (dangerous person), "backslider" (weak person), "red tape," "floating fraternity" (transients), "boomer" (same but also part-time railroad worker) and "killing time."

In conjunction with the evolution of the pop culture phenomenon of hoboing at the turn of the century came the birth of several hobo or transient-oriented associations. Fraternal organizations were a minor rage in America at the turn of the century and hobos were no different than others. Most famous of these was the I.W.W. - the Industrial Workers of the World ("Wobblies" or "Wobs"). The I.W.W. was formed in Chicago in July 1905 and was variously regarded as everything from a bonafide unskilled workers' union to a Marxist subversion of American capitalist values ("I Won't Work" or "I Want Whisky"). Wobblies traveled the country by rail in search of jobs. By 1906 they carried the "Little Red Card" which often made the difference between being thrown off a train or being allowed to ride.

The International Brotherhood Welfare Association (I.B.W.A.) was a smaller and strictly hobo organization which formed "Hobo Colleges" throughout the country. The IBWA was formed by the son of a wealthy St. Louis family, James Eads How. Its purpose was to improve the lives of hobos by enabling them to obtain medical and legal aid, higher wages and better working conditions. Hobos stopped in to discuss topics of current interest. In the public's eye the group's political leanings appeared too close to socialism and the I.W.W. The outfit ultimately failed.

In 1908 a young Ohioan named Jeff Davis formed Hobos of America, Inc. with 32 members in Cincinnati. Davis' group became one of the better known hobo associations. Davis published his own newspaper, *Hobo News*

Review, and opened several hostels collectively called "Hotel de Gink." This was another short-lived operation.

A 1918 spin-off of the IBWA was the Migratory Workers' Union (M.W.U.), which was also short-lived. The Benevolent and Protective Order of Ramblers ("Hail! Hail! You ought to be a Rambler") was a semi-secret society in Chicago with the sole mission of helping its members in trouble.

Not all railroadmen were sympathetic to hobos, Little Red Card (or similar affiliation) or otherwise. By the turn of the century few trains were without freeloaders (read Jack London's *The Road* - 1907). In 1898 a Santa Fe train was documented pulling into Newton Kansas with 200 men riding it. Trainmen were generally kind to crippled and unemployed hobos looking for work, but just as often vented their ire on drifters and bad actors. One trainman boasted in 1893 he'd "looped a rope around the bastard's head, led him to the edge of town and choked him 'til his tongue stuck out like a bull calf's."

By the 1890s hobos were resorting to legal means to bring indictments against railroaders who used too much force in ejecting them from trains moving too fast. The practice of trainmen charging to look the other way also began during this period - standard fare being $1.00 per division (~100 miles) or by the trip. In general hobos avoided trouble with employees because they knew they got something for nothing.

Estimates of people riding the rails during the mid-1890s range from a low of 60,000 to a high of 300,000. By the turn of the century easily one million men were on the road. Contact with a wandering hobo was a common experience during the last decade of the 19th century. Most hobos knew the meanings of a variety of cryptic symbols scratched on the gate of a residence or barnyard, or somewhere conspicuous in the yards. These symbols meant things like "good place for a handout," "you can sleep in this farmer's barn," "doctor treats hobos free," "fake illness here," "kind man lives here," "tell a hard-luck story here," "only bread given here," "set-down meal given here," "good chance money given here," "work for a meal," "hobos will be arrested on sight," "people who live here may treat hobos violently," "owner has a bad temper," "religious people - be sanctimonious," "kind woman," "dishonest man - don't ask for work," "bad bull - stay out of the yards," "keep quiet," "poor water," "get out of here fast," "these people will help you if you're sick," "police officer lives here," "police watch for hobos here" "police do not bother hobos here" and "good jungle - make yourself at home." Hobos created signals in trees by bending young branches with string or rope. The branch would mature and remain permanently bent, meaning its owner was sympathetic.

After the recession of 1904-1905 a slow return to economic health and favorable weather patterns occurred. The hobo ranks declined once again. Work became increasingly plentiful between 1907-08 and 1918. Progressive Era reforms eliminated or greatly curtailed many labor practices which maimed thousands of workers leaving them no alternative but to wander. The call-to-arms of 1917-1918 scooped up even the most economically dispossessed.

All this changed after the Treaty of Versailles. A number of things happened at once. Just as after Appomatox a surplus of ex-soldiers competed for fewer postwar jobs. Our chief foreign market, Europe, was decimated. A pronounced economic recession extended from 1919 to 1922. Spanish Influenza ravaged one out of three American households.

Weather patterns in the Midwest changed for the worse. During the war farmers were wooed out onto marginal tracts of western high prairie during years of plentiful rain and enormous European demand for American foodstuffs. When the rains and lading orders dried up in the Twenties farmers from Texas to Alberta had to pull up stakes. In fact except in California the Roaring Twenties never came to the North American farm.

Hobo ranks swelled for a fourth time. Estimates (always rough approximations due to the underground nature of the life) run between 100,000 and nearly half a million men riding the rails on *any given day*. For example in the one month of October 1921 on only *one* railroad - the Southern Pacific - 20,643 "undesirable persons" were kicked off railroad property. The situation stabilized toward the end of the twenties only to be rocked again by the Great Depression and the Dust Bowl.

The period between 1930 and 1942 represents the climax of the American hobo experience. By *any* estimate easily more than one million and perhaps as many as three million people (men, women *and children*) were riding the rails in search of work. Estimates come from extrapolations of hobo counts made by railroadmen, arrest and jail records and a variety of literature. California in particular provides a fairly accurate count of migrants. The state was harsh with hobos. The California Highway Patrol and State Police turned people back at the state line and told them to come back to California only when they could do so "like a man." In 1935 alone over 135,000 such contacts were made.

One thing is clear. Many more Americans fled catastrophe by *railroad* than ever followed Tom Joad down the road in a jalopy. Those who did flee by automobile were called "rubber tire hobos." This unsung rail migration is one of the most intriguingly nonexistent phenomena of 20th century American History. Data on hoboing during the Depression is both scant and contradictory.

Some things *are* clear however. Work programs, relief agencies, "Transit Bureaus" and sympathetic townspeople sustained migrant workers as they traveled. The Transit Bureaus were government-sponsored shelters for men on the road and merchant mariners without a current berth. Those in charge sought to find travelers temporary work in city parks, repairing streets or other community projects - for a dollar a day and a sack of Bull Durham. Hot meals, clean dry warm dormitories and clothes-cleaning/delousing facilities were available. All except skilled craftsmen were required to move on after three days.

Given the broad spectrum of participants in the mass migration - skilled and unskilled workers alike - the quality of hobo life in general reached unprecedented levels of sophistication. Hobo jungles became unlikely models of comfort and elaborateness, replete with permanent structures, furniture, kitchenware - even heating and running water.

The political consciousness of the hobo also reached new heights during the Depression. Rumblings of socialism, communism and rebellion were neither uncommon nor unexpected. These were also years when railroads reached unparalleled levels of intolerance for non-paying passengers. A 12-year war broke out on the railroad between hobos, bulls and RCMPs (Royal Canadian Mounted Police). Riding the rods, blinds, bumpers and decks became a way of *survival* as well as travel for millions of North Americans. When the smoke cleared in the early 1940s no one would be declared the winner.

In contrast during the same 20-odd year period (1921-1940) other forces were at work in North America which resulted in fewer workers being forced to travel than had previously. The continent's economic emphasis shifted to industrial production in larger towns and cities beginning during World War I and continuing through the Roaring Twenties and Depression. According to the 1920 Census for the first time more than half of all Americans lived in towns and cities rather than on the farm. Jobs became more permanent in metropolitan areas.

Finally Roosevelt, *arguably* the New Deal, World War II, farm mechanization and irrigation, price support systems and regulation of shipping brought increased productiveness, predictability and profitability to the farm. Along with this however came a huge wave of farm consolidations. Fewer farmers grew more food. Today only 5% of Americans are farmers - and many are still tenants.

The need to travel for work diminished with this economic shift. Average workingmen and women bought or rented homes in growing communities and put down roots as never before. This move to permanence meant fewer and fewer hobos rode the rails - with one minor exception.

Following World War II a sixth but smaller increase in the number of hobos occurred with the return of soldiers from the wars and the recession of 1946-48. Since the 1950s however the number of *professional* hobos has steadily declined. By my estimate today somewhere in the neighborhood of 5,000 to 10,000 folks make riding trains a full time job. This is a very generous estimate. By "full time" I include all migratory farm laborers who move by train, all folks who stay in rescue missions but ride trains back and forth and all folks who stop to perform unskilled piecework. I also include people who have a home but consider themselves first and foremost traveling hobos - *and* ride trains. Let's not forget undocumented workers who might number as many as 10,000 on a given day. By my estimate since 1970 (when I started riding trains) this total figure has declined from around 30,000 mainly due to old age and death. I would also estimate there are 20,000 to 40,000 sportsmen like me who ride the rails for fun. This number is definitely growing.

All told down through the years between 5 and 25 million Americans and Canadians have ridden the rails. Many have long since passed away. If you'd like to take a look at some of their faces however, examine photographs at the Smithsonian taken (among others) by Walker Evans and Dorothea Lange for the Farm Security Administration in the late 1930s. You'll see scores of hobos lined up for a brief rendezvous with immortality.

Take a look at these people standing proudly next to their trains - men, women, children and all their worldly possessions lined up at trackside. Six waves of hoboing should impress upon us the fundamental impact of the North American railroad in general, and in particular the hobo experience in North America.

XXI

COMMON MISCONCEPTIONS

BUT DON'T JUST BUMS RIDE FREIGHT TRAINS?

No. Down through the decades of the Iron Horse and right up to today some of our most eminently respectable citizens have jumped freights. Anybody who's read a book by a decent American author knows some pretty heavyweight folks have ridden the rails. How about Jacks London and Kerouac? (O.K., I know Kerouac traveled by bus. But he was a freight brakeman and had enough imagination to throw in freight scenes.) How about Johns Dos Passos and Steinbeck? Don't forget Walt Whitman, Mark Twain, Upton Sinclair, Zane Grey, Vachel Lindsay, Robert W. Service, John Fante and Bret Harte. Don't overlook Frank Capra, Clark Gable, Melvin Belli, Ernie Buschmiller and former U.S. Supreme Court Justice William O. Douglas! The profusion of literature on the subject alone high-lights the sense of adventure in riding the rails as well as its appeal to the intellect and imagination.

So who rides freight trains? Let's begin with childhood. Kids who live near a railroad jump freights for short rides all the time - just plain kids falling in for one of America's favorite what-the-hells: Bilking the railroad out of a few free miles of kicks. Whether urban or rural, ghetto or farm, kids can't seem to resist the temptation of climbing on a slow-rolling freight train and taking a ride. The same holds true for adventurous adolescents.

Kids of all ages *love* the idea of adults riding freights. Prove this to yourself. Next time you're on a freight paralleling a highway stand on your car where motorists can see you. They'll pull even with you. There's Dad behind the wheel, faithfully minding the roadway and trying not to snuff out the family. There's Mom in the front passenger seat yacking away about the bad food back at the last cafe. Then there's Brother and Sister in the backseat. Guaranteed - *every time* the kids will be watching the train. They'll spot you first.

When they do they simply go *ape* in the backseat. "Mom and Dad! Look! There's a *guy* on that train!" As they watch you rolling along they point frantically with their noses glued to the window. They wave, bounce up and down and create general tumult in the backseat. Mom and Dad glance at you briefly then dismiss you for fear their children might be tempted to do something disgraceful like that someday. "Only bums do that dear" counsels Mom. Of course you the Bum wave back and reassume your position as The Cool Adventurer. This completely makes the kids' day. Now no one is suggesting kids should emulate The Cool Adventurer. No one has to - they do it anyway.

You'll meet some very interesting people riding freight trains - especially lately because it's getting popular as a sport. We're talking doctors, lawyers, Indian Chiefs and amateur peripatetic philosophers - people with every kind of job and background imaginable. In science, medical and legal circles growing numbers of young people who work together are taking off and hitting the highline. Some professionals call them "yuppie hobos." According to one hobo their ranks include bored computer programmers, college professors, business executives, professional people and even working mothers. (This is a fact from my own experience. I recently introduced the sport to a working mother. She loved it and we'll be catching out again soon.) These folks don't *have* to do this with their spare time. They do it because they like it. They do it because they know how hard it is to find real adventure in North America anymore.

If you're a club kinda gal or guy there are clubs to join formed by people who enjoy riding freights. Induction requires you pay some money and at least *claim* to have ridden a freight train. The largest is the "National Hobo Association" (N.H.A.) which touts 3,800 members. Then there's the "Beverly Hills 'Bos" with around 500 members. Another group is the "Freight Train Riders Association" (F.T.R.A.). I'm told these folks' calling-card is to wear a bolo tie. If you're passing through Brainerd Minnesota drop in and visit Buzz Potter at the Depot Inn (aka the "Hobo Club").

I also hear hobo clubs are forming in major cities nationwide and can be contacted through the N.H.A. These clubs *quietly* encourage members to ride trains then come back and share the experience or write about it in the club rag. They also sponsor group rides like from Los Angeles to Las

Vegas. The N.H.A. publishes a bi-monthly newsletter called "Hobo Times" filled with anecdotes, yarns, hobo *argot* and memorabilia. (Write or call Captain Cook, Hobo Times, World Way Center, Box 90430, Los Angeles, CA 90009 - $18 a year for non-hobos and $6 for hobos.) Note each edition of "Hobo Times" ends with the following disclaimer: "And always remember, the N.H.A. does not advocate railriding - it is illegal and dangerous. Safety first!!" I wonder who their lawyer is? I'm sure I'll be hearing from him or her soon. There's even a *toll-free hobo hotline* (800/622-HOBO). Call for information you might be interested in.

Each August for the last 92 years professional and amateur hobos and *aficionados* have held a convention in the north-central Iowa town of Britt. It's a small town on the Soo Line 32 miles west of Mason City. I've been through Britt but never during the convention. Thousands of people attend the weekend festival. It's a photo op and you can help yourself to some real Mulligan stew or "combination" and vote for the annual King and Queen of the Hobos. Another convention, "Pufferbilly Days," is held annually in Boone Iowa, 14 miles west of Ames on the Chicago & North Western line. Here you can ride around in a *passenger* car while conductors playfully toss "'bos" off. Other festivals are held each year in Dunsmuir California, Amory Mississippi, Gaylesburg Illinois and North Vernon and Logansport Indiana.

So no - not just bums ride the rails. Rather it's anybody who has a flair for excitement, for the unknown, for danger and for the novel.

I can tell you this too: Riding trains is real life alright. No question about it. You can read all the books available on the subject including this one. Reading about it is a handy means of escape. But when you're out there *doing* it it's pretty damned real. It's hot, it's cold, it's lonely, it's intimate, it's fun, it's scary, it's exhilarating, it's a drag, it uplifts, it depresses, it invigorates, it enervates. But above all it's *real*.

Other sports of course have varying degrees of adventure. But the adventure is often contrived in comparison to freight train riding. So do adventurers and risk-takers. What's more the price is right.

But Isn't Riding the Rails Just for Guys?

No. This is a definite misconception. By all means women who want to experience this adventure should *go for it*. I've met a number of women riding the rails. Several have accompanied me. Women are every bit as adventurous as men and get an equally big kick out of this sport. A woman is quite as capable of physically riding a freight train as she is in roles such as combat, submarine, tank, artillery, fighter pilot, peace officer, construction worker and railroad personnel. A few common sense observations however are in order.

Women should travel together or with one or more men, just as in hitchhiking. This isn't peculiar to women on the railroad. The ideal traveling arrangement *female or male* is to travel as a team. One person stays with the gear while the other buys groceries, hunts up information, looks for a car, etc. The only quick ways to really get to know someone are (1) get married; (2) live together; or (3) ride together on an extended freight train journey.

I also guarantee you workers and even bulls will be courteous when you're courteous to them. It's your business if you want to bring an "equalizer" such as mace, a knife or gun. Personally I hate guns and knives. They usually create more problems than they solve and are not recommended.

Personal hygiene is just as simple for a woman as a man on the rails. Use an empty cardboard juice container to urinate. Defecate on newspaper, a piece of wood or in a "No. 10 gunboat" can. Simply empty or toss it off the side. Bring the essential toiletries but keep it light. A hat or scarf will minimize grit getting into your hair.

Riding freights is not a sport for trixie, candy-assed fifi *femmes* of the spike-heeled, heavily made-up persuasion. We've all met them but not on the railroad. Ride a freight train when you want to renew your self-image of being a gutsy person. Women have every bit as much moxie as men. It's a sport for anybody with gumption.

BUT WON'T I GET MUGGED?

One common misconception about railriding is that you'll get jacked up, mugged, drugged or generally jerked around by nasty old hobos. Baloney. All the junk literature out there about shifty, dangerous hobos is nothing more than multimedia malarkey.

Most professional hobos stick to themselves or only congregate with people they know. Many of them are out-and-out loners. I don't care what others before have said. The *last* thing a hobo wants is to create a problem for himself by hassling someone else. The maxim "If you live outside the law you must be honest" applies here. Professional hobos have enough problems already. They don't need us as another one. As long as you bring your common sense along for the ride you'll be fine.

There is a type of character mentioned earlier known as the streamlined jackroller. This is a fellow who carries little gear of his own but wants yours. Keep an eyelid peeled for him. Of course there will be no problem with the new breed of wayfarer - people like me who are just out for a good time.

But Won't I Die From the Heat or Cold?

Not if you're prepared in advance. The weather has a lot to do with who we meet and whether we have fun riding the rails. For most hobos it's a seasonal sport - i.e., when the sun's out. Nice weather means we can wear light clothing and bask in the sunshine. We can float about and examine Mother Nature in all her manifold and great bounty. We can also ride any kind of freightcar we want. So it's great - spring, summer and fall. All pretty nice.

At times the weather gets too cold to play unless you're an avid member of the Polar Bear Club who thrives on frigid temperatures. We're talking about when it gets so cold that when you touch metal with your hand then remove it the skin sticks to the metal. We don't like when this happens.

In the winter for obvious reasons the West Coast and Southwest have the most pros. San Antonio, El Paso, Tucson, Phoenix, Yuma, Indio, Los Angeles, Santa Barbara, San Luis Obispo, Salinas, Watsonville, San Francisco, Roseville, Dunsmuir, Bend, Portola, Portland, Wishram and Seattle fill up with pros during the cold months. But in the spring, summer and fall hobos branch out all over the country.

Although there are exceptions hobos are generally a hardy breed. Many of them can live outside in weather you'd think would kill off anybody. Some even know how to ride across Minnesota in a boxcar in January and still have at ball. When you meet these hardy souls they look pretty bizarre. They're wrapped up in tons of clothes and often wear heavy beards. They resemble mountainman furtrappers coming down out of the Rockies in the 1840s. When winter's chill sets in however the great majority of regulars head for where the weather suits their clothes.

But Isn't It a Hassle Riding with Unknowns?

Yes unless we abide by traditional *boxcar etiquette*. If you're riding alone you can conduct yourself in pretty much any manner you choose (except for excretory functions in light of people using your car in the future). If you're accompanied by anyone however certain customs must be adhered to.

Number one if your car is already occupied by someone you should defer to their choice of positioning. It's first-come-first-served on the railroad. Number two if somebody doesn't feel like talking don't insist upon it. Number three never pee or shit *any portion* of the car (pee down the boxcar door and off-load feces). Number four don't pry into other people's backgrounds. They'll tell you what you need to know. Number five when asked always give any information you have. Number six don't be a jerk. Number seven help people whenever possible. And number eight be courteous to the workers.

These are the same manners we use hitchhiking. We always let the first person there have the best position. We stand politely. We strive to position ourselves so they can see us well in advance (to make up their minds). We try to give cars a safe place to pull over. We hold signs to let them know where we'd like to go. We place our gear in the vehicle politely. We ride where asked to. We try to hold up our end of the conversation. We suggest they stop for others. We never ask for spare change. We don't expect them to buy us food. We help them drive on request. We help keep them awake. We don't sleep unless it's unavoidable and at ride's end we thank them profusely (so they pick up the next traveler).

But Isn't It Illegal?

Finally another question I get all the time is "Isn't it against the law?" Friends it most assuredly is. This is *not* a misconception. The illegality aspect is simply way overblown. Riding the rails is one of the most innocuously illegal things you can do in America.

Freight train riding is definitely illegal. Be careful. It's like being a stowaway or joyriding railroad-style. Riding the rails is not for the fainthearted. You must be willing to accept the fact you're transgressing one of Western Civilization's most hallowed and tenaciously protected institutions - private property.

Before you throw up your hands and declare abject fainthearted-ness, let's examine the property interests we impose upon when riding the rails. Once we've assessed these interests *you* be the judge whether you're harming anyone's *legitimate* property interests. Let's examine what kinds of property are involved.

Railroads own or possess three distinct kinds of property: Land, equipment and freight. Let's take them in order.

LAND

Recall our discussion of the manner in which the majority of track-age was acquired by the railroads in North America (land grants), then you be the judge whether you're seriously impacting upon someone's legitimate property interests by walking on railroad land. Did they save up and buy it like everybody else? Enough said.

EQUIPMENT

The railroads' equipment property interests include their rolling stock, rails, ties and ballast, vehicles, depots, sheds, barns, towers, other buildings, signals, switches and everything else they use to conduct business and run safe trains. As opposed to their property interests (which command dubious respect) railroad equipment interests deserve great respect - if for no other reason because we endanger the lives of others and ourselves if we mess with them.

When you consider the railroads' concerns about equipment con-sider their three main worries: Fire, theft and vandalism (sounds like an insurance contract doesn't it?) These are legitimate concerns and should be closely examined. Let's start with fire.

FIRE

People usually build fires to stay warm or cook food. Perhaps at times they're trying to sell something to the insurance company (under the terms of a contract they understand only well enough to know that if the arson investigators don't latch onto what happened they collect). Since we don't *own* anything on the railroad we build a fire to stay warm or cook food.

First off everybody likes a nice outdoor fire. There's a certain intimacy enkindled in sitting around a fire under the wide open sky. As

Smokey the Bear has pointed out since getting his butt singed in New Mexico in 1912 however, fires have an annoying tendency to get out of control.

The basic rule of thumb on the railroad is: *Don't build a fire unless you really need one.* "Really need one" means when you're cold or have grub you *have* to cook to eat. In either case build your fire in a safe place - where others have built fires before you. Otherwise don't build fires on the railroad.

Every freightyard across the country has a well-used place where thousands of fires have been built in the past. It's tucked away somewhere out of sight of the station and away from roads the bull uses. The center-piece of this venue is a blackened fire pit surrounded by discarded odds and ends. Build a fire here.

The place we're talking about is the hobo "jungle" which I've mentioned. Don't ask me where this appellation comes from. I don't know. I've asked many people and looked it up but nobody has a convincing answer. It's something akin to the pitchers' bullpen because like waiting relief pitchers the jungle is where we wait for trains in our sport. When we're waiting or sleeping in the jungle we're "jungling out" or "jungled out" until train time. Since we should only build fires in the jungle let's digress for a moment and round out the concept of the North American Hobo Jungle.

THE HOBO JUNGLE

You may have thought North America didn't have any jungles (except Hawaii). Not true. We can find a jungle continent-wide wherever freight trains stop.

Hobo jungles have a very interesting history. In every railroad town across the continent jungles sprang up to provide safe haven for the migratory masses as a result of continuous cycles of boom and bust. Early jungles were primitive, consisting of a fire pit and a couple of logs to sit on. Over the decades however they became more elaborate and grew into regular vagabond communities with constantly changing inhabitants.

Almost immediately after railroads realized they had non-paying passengers on their freights they hired bulls to keep hobos off. This meant hobos needed secluded spots near the yards to rest and wait for trains in safety. In the old days bulls seldom had the guts to break up a jungle, mainly because they were far outnumbered - and often outgunned. Jungles were found under a nearby bridge, down on a stream or river, in a grove of trees or in an abandoned building - always as far out of sight from the bull as possible. Whenever a railroad declared war hobos found increasingly clever hiding places.

Although infrequently a railroad ordered a jungle be razed, as a general rule - particularly out West - they acquiesced in the scheme. Farmers needed workers to get to the job and railroads needed farmers. Jungles became established over the decades, particularly during the six great waves of hobodom. The Hoovervilles of the Great Depression didn't materialize out of thin air. They were logical extensions of North America's prior experience with the hobo jungle. After World War II jungles fell into disuse and disrepair - but never completely.

Today jungles are found at every stop-off point along the major rail routes across the continent - many in the same place they've been for over 100 years. Just sniff around the yards if you want to build a fire or take a load off. Sooner or later you'll come across the jungle. You'll develop a second sense for where they'll be.

Jungles today however are a far cry from their sophisticated predecessors. In the West there are some big permanent jungles. But the average jungle might have a resident every second or third day and then only during travel seasons. The discipline required to run a shipshape operation has evaporated. Today's jungle is often strewn with empty cans, broken bottles, feces and discarded clothing. More often than not the jungle is a pretty wretched place.

Kick around and get a feel for the desperate plight people have had through the years on the move by freight. One envisions them huddled together at night, their faces illuminated by a small, flickering fire, talking about their prospects and outlook on life. That's exactly right. Fire is the thing which unites hobos at night like thousands of years ago for cave dwellers.

Despite what people say about slash-and-burning of the world's jungles, on the railroad don't build a fire anywhere else. You don't have to stay or sleep in the jungle but always build your fire there. Many bulls leave us alone in the jungle. It's definitely the only place they tolerate a fire. Sometimes they tolerate us *until* we build a fire. Then they come over and tell us to put it out, or put it out and leave. Without exception whenever *you* leave make sure your fire is all the way out.

Keep an eye on your fire. Don't let it get out of control. Make sure the wind doesn't take it somewhere else. These are the same basic ideas we follow when camping. Be fire-smart/fire-cautious.

Under no circumstances build a fire on a freightcar.
Even though you'll see the odd hobo do this to keep warm or cook
don't follow his or her example. Not only will you incur the undying
wrath of the carrier; you could very easily incinerate yourself. Freightcar
floors built of wood are highly flammable. When you get the wood hot
enough a fire will quickly get out of control because the floors are soaked in
creosote. Even new cars have wooden floors. *Don't build fires on trains.*
Crews are taught to watch for fire on trains. If they spot yours you almost
certainly will get arrested.

Keep your jungle fire small and functional. Bonfires will not
score any points and have the annoying tendency of drawing un-
wanted attention. Fires are also usually unnecessary unless you haven't
anticipated the weather or a hot lunch is a must for you. The watchword is
common sense. Don't build a foolish fire. Remember what the Indians
said about the white man's fire - when stealth was important we built
ours too big.

THEFT

Theft is a serious concern for railroads. They lose *beaucoup dinero*
each year from people stealing parts and equipment. Railroads have loads of
interesting bits and bobs one could make away with if one had a use for
them. Most railroad equipment is highly specialized however and is of no
use to us. Not surprisingly most *equipment* theft is conducted by employees.

Stay out of railroad buildings unless it's freezing, raining or you
need a place to hide. If you *do* need to get inside a building keep your hands
off anything inside. It's like stealing the basketball from the local parks and
recreation department. Pretty low rent stunt, right? Don't lend credence to
the railroads' argument hobos are responsible for theft losses. Respect their
equipment and facilities and keep your hands off it.

Are we stealing services from the railroad when we latch onto one
of their cars and take a ride? I suppose so to the tune of about 2¢ per 1000
miles. It's ridiculous to imagine the weight of one wayfarer increases a
railroad's fuel expenditure. It's certainly tough to wear out a railroad
freightcar. I've spent many hours in quiet meditation on this subject and I
can't come up with any other way we impact a railroad besides a pittance of
fuel. Let your conscience be your guide.

VANDALISM

Vandalism is another big problem on the railroad. Most of it is caused by kids, punks, disgruntled employees or sickos who get off on wrecking things. These are the same people we're trying to escape when we ride freight trains to begin with. Nevertheless people regularly wreck things.

The most common vandals are kids. Their tool of choice is the rock since there are so many at hand. They lie in wait for the local to express their creativity by showering it with a hail of rocks from secluded locations. Look out because kids in North America love to pelt trains with rocks.

We talked about rocking earlier. I admit as a kid my buddies and I used to riddle trains with rocks during Boy Scout campouts. But we just liked hitting boxcars to see the sparks fly. I've seen kids doing the same thing all over the continent. When a train comes along they pepper it with rocks as if it was the just-married couple exiting an industrial marriage. We all know rocks are bigger than rice so you are hereby put on notice:

When riding the rails you run the risk of getting riddled with rocks from right arms of America's rockers, rendering forth with pocket rocket projectiles ricocheting randomly around. Look out for these kids. They're not looking out for you. But if they see you they'll take aim. It's adventure like shelling gunboats on the Mississippi at Vicksburg. Sometimes we're sitting ducks on sideless cars if the train's going slow. I'm not saying we run the risk of getting nailed by a rock everytime we ride a train. I'm saying it's something to look out for.

Another form of vandalism is graffiti. Like public transit freightcars offer an irresistible canvas for all manner of "creative" scrawling and doodling. Some of it is good; most of it isn't. The mediums of choice are chalk and spray paint. I've never heard anybody express much concern about graffiti on freightcars. Nevertheless you'll irritate someone if you get caught. I'd counsel against it.

One must admit some good artists are at work on the railroad. There's no harm in admiring their work. After a while you'll recognize certain particularly prolific artists. "Herbie" is specially productive with his sombrero/siesta motif. Graffiti artists' creations are branched out across the country. Sometimes they sign their works, but usually with a *nom de graffiti* like "Pepe" or "Slowshoe." Sometimes you'll see railroad workers' beefs with the company or a supervisor eloquently inscribed on the sides of cars - things like "Fuck you Jack." Graffiti is the most innocuous form of vandalism going on over at the railroad - but leave it to others.

What's more serious is the physical damaging or destruction of equipment found in the yards, on trains and over the road. I would like to *strongly discourage* you from breaking or changing things in the yards or over the road. You could get somebody killed - including yourself.

The equipment railroads use has been specially designed to provide safety and efficiency in their operations. (No, this is not a plug for the railroads. As you can well imagine I'll never see a plugged nickel from them.) If you compromise their system you run the risk of fouling up the whole shooting match. You'll also wait with everybody else until they send somebody out to repair what you've wrecked. Resist the temptation to throw the odd switch, pull the whistle or put something bigger than a penny on the rails (a thick coin can lift the engines' treads far enough off the rail to shatter it when they come back down). Don't fool with the signals and signs, break windows, wreck abandoned buildings or trash things.

I'm not advocating the Boy Scout approach: "Leave your campsite cleaner than you found it." You certainly don't have to police the area for anyone. Just don't fiddle with the devices or fool with the premises and you'll have the same fun as if you did.

All of which goes by way of saying *don't mess with railroad equipment.* Look at their role in your sport as being the friendly provider of turf. Give them the respect you'd give anyone "generous" enough to make sporting space available and have good, clean, unharmful-to-others fun.

FREIGHT

As we've seen a wide variety of products is shipped by rail. If the shipment is large enough *anything* in the way of raw materials or finished products will go by freight. The big rule is: Don't be overly interested in what railroads ship. As a matter of fact a healthy degree of *disinterest* will hold you in good stead. Mess around with freight and sooner or later you'll get into trouble - probably big trouble.

Professional thieves make a living breaking into freightcars and making off with the goods. Theft is the Number One liability railroads incur each year. They blame hobos for a large percentage of the loss, claiming they damage things by pawing through freight on cars until they find something interesting. Of course this is nonsense. One look at the average professional hobo puts the lie to this accusation. They're simply trying to get from here to there.

The big losses come from the big thieves - professional crooks with advance information from warehouse buddies about what a car is carrying. Since freightcars never advertise what they're loaded with (except hazardous materials [supposedly]), crooks know what they're looking for from inside information. They come in with trucks, break into cars and make off with the goods. *They* are the people railroads should be concerned about, as any honest bull would admit. At times you'll see professional heisting in progress. When you do, do yourself a big favor: Turn around and *walk the other way.*

Even if you're the thieving type without inside information chances are *you* won't find anything worth stealing. In smaller quantities most valuable freight in America isn't shipped by train anymore. Anything you'd run across wouldn't be worth taking - unless you have a very great need for paper, pipes, minerals or lumber and also have a *very big* wheelbarrow to cart your booty away with. I certainly wouldn't try walking off with a refrigerator.

Most of the good freight is too big to move or is locked in cars you'd have a hard time getting into. Good luck trying to figure out which car to get into without the inside dope. Appliances and beer are hot commodities. I've heard some good stories about things people have turned up with carousing around the yards. But *leave the theft action to the pros.* Don't be a chump. The attitude test and any other ass-saving technique goes out the window if you commit a theft crime on the railroad.

Let's sum up then on the legality and various private property interests you impact by riding freights: It's illegal. For all the reasons indicated however don't fret about walking on railroad land. The mere trespassing aspect of your sport is *reductio ad absurdum* (reduction to an absurdity). Trespass however with respect for things you come across. Riding a freight train while illegal is not only an historical reality but a great American adventure. Any destruction or loss you wreak along the way is unforgivable. Keep these distinctions in mind and you'll have a great trip.

That's all the advice I have except that you owe it to yourself to See America First. All pretty nice.

"Highball!!"

APPENDIX

Here's a list of towns in each of the 50 states and 6 western provinces and territories of Canada (I've never been east of Manitoba) where we stand the best chance of catching a freight train when it stops. Also listed are a couple of bigger cities where, as this book goes to press, no hassle has developed. (PLEASE NOTE: Some of the "towns" listed below aren't towns in the traditional sense; they're merely junctions where railroads stop to exchange cars.) "Nighttime only" means we have to be wary of the bull.

Alabama: Frisco City, Phenix City, Bridgeport, Piedmont, Troy, York, Dothan, Decatur (Tennessee River railroading), Hybart, Muscle Shoals, Jasper, Cromwell, Leeds, Linden, Atmore, Anniston, Wellington, Flomaton, Stevenson, Boligee, Birmingham (Duncan, Norris, Thomas, Woodlawn Junction, Irondale Junction, 14th Street, 27th Street, Fourteenth Tower Yards - nighttime only), Sheffield Yard, Bessemer, Mobile, Montgomery, Ensley, Wilton, Kimbrough, Demopolis, Childersburg, Parkwood, Green Tree, Tuscaloosa, Tuscumbia, Talladega, Georgiana, Andalusia, Attalla, Calera, Cordova, Opelika, Sylacauga, Magnolia and Selma.

Alaska: Fairbanks (check out the midget trees), Eielson, Healy, Nenana, McKinley Park, Cantwell, Curry, Talkeetna, Willow, Matanuska, Anchorage, Portage, Palmer, Whittier, Moose Pass, Seward (watch out for landslides into Kenai Lake) and Skagway (over to White Horse Yukon Territory - a great narrow gauge ore-car ride - *if they ever reopen it*).

Arizona: Kingman, Flagstaff (rimtop railroading), Winslow (Santa Fe - hot yard), Williams Junction, Ash Fork, Parker, Phoenix (Taylor Yards), Yuma (bring water for sure), Gila, Magma, Casa Grande, Picacho, Tucson, Benson, Bowie, Douglas, Miami, Globe, Palo Verde, Vicksburg, Wickenburg/Matthie, Drake and Nogales.

Arkansas: Jonesboro, Paragould, Benton, Fort Smith (Boston Mountains to the north), Fayetteville, Blythville, Batesville, Lewisville, Russellville, El Dorado, North Little Rock (nighttime only), Camden, Cotter, Mena, Crossett, Texarkana, Marianna, Marion, Monticello, Forest City, Ashdown, Fairoaks, Fordyce, Hope (say "hi" to Billy and Hillary), Pine Bluff (Gravity Yards; catch a hotshot Southern Pacific freight all the way to Los Angeles), Stuttgart, Bridge Junction (West Memphis), River Junction, McGehee, De Queen, Hoxie, Diaz Junction/Newport, Smackover, Stamps and Bald Nob.

California: Indio (bring water), West Colton, Barstow (nighttime only), Needles (nighttime only; bring water), Santa Barbara, Bakersfield (nighttime only), Exeter, San Luis Obispo (real nice venue), Santa Margarita (they pull pusher units off here), Loma Linda, Watsonville, Oroville, Marysville, Roseville, Sacramento, Salinas, San Bernardino, Los Angeles (Glendale "C" Yards - nighttime only), Warm Springs, Westwood (not in Los Angeles), Oakland (nighttime only), Fresno, Richmond (nighttime only) Hanford, Merced, Long Beach (Dolores Yards - nighttime only), Stockton, Portola, Tracy, Truckee, Norden, Keddie Wye, Tehama, Bieber, Cadiz, Yermo-Daggett, Davis, Willits, Redding, Dunsmuir (go fishing between trains), Eureka, Mojave, El Centro and Santa Clara.

Colorado: Trinidad, Pueblo (straight shot west up the Arkansas), Denver (Cherry Creek, North, Nineteenth Street, Twenty-Third Street, Thirty-First Street Yards - nighttime only), South Denver, Boulder, La Junta, Walsenburg, Julesburg, Alamosa, Avondale, Salida, Minturn, Craig, Delta, Dotsero, Grand Junction (hotshots go all the way to Oakland CA), Sterling, Fort Collins, Fort Morgan, Tabernash, Tennessee Pass, Lamar, Limon, Burlington, Eads, East Brush, Steamboat Springs, Colorado Springs and Glenwood Springs (cross the river and take a hot mineral bath).

Connecticut: Stamford, South Norwalk, Bridgeport, New Haven, New London, New Britain, Hartford, Milford, Groton, Norwich, Willimantic, Waterbury, Westbrook, Derby, Danbury, Stonington and Meriden.

Delaware: Wilmington, Dover, Harrington, Clayton, Townsend, Newport, Frankford, Seaford and Newark.

Florida: Pensacola, Palatka, Plant City, Panama City, Chattahoochee, Tallahassee, Okeechobee (bring insect repellant), Drifton, Baldwin, Lake City, Live Oak, Wildwood, Hampton, Ocala, Orlando (Taft Yards; catch the "Orange Blossom Special" - now a freight train), Hialeah, Lakeland, Winter Haven, Bartow, Arcadia, Ft. Myers, Daytona Beach, Greenville, Jacksonville (nighttime only), Graceville, Titusville/Jay Jay (hit the beach between trains, or watch a shuttle launch), Jasper, Marcy, Auburndale, Cottondale, Crawford, Sanford, St. Augustine, St. Petersburg and Tampa.

Georgia: Columbus, Cordele, Vidalia, Valdosta (Langdale Yards), Marietta, Helena, Junta, Jesup, Dublin, Dalton, Bainbridge, Brunswick, Griffin, Newnan, Ft. Valley, Cartersville, Thomasville, Gainesville, Lamarville, Cedartown, Fitzgerald, Manchester, Rome, Athens, Albany, Americus, Augusta, Atlanta (Pot, Inman Yards - nighttime only), Elberton, Macon (Bronson, Brosnan, Macon Junction Yards), La Grange, Waycross (Rice Yards), Savanna (boat over to Jekyll Island and fish) and Everett City.

Hawaii: Forget it and go to the beach or a volcano (no freight railroads).

Idaho: Sandpoint (go boating on Lake Pend Oreille), Bonner's Ferry, Grand Junction, Moscow (go from college town to college town over to Pullman Washington), Twin Falls, Idaho Falls, Lewiston, Burley, Blackfoot, St. Anthony, Grangeville, Eastport (Kingsgate, B.C.) (bring your passport), Montpelier, Caldwell, Coeur d'Alene, Pocatello (Union Pacific - hot yard), Payette, Humphrey, Spencer, Boise and Nampa.

Illinois: Rock Island (salute the first bridge over the Mississippi), Kankakee, Paducah, Marion, Markham, Harrisburg, Mt. Vernon, Mt. Carmel, Salem, Centralia, Tuscola, Peoria, Aurora, Tolono, Belleville, Danville, Bensenville, Jacksonville, Waltonville, Grayville, Edwardsville, Edgewood, Litchfield, Springfield, Decatur, East Dubuque, Lincoln, Luther, Berkeley, Champaign, Berment, Villa Grove, Hoopeston, Venice-Madison (nighttime only), Canton, Clinton, Bloomington, Charleston, Sommer, Gilman, Crown 3 (tip your hat), Cicero, Gibson City, Fairmont City, Farmer City, Mound City, Carbondale, Metropolis, Blue Island, Quincy, Streator, Freeport, South Pekin, Virden, Ottawa, Shattuc, Virden-Girard, Davis Junction, Moline, De

Kalb, Rockford, Rochelle, Elgin (check the time), Paxton, Bushnell, Waukegan, Savanna, Woodlawn, East St. Louis, St. Elmo, Galesburg, Effingham, Odin, Joliet, Ashley, Cairo (watch out for pronunciation - it's KAY-row), Chicago Heights, and, of course, **CHICAGO** (Roosevelt Road, Union Avenue, Corwith, Halsted Street, Western Avenue, Cicero, Berwyn, Belwood, Clyde, Hanson Park, Brighton Park, Auburn Park, Schiller Park, Calumet, Riverdale, Bryn Mawr, Proviso, Pullman Junction, IC Junction, Wood Street, Landers, Hazel Crest, South Holland, South Chicago, West Chicago, Union Station, La Salle Street Station, Forth-Seventh Street, Seventy-First Street Yards, to name a few).

Indiana: Evansville (take a raft trip down the Ohio), Connersville, Princeton, Bloomington, Linton, Fulton, Washington, Youngtown, Bedford, New Albany, New Castle, Odon (all coal trains), Madison, Columbus, Richmond, Muncie, Anderson, Frankfort-WY, Lawrenceburg, Kokomo, Marion, Sullivan, Mitchell, Vincennes, Terre Haute/Spring Hill, Lafayette, La Porte, Peru, Valparaiso, Wabash, Gary, Seymour, Richmond, Fort Wayne-New Haven-Four Mile Road, Indianapolis (Big Four, Avon Yards - nighttime only), South Bend and Elkhart.

Iowa: Burlington, Red Oak, Ottumwa, Keokuk, Britt (don't miss the annual Hobo Convention in August), Fort Madison, Fort Dodge, Tara, Davenport, Ebner, Marshalltown, Hinton, Creston, Clinton, Chariton, Cherokee, Sheldon, Des Moines, West Des Moines, Dubuque, Le Mars, Muscatine, Moulton, Manly, Bettendorf (all coal trains), Atlantic, Cedar Rapids, Cedar Falls, Waterloo, Webster City, Iowa City, Charles City, Mason City, Sioux City, California Junction, Boone, Ames (stop off at a college party), Council Bluffs and Albia.

Kansas: Arkansas City, Garden City, Dodge City, Junction City, Scott City, Kansas City (Armourdale, Armstrong, Argentine, Kenokee, 18th St. Yards), Coffeyville, Marysville, Pittsburg, Esbon, Hutchinson, Newton, Hoisington, Herington (world's greatest milkshakes), Wellington, Pratt, Winfield, Independence (hardly), St. Francis, Cherokee, Chanute, Columbus, Council Grove, Fort Scott, El Dorado, Great Bend (breaks the monotony), Goodland, Parsons, Ft. Scott, Augusta, Concordia, Emporia, Fredonia, Almena, Salina, Hiawatha, Kiowa, Ottawa, Paola, Iola, Wichita,

Topeka, Neodesha, Lawrence, Abilene, Leavenworth, McPherson, Phillipsburg, Atchison, Kingman, Lorraine, Cherryvale, Maran, Selden, Oakley, Colby and Liberal (a real western town).

Kentucky: Hopkinsville, Danville, Nortonville, Louisville, Bowling Green, Middlesboro, Beaver Junction (take a hike in the Appalachians), Paducah, Corbin, Central City, Elkhorn City, Cecilia, Ravenna, Henderson, Frankfort, Hickman, Hazard (bring your coal shovel), Ashland, Loyall, Ft. Hamel, Russell, Winchester-Patio, Shelby, Youngtown, Williamstown, Elizabethtown, Lexington, Covington-Newport, Fulton and Berea.

Louisiana: Lake Charles, Opelousas, Orange, Oakdale, Crowley, Lafayette, New Iberia, Plaquemine, Tallulah, Gretna, Ferriday, Monroe, Minden-Sibley, Lobdell, Geismar, Baton Rouge, De Quincy, Morgan City (go swamp tunneling), Gramercy, Reserve, Livonia, Leesville, New Orleans (get ready for some long bridge walks), Alexandria, Winnfield and Shreveport.

Maine: Bangor, Waterville, Jackman Station, Saco-Biddeford, St. Francis, Lewiston-Auburn, Augusta, East Deering, Fort Fairfield, Gardiner, Rumford, Brunswick, Belfast, Searsport, Rockland, Portland (Rugby Yards), Millinocket, Mattawamkeag, Madawaska, Old Town, Oakfield, Houlton, Hermon, Limestone, Caribou, Vanceboro, Van Buren (bring your passport), Calais, Stockholm, Danville Junction, Milltown Junction, Yarmouth Junction and Brownville Junction (bring your passport).

Maryland: Westernport, Centreville, Cumberland, Hagerstown, Brunswick, Cambridge, Relay, Snowhill, Salisbury, Harve de Grace, Aberdeen (take the CSX Transportation tracks, not Amtrak's), Deer Park, Massey, Point of Rocks, Pocomoke and Denton.

Massachusetts: Athol (always loved this town), Ayer, North Adams (if headed east, get ready for the Hoosac Tunnel), Holyoke, Greenfield (take a stroll down a true New England mainstreet), Westfield, Springfield, Pittsfield, East Deerfield, Clinton, Lawrence, Lowell, Lynn, Attleboro, Fitchburg, Northbridge, Cambridge, Southbridge, New Bedford, Milford, Millers Falls, Waltham (check the time), Framingham, Selkirk, Readville, Somerville, Braintree, Salem, Webster, Worcester, Palmer, Gardner and Chicopee.

Michigan: Battle Creek (bring a spoon), Kalamazoo, Standish, Port Huron, Benton Harbor, Ann Arbor, Albion, Jackson, Wyandotte, Pontia, Nestoria, Ionia, Escanaba, Holland, Houghton, Hancock, Hamtramck (have a Polish), Highland Park, Muskegon, Ontanogan, Detroit-Ferndale (Moterm Yards - nighttime only), Big Rapids, Grand Rapids, Alma, Fling, Ludington, Manistee, Woodhaven, Traverse City (go boating), Bay City, Reed City, Mackinaw City (cross the Strait of Mackinac and keep going to the U.P.), Petoskey, Cheboygan, Saginaw, Sault Ste. Marie, Marquette (beware of deer hunters), Cadillac, Pontiac, Lapeer, Sterling, Ishpeming, Channing, Iron Mountain, Flat Rock, Gladstone and Lansing.

Minnesota: Austin (nice rolling farmland), Mankato, Minneapolis (St. Croix Tower, Westminster Street, Dale Street, Midway, Saint Anthony, Union, Minneapolis Junction, Hopkins, Van Buren Street Yards - nighttime only), Waseca, Winona, Red Wing, Hastings, Fairmont, Albert Lea, St. Cloud, St. Paul (nighttime only), South Moorehead, Stillwater, Staples, Savage, Shakopee, Little Falls, Fergus Falls, Hanley Falls, Thief River Falls, International Falls (bring a jacket), Taconite Harbor, Coon Creek, Bayport, Dilworth, Erskine, Two Harbors, Montevideo, Brainerd, Cloquet, Ortonville, Willmar, Duluth, Bemidji (never got a straight answer on how to pronounce this), Keewatin, Carlton, Appleton, Brookston, Crookston, North Crookston Junction, Detroit Lakes, Cass Lake, Hibbing, Gunn, Virginia, Forbes, Eveleth, Ely, Willmar, Owatonna, Ortonville, Warren, New Ulm, Noyes, Staples and Glencoe.

Mississippi: Tupelo (buy some honey), Clarksdale, Greenville, Greenwood, Yazoo City, Natchez, Hattiesburg, Vicksburg (visit the battlefield), Laurel, Holly Springs, New Albany, Amory, Aberdeen, Columbus, Gulfport (sleep in the pines across from the beach), Lake Cormorant, Pascagoula, Brookhaven, Meridian-Shops, Jackson (nighttime only), Winona, Canton, Corinth, Grenada, Biloxi, Picayune, Roxie and McComb.

Missouri: Kansas City (Avondale, Knoche, East, Neff, Murray, GWWR Yards), North Kansas City, Springfield Yard, Pacific, La Plata, Nevada (go east into the Ozarks), Sedalia, Louisiana, Aurora, Carthage, Hannibal, West Alton, Illmo, Mexico, Maryville, Marshall, Marceline, Moberly, Macon,

Neosho, Jefferson City, Monroe City, Crystal City, Harrisonville, Owensville, Brookfield, Horine, Lamar, Kelly, Stanberry, Poplar Bluff, Chillicothe, St. Louis (Lindenwood Yards - nighttime only), St. Joseph, St. Genevieve, Slater, Thayer, Lock Springs, Independence, Chaffee, Sikeston, Joplin, Teed, Cape Girardeau (take a swim in the Mississippi), Valley Park, West Quincy and West Plains.

Montana: Williston, Lewiston, Livingston, Libby (watch out for the Flathead Tunnel to the east), Logan, Bozeman, Garrison, Dillon, Wolf Point, Glasgow, Glendive, Malta, Terry, Miles City, Huntley-Jones Junction, Billings (visit my Mom), Butte, Silver Bow, Bainville, Sweet Grass, Silver Bow, Cut Bank, Great Falls, Three Forks, Fort Benton, Havre (watch out for grass fires), Conkelley, Shelby, Whitefish, Whitetail, Missoula (go to another college party) Laurel, Forsyth, Essex and Helena.

Nebraska: Scottsbluff, Oshkosh (buy a new pair of overalls, b'gosh), Orleans Junction/Flynn, Omaha, South Omaha, O'Neill, O'Fallons, McCook, Ravenna, Grand Island, Holdrege, Chadron, Fairbury, Beatrice, Falls City, Nebraska City, Central City, David City, Sioux City, South Sioux City (Ferry), Fremont, Ashland, Kearney, North Bend, North Platte, North Port, Crete, Long Pine, Broken Bow (notice no one lives out here?), Hastings, Huntsville, Louisville, Columbus, Sidney, Norfolk, Alliance (Emerson, Third Street, West Alliance Yards; great big hobo jungle), Crawford, Superior, Valentine and Lincoln (Hobson, Cushman and Carling Yards).

Nevada: Sparks (go across the street and try your luck), Las Vegas (don't even have to cross the street), Winnemucca (runnamucka in), Golconda, Carlin, Battle Mountain, Beowawe, Hazen, Boulder Junction, Elko, Mina, Flanigan, Wells, Gerlach, Caliente and Moapa (Union Pacific - hot yards).

New Hampshire: Franklin, Lebanon, Woodsville, Woodstock, Whitefield, Berlin (any way you go, be ready for some rugged country), Groveton, Laconia, Nashua, Huzens, Manchester, Portsmouth, Plymouth, Somersworth, Rochester, Hartford, Claremont, Concord, Dover and Exeter.

New Jersey: Jersey City, Paterson, Clifton, Passaic, Montclair, Bloomfield, Dover, Orange, East Orange, Elizabethport, Perth Amboy, Red Bank, Hoboken (nighttime only), Bound Brook, Roselle, New Brunswick, Newark (Oak Island Yards - nighttime only), Trenton, Vineland, Camden, Phillipsburg, Woodbury, South Kearny, North Bergen, South Amboy, Winslow, Millville and Bridgeton.

New Mexico: Gallup (red rock cliff dwellings to the west), Grants, Belen, Vaughn, Clovis, Santa Rita, Rincon, Las Cruces, Carlsbad, Roswell ("Little Texas"), Whitewater, Tucumcari, French, Texico, Alamogordo, Las Vegas, Raton, Carrizozo, Deming and Lordsburg.

New York: Albany-Rensselaer, Poughkeepsie, New Rochelle (visit your poor cousins in Weschester County), Peekskill, Watertown (go east into the Adirondacks), Kingston, Newburgh, Beacon, Schenectady-South Schenectady, Hoosic Junction, Hornell, Hudson, Rome, Troy, Syracuse, Saratoga Springs, Elmira, Massena, Lackawanna, Batavia, East Salamanca (sip a Genessee Beer), Utica, Ravena, Oneonta, Olean, Ossining, Silver Springs, Little Falls, Niagra Falls (stay low if you sleep in the park by the falls), Waterboro, Post Road Crossing, Corning, Gang Mills, Cortland, Lancaster, Buffalo (Bison Yards - nighttime only), Lockport, Endicott, Mount Vernon, Mechanicville, Hicksville, Port Jervis, Rotterdam Junction, Rouses Point, White Plains, White Hall, Rochester, Binghamton, Plattsburgh, Selkirk and Dunkirk.

North Carolina: Wilmington (resist the urge to stowaway on something), Rocky Mount, Wilson, Weldon, Goldsboro, Dillsboro, Wadesboro, Greensboro, North Wilkesboro, Greenville, Reidsville, Thomasville, Statesville, Fayetteville, Hendersonville, Ashville Yard (by all means go see those Great Smoky Mountains), Burlington, Durham, East Durham (buy a sack of rolling tobacco), Duke, Hamlet, Hickory, High Point, Kannapolis, Barber, Concord, Chocowinity, Mount Airy, Salisbury, Selma, Shelby, Star, Lee, Gastonia, Marion (visit a southern plantation), Raleigh, Spencer, Winston-Salem (don't start any anti-smoking conversations), Charlotte, Pembroke, Aberdeen, New Bern, Norwood and Fair Bluff.

North Dakota: Williston, Minot, Grand Forks, West Grand Forks, East Grand Forks, Surrey, Fargo, Vance, Valley City, Watford City, Northgate, Grenora, Harvey, Jamestown, Grafton, Carrington, Casselton, Dickinson (you are completely in the middle of nowhere here), Wahpeton, Surrey Line Junction, Oakes, Ardoch, Lansford, Kenmare, Enderlin, Drake, Devils Lake (watch out for grass fires from hot brakes), Oakes, Rogers, Portal (bring your passport), Bismarck-Mandan, Killdeer, Beach and Hettinger.

Ohio: Toledo (Stanley Yards - nighttime only), Defiance, Fostoria, Lima, South Lima, Urbana, Piqua, Ashtabula, Ravenna, Delta, Arcadia DA, Mingo Junction, Delmont Junction, Montpelier, Findlay, Bucyrus, Justus, Dunkirk, Delaware, Sidney, Springfield, Mansfield, Sandusky, Norwood, Washington Court House, Middletown, Youngstown, Hamilton, Canton, Dayton, Akron, Marion, Massillon, Vermilion, Newark, Alliance, Ridgeway, Evendale, Cuyahoga Falls, CW Tower, Conneaut, Cleveland (Collinwood Yards - nighttime only), Columbus (Buckeye Yards - nighttime only), Cincinnati (Queensgate Yards - nighttime only), Chillicothe (nice country), Clare, Crestline, Steubenville, Zanesville, Sciotoville, Bellefontaine, Bellevue Yard, Gallipolis, Greenwich, Portsmouth, East Portsmouth, Wallbridge, Willard, Liverpool and Lorain.

Oklahoma: Guymon (don't blink), Woodward, Poncha City, Elk City, Custer City, Oklahoma City (north, south, east or west - take off), Duncan, Durant, El Reno, Enid (watch for trains headed for Mexico), Guthrie, Seminole, Muskogee (don't burn Old Glory down at the Courthouse), Pawnee, Chickasha, Tulsa (Cherokee Yards), Heavener, Henryetta, Nowata, Vinita, Sapulpa, Panama, Waynoka, Ada, Alva, Avard, Altus, Afton Junction, Ardmore, Claremore, Clinton, Lawton, Frederick, Madill, Hugo, Perry, Bartlesville, Holdenville, McAlester and Howe.

Oregon: Klamath Falls (wave to the Three Sisters Peaks), Bend, Eugene, Hillsboro, Hermiston, Pendleton, Medford, Corvallis, Albany, Astoria, Ashland (Shakespeare in the pines?), Oregon City, Chemult Junction, Cascade Summit, Hinkle, Roseburg, Reedsport, Troutdale, Springfield, Umatilla, The Dalles (salute the Grand Columbia), Portland (Brookland Yards - nighttime only), North Portland Junction, Salem, La Grande, Baker, Burns (deserts this far north?), Ontario, Oakridge, Westfir and Madras.

Pennsylvania: Altoona, Myrtle Point, Union City, Oil City, Albion, Erie, Ridgway, Brockway, Conway, Reading, Du Bois, Dunmore, Lebanon, Lock Haven, Lancaster, Warren, Washington, Freeport, Williamsport, McKeesport, Harrisburg, Lewisburg, Wilkinsburg, Greensburg, Chambersburg, Indianapolis, Pittsburg (Rook Yards - nighttime only), Sunbury, Scranton, Easton, Pittston, Allentown, Johnstown, Norristown, Lewistown, Punxsutawney (say "hi" to Punxs. Pete), Clearfield, Butler, Kittaning, Beaver Falls, Braddock, Bradford, Brookville, Coatesville, Connellsville, Meadville, Morrisville, Shippenville, Reynoldsville, Tyrone, Monessen-Charleroi, New Castle Junction, York, Hyndman, Bethlehem, Nanticoke and Wilkes Barre.

Rhode Island: Cranston, Providence, East Providence, Woonsocket, Pawtucket, Central Falls, Newport (nice houses, huh?), Westerley and West Kingston.

South Carolina: Abbeyville, Warrenville, Greenville (getting tired? Take a run up to Travelers Rest), Greenwood, Orangeburg, Spartanburg-Hayne Junction, Laurens, Newberry, Columbia (Andrews Yards; stately old Southern city), Chester, Carlisle, Clinton, Charleston, Darlington, Denmark, Dillon, Florence (thumb down to Myrtle Beach and meet a waiter or waitress), Fairfax, Sumter, Rock Hill and Yemassee.

South Dakota: Rapid City (go see Mt. Rushmore on its 51st B-day), Pierre (feel isolated? you should), Huron, Canton, Edgemont, Yankton, Watertown, Chamberlain, Brookings, Elk Point, State Line, Belle Fourche, Philip, Mobridge (hope you've got company or a good book), Aberdeen, Mitchell, Milbank, Sioux Falls, Napa and Wolsey.

Tennessee: Johnson City, Morristown, Nashville, Knoxville (Sevier Yards), Chattanooga (CT Tower, Pratt, De Butts Yards), Athens, Erwin, Tullahoma, Etowah, Dyersburg, Murfreesboro (visit the battle site), Capleville, Clarksville, Kingsport, Bristol, Oakdale, North Oakdale, New Line, Cleveland, Dossett, Harriman, Bulls Gap, Emory Gap, Morley, Frisco, Jackson, Memphis (Tennessee Yards - or wait for a tie-up at the Harahan Bridge), Milan and Rockwood.

Texas: El Paso (Cotton Avenue Yards), Amarillo, Waco, Del Rio, Presidio, Laredo, San Antonio (Kirby Yards), San Angelo, Texline,

Texas City, Pecos, Palestine, Valentine (watch out for Border Patrol), Alpine, Sanderson, Houston (New South Yards—nighttime only), Beaumont, Orange, Brownwood, Waxahachie, Chillicothe, Victoria, Texarkana (hop a fast freight to California), Corsicana, Toyah, Sierra Blanca, Flatonia, Odessa, Mineola, Tenaha, Wichita Falls, Dalhart, Denison, Dimmitt, Dallas (T&P Junction, Ninth Street, North, Irving Yards - nighttime only), Ft. Worth, Saginaw (North Ft. Worth), Cleveland, Childress, Corpus Christi, Carollton, Cleburne, Yoakum, Mesquite, Galveston, Monahans, Port Authur, Bryan, Tyler, Marshall, South Sherman Junction, Hodge Junction, Big Spring, Eagle Pass, Ranger, Silsbee, Eastland, Sweetwater, Abilene, Harlingen, Hearne, Bowie, Teague, Lufkin, Longview, Plainview, Enise, Estelline, Lubbock, Paris, Bay City, Robstown, Greenville, Brownville, Gainesville, Houlderville, Austin and Temple.

Utah: Wendover, Spanish Fork, Murray, Logan, Soldier Summit, Nephi, Garfield, Provo, Ogden (nighttime only), Salt Lake City (Roper Yards - nighttime only), Brigham City, Milford (you are further away from another RR than anywhere else in the USA), Delta, Helper and Green River.

Vermont: Burlington (take a [brief] dip in Lake Champlain), Bennington, Montpelier, Rutland, Windsor, Brattleboro, Middlebury, Bellows Falls, Wells River, White River Junction, Island Pond, Springfield, St. Albans, St. Johnsbury (wild and wooly country), Newport, East Alburgh, South Vernon, Hartford and Richford (bring your passport).

Virginia: Alexandria-Arlington (Potomac Yards), Lynchburg, Fredericksburg, Petersburg, Harrisonburg (head west into the Shenandoahs), Danville, Charlottesville, Burkeville, Keysville, Gordonsville, Bluefield (don't confuse with West Virginia), Shenandoah, Kinney, Andover, Abilene Connection, Buchanan, Narrows, Richmond, Chesapeake (Portlock Yards), Pulaski, Radford, Hampton, Staunton, Covington, Walton, Norton, Monroe, Gladstone, Winchester, Crewe, Dundee, Manassas Junction (visit Bull Run), Newport News, Clifton Forge, Lamberts Point, Norfolk (Conneaut Yards - headed for the Old World?), Suffolk, Portsmouth, Roanoke, West Roanoke (visit the Blueridge Trail) and Bristol.
Washington: Spokane (Sunset Junction, Hillyard and Yardley Yards), Ritzville, Oroville, Richland, Pasco, Sumas, Cheney, Longview,

Grandview, Olympia, Tacoma, Yakima, Walla Walla, Lamona, Centralia, Riparia, Attalia-Wallula, Aberdeen, Anacortes, Blaine, Black River, Sunnyside, Hooper, Hoquiam, Wishram (again, salute the thundering Columbia), Bellingham, Pullman Bremerton, Lakeside-Latah Junction, Vancouver, Seattle (Twenty-Third Street, Balmer, Interbay, Garfield Street, North Portal, King Street Station, Whatcom Yards), Cherhalis, Everett, Kettle Falls and Wenatchee (drop in for the annual late-summer Apple Blossom Festival).

Washington, D.C.

West Virginia: Huntington, Princeton, Grafton, Hinton, Charleston, Mannington, Morgantown, Tunneltown, Williamson, East Williamson (go visit Colonel Sanders or the Hatfields and McCoys), Nitro, Logan, Bluefield (beautiful countryside in through here), Kelleysville, Moundsville, New Martinsville, Barboursville, Adrian, Beckley, Elkins, Elmore, Keyser, Pleasant, Deepwater, Richmond, Bellaire, Gauley Bridge (look for tri-county bluegrass festivals), St. Albans, Kenova, Parkersburg, Clarksburg, Martinsburg, Landisburg, White Sulphur Springs, Wharncliffe and Wheeling-Benwood.

Wisconsin: Superior-Boylston (East End, Hill Ave. Yards), Ladysmith, Chippewa Falls, Baraboo, Oshkosh (b'gosh), Manitowoc, Sheboygan, Kenosha, Wauwatosa, Waukesha, Wausau (forget the insurance - keep riding), Manitowac, Kewaunee, Allouez/Itasca, Beloit, La Crosse, Marinette, Racine, Prairie du Chien, Eau Claire (Altoona), Fond du Lac, Portage, Rhinelander, Plymouth, Sparta, Merrill, Marshfield, Adams, Ashland, Stevens Point, Spooner, Port Edwards, Appleton (watch out for hunter trafficjams in early Fall), Bradley, West Allis, Milwaukee (Muskego Yards±—nighttime only), North Milwaukee, Madison (go to a frat party in "Mad" Town), Watertown, Wisconsin Rapids, Spooner, Stevens Point, Janesville and Green Bay-Howard.

Wyoming: Cheyenne, Laramie, Rawlins (do not become stranded here - State Prison), Granger, Casper, Wendover, Gillette (take a coal train anywhere east or south), Bridger Junction, Donkey Creek, Sheridan, Shawnee,

Bill, Orin, Cody, Evanston, Rock Springs, Green River (arguably America's crookedest town), Douglas, Greybull, Guernsey and Shobon.

Now for our Canadian friends here's a group of towns in the Canadian West where you can catch out on a freight. I only list towns in the West because I've never ridden any Canadian freights east of Winnipeg.

Alberta: Peace River, Keg River, Meander River, High River, McLennan, Fort McMurry ("Waterways"), Fort MacLeod, Smith, Edmonton, South Edmonton, Lloydminster, (on the line with Saskatchewan), Camrose, Consort, Stettler, Hanna, Calgary (Alyth Yards - nighttime only), Manyberries, McLennon, Brooks, Banff, Red Deer, Dinosaur Junction, Lethbridge, Medicine Hat, Wainwright, Windfall, Lac la Biche, Grande Prairie, Grand Centre, Vegreville, Vermilion, Innisfail, Brazeau (Nordegg), Blairmore, Edson, Drumheller, Jasper, Hythe, Athabasca, Wetaskiwin, Bassano and Taber.

British Columbia: Golden, Revelstoke, Vernon, North Kamloops, North Bend, Blue River, Blackpool, Boston Bar, Kelowna, Chilliwack, Penticton, Trail, Creston, Cranbrook, Grand Forks, Ashcroft, Lytton, Yale, Hope, Fernie, Field, Red Pass, Princeton, North Vancouver (nighttime only), Roberts Bank (all coal trains), New Westminster, Kingsgate, Kimberley, Squamish, Lillooet, Endako, Clinton, Williams Lake, Bear Lake, Burns Lake, Basque, Quesnel, Prince George, Prince Rupert, Ridley Island, Vanderhoof, Smithers, Hazelton, Armstrong, Terrace, Fort St. James, Fort St. John, Fort Nelson, Port Coquitlam ("Poco"), Port Mann, Middle River, Takla Landing, Tacheeda (all coal trains), Driftwood, Chetwynd, Castlegar, Beatton River, Fontas, Dawson Creek, Mcbride, Tete-Jaune-Cache, Stuart, Sinclair Mills, Victoria, Courtenay and Nanaimo.

Manitoba: Swan River, Lynn Lake, Optic Lake, Snow Lake, Dunlop, Thicket Portage, Amery, Rafter, Churchill, Gladstone, Winnipegosis, Winnipeg (Symington Yards - nighttime only), Neepawa, Minnedosa, North Transcona, Dauphin, Portage-la-Prairie, Beausejour, Souris, Boissevain, Boniface, Sprague, The Pas, Brandon, Carman, Carberry, Morden, Methven Transfer, Morris, Russell, Paddington, Thompson, Gillam, Virden, Gypsumville, Wabowden, Flin Flon, Rivers, Emerson/ Emerson Junction and Killarney.

Northwest Territories: Hay River and Pine Point.

Saskatchewan: Estevan, Bienfait, Govenlock, Shaunavon, Assiniboia, Weyburn, Maple Creek, Swift Current, Meadow Lake, Watrous, Carrot River, Moose Jaw, Regina, Indian Head, Melville, Yorkton, Young, Canora, Sturgis, Speers, Nokomis, Wynyard, Wayburn, Lanigan, Nipawin, Moosomin, Beechy, Wadena, Conquest, Humboldt, Saskatoon, Biggar, Wilkie, Battleford, North Battleford, Northgate, Rosthern, Rosetown, Shellbrook, Lloydminster, Prince Albert, Tisdale, Tyson, Kamsack, Hudson Bay, Maple Creek, Broadview, Willowbunch and Kindersley.

Yukon Territory: White Horse (the narrow-gauge ride mentioned earlier going over to Skagway Alaska - *if they ever reopen it*).

GLOSSARY OF TERMS

-ABD freight brake: Refined Westinghouse AB freight brake, first adopted in the 1930s. See AB freight brake.

-ABDW freight brake: Further refined ABD freight brake, now standard on North American freightcars. Same Westinghouse principles apply.

-AB freight brake: The original Westinghouse automatic air brake, first adopted on the Pennsylvania Railroad in 1876. See Automatic air brake.

-A.B.S. - Automatic block system: Signaling system commonly used on over-the-road track. Electric current running in a circuit through the rails is interrupted, or "shunted" by a train's wheels, telling signal to display a red aspect. See Shunt.

-Absolute signal: A signal which when displaying a red aspect means "stop-and-stay" stopped until the aspect changes to yellow or green, or is superseded by an override order. See Override order and Stop-and-stay.

-Ace Centerflow hopper: A widely-used closed hopper which has body bolster top shear plates and is rideable. See Body bolster top shear plates.

-Accommodation car: Old term for caboose.

-Advertised freight service: Industry parlance for a regular freight train. See Regular freight.

-A-end: The end of any freightcar which does *not* have the handbrake. See B-end.

-Agro-industrial workweek: Author's conceptualization of the manner in which the ebb and flow of agricultural and industrial production variables impact North American railroads.

-Air brake valve: Valve underneath each freightcar (except hoppers) which allows air to pass from air reservoir to brake cylinder, setting brakes.

-Aired-up: A train which has legal air and is ready to depart. See Legal air.

-Airhorn: Modern-day equivalent of a steam locomotive's whistle, which warns passersby of presence or approach of a train and signals orders to distant crewmembers.

-Air reservoir: Reserve of air underneath each freightcar (except hoppers and certain specialized cars) which releases air into the cylinder through the air valve when air pressure is reduced in the brake cylinder, setting brakes.

Alertor: A safety device attached to an engineer's throttle handle and brake valve throttle which requires the engineer to hold and release each throttle in a prescribed sequence to confirm he is alert and attentive.

-Alternator: Converts high-horsepower diesel-electric engine's crankshaft motion into electricity (600 volts DC). See Generator.

-Ammeter: A gauge inside the cab which indicates how much current is running through the electric traction motors and thus how hot they are. See Electric traction motor.

-Amtrak: National Passenger Rail Corporation.

-Anchor plate: The metal plate which sits atop the face of a railroad tie upon which the rail is laid. See Tie and Tie-plate.

-Anti-creeper: Spring clips which snap onto the base of a rail and come up against the tie to prevent rail creep. See Rail creep.

-Apex: The topmost part of a freightyard hump. See Hump.

-Appliances: Equipment designed for workers to work. Includes brakewheels, footboards, grab irons, ladders and stirrups. See each and Running gear.

-Apron: Small metal "lip" around open sides of some freightcars, provided to keep loads (and therefore wayfarers) aboard trains.

-Arrival yard: When a train reaches its ultimate destination it stops and waits in the arrival yard until switched out of existence.

-Ash cat: Old term for railroad fireman. See Fireman.

-Aspect: The color of a signal's light: Red for stop, yellow for caution and green for go or proceed.

-Association of American Railroads (AAR): American member railroads' industry trade group, statistician, lobbyist and coordinator.

-Automatic Air Brake: Invented by George Westinghouse in 1869 and first used in 1876. A continuous serial action railroad brake system which uses increased air pressure to release brakes and reduced air pressure to set brakes. See Straight air system, Continuous air brake and Serial action.

-Automatic brake valve throttle: A throttle inside the cab the engineer uses to set and release brakes on his train.

-Automatic coupler: First universally-adopted coupling system patented by Eli H. Janney in 1868. Eliminated necessity of standing between cars to couple or uncouple cars. See Glad hands, Knuckles and Link-and-pin coupler.

-Auto rack: Generic term for a bi- or tri-level freightcar which hauls new cars and trucks.

-Auxiliary-emergency air reservoir: Backup air reservoir underneath each freightcar (except hoppers) which applies brakes in emergency stops and during failure of standard air brake system.

-Babbit-faced bearing: A bearing made of tin, copper and antimony which reduces friction between axle and bearing in a friction-bearing journalbox. See Friction-bearing journalbox.

-Back over: (Verb) To return a switch to its original position after passing over it, e.g., "Throw it *back over* to the main after the rearend clears."

-Bad order: Any track or equipment problem which impacts optimum performance, rendering it substandard, defective, dangerous or shot.

-Ballast: Crushed rock, slag, shell or gravel spread beneath railroad track, designed to anchor down the track, spread a train's weight over a larger area and provide track drainage.

-Ballasting: Extra metal plating installed on diesel locomotives to increase their weight ergo traction. See Wheel slippage.

-Ballast tamping machine: A track-conveyed hydraulic tamping machine which repacks ballast under the track to prevent rail creep and maintain track alignment. See Rail creep.

-Balling the jack: A freight train which is rolling fast. See Highball.

-Ball the jack: (Verb) To drive a train at high speeds, e.g., "They were *balling the jack* at the time of the wreck."

-Banjo: A small portable frying pan.

-Bathtub gon: A coal gondola with higher sides than an ordinary gondola, often equipped with a rotary coupler for roll dumping. See Gondola, Roll dumping and Rotary coupler.

-Bays: Chutes underneath hopper cars which allow gravity to unload the car's lading.

-Bat out: (Verb) To push or hump freightcars toward a new train, e.g., *"Bat out these last five cars to the local on Track 3."* See Hump (Verb) and Kick cars.

-Behind time: An engineer running behind schedule.

-B-end: The end of any freightcar which has the handbrake. See A-end.

-Bender: A railroad track alignment worker.

-Big box: Intermodal container which covers the entire floor of its platform (flatcar or well car). See Platform and Well car.

-Big hole in the sky: See Westbound.

-Big hole position: An emergency stop.

-Bi-level auto rack: Industry parlance for a double-decked auto rack.

-Billygoat: Familiar term for a yard switching unit. See Yard switching unit.

-Bleeding air: Releasing air from each brake cylinder along a string of freightcars scheduled to be humped, to release the brakes and allow the cars to roll freely in the yards.

-Bleed rod: The rod located near mid-car underneath the floor of a freightcar which a worker pushes to bleed brake cylinder air.

-Blind baggage: Old term for hopping a train and riding the footboard behind the coalcar and in front of the first freightcar (a baggage car on passenger trains). Also perhaps riding outside on a passenger train. "Blind" because of reduced vision.

-Block: A series of freightcars with the same destination coupled together consecutively. See Blocking.

-Block: A section of over-the-road track divided into roughly 2 mi. lengths. See Block system.

-Blocking: The method by which freightcars are coupled together to form a train. See Consist.

-Block system: Track signaling system where over-the-road track is divided into blocks, each block having signals warning of a train's presence on the block or in the immediate vicinity. See A.B.S., Block, CTC and Shunt.

-Blowers: Large fans which cool a diesel-electric locomotive's electric traction motors. See Electric traction motor.

-Body bolster top sheer plate: Industry parlance for platforms over the wheels of rideable hoppers which provide traveling accommodation for wayfarers.

-Bolted-rail track: Track made of rails in lengths of 39, 45, 60 or 79 ft. which are bolted together at each end by fish-plates. See Fish-plate and Joint rail.

-Book of Rules: A rule book which governs all facets of railroad activity. Each railroad has its own book, which must conform to minimum FRA safety standards. See Federal Railroad Administration.

-Bottoms: See Bays.

-Bouncer: Old term for caboose.

-Bowl: The part of a gravity freightyard which receives cars which have been humped. See Gravity yard and Hump (Verb).

-Bracing: Any of a variety of freight packing schemes which prevents a load from shifting. See Dunnage.

-Brake chain: Chain attached to brakewheel, brake cylinder push rod and brakes which pulls brakes onto wheels when brakes are set.

-Brake cylinder: Cylinder underneath each freightcar (except hoppers and specialty cars) which fills with air to release brakes, then releases air and is refilled by air reservoir to set brakes. Cylinder is refilled by engine air, forcing reserve air back into air reservoir to release brakes again.

-Brake cylinder push rod: Push rod connecting brake cylinder to brake chains which pulls on or releases chain to set and release brakes.

-Brakeman: Train crewmember responsible for track and car management. See Switchman.

-Brakeman's cab: Old term for caboose.

-Brakeman's club: An oak staff carried by 19th century brakemen to securely set handbrakes when they'd "wind 'em up." See Wind 'em up.

-Brakeman's platform: A metal platform at the B-end of a walled freightcar or tankcar a brakeman stands on while switching or setting/releasing handbrakes.

-Brake rigging: Generic term for all components of a railroad brake system on a freightcar.

-Brake staff: See Brakeman's club.

-Brake throttle: Engineer's hand lever which sets and releases air brakes or electropneumatic brakes.

-Breaking the air: Rapid release of pressurized air from an air brake system, either when units uncouple, an air hose bursts or a break-in-two occurs.

-Break-in-two: When a coupler on a moving train fails and the train breaks into two sections.

-Break-of-gauge point: The location where railroads of different track gauges meet. See Track gauge.

-Bridge hog: Railroad bridge worker.

-Bridge plate: Metal plate at the end of some piggybacks which snaps down to bridge gap between cars so trailers can be driven from one piggyback to the next. See Circus loading and Piggyback.

-Brotherhoods: Twenty-One traditional unions which represent the various occupational "trades" on the railroad, i.e., Brotherhood of Railroad Brakemen, Brotherhood of Engineers, etc. See United Transportation Union.

-Buff: Compression of railroad car couplers and draft gears during slowing or stops. See Draft.

-Buff in: (Verb) To compress or bring together a train's slack during slowing or stops, e.g., "You *buffed her in* nicely down that last grade."

-Buggy: Old term for caboose.

-Bulkhead flats: Flatcars equipped with "bulkheads" or walls at each end.

-Bulkheads: Vertical end-walls on flatcars which prevent loads from shifting forward or backward off the car.

-Bull: Non-union railroad employee hired to protect a railroad.

-Bullet train: "Shinkasen" - Japanese high-speed electric train opened in 1964 which connects all major cities of central Japan.

-Bull local: See Drag freight.

-Bull's-eye signal: See Searchlight signal.

-Bum: (Verb) To live by begging or sponging off other people, e.g., "Can I *bum* a dime off you?" A person who engages in bumming. In literary circles a person who "drinks and wanders (riding trains)." See Hobo and Tramp.

-Bumpers: Freightcar couplers. See Draft gear, Draw-head and Riding the bumpers.

B-unit: Multiple cabless engines coupled together to an on-the-point unit (e.g., original diesel designs of the 1950s and 1960s; new models also have B-units). See On-the-point unit.

-Bunk down (Verb) To hide in an end or ice compartment of an old refrigerator car for safety, e.g., "Don't forget to *bunk down* heading into the yards." See End bunker and Reefer.

-Bunkhouse: Hobo term for refrigerator car's end or ice compartments, which when empty provided a safe place to ride a train. See End bunker and Reefer.

-Bunt: See Bat out and Kick out.

-By the Book: When railroad workers work exactly as prescribed by the Book of Rules, usually during periods of labor-management friction. See Book of Rules.

-Cab: The crew compartment on any type of locomotive.

-Cab-forward: Steam locomotive design placing the cab ahead of the boiler and smokestack, to prevent smoke asphyxiation in long Western tunnels.

-Cabin car: Old term for caboose.

-Cab signaling: A modern signaling mechanism which brings signal aspects (colors) up into the cab. Often combined with an auditory alert system.

-Call a train: (Verb) To schedule a traincrew to come on duty at a specific time, e.g., "When is the next train to Memphis *called*?" See Call for.

-Call boy: A messenger (no longer used) who ran messages from depot to traincrew and back.

-Call for: (Verb) Time when a traincrew is scheduled to go on duty, e.g., "This train is *called for* 10 p.m."

-Call Sheet: Printed train schedule obtainable in freight office.

-Canned heat: See Tokay blanket.

-CalTrain: Commuter/passenger system serving the San Francisco Peninsula.

-CAPY - freight weight capacity: Total freightcar weight allowable on the rail, as indicated on each side of a freightcar, e.g., a 125-ton car carries 250,000 lbs. plus the weight of the car = CAPY 375,000. See LD LMT/LD LT and LT WT.

-Car foreman: Freightyard worker who supervises work of Carman/Car knocker.

-Car knocker: Freightyard worker who readies a train for departure and inspects cars. Synonymous with "Carman."

-Carman: See Car knocker.

-Carriage: The floor of a freightcar which rides atop the trucks. See Chassis and Truck. Also British name for a railroad passenger car.

-Catch out: (Verb) To hop or jump a freight train, e.g., "I *caught out* in Omaha and rode it all the way to Oakland."

-Catenary: The overhead electrical wire from which an electric train derives its energy. See Pantograph.

-Center Beam Bulkhead Flat Car: New bulkhead flatcar with a center beam running down the middle of the floor, for easier forklift loading and load strap-down. Popular with lumber manufacturers. See Bulkhead flats.

-Chassis: The floor of a freightcar which rides atop the trucks. See Carriage and Trucks.

-Circus loading: Older method of loading trailers onto piggybacks where trailer is driven across one piggyback to another over bridge plates. See Bridge plate and Piggyback.

-Classification yard: A freightyard where trains are assembled for departure. See Marshaling yard.

-Classify: (Verb) To assemble and make ready a group of freightcars for departure on a train, e.g., "*Classify* the 8915 section next." See Marshall and Hump (Verb).

-Clasped hands principle: The design principle on all North American coupling schemes for couplers and air hoses, like two hands clasped together with knuckles wrapped.

-Class 1 Line Haul Railroad: Any railroad which generates roughly $100,000,000 in gross revenue annually (currently 14 in North America).

-Claw spike: An angular railroad spike which has a wide, flat head. When sunk into a tie the "claw," or head holds rails and tie-plates down on the tie.

-Climb the rails: (Verb) To derail a train by any cause, e.g., "We were damned lucky to come out alive when that sucker *climbed the rails*."

-Coach: See Carriage.

-Cocked position: Prepositioning of the pin prior to coupling in the link-and-pin coupling system. See Link-and-pin.

-COFC - Container On Flatcar: Container shipped on a railroad flatcar. See Intermodal freight and Platform.

-Coffin Bill of 1893: The federal Act mandating use of Janney automatic couplers on all railroad cars, named after the coupler's advocate, Lorenzo Coffin. See Federal Appliance Safety Act of 1893.

-Colored position signal: Complex and rarely-used signal system outside the scope of this text.

-Combination: Hobo Mulligan stew, generally meat, potatoes and whatever else is at hand. See Hobo stew.

-Combing: See Apron.

-Comes out of: (Verb) Used to describe the freightyard from which a freight train originates, e.g., "This train *came out of* the Argentine Yards."

-Communication center: Traffic management center on CTC-controlled track. See CTC.

-Compromise car: A 19th century railroad car with a wide wheel tread designed to operate over tracks of close but different gauges. Abandoned in 1880s after one-too-many spectacular wrecks. See Break-of-gauge point and Wheel tread.

-Conductor: Train crewmember who is train boss, orders movement, cut-outs and pick-ups and assists other crewmembers. See Engineer and Trainmen.

-Conductor's van: Old term for caboose.

-Condemn: (Verb) To scrap an old, bad order or unprofitable freightcar, e.g., "We had to *condemn* all our old reefers."

-Consist: Term for the engines and freightcars a given train is made up of, e.g., "This train's *consist is* two units and 47 piggybacks."

-Console: The position in the cab where an engineer sits to drive his train.

-Constant-lit signal: A signal which remains lighted regardless of whether any trains are in the vicinity (usually stays green).

-Continuous brakes: Mechanical air brakes which set and release practically simultaneously. May also be electrical or electropneumatic.

-Continuous-welded rail: Industry parlance for ribbon rail. See Ribbon rail.

-Control stand: See Console.

-Coolers: A water system which cools a diesel-electric engine's lubrication system.

-Cornfield meet: A head-on train collision. See Head-on and Prairie meet.

-Coupler fixtures: The moveable parts of a coupler, e.g., the hands, locking pin and brake lever bar. See, e.g., Cut lever and Glad hands principle.

-Crew Car: Old term for caboose.

-Crew change: See Crew division.

-Crew division: Industry parlance for where railroads change crews on an over-the-road freight train. See Division.

-Cross-over track: On double-track mainline a track which runs from one track across to the other, facilitating switching and traffic routing of trains around one another.

-Crumb boss: The designated chef in a hobo jungle. See Gang cook and Jungle.

-Crummy: Old term for caboose.

-CTC - Centralized Traffic Control: Modern signaling system wherein all signals and switches in freightyards and for up to hundreds of miles of over-the-road track are connected to and controlled by a centralized traffic monitoring facility or "Communications center." Often fully computerized.

-CU FT - cubic foot capacity: Total cargo space available in cubic feet as indicated on each side of a freightcar, e.g., "CU FT 3713."

-Cummings Diesel: The diesel engine which powered original General Electric freight train locomotives.

-Cushion car: A rubber- or hydraulically-cushioned freightcar (usually boxcar) used for shipment of sensitive freight.

-Cushioning unit: A modern cushioning device at the center undercarriage of a freightcar which works in conjunction with a sliding center sill to provide cushioning during slows or stops. May be rubber or hydraulic. See Sliding center sill.

-Cut: A freightcar or cars uncoupled from a string which is/are taken to or left at a certain location or coupled onto another train.

-Cut in: One or more additional cars or engines placed onto an existing train.

-Cut lever: The lever at one end of the side of all freightcars which a brakeman pulls up on to uncouple two freightcars.

-Cut out: (Verb) To drop off one or more freightcars for a customer on a siding or in a freightyard, e.g., "I got *cut out* in the middle of nowhere."

-Cutting slack: Reduction of tension in a train's couplers and draft gears when a train slows or stops, allowing cars to be uncoupled. See Buff and Slack.

-CYA - Cover Your Ass: The fundamental assumption of North American railroad signaling systems which assumes trains are moving in either direction on either side of a train and requires operation of all signals in the vicinity to reflect this reality (or fiction).

-Dark track: Track which has no signaling system. Speed limit 49 MPH.

-Dashboards: Railroad employee coveralls.

-Deadend siding: A siding which leaves the mainline and doesn't come back to meet it at the other end. See Double-ended siding.

-Dead head: (Verb) To move a new crew ahead of their train by auto or another train, e.g., "We were *dead headed* to Altoona to meet that train."

-Deadman's pedal: A safety pedal at the foot of an engineer in older diesel-electric engines which must be depressed at all times the engine is in motion; otherwise the engine automatically sets brakes and stops.

-Dead on the clock. By FRA rules when a traincrew works one minute over 12 hours they go "dead on the clock" and must immediately cease operations and wait for a new crew. See Federal Railroad Administration.

-Dead string: A string of freightcars which is scheduled to be separated (humped) and placed on different new trains. Also a string of cars which is bad order or has been redlined. See Bad order, Condemn, Hump and Redline.

-Decelostat: A brake sensor device on freightcars which slightly decreases brake pressure on a wheel when it senses the wheel has stopped turning and is sliding down the rail, rendering it flat. The easing of pressure frees up the wheel to roll again. See Flatwheeler.

-Deck: The floor of a flatcar. See General service flatcar.

-Deck: The roof of any railroad car (freight or passenger). See Riding the deck.

-Dedicated piggyback train: A regularly-scheduled train comprised exclusively of piggybacks with the same origin and destination. See Piggyback.

-Dedicated track: Track used exclusively for one type of rail service, e.g., commuter/passenger train service.

-Deferred maintenance: An industry euphemism for track or equipment which is bad order and failure prone but whose repair is deferred for fiscal reasons.

-Demurrage charges: Tariffs set and assessed by railroads and enforced by the ICC which encourage shippers to load and unload freightcars quickly and return them to revenue service.

-Departure yard: The freightyard from which a newly-assembled train leaves. Usually a special yard in a large freightyard.

-DF-XL load restraining device: Lateral moveable walls in boxcars which protect sensitive freight from damage. Walls slide up and down the car and secure in holes in the roof and floor. See Less-than-full-car.

-Dick: Older term for railroad bull. See Bull.

-Diesel-electric engine: A diesel- and electric-powered locomotive. Diesel fuel is converted into electrical energy to drive electric traction motors which turn the engine's axles.

-Dirt stiff: A railroad right-of-way blaster, grader or filler.

-Dispatcher: A freightyard or over-the-road worker who orders, monitors and records train departure and movement.

Ditch Lights. New dual lights affixed low on a diesel-electric near its coupler and cowcatcher.

-Division: The locale where railroads change crews on an over-the-road freight train. Usually 150 to 300 miles between each.

-Division point: See Division.

-Doubled over: A train which is too long for one yard siding and sits on two or more sidings.

-Double-ended siding: A siding which leaves the mainline but comes back to meet it at the other end. See Deadend siding.

-Double heading: In the days of steam the coupling of two locomotives together to pull a heavy train up a steep grade.

-Double-stack: The latest innovation in intermodal freight where containers are stacked on top of one another on a platform or well car. See COFC, Intermodal freight and Well car.

-Double-track mainline: Mainline track composed of two or more tracks, greatly facilitating train traffic routing. See Cross-over track.

-Doubling the hill: If a train's power is insufficient to pull a train up a grade, the crew splits the train in two, pulls the front end over the top and returns for the back end. See Power.

-Draft: The pulling apart of railroad car couplers and draft gears during start-ups, humping and switching. See Buff.

-Draft gears: Modern coupler appliance which recoils and slides along a pocket underneath a railroad car's floor, cushioning impact and providing slack. See Bumpers, Draw-head and Slack.

-Draft out: (Verb) To stretch out the play or travel in the couplers and draft gears of a string of cars, e.g., "He *drafted that string out* in about 5 seconds and took off like a bat out of hell." See Play and Travel.

-Drag freight: A local work train which stops frequently to cut out and pick up customers' cars. Also a long or heavy train which moves slowly. See Hotshot and Regular freight.

-Draw-head: An out-dated coupling/cushioning scheme for freightcars. See Draft gear and Link-and-pin coupler.

-Drift a train: (Verb) To slow a train way down but continue rolling toward a switch while a brakeman runs out in front to throw the switch, e.g., "The way that bastard *drifts* a train I have to run like a dog."

-Drop: The exact spot where humped and now-rolling freightcars collide and couple with other cars. See Hump.

-Drop-on point: See Drop.

-D-Rye-O-Grandee: Familiar term for the Denver & Rio Grande Western Railroad.

-Dunnage: Wooden or metal packing (similar to a pallet) underneath freight to prevent damage in transit. See Bracing.

-Dutch clock: A primitive form of speedometer placed in 19th century cabooses to monitor train speeds and discipline offending engineers. Often tampered with by conductors.

-Dwarf signal: A low-lying signal found close to trackside in freightyards and on over-the-road switches.

-Dynamic brake: A modern diesel-electric engine's brake system which converts the traction motor from a propulsion source to a braking source on downhills and emergencies. See Traction motor.

-Dynamite: (Verb) To uncouple the headend from a train, e.g., "We *dynamited* her, pulled off it and derailed."

-Dynamite car: A freightcar whose air hose bursts, bringing a fast-moving train to a grinding halt and at times shattering coupler or worse.

-Electric bond wires: Wires affixed to each end of a rail which pass electric current from rail to rail in the A.B.S. signaling system. See A.B.S. and Track circuit.

-Electric traction motor: Electric motors of a diesel-electric engine (one for each axle) which convert diesel power into motive power.

-Electro-Motive: Short name for a diesel-electric engine manufactured by the Electro-Motive Division of General Motors in McCook Illinois.

-Electronic classification yard: Industry parlance for a computer-assisted gravity yard to form new trains. See Gravity yard and Hump.

-Electropneumatic brake: Air brake system on passenger trains which uses either air pressure, electronic signals, or both to set and release brakes.

-EMD - Electro-Motive Division of General Motors: See Electro-Motive.

-Enclosed bi-level auto rack: Industry parlance for a double-decked auto rack with siding and end-doors, preventing damage, theft and entry. See Auto rack.

-Enclosed tri-level auto rack: Industry parlance for a triple-decked auto rack with siding and end-doors, preventing damage, theft and entry. See Auto rack.

-End bunker Compartment at each end of an obsolete ice refrigerator car where blocks of ice were placed to cool the perishable freight. See Reefer.

-End CTC: Trackside sign which indicates a train is leaving track which is governed by CTC. See CTC and Start CTC.

-End-doors: Large metal doors at each end of an auto rack which either swing shut or slide down into position, preventing damage, theft and entry. See Auto rack.

-Engineer: Train crewmember who drives train and is the crew's boss. See Conductor.

-Enginehouse: Area where "off-shift" locomotives are stored, inspected, repaired and/or refueled. See Roundhouse.

-Engineman: Recently-inaugurated title for train crewmember, e.g., brakeman, engineer, fireman or conductor. See Trainman.

-EOT - End-Of-Train Device: A flashing red light with a variety of sensors placed on the back car of a freight train, signifying its rearend and replacing the need for a caboose and rearend crew.

-Exhausted air: Air vented out of an air brake system into the atmosphere. See Bleed rod and Vent.

-Expedited freight: Industry parlance for a hotshot. See Hotshot.

-Extra: A regular freight which runs as an extra train when sufficient overload business stacks up. See Regular freight and Section.

-Extra board: A means of prioritizing new railroad workers by seniority on a short-notice, as-needed basis.

-Face thickness: Thickness of top side of a railroad tie spikes are driven into. Usually nine inches. See Tie face.

-Facing-point siding: A siding which an engine can roll directly onto without having to back up. See Trailing-point siding.

-Failure prone: The degree to which any piece of railroad equipment (e.g., coupler or track) will or will not fail under stress.

-Federal Appliance Safety Act of 1893: The federal Act mandating use of the Westinghouse continuous air brake on all railroad cars. See Coffin Bill.

-Federal Railroad Administration (FRA): The federal Agency which regulates railroads. It also intermediates between railroad management, labor and the government, particularly during strikes. Also oversees all freightcar design and maintenance.

- Federal Trade Commission (FTC): The federal Agency which enforces antitrust legislation, now applicable to railroads since 1980.

-Field welding: Welding joint or bolt rail into ribbon rail at its installation site. Often used to convert joint rail into ribbon rail and connect sections of ribbon rail. See Bolt rail, Joint rail and Ribbon rail.

-15-year overhaul: An AAR/FRA mandatory overhaul of all moveable parts of a freightcar (e.g., running gear, doors, handbrakes, coupler fixtures and chutes) every 15 years. See Appliances.

-Fireman: Train crewmember responsible for firing a steam locomotive. Today where extant responsible for track and car management. See Ash cat and Brakeman.

-First class train: Industry parlance for a hotshot. See Hotshot.

-Fish-plate: Sturdy metal bars bolted to either side of a joint in a rail which prevent the weight of a train from knocking the rail over or disturbing the underlying ties and ballast.

-Flag: See Flagman.

-Flagman: Railroad worker who manually signals presence and movement of trains. Now largely obsolete.

-Flanged wheel: The means by which a train stays on the track. A flange extends down the inside of the wheel tread to guide the train between the rails. See Wheel tread

-Flat: Generic term for any type of flatcar designed exclusively to haul a truck trailer. See Piggyback.

-Flat-bottom rail: A universally-adopted rail design which uses an inverted "T" shape. The wide horizontal is the rail foot, while the narrow is the railhead. See Rail foot and Railhead.

-Flat-switching: Humping a new train together without use of an elevated hump. See Hump.

-Flat-switching yard: A switching yard without a hump. See Hump.

-Flatwheeler: A freightcar with one or more flat wheels. Usually caused by a brake clamping down too hard, freezing rotation and causing the wheel to slide down the rail on a braking train. The wheel is ground flat and the car is bad order. Not fun for wayfarers. See Out-of-round wheel.

-Flying switch: A means of switching freightcars onto a siding whereby the engine accelerates rapidly, brakes, uncouples quickly from the car(s), accelerates again out ahead of the car(s) and passes a switch thrown to lead the car(s) onto the siding. Dangerous, increasingly limited use and frequently forbidden.

-Footboard: Metal catwalk on locomotives and freightcars provided for walking, standing on and riding along with equipment.

-Foreign car: A freightcar which is currently in the possession of a railroad which does not own it.

-Forwarding yard: See Departure yard.

-FRED - Fucking Rear End Device: Western parlance for an End of Train Device. See EOT.

-Free slack: The distance between the closed knuckles of a coupler (1/4th to 3/4ths of an inch). Built-in to ease impact pressure, allow smoother departure of freight trains and avoid break-in-twos. See Break-in-two and Slack.

-Friction-bearing journalbox: Pre-1963 journalbox which uses gearlube and woolen "waste" to apply grease between a babbit-faced bearing and its spinning axle.

-Frisco Line: Familiar term for the St. Louis-San Francisco Railroad.

-Frog: The static portion of a switch which allows the wheel tread of a railroad car to cross from one track to the next. See Guard rail, Points and Wheel tread.

-Front runner: A shorter, lighter piggyback which accommodates only one truck trailer of up to 53 feet in length. See Piggyback and Standard flat piggyback.

Fuel foiler: See Front runner (manufacured by AT & SF).

-Full shout: When diesel-electric engines are operating at full capacity they operate at "full shout."

-Full-tilt speed: The top average speed of a given freight train

-Gang cook: The designated chef of a track-laying party in the 19th century.

-Gandydancer: A railroad track layer. See Stake artist.

-Gantry loading: Loading of truck trailers and containers onto freightcars by an overhead gantry crane.

-GEEP: Familiar term for a "general-purpose" diesel-electric engine, manufactured by EMD of General Motors. See EMD.

-General service flatcar: Any non-bulkheaded flatcar which hauls a wide variety of cargoes, i.e., construction materials, heavy vehicles or equipment, steel coils, etc.

-Generator: Converts a diesel-electric engine (except recently-built high-horse-power units) crankshaft motion into electricity (600 volt DC). See Alternator.

-Get the Bell (Verb): Familiar term from 19th century railroading for orders or signal to depart, e.g., "*Get the bell* - let's get outta here."

-Glad hands: The moveable parts of the automatic coupler which fold around each other and lock into place. See Knuckles.

-Goat: Familiar term for billygoat. See Billygoat.

-Gon: Familiar term for gondola. See Gondola.

-Gondola: A roofless (with minor exceptions) low-walled, flat-bottomed freightcar designed to haul coal, steel, pipe, recyclables, etc.

-Grabirons: Handholds provided on all railroad cars which allow workers (and hobos) to hold onto cars while ascending, descending or riding cars.

-Grabs: Familiar term for Grabirons. See Grabirons.

-Gravity yard: A freightyard which uses an elevated hump to form new trains. See Hump and Flat-switching yard.

-Grind-wheel smoke: The smoke created by a Speno Track Grinding Car. See Speno Track Grinding Car.

-Grips: The bags trainmen bring their personal belongings in for over-the-road work. Often black.

-Group retarder: The second retarder brake which slows freightcars which have been humped as they roll into the bowl, controlling speeds for 5 to 9 yard tracks. See Master retarder and Retarder brake.

-Guard rail: An extra section of rail placed inside the rail opposite a switch frog which prevents wheel flanges from taking the wrong path at the frog point.

-Gung-ho bull: A bull who takes his job seriously and apprehends hobos, thieves and trespassers. See Bull.

-Handcar: An old-fashioned railroad pushcart used to inspect track or travel over it by pumping up and down on a see-saw handlever.

-Hands: The parts of a freightcar coupler which fold around each other. See Knuckles.

-Happy Hooligan: The hero/antihero of a hobo comic strip of the same name, popular at the turn of the century and drawn by Zim and Opper. See Weary Willie.

-Head block ties: Low-lying railroad ties which protect the operating rod connecting a manual or automatic switch stand to the points. See Operating rod, Points and Switch stand.

-Headend: The end of a train the engines couple onto.

-Headlamp: One or more high-intensity white lights on the headend of a train or engine.

-Headlight: See Headlamp.

-Head-on: A headend to headend collision of two trains. See Cornfield meet.

-Helper unit: Any diesel-electric engine coupled behind the lead unit but at the headend of the train. See Pusher unit and Slave unit.

-Herder: A freightyard worker who aligns track for arriving and departing trains. See Lining track and Switchman.

-Highball: The conductor or dispatcher's order that an engineer begin driving a train out of the yard or station. Also the engineer's acknowledgment of and compliance with such an order.

-Highball: (Verb) To order a train to start, go faster or proceed at full-tilt speed, e.g., "He *highballed* it right past the stationmaster." See Full-tilt speed.

-Highiron: A familiar term for mainline track, so named because mainline track is made of heavier poundage and trains stands higher off the ties than on yard track or spur lines. See Poundage and Railhead.

-Highline: A familiar term for mainline track.

-Highline: (Verb) Hobo jargon for riding a fast freight train, e.g., "To *highline* it down the track," or "*highlining* it."

-High Line: A familiar name for the Great Northern Railway.

-High rail: On a curve the rail on the banked or uphill side of the track. See Low rail.

-Hinged-lid journalbox: The housing which contains a friction-bearing journalbox with a lid railroad workers lift up to pour in gearlube. See Friction-bearing journalbox.

-Hit a siding: (Verb) To reach a siding, e.g., "He always *hits those sidings* so fast it makes you think you're gonna climb the rails."

-Hobo: 19th century Americanism (origin unknown) for migrant worker who travels by freight train. Perhaps from "Ho! Beau!" - ("Ho, pretty or beautiful" in French), a call of greeting between such workers, or "hoe-boy" for men who carried and worked with hoes, or "hi, boy" which evolved into "hi bo" then "ho bo" out of consideration for manliness. In literary circles a person who "works and wanders (by train)." In reality anyone who rides freight trains. See Bum and Tramp.

-Hobo alarm clock: A familiar hobo term for a remote-controlled switch which when activated awakens a sleeping hobo and alerts him to the approach of a train.

-Hobo Convention: The Crown Jewel of hobo conventions. A hobo and spectator convention held in Britt, Iowa each August, where the local Chamber of Commerce sponsors a parade and spectators listen to "hobo" lore, sample Mulligan stew and elect a "King and Queen of the Hobos."

-Hobo graveyard: Trackside burial site of a deceased wayfarer - usually at or near the site of his or her demise.

-Hobo stew: A stew cooked in a large pot made of small pieces of meat, potatoes, onions, carrots or other vegetables and herbs found in the area. See Mulligan Stew.

-Hog: Familiar term for a railroad locomotive.

-Hogger: Familiar term for an engineer.

-Homeguard: In literary circles a person who drinks in freightyards. In the 19th century a vagrant who never left town. In reality today a garden-variety drunk who hangs out in freightyards but never rides trains (also known as a "hanger-on").

-Hood: Any part of a diesel-electric engine which is above floor level and houses engine equipment rather than the crew. See Cab.

-Hopper: Roofless (open) or roofed (closed with hatches) freightcar designed to haul bulk commodities (i.e., coal, grain, cement, sand). Key features are "V"-shaped cut-ins at each end, slope-sheet floors and gravity chutes for offloading.

-Hosed-up: Familiar term for being able to tell when a train is readied to depart. All the cars' hoses are connected and it's "hosed-up."

-Hotbox: An overheated journalbox which if not detected in time can cause fires and derailments. See Journalbox.

-Hotbox alarm: Two capsules of liquid which melt when a friction-bearing journalbox overheats. One produces a foul smell while the other a blue smoke to alert the crew to the problem.

-Hot freightyard: A freightyard which employs one or more gung-ho bulls. See Bull and Gung-ho bull.

-Hotshot: Familiar railroad worker and hobo term for a fast train with high priority, known by the industry as an "Expedited Freight" or "First Class Train." An old term was "Red Ball Manifest." See Drag freight, Priority and Regular freight.

-HSC electropneumatic brake: An electropneumatic diesel-electric engine brake required to pull passenger cars. Standard on both passenger and freight locomotives since the 1950s.

-Hump: Familiar term for a mountain pass which a freight train crosses over, often requiring warm clothing or other warmth-retention measures taken by wayfarers. See 1000-mile paper, Tokay blanket and Westbound.

-Hump: The elevated portion of a gravity yard that an old train's freightcars are pushed over, uncoupled from the rest of the train, and sent rolling to couple onto new trains. See Arrival yard, Bowl and Departure yard.

-Hump: (Verb) To uncouple an old train's freightcars from one another and couple them onto new trains for further travel, e.g., "The cars on Track 23 have to be *humped* next before the 8:15 can leave."

-Hump engine: A freightyard switchengine which pushes a string of cars over the hump during humping in a gravity yard, or pushes and pulls them back and forth in flat-switching. See Billygoat, Flat-switching and Gravity yard.

-Humping: The means by which an old train's freightcars are batted out and coupled onto new trains for further travel. See Flat-switching and Gravity yard.

-Hump it up: (Verb) To perform a task or move a train faster than at present, e.g., "We better *hump it up* if we're gonna make Clinton by one-thirty."

-Hump master: The freightyard worker who has final authority over all aspects of humping. See Humping.

-Hump up: (Verb) To assemble a new train by means of humping freightcars from old trains onto it, e.g., "Have you guys *humped up* that local called for 10:30 yet?"

-Hydraulic tamper: A large hydraulically-driven tamping machine which repacks ballast firmly underneath a track.

-Ice: (Verb) To place blocks of ice into the end or ice bunker of an old reefer car, e.g., "Yeah, they've been *iced* alright, but I don't know if they'll make it to Dallas." See Reefer.

-Ice bunker: See End bunker.

-IH - in-height: The height of a freightcar from the railhead to its topmost point, as indicated on each side of the car, e.g., IH 15 ft. 6 in. See Railhead.

-IL - in length: The length of a freightcar at its longest point (excluding couplers), as indicated on each side of the car, e.g., IL 50 ft.

-Industry switcher: Industry parlance for a drag freight. See Drag freight.

-Infrared heat sensors: Low-lying trackside infrared sensors which journalboxes pass over in transit. Upon detecting a hotbox a signal alerts the crew in the cab.

-Inspection pit: A pit located underneath tracks leading up to the apex of a freightyard hump, where car inspectors inspect running gear for bad orders. See Bad order and Running gear.

-INS/USBP - Immigration and Naturalization Service/United States Border Patrol: The federal Agency responsible for preventing illegal immigration and whose agents are commonly encountered in the southern US when wayfarers ride freight trains.

-Intermodal containers: Intermodal freight in box form. Containers can be shipped interchangeably by rail, ocean-going vessel or truck.

-Intermodal freight: Freight moved in a shipping container (i.e. truck trailer or box) which is easily switched from one conveyance to another (i.e. train to boat or truck to train).

-Interstate Commerce Commission (ICC): The federal Agency originally created to regulate railroads and which now oversees all interstate transactions. Its purpose is to ensure fairness in all such transactions.

-In the hole: Familiar term for a train which is standing on a siding waiting for another train to pass, conduct business or repair an equipment failure, e.g., such a train is "in the hole."

-Into the hole: Familair term for when a train goes onto a siding, either to let another train pass, conduct business or repair an equipment failure, e.g., it goes "into the hole."

-IW - in width: Width of a freightcar at widest point, as indicated on each side of the car, e.g., IW 10 ft. 6 in. (maximum allowable width).

-IWW - Industrial Workers of the World ("Wobblies"): A militant and controversial unskilled worker's union (1905 - 1918) which advocated shorter hours, higher wages and union recognition. Many hobos during this period were Wobblies.

-Jerking: Author's conceptualization of how a stationary freightcar or string of cars can suddenly jerk violently but doesn't move when another car, string of cars or engine collides and couples with it. Jerking can cause serious injury to a person on a car. See Sudden takeoff.

-Jerry gang: See Gandydancer.

-Joint: The point in bolted-rail track or "joint rail" where two rails meet and are bolted together. Joints cause the railroad's clickity-clack. See Bolted-rail track, Fish-plate and Joint rail.

-Joint bar: See Fish-plate.

-Joint rail: Familiar and hobo term for bolted-rail track. See Bolted-rail track.

-Journalbox: Point of contact between freightcar trucks and axles where internal lubricants reduce friction heat and provide for a smooth ride. See Truck.

-Jungle: The place in or near a freightyard where hobos wait for trains, rest, cook meals, read, sleep and congregate.

-Jungle out: (Verb) To wait or sleep in a jungle, e.g., "I was *jungled out* when the Border Patrol rousted me." See Jungle.

-Junk train: See Drag freight.

-Katy: Familiar term for the Missouri-Kansas-Texas (M-K-T) Railroad.

-Kick cars: (Verb) To push or hump freightcars toward a new train, e.g., "We *kicked* that last string in less than an hour." See Bat out and Hump.

-Knocked into the hole: Familair term for a train order or signal which requires that the train go into a siding to allow another train to pass on single-track mainline, e.g., "We got knocked *into the hole* for five hours."

-Knock out: (Verb) See Bat out and Kick cars.

-Knuckles: The moveable parts of a freightcar coupler which fold and lock around each other. See Glad hands.

-Land-bridge train: An intermodal box train which originates in one of four American East Coast ports, with a destination at one of four West Coast ports or vice versa, with freight destined for the Orient or Europe. Eliminates ocean vessel passage through the Panama Canal.

-LD LMT/LD LT - load limit: The total load weight allowable on a freightcar, i.e., the difference between its empty (light) weight and its capacity (total load on the rail) as indicated on each side of the car, e.g., LD LMT 201600. See CAPY and LT WT

-Legal air: The amount of air pressure which must fill a train's braking system as mandated by the FRA. Legal air is determined by length and weight of train and terrain to be crossed, between 70 and 90 psi.

-Less-than-full car: A shipment which does not entirely fill a freightcar. Often small shippers combine to fill a car. See DF-XL load restraining device.

-Light-running units: Diesel-electric engines which run back to one end of a railroad's line without a train because they're needed at that end but have stacked up at the other.

Lining track: (Verb) To throw a track switch so that a train leads onto the right designated track, e.g., "I *lined* him onto track 27 and then the damned Yardmaster changed his mind." See Herder.

-Link-and-pin-coupler: An outmoded method of coupling freightcars together using draw-heads, slots, links and pins. Responsible for death and injury of thousands of railroad workers in the 19th century.

-LIRR - Long Island Railroad: The commuter/passenger system serving Long Island.

-Little Red Card: The membership card of the IWW union ("Wobblies"). See IWW.

-Load blocking: One means by which cargo on open-air cars (e.g., flatcars) is held in place, by nailing blocks of wood into the floor of the car to restrain the load. See Bracing and Dunnage.

-Local switcher: See Drag freight.

-Local times: Over 100 different time settings throughout America and Canada, by regions, communities and railroads, before adoption of Standard Time in 1883. See Sun times.

-Lock: The modern-day "pin" which locks freightcar couplers together.

-Long end: The longer paneled console of a modern diesel-electric road switcher which houses the diesel power, electric traction, braking and air systems. See Road switcher.

-Long Hood: See Long end.

-Long-haul train: A long-distance train - minimum 500 miles.

-Long walk: Familair term. In the absence of a caboose on modern freight trains crewmembers are often required to walk the entire train to return to the headend after conducting switching at the rearend of the train. On some railroads crews back the train to the stranded crewmember.

-LO small cube covered hopper car: Closed, rideable hoppers carrying bulk commodity ladings which require protection from the weather. See Hopper.

-Lowball: Famialir term for an old signal positioning of a ball on a mast. When the ball dropped down the mast this signified slow down or stop. See Highball.

-Low joints: Joints in a rail which are pounded up and down by wheels passing over them, putting greater stress on the underlying ties and ballast. Corrected only through frequent respiking, fish-plate tightening and ballast tamping. See Fish-plate and Hydraulic tamper.

-Low-line: (Verb) To leave a freightyard quickly, e.g., "There's the bull. Let's *low-line*."

-Low Line: Familiar term for the Northern Pacific Railroad. See High Line.

-Low rail: On a curve, the rail on the downhill side of the track. See High rail.

-LT WT - light weight: The empty weight of a freightcar (must be reweighed after repairs or modification), as indicated on each side of a freightcar, e.g., LT WT 47000 NO (New Orleans) 8-88. See CAPY and LD LMT/LD LT.

-Make up: (Verb) To prepare a train for departure, e.g., "That train will be *made up* on Track 18."

-Magnetic levitation ("Maglev"): The theoretical means of powering electric trains by use of electromagnetism to physically hold the train off the track while moving forward.

-Manifest: Industry parlance for a regular freight train. See Regular freight.

-Manual block system: A signaling system whereby a passing train mechanically changes a semaphore or signal aspect, which must then be reset by a signal operator or dispatcher. See Dispatcher.

-Marked up: (Verb) To be assigned a shift on the Extra Board, e.g., "I got *marked up* on my birthday and had to leave the party." See Extra Board.

-Marshal: (Verb) To assemble and make ready a group of freightcars for departure on a train, e.g., "Is that Vermont train *marshaled* yet?" See Classify and Hump.

-Marshaling yard: A freightyard where trains are classified for departure. See Classification yard.

-Master retarder: The first retarder brake used to slow freightcars which have just been humped and are rolling into the bowl. See Apex, Group retarder and Retarder brake.

-Metra: The commuter/passenger system serving the greater Chicago area.

-Micro land-bridge train: A land-bridge train with freight originating from the Orient or Europe but destined for a city in the interior of North America.

-Midnight creeps: Familiar term for a freightcar rolling silently through a freightyard (day or night) which can sneak up on an unsuspecting person too close to its track and cause serious injury or death.

-Mileage charges: Fees assessed per mile that a non-owning railroad incurs while moving a foreign freightcar along its system. See Foreign car.

-Mill gon: Familiar term for a subcategory of gondola designed to haul coal, coking materials, rock, etc. Often coupled together in unit trains and equipped with rotary couplers for roll dumping. See Gondola, Roll dump, Rotary coupler and Unit train.

-Milwaukee Road: Familiar term for the Chicago, Milwaukee, St. Paul and Pacific Railroad (CMSP&P).

-Mini-land bridge train: A land-bridge train with freight originating from the Orient or Europe but destined for and terminating at a city on the opposite American coast. See Land bridge train.

Montana bindle: Familiar term for a hobo's traveling accessories when they are substantial. Often includes tools of a trade, many changes of clothes or footwear, and practically everything else the traveler owns. See Streamliner.

-Mo-pac: Familiar term for the Missouri Pacific Railroad (MP).

-Mopy: See Mo-pac.

-Motor car: A small gasoline-powered railcar used by track inspection teams to survey sections of track.

-MTA - Metropolitan Transit Authority: The commuter/passenger system serving the greater Boston area.

-Mud chicken: Familiar term for a railroad tunnel worker.

-Mulligan stew: A traditional railroad worker stew cooked in a large pot. Allegedly first concocted by a gandydancer named Mulligan on the Union Pacific Railroad while building the first transcontinental in the 1860s. The stew consists of large chunks of beef, buffalo (when available) or hamburger, potatoes, onions, carrots or other vegetables and seasonal herbs. See Hobo stew and Gang cook.

-MU - multiple unit: Two or more diesel-electric engines coupled together which are equipped to run in tandem. Usually only road switchers. See Road switcher.

-National Railway Labor Conference Organization (NRLCO): An industry-wide management body which bargains with The Brotherhoods and UTU. See Brotherhoods and UTU.

-NFL - No Field Lubrication journalbox: A roller-bearing journalbox certified to run 10 years before disassembly and refurbishing. No field lubrication (i.e., out in the freightyards) need be performed.

-Nickel Plate Road: Familiar term for the New York, Chicago & St. Louis Railroad.

-NICTD - Northern Indiana Community Transit District: The commuter/passenger system serving the northern Indiana area.

-NJT - New Jersey Transit: The commuter/passenger system serving the northern New Jersey area.

-Non-constant lit signal: A signal which stays dark unless a train is in the vicinity. See Constant-lit signal.

-Nose: The outside portion of the short end of a road switcher. See Road switcher and Short end.

-Nose herald: The name, abbreviated name or logo of a railroad company painted on the nose of a road switcher. See Road switcher.

-No 10. gunboat can: Number 10 can used for brewing coffee, cooking, urinating and defecating.

-Off-shift: A locomotive which is not in service.

-Oilcan train: Familiar term for a train made up mainly or exclusively of tankcars.

-Old Gold Mountain: Familiar Cantonese expression for North America.

-One-eyed bandit: Author's term for a boxcar with one door open and the other door shut.

-On the fly: See On the run.

-On the point unit: The lead diesel-electric engine at the headend of a train where the engineer and crew ride.

-On the run: Getting on or off a freight train which has slowed but not stopped.

-Operating air pressure: See Legal air.

-Operating rod: A metal rod which connects the switch stand of a railroad switch to the points. See Points and Switch stand.

-Opposing train: A train which approaches your train from the opposite direction.

-Ordinance yard: See Classification yard.

-Outlet gates: See Bays.

-Out-of-round wheel: A wheel on a freightcar or engine which has gone out-of-round after years of grinding by the rails. See Flatwheeler.

-Override order: A specific train order issued by a dispatcher or traffic coordinator which takes precedence or overrides a signal aspect, e.g., to proceed past an absolute red signal.

-Over the road: Any track outside yard limits. See Road master and Yard limit.

-Pantograph: The spring-loaded shoe atop an electric locomotive which presses against and slides under the overhead electrical wire to receive motive power. See Catenary and Third rail.

-Passing track: A long stretch of track (3 to 5 mi.) left in place after a railroad tears out double-track which allows trains to pass each other without stopping on single-track. See Double-track mainline and Single-track mainline.

-Peddlar: See Drag freight.

-Pensy: Familiar term for the Pennsylvania (PRR) Railroad.

-Performance: Author's conceptualization of how fast or slow an over-the-road freight train goes and how many or few stops it makes.

-Permissive signal: A signal which, when displaying a red aspect means "stop-and-proceed." The engineer must fully stop the train but then may proceed with caution (usually 15 MPH max.) past the signal, ready to stop on a moment's notice. Signal identified by a staggered lower light or a marking on its mast.

-Pick up: (Verb) To cut in one or more freightcars on a train from a customer, a siding or a freightyard, e.g., "We'll be *picking up* 7 cars out at the GM plant."

-Piggly-wiggly: Author's term for a front runner piggyback which, because shorter and more flexible than a standard flat piggyback torsions around curves more easily. See Front runner and Standard flat piggyback.

-Piggyback: A railroad flatcar or "flat" which is designed exclusively to haul truck trailers and intermodal containers. See COFC, Flat and TOFC.

-Piggybacker: A large forklift-type loading device which picks up truck trailers or intermodal containers and loads them onto or off-loads them from TOFCs and COFCs (piggybacks). See COFC, Side loading and TOFC.

-Pinch (Verb): To be injured while switching freightcars, often losing a finger, hand, leg or foot, e.g., "Not nearly as many of us get *pinched* as we used to."

-Pinched: An older familiar hobo term for being jailed.

-Pin-puller: Familiar term for a brakeman or switchman.

-Platform: A generic term for any type of flatcar which hauls a modular container.

-Play: The amount of "give," "slack" or "travel" in a freightcar's couplers and draft gears, ranging from 15 to 30 inches. See Travel.

-Plug door: A boxcar door which is forced inward by its doorlatch bulkheads after being slid into the closed position.

-Pneumatic pressure: Air pressure.

-Pocket: The housing of a draft gear under the floor of a freightcar. Designed to provide friction to cushion impact on coupling, starts and stops.

-Points: The moveable portion of a switch which allows the flanged wheel tread of a railroad car to cross from one track to the next. See Frog.

-Point unit: See Headend unit.

-Position light signal: Second-most widely-used signal design, consisting of an oblong black backing surrounding three signal lights - red on top, yellow in the middle and green on the bottom.

-Power: A train's locomotive or series of locomotives. See MU.

-Power sharing: Agreements between various railroads to use each other's diesel-electric engines on an as-needed basis.

-Prairie meet: When two trains meet headend to headend on single track mainline. See Cornfield meet.

-Preference: Industry parlance for priority of trains. See Priority.

-Priority: Railroad company decisions as to which train passes which on single-track mainline. Based on profit, time of day, day of week, eastbound/westbound, uphill/downhill, etc.

-Private Varnish: A privately-owned beautifully-appointed passenger car which is leased or rented to individuals or corporations for "railfan" traveling. May accompany an Amtrak train or a freight train - usually at the rear.

-Pull-apart: An improperly-welded rail breaks at a field weld of two joints due to rail shrinkage when the temperature drops significantly. See Field welding, Joint rail and Ribbon rail.

-Pulled coupler: A broken coupler, usually at the knuckle, from excess forward stress placed on the coupler which results in a break-in-two. See Break-in-two.

-Pulling pins: The act of uncoupling railroad cars. See Cut lever and Pin puller.

-Pusher unit: Any diesel-electric engine behind the lead unit but at the headend of the train. See Helper unit and Slave unit.

-Q: A familiar term for the Chicago, Burlington & Quincy (CB&Q) Railroad.

-Quincy: See Q.

-Rail anchor: See Anti-creeper and Rail creep.

-Rail creep: The lengthwise movement of rail due to downhill passage of heavy trains or trains braking in one direction, which causes stress on switches and sideways buckling of track.

-Rail foot: The wider section of the inverted "T" portion of track which is cradled on the anchor plates and spiked down onto the ties. See Railhead.

-Railhead: The narrower section of the inverted "T" portion of track which a railroad car's wheel tread rolls over (usually shiny if frequently used). See Rail foot and Wheel tread.

-Rail heat: A "batch" or "production" of rail from a particular steel mill during a specific production period. Absent modern detection devices, when transverse fissures developed and a rail broke an entire "heat" would be pulled up and replaced by new rail. See Sperry Detector car and Transverse fissure.

-Railroad red: The rust-colored brown which most rolling stock is painted.

-Rail-train: A series of flatcars dedicated exclusively to hauling ribbon rail out to the point of installation. See Ribbon rail.

-Rattler: Familiar term for a freight train comprised mostly or completely of empties which rattle down the track at high speeds.

-Rattle the hocks off her: (Verb) To drive a freight train at high speeds causing freightcars to shake, rattle and roll, e.g., "He was *rattling the hocks off her* all the way down the mountain." See Ball the jack and Highball (Verb).

-RBL Boxcar: Insulated boxcar which maintains the same temperature for several days. Popular with shippers of beer and other canned perishable goods.

-Rear-on: A headend to rearend collision, i.e., one train plowing into the rear of another.

-Receiving yard: See Arrival yard.

-Redball: See Red ball manifest.

-Red ball manifest: Industry parlance and old hobo parlance for a hotshot. See Hotshot.

-Redline: (Verb) To condemn or scrap an old or unprofitable freightcar, e.g., "Many reefers are being *redlined* today."

-Red plaque: A red symbol placed on the back car of a freight train by day, signifying its rearend and replacing use of a caboose or an EOT. See EOT and FRED.

-Reefer: Familiar term for a refrigerator car (ice or mechanical) which hauls perishables (e.g., fruit, meat, flowers).

-Reefer train: A freight train comprised exclusively of reefers. See Reefer.

-Regional railroad: A smaller-than-Class 1 Line Haul railroad which serves a specific region, e.g., New England, the Carolinas or Montana. See Class 1 Line Haul Railroad.

-Regular freight: An over-the-road freight train of average length and speed which makes fewer business stops than a drag freight. The most frequently encountered type of train, consisting of any and all types of cars. See Drag freight and Hotshot.

-Re-ice: (Verb) To replace melted ice in an ice reefer, e.g., "They *re-ice* all their salad-bowl trains in OK City." See End bunker and Ice.

-Relay rail: Worn-out over-the-road joint rail which is torn up and reused elsewhere - usually in freightyards. See Joint rail.

-Release valve: A valve underneath each freightcar (except hoppers and specialty cars) which releases air from the brake cylinder when the engineer activates the brake throttle, triggering the air reservoir to refill the brake cylinder and set brakes.

-Reporting marks: Two through four-letter and two through six-number designations of ownership and inventory on each side of a freightcar, e.g., "IC 4615" (Illinois Central), "TTX 669880" (Trailer Train Corporation), or "CSXT 55286" (CSX Transportation, Inc.).

-Retarder brakes: Hydraulic brakes which slow freightcars rolling from the apex of the hump on their way to new trains. See Apex and Hump.

-Retarder yard: A gravity freightyard which has retarder brakes. See Hump and Retarder brakes.

-Return springs: Large coiled springs used to recenter older draft gears (in the absence of a sliding center sill) after buffing or drafting. See Buff and Draft.

-Revenue trip: A loaded freightcar which generates revenue for each railroad which hauls it.

-Reverse/selector handle: A handle inside the cab which allows the engineer to reverse drive direction of the electric traction motors for backing up, switching and emergency stops.

-Ribbon rail: Joint rail which has been welded into continuous lengths of roughly 1500 ft. either at the steel mill and brought out to the installation site on a rail train or by on-site field welding. Reduces maintenance and provides for a smoother ride.

-Ride the cushions: Familiar term for riding a passenger train. See Varnish.

-Riding the blinds: See Blind baggage.

-Riding the bumpers: Familiar term for riding a freightcar by straddling its coupler with one's legs. No longer popular and not safe. See Bumpers.

-Riding the deck: Familiar term for riding any railroad car on its roof. Not safe.

-Riding the rod: Familiar term for riding a freightcar underneath the floor of the car atop one of the car's structural rods. No longer possible. See Rod.

-Rip-track: A freightyard track reserved for freightcars which are bad order and/or scheduled for repairs. See bad order.

-Rip-track worker: A freightyard worker who repairs bad order freightcars and/or cars scheduled for repairs.

-Road foreman: See Road master.

-Road grime: The dirt, grease, dust and grit which railroad equipment accumulates over time.

-Road master: A freightyard worker who supervises all aspects of over-the-road train movement outside the yard limits. See Yard limit.

-Road power: An engine or engines which pull a train out over the road. See MU.

-Road switcher: Industry parlance for an over-the-road diesel-electric engine. See MU.

-Rock and roll: A resonant rocking of cars which pass over a low joint, further damaging the underlying ties and ballast. See Low joint.

-Rock slide detector fence: Tall poles strung together by sensor wires which rapidly change all nearby signals to red if struck by rock, earth, vegetation or snow. Common along mountainous stretches of track.

-Rod: The metal struts underneath the floor of old freightcars which provided structural integrity. See Riding the rod.

-Rollability: The ability of a freightcar or cars to roll after being humped, based on the number of cars, their combined weight and travel distance.

-Roll dump: A method of unloading a hopper or gondola. The car is physically tipped-over sideways then righted. Must be equipped with rotary couplers. See Rotary coupler.

-Roller-bearing journalbox: Post-1963 self-contained journalbox which is self-lubricating much like an automotive wheel bearing. See Friction-bearing journalbox and Hotbox.

-Rolling a train: For a hobo, familiar term for canvassing a train for prospective freightcars to ride; for a crew, inspecting a passing train for equipment or cargo problems.

-Rolling stock: All of a railroad's engines, freightcars, cabooses and other equipment which rolls on a railroad track.

-Roofwalks: Wooden catwalks down the center of old boxcar roofs, used by 19th century brakemen to run from boxcar to boxcar to set and release handbrakes.

-Rotary coupler: A coupler of a freightcar which allows the car to be dumped sideways to offload cargo. Typical on unit train hoppers and mill gons. See Roll dump and Millgons.

-Roundhouse: Older term for area where "off-shift" locomotives are stored, inspected, repaired and refueled. "Round" because the housing was built around a turntable to turn an engine around facing the right direction. See Enginehouse and Off-shift.

Rubber tire hobo: Familiar term for hobo who travels by motor vehicle rather than train.

-Run-around track: A freightyard track left open and reserved for switchengines to travel from one end of the yard to the other.

-Running gear: The wheels, brake equipment, springs, couplers, draft gears, sliding center sills - everything underneath a freightcar which assists in starting, rolling or stopping it.

-Running in slack: See Cutting slack.

-Running switch: See Flying switch.

Run the line: (Verb) To ride freight trains, e.g., "That old 'bo's been *runnin' the line* since the time you was knee-high to a grasshopper."

-Run through train: See Through train.

-Runways: The narrow paths between freightyard tracks used by workers on foot or in go-carts to block and inspect freightcars, prepare them for departure or bleed their air for humping.

-SAM - Shipper Assist Message: An AAR-sponsored service in Washington D.C.

offered to subscribing railroads which assists railroads and shippers in locating freightcars or carloads of particular interest to them.

-Sanders: Compartments on diesel-electric engines containing sand which is poured on the railhead in front of the engine's wheels, enhancing traction on wet track to prevent wheel slippage. See Wheel slippage.

-Saw-by: When two freight trains meet on single-track mainline and one too long for the siding has to go into the hole, the shorter train passes the near end of the longer train which is clear on the siding. While the shorter train approaches the far siding the longer train snakes through the siding and clears that end for the shorter train.

Sawing a train: Separating cars on a stopped train which are blocking a town's thoroughfares.

-Scenery Bum: Familiar term for a voluntary hobo.

-Scenic cruiser: Author's term for a boxcar with both doors open.

-Searchlight signal: The most widely-used signal design, consisting of a circular black backing surrounding one high-intensity polarized signal light with three interchangeable color lenses - red, yellow and green.

-Second-nighter: Familiar term for a hobo refused entry into a rescue mission.

-Section: A regular freight which is divided into two or more trains due to an excess number of cars. See Extra.

-Section foreman: An over-the-road railroad track repair supervisor.

-Section hand: An over-the road railroad track repair worker.

-Semaphore signal: An old-fashioned mechanical signal used on a few railroads which consists of a large bar or "arm" which changes position. The vertical position means go, 45 degrees means caution and horizontal means stop.

-SEPTA - Southeast Pennsylvania Transit Authority: The commuter/passenger system serving the greater Philadelphia area.

-Serial action: The means by which continuous air brakes set and release rapidly, even on very long freight trains.

-Service application: The setting of air brakes by use of the brake throttle.

-Service position: Any position on the brake throttle which sets the air brakes.

-Service range: See Service position.

-Set out: See Cut out.

-Shack: Familiar term for brakeman.

-Shatter cracks: See Transverse fissures.

-Shinkasen: See Bullet train.

-Shopmaster: A railroad employee who oversees the work of shopworkers. See Shopworker.

-Shopworker: A "non-railroad" freightyard worker who builds, rebuilds or repairs rollingstock, e.g., machinists, electricians, sheet metal workers, boilermakers, blacksmiths, painters, pipe fitters and their apprentices.

-Short end: The shorter paneled console of a modern diesel-electric road switcher which often houses the crew bathroom and air equipment. See Long end and Road Switcher.

-Short hood: See Short end.

-Short line railroad: A very small railroad with track from 1 to 150 miles in total length. Many are owned by a mine or manufacturing plant. See Regional railroad.

-Shunt: (Verb) To interrupt A.B.S. electric current passing through a block's rails with the wheels of a train. The train "shunts" the current up through its wheels, interrupting the circuit through the rails. Interruption triggers the track relay to cause nearby signals to change aspects to reflect the train's presence, e.g., "How come I never git a shock when we *shunt* those dang things?" See Automatic Block System and Track relay.

-Side door Pullman: Traditional hobo term for a rideable boxcar.

-Side loading: The loading of truck trailers and containers onto freightcars from the side by a Piggybacker. See Piggybacker.

-Side-on: A headend collision by one train into the side of another.

-Siding: A section of track to the side of a mainline used to stop a train or one or more of its cars without blocking the mainline.

-Signal: Any of a large variety of means used to route railroad traffic.

-Signal aspect: See Aspect.

-Signal bridge: Overhead span housing traffic signals.

-Signal maintainer: A railroad worker who inspects and maintains signaling equipment.

-Signal mast: Metallic light standards or poles placed at trackside. The signal is affixed to the mast's top.

-Single-point hitch: A fold-up - fold-down hitch on a piggyback flat which holds the wheelless end of a trailer upright during transit. See Flat and Piggyback.

-Singleton door opening system: A method of manually opening or closing a boxcar door by means of a wheel which moves the door along its track.

-Single-track mainline: Mainline composed of only one track.

-Skipper: Familiar term for conductor.

-Slack: "Play," "give" or "travel" built into a train's coupling system to cushion impact and ease starting and stopping.

-Slave unit: Any crewless MU road switcher behind the lead unit and separated from other headend units by some or all of the train's cars (i.e., in the middle or back of the train). Run in tandem by radio signal. See Helper unit, MU and Pusher unit.

-Sliding center sill: A modern draft gear/pocket coupler design which extends into the center of the freightcar underneath its floor, providing additional cushioning during slows or stops. See Pocket.

-Slip-by: When the knuckle of one coupler rides too high or too low in relation to the other knuckle they "slip-by" each other resulting in a break-in-two. See Break-in-two.

-Slippery: An engine which is too light for the load it's hauling. See Wheel slippage.

-Slope-sheet floors: Slanted floors of hopper cars which funnel ladings out through the gravity chutes. See Gravity chutes.

-Slow order: An order requiring engineers to reduce speeds over bad order track. See Bad order and Slow order track.

-Slow order track: Railroad track which is bad order. Engineers are ordered to reduce speeds over this track until it is repaired or replaced. See Bad order.

-Slug unit: A ballasted 4- or 6-axle unit which has traction motors but no cab, engine or generator. When heavy loads must be hauled at medium speeds a road "slug" is "married" to a road switcher for additional tractive force. Generally an older MU configuration used east of the Mississippi. The hood of the unit stands only three or four feet higher than the platform. See Ballasting.

-Smoke and Headlight Rule: The most primitive railroad signaling system - none. Engineers were required to watch for approaching trains' smoke by day or headlight by night to avoid cornfield meets. See Cornfield meet and Prairie meet.

-Smoker: See Hotbox.

-Snag: Anything (i.e., metal straps, loads, wood or wire, etc.) hanging off the side of a freightcar which could hit and injure someone walking or standing nearby. A brakeman's and hobo's headache.

-Spare board: See Extra board.

-Speno Track Grinding Car: A track maintenance car or series of cars which grind rail back into smoothness and continuity. See Railhead.

-Sperry Detector Car: A track inspection car which seeks out defective or flawed rail by the use of magnetic and/or ultrasonic tests.

-Spot: (Verb) To position a freightcar at a desired location, e.g., "Harry always *spots* a car dead-on target."

-Spotter: A late-19th-century and early-20th century railroad-employed bull whose job it was to infiltrate railroad unionization efforts and identify the perpetrators for blackballing. See Bull.

-Spring-loaded wick-fed lubricator pad: An improvement over the simpler waste-ladened friction-bearing journalbox. Gearlube is fed onto a wick which is held against the axle with spring-loading. See Friction-bearing journalbox, Hinged-lid journalbox and Journalbox.

-Spur line: A track of roughly 5 mi. in length or longer which is classified as neither a mainline nor a siding. Spur lines often lead to a nearby plant, mine or other large railroad customer.

-Stack train: Familiar term for a train which is all or mostly double-stacked intermodal containers. See Double-stack and Intermodal containers.

-Staggered rail: Joint rail which is staggered, i.e., laid so one joint is midway along the solid rail on the other side of the track, minimizing resonant rock and roll and resulting track/ballast damage. See Rock and roll.

-Staggers Act of 1980: The federal Act chiefly notable for deregulating railroad operations and rate schemes.

-Stake artist: Railroad track layer. See Gandydancer.

-Stake pockets: Pockets on the sides of flatcars which upright wooden stakes are fitted into to prevent loads from shifting sideways on a car.

-Standard flat piggyback: The original modern piggyback - 89 ft. long and designed to accommodate two 40 ft. long truck trailers. See Piggyback.

-Standard Gauge: A track gauge of 4 feet, 8-1/2 inches (1435 mm), adopted throughout many industrialized nations.

-Start CTC: Trackside sign which indicates a train is entering track which is governed by CTC. See CTC and End CTC.

-Steel chair: See Anchor plate.

-Steel wheel technology: The use of new metallurgical processes to create railroad wheels which generate less friction and withstand longer use.

-Sterno drunk: Familiar term for a transient who drinks sterno, cheap wine, shoe polish or anything else he can get his hands on. See Sterno stove.

-Sterno stove: A traditional term for the hobo's portable cooking stove. Usually fueled with sterno, an alcohol-based flammable which was often imbibed when money was short.

-Stirrup: A metal step shaped like a flat "U" which is affixed to the underside of each end of both sides of a freightcar, used to step onto and off of the car.

Stool pigeon: See Bull and Spotter.

-Stop-and-proceed: A rule which requires the engineer to stop when a permissive signal displays a red aspect, but then may proceed. See Permissive signal and Stop-and-stay-stopped.

-Stop-and-stay-stopped: A rule which requires that when an absolute signal displays a red light the engineer must stop and stay stopped. See Absolute signal, Dispatcher, Override order and Permissive signal.

-Straight Air System: A railroad brake system which uses pressurized air to apply brakes, then releases the pressure to release brakes. Used today on locomotives only. See Automatic Air Brake.

-Strap-down: (Verb) To secure a load on a flatcar by use of flat metal bands tightly strapped around the load, e.g., "*Strap-down* this lumber before the local gets here."

-Strap rail: Pre-iron rail made of hard wood with a strap of iron affixed to its top. These straps often peeled up and ripped through car floors.

-Streamlined jackroller: Familiar term for a hobo thief who travels light. See Streamliner.

-Streamliner: Familiar term for a hobo who travels light or with next to nothing (or nothing).

-Stretch out: (Verb) To draft out the slack in a train in anticipation of leaving the station. A delicate operation to avoid break-in-twos, e.g., "I *stretched it out* as gentle as I could but the sucker snapped anyway." See Break-in-two and Slack.

-String-lining: The tendency of cars toward the middle of a train to jump the inside rail on a curve because the headend is pulling harder than the rearend can travel. Absent a break-in-two string-lining leads to derailments. See Break-in-two, High rail and Low rail.

-Sub ballast: The bottom layer of crushed rock, lava, slag or shells upon which top ballast is poured and the track is laid. See Top ballast.

-Sudden takeoff: Author's conceptualization of a stationary freightcar or string of cars suddenly jolting into motion, by collision and coupling by a car, string of cars or an engine causing serious danger to a person on a car. See Drop, Drop-on point, Hump and Jerking.

-Sun times: Over 50 different time settings throughout North America before the adoption of Standard Time in 1883. See Local times.

-Superiority of trains: Industry parlance for priority of trains. See Priority.

-Surface Transportation Act of 1982: The federal Act which allows trucks to haul 45, 48 and 53 ft. long trailers (often in tandem) causing railroads to rethink piggy-back length and design schemes. See Front runner, Fuel foiler and Piggyback.

-Switch: A section of railroad track which allows a train to change tracks.

-Switchengine: See Billygoat.

-Switching: Process of moving a car or train from one track to another, or assem-bling or reassembling the consist of a train. See Consist, Frog and Points.

-Switch leader: A freightyard track which leads from one yardtrack to the next and connecting many tracks together at its switches. See Switch.

-Switchlist: A list of freightcar numbers which assists switchmen and brakemen in determining which car(s) should be directed toward which track or customer. See Reporting marks.

-Switchman: A freightyard worker who assists in assembly of trains and alignment of tracks as ordered.

-Switch rails: See Points.

-Switch stand: A manual (hand-thrown) or automatic (power-thrown) mechanism located at the points end of a switch. This mechanism throws switches from one track to another by means of the operating rod. See Operating rod, Points and Switch.

-Symbol: Industry parlance for a regular freight train. See Regular freight.

-Tailend: The end of a train opposite that to which the engines are coupled (which has either a caboose, red plaque or EOT/FRED device). See EOT, FRED and Red plague.

-Taking in slack: See Cutting slack.

-Tallowpot: Familiar term for railroad fireman. See Ashcat and Fireman.

-Tank train: See Oilcan train.

Target signal: See Searchlight signal.

-Telephone lineman: A railroad worker who installs, inspects and maintains railroad telephone equipment.

-Tender: A steam locomotive's fuel car (wood, coal or oil).

-Testify: (Verb) To accept the pastor's call at a religious rescue mission to admit the error of one's ways and ask The Lord to come into one's life, e.g., "I been drinkin' an' runnin' aroun' fer years and I ain't ashamed to *testify* that the Good Lord don't look any too kindly on it."

-TGV - Train à Grande Vitesse (literally "Train of Great Quickness" or High Speed Train): French high-speed electric train which reaches speeds exceeding 180 MPH on dedicated track. Currently being built in Texas and throughout Europe.

-The big hook: A giant railroad crane used to clean up railroad wrecks.

-The Rock: Familiar term for the Chicago, Rock Island & Pacific Railroad ("CRI&P").

-Third rail: A low-lying rail next to an electric train's track which is electrified and provides motive power for the electric locomotive. See Pantograph.

-Thoroughfare track: See Run-around track.

-1000-mile inspection: An ICC/FRA mandatory inspection of all engines and cars on any train which has traveled 1000 miles.

-1000-mile paper: Thick craft paper or cardboard used to lie down on freightcars for cushioning, insulation and cleanliness.

-Throttle handle: A throttle inside the cab which the engineer uses to accelerate the train.

-Through-route: The route a train takes over two or more railroads' track.

-Throw the points: (Verb) To throw a switch, e.g., "If he doesn't get that *point thrown* in about 3 hot seconds we're gonna split the difference."

-Ticket to ride: Familiar hobo term for ready access to a rideable freight train.

-Tie: The long, squared wooden (or in places concrete or steel) cross-section upon which railroad track is laid.

-Tie face: The topside of a railroad tie, on top of which the anchor plates are placed and into which the track is spiked. See Anchor plate and Tie.

-Tie-plate: See Anchor plate.

Tilting train: Passenger or freightcars which tilt on curves to offset centrifugal forces and take curves more easily.

-TOFC - Trailer On Flatcar: A railroad flatcar designed exclusively to haul truck trailers. See Piggyback and Platform.

-Tokay blanket: The use of intoxicants to fend off cold weather riding freight trains. See Canned heat and Hump.

-Top ballast: The top layer of crushed rock, lava, slag or shells poured over the sub ballast and upon which the track is laid. See Sub ballast.

-Top end: The end of a freightyard which is opposite the end freightcars are being humped off or onto strings of cars. See Trimmer.

-Top sill: The topmost widened portion of the four walls of a gondola. See Gondola.

-Torsion: The flexing or bending of a freightcar when rounding a curve. See Front runner.

-To Rule: See By the Book.

-Tower: The base of operations in a larger freightyard - always elevated over the tracks.

-Tower operator: A freightyard worker who governs arrival, departure and assembly of trains from a yard tower.

-Track circuiting: The means by which low-voltage electric current passes through rail to form the basis of the A.B.S. signaling system. See A.B.S. and Electric bond wires.

-Track fastener: See Claw spike.

-Track Gauge: The distance between inside edges of railheads, standardized in North America at 4 ft. 8-1/2 in. (1435 cm.).

-Track geometry car: A track maintenance car which gauges whether track is properly aligned.

-Track patrolman: An over-the-road railroad track inspector.

-Track relay: A sensing device in the A.B.S. system which notes when a train has interrupted or "shunted" the current on the block, which causes nearby signals to change aspects to reflect the train's presence. See A.B.S., Aspect and Shunt.

-Track section system: See A.B.S. and Block system.

-Trackwalker: Freightyard and over-the-road worker who inspects and repairs track.

-Tractive Effort Booster Unit (TEBU): See Slug unit.

-Trailing-point siding: A siding which requires the engineer back up to get on it. See Facing-point siding.

-Train: Anything on wheels on a railroad track which has a white light at the headend and a red plaque or light at the rearend - including a hand car.

-Train car: An old term for a caboose.

Trainman: Any member of an over-the-road train crew. See Engineman.

-Tramp: In literary circles eulogizing the hobo a person who "dreams and wanders." In common usage a person who travels about on foot doing odd jobs or begging for a living, e.g., a vagrant. In reality a minuscule yet notable minority of Americans seeking a better way in life. East of Chicago hobos supposedly work. West of Chicago tramps work. See Bum and Hobo.

-Tramp: (Verb) To ride freight trains, e.g., "I been *trampin'* for 47 years."

-Transposed rail: Rail shifted from the high rail or low rail side of a curve or to a different location to prolong rail life. See High rail, Low rail and Relay rail.

-Transverse fissure: Minuscule cracks which develop within the railhead of a rail owing to impurities or air in the steel. Over raillife these cracks expand outward under intense usage, ultimately causing the rail to break. See Rail heat.

-Travel: The amount of "play," "give" or "slack" in a freightcar's couplers and draft gears, ranging from 15 to 30 inches per car. See play.

-Tread: See Wheel tread.

-Tri-level auto rack: Industry parlance for a triple-decked auto rack. See Auto-rack.

-Trimmer: A freightyard switchengine which runs up and down tracks at the top end of a freightyard, forcing new strings of cars together to ensure they are coupled securely or rearranging strings of cars not yet properly blocked. See Blocking, Hump and Top end.

-Truck: The portion of the running gear on a freightcar which connects the chassis to the wheel axles. Also called a "car truck." See Chassis.

-Trunk route: Any major rail thoroughfare which connects distant regions.

-Turn: See Drag freight.

-26L engine brake: A modern electropneumatic diesel-electric engine brake. See Electropneumatic brake.

-Type-5 unit: A modern yard switchengine. See Billygoat and Yard switching unit.

-U-boat: Familiar term for General Electric locomotive products produced through the mid-1980s.

-Uncoupler lever: See Cut lever.

-Undercarriage: That portion of a freightcar underneath the floor or chassis. See Chassis.

-Unit: A diesel-electric engine. See MU.

- United States Railroad Administration (USRA): The federal agency created in 1918 to run railroads during World War I. Dissolved in 1920.

- United Transportation Union (UTU): The umbrella union group which represents the Brotherhoods and bargains nationwide with railroad management. See Brotherhoods.

-Unit train: A train comprised of only one type of car which travels back and forth from one customer to another (e.g., from coal mine to power plant and return).

-Upper quadrant signal: See Semaphore signal.

-Varnish: A passenger train. See Ride the cushions.

-Vent: (Verb) To exhaust air into the atmosphere - most often from a train's air brake system, e.g., "*Vent* it some more 'er we won't be able to bat 'er out."

-Waybill checker: A railroad officer worker who verifies pick-up and delivery of freightcars.

-Way car: An old term for caboose.

-Wayside signals: Trackside railroad signals, either lighted, manual or mechanical. See Signal.

-Way train: See Drag freight.

-Weary Willie: Happy Hooligan's sidekick in their manifold wanderings across the turn-of-the-century American terrain. See Happy Hooligan.

-WeePee: Familiar term for the Western Pacific (WP) Railroad.

-Well car: The newest intermodal container platform with a floor lowered down toward the track to accommodate double-stack boxes. Often coupled together in units of four, five or more with articulated wheel trucks. Some have open floors and others have closed, rideable floors. See Double-stack and Stack train.

-Westbound: The train a hobo dies on. See Big Hole in the Sky.

-Wheel tread: The smooth, nearly-flat and high., polished surface of a freightcar wheel which travels over the railhead. See Railhead.

-Wheel slip light: A light inside the engine cab which alerts the engineer that one or more of his engines' wheels is slipping. See Wheel slippage.

-Wheel slippage: When a diesel-electric's wheels slip on the rail, due either to insufficient engine weight-to-tonnage, excessive acceleration or snow, ice or water on the track. See Ballasting.

-Whistle down: A short cadence of whistle blasts which signaled brakemen on moving trains in the 19th century to manually set handbrakes. See Whistle up.

-Whistle up: A short cadence of whistle blasts which signaled brakemen on moving trains in the 19th century to manually release handbrakes. See Whistle down.

-White puke: Familiar term for muscatel.

-Wind 'em up: (Verb) To set handbrakes manually with a brakewheel and winding staff, e.g., "We had to *wind 'em up* 17 times that night."

-WPLJs: Familiar term for white port and lemon juice - a favorite hobo concoction.

-Wobblie: A member of the IWW union. See IWW.

Woodchip gon: A very high-sided gondola used to carry woodchips, sawdust and other wood waste products for remanufacturing. Lading is secured from wind loss by heavy netting across the top sills. See Gondola and Top sills.

-Work train: See Drag freight.

-XF food service boxcar: Boxcars with seamless plastic linings and plug doors to prevent contamination and provide smooth interior wall surfaces for food product lading. See Plug door.

-XM combination door boxcar: A standard boxcar with two doors on each side. One slides shut and the other is sealed in place with bulkheads.

-XM free-running boxcar: A standard boxcar with two ordinary sliding doors.

-Yard air: Pressurized air supplied in larger freightyards to fill a train's air brake system to legal air. Can be done more quickly than units themselves. See Legal air.

-Yard billy: See Billygoat.

-Yard foreman: A freightyard worker who supervises all aspects of yard operations within yard limits.

Yard limit: The two edges of a freightyard, delimited by yard limit boards or "Y's."

-Yard limit board: A trackside "Y"-shaped sign delimiting the boundaries of a yard and the jurisdiction between a yard master and road master. See Road master and Yard foreman.

-Yardman: Any freightyard worker.

-Yard master: See Yard foreman.

-Yard office: The nerve center of a switching yard's operations. Often a simple depot; equally often a tower or communications center.

-Yard switching unit: Industry parlance for a yard switchengine or billygoat. Usually unable to run as an MU unit because not electrically-equipped to run in tandem. See Billygoat and MU.

-Yegg: Familiar turn-of-the-century moniker for a criminal hobo who preyed on other migrants.

-Yoke: The part of a freightcar coupler which attaches the draft gear to the under-carriage. See Draft gear and Pocket

SELECTED BIBLIOGRAPHY

Books

Alexander, E.P., *Iron Horses, American Locomotives 1829-1900*. New York: Random House 1941.

Anderson, Nels, *The Hobo: The Sociology of the Homeless Man*. Chicago: The University of Chicago Press 1923.

Armstrong, John H., *The Railroad - What It Is, What It Does*. Omaha, Nebraska: Simmons-Boardman Books, Inc. 1990.

Buck, Solon J., *The Granger Movement*. Cambridge, Massachusetts: Havard University Press 1913.

Campbell, Lindsay, and Heath, Erle, *Trail to Rail*. San Francisco: The Southern Pacific Company 1930.

Conover, Ted, *Rolling Nowhere*. New York: Penguin Books 1984.

Davies, William Henry, *The Autobiography of a Super-Tramp*. London: McKenzie Flowers & Co. 1897

Ducker, James H, *Men of the Steel Rail*. Lincoln, Nebraska: University of Nebraska Press 1983.

Farrington, S. Kip Jr., *Railroads of Today*. New York: Coward-McCann, Inc. 1949.

Galloway, John Debo, *The First Transcontinental Railroad . . . Central Pacific, Union Pacific*. New York: Simmons-Boardman Publishing Corp. 1950.

Graham, "Steam Train" Maury and Hemming, Robert J., *Tales of the Iron Road*. New York: Paragon House 1990.

Grosfield, Byron, *Buckaroos and Boxcars*. Big Timber, Montana: Pioneer Publishing Co. 1981.

Hinckley, Thomas K., *Transcontinental Rails*. Palmer Lake, CO: Filter Press 1969.

Holbrook, Stewart H., *The Columbia*. New York: Rinehart Books 1956.

Holbrook, Stewart H., *The Story of American Railroads*. New York: Crown Publishers, Inc. 1947.

Holland, Rupert Sargent, *Historic Railroads*. Philadelphia: MaCrae Smith Company 1927.

Jensen, Oliver, *Railroads in America*. New York: American Heritage Books 1981.

John, Midwest, *My Life as a Hobo*. Unknown

Kneiss, Gilbert H., *Bonanza Railroads*. Stanford, California: Stanford University Press 1941.

Leen, Daniel, *The Freight Hopper's Manual for North America*. London: Travelaid 1981.

London, Jack, *The Road*. Santa Barbara and Salt Lake City: Peregrine Smith, Inc. 1978.

Marshall, James W., *Santa Fe, the Railroad That Built an Empire*. New York: Random House 1949.

Marshall, John, *The Guinness Railway Book*. Middlesex, England: Guinness Publishing Ltd. 1990.

Martin, Albro, *Enterprise Denied: Origins of the Decline of American Railroads*. New York: Columbia University Press 1971.

Mathers, Michael, *Riding the Rails*. Boston: Houghton Mifflin Co. 1974.

Merk, Frederick, *History of the Westward Movement*. New York: Knopf Press 1978.

Rorer, David, *The Law of Railways* (2 vol.). Chicago: Callaghan & Co. 1884.

Stevens, Irving L. ("Fish Bones"), *Hoboing in the 1930s*. Milo, Maine: Irving L. Stevens 1982.

Stover, John F., *American Railroads*. Chicago: University of Chicago Press 1961.

Wilner, Frank N., *Railroad Land Grants*. Washington, D.C.: Association of American Railroads 1984.

Wilson, Neill C. and Taylor, Frank J., *Southern Pacific - The Roaring Story of a Fighting Railroad*. New York: McGraw-Hill Book Company, Inc. 1952.

Yenne, Bill, *History of North American Railroads*. New York: Gallery Books 1986.

Periodicals

A Basic Guide to Railroad Crew-Change Points and Jumping Freight Trains in North America, Paul Norton. (unpublished and not wanted to be).

The Best of Mainline Modeler's Freight Cars Vols. One, Two and Three, (no set sequence), Phoenix Publishing, P.O. Box 3260, Friday Harbor, WA 98250.

CTC Board, (monthly), CTC Board, P.O. Box 55, Denver, CO 80201.

Handy Railroad Atlas of the United States. Chicago: Rand McNally & Co (1973 and 1991.) Chicago, New York, San Francisco.

Hobo Times, (bi-monthly), Captain Cook, Editor-Publisher, World Way Center, P.O. Box 90430, Los Angeles, CA 90009.

The Official Railway Guide, Freight Service Edition, (bi-monthly), K-III Information Company, Inc., 424 W. 33rd St., New York, NY 10001-2604.

Railroading in the Good Old Days (defunct quarterly), Railroad Good Old Days, P.O. Box 428, Seabrook, NH 03874.

The Short Line, (bi-monthly), Garreth M. McDonald, Editor-Publisher, P.O. Box 607, Pleasant Garden, NC 27313.

Trains Illustrated, (quarterly), Kalmbach Publishing Co., 21027 Crossroads Circle, Waukesha, WI 53187.

Trains: The Magazine of Railroading, (monthly), Kalmbach Publishing Co., 21027 Crossroads Circle, Waukesha, WI 53187.

INDEX

175, 232, 234
combination door, 89
cushion car, 57
DF, 89
doorlatch, 84, 86-87
etiquette, 266
floors, 88-89
food service, 89-90
forklift, 109
hasp, 84
less-than-full-car, 89
One-Eyed Bandit, 84, 86, 142, 167, 173
open door, 87-88, 173-175
plug door, 89, 108
RBL, 109
roofwalk, 68
Scenic Cruiser, 84, 142, 167, 173
Side Door Pullman, 84
Singleton door opening system, 85
XF, 89-90
XL, 89
XM, 89
Boy Scouts of America, 271-272
bracing, 57, 89, 188
Brake: 64-78
AB, 73
ABD, 73
ABDW, 73
A-end, 75, 175, 180
air increase, 77, 205-206
air release, 78
air test, 77
automatic air brake, 71
automatic brake valve handle, 71
auxiliary air reservoir, 71
B-end, 75, 92, 98, 180
big hole position, The, 73, 134, 139
bleed the air, 205
bleed rod, 59
brakechain, 92
brakeshoes, 76
break the air, 78, 139, 205
club, 67
compressor, 70-71, 129
cut lever, 52, 60, 210
cutting slack, 52
cylinder, 70-71, 78-79, 92
dragging your foot, 68, 73

dynamic, 129
dynamite, 205
dynamite car, 78
electropneumatic, 73
glad hands, 70
hoses, 70-71, 79, 151
hosed up, 76, 202
HSC Electro-Pneumatic Brake, 74
legal air, 77, 205
manual brakewheels, 67-69, 75-76, 80, 211, 214
operating pressure, 77
pneumatic pressure, 70
pushrod, 92
reservoir, 71, 75, 78-79, 92
retarders, 60, 78
return springs, 57
rigging, 183
rod, 38
service range, 71
slack, 56-58, 60, 165, 178, 210
springs, 70, 77
staff, 67, 75
steady air, 76-77, 205-206, 237
steam, 71
Straight Air System, 70-71
throttle, 70-71
26L Brake, 73
valve, 92
vent air, 59, 71
Westinghouse Air Brake, 70-73
Westinghouse Air Brake Company, The, 71
Westinghouse Continuous Automatic Air Brake, The, 72
Westinghouse, George C., 70-74
whistle down, 67-68
whistle up, 67-68
yard air, 76
brakeman, 136, 142, 185, 207-212
brakeman's cab, 66
British cattle speculators, 244
British Columbia Railway (BC Rail), 112
Britt, Iowa, 263
Brotherhoods, The, 22, 255
Bryan, William Jennings, 255
Bryan, Wyoming, 29
buffalo, 199, 215
Buffalo, New York, 215
buggy, 22

ABOUT THE AUTHOR

Douglas C. "Duffy" Littlejohn was born in Pacific Palisades California in 1953. He attended St. Matthew's Elementary School, Paul Revere Junior High School and Palisades Highschool, graduating in 1971. He also attended the University of California at Los Angeles during the twelth grade.

After high school he hit the road, living for brief times over the next five years in Santa Fe New Mexico, Las Vegas New Mexico and Colorado Springs Colorado. He attended the New Mexico State Highlands University in Las Vegas for four quarters. At one time or another he has passed through every state of the Union except Hawaii and all the provinces and territories in Canada west of Ontario. In the first six months of 1976 he traveled from Mexico to Bolivia and back.

He graduated from the University of California at Santa Barbara in 1979 with degrees in History and Dramatic Arts, traveling and working each summer between quarters. He worked as a legal secretary in San Francisco in 1979-80 before taking a five-month tour of Europe. He then entered law school at the University of California at Davis and graduated in 1983.

He worked for two years in private practice in San Francisco as an insurance defense counsel before joining the District Attorney's Office there in 1985. He served as an Assistant D.A. until 1987 before transferring to the Alameda County District Attorney's Office as a Deputy D.A. He served in this capacity until 1989.

He opened his own practice in criminal law in 1989 and practiced until 1990. He then moved to Paris France where he resided for two and a half years. This book was written in Paris. He rode freight trains in France. He returned to the United States in April, 1992 and continues to ride the rails on a regular basis. Last heard his whereabouts were unknown although he assures us his pulse is checked on a regular basis.